Daisy Yulin Tsai
Human Rights in Deuteronomy

Beihefte zur Zeitschrift für die alttestamentliche Wissenschaft

Edited by
John Barton, Ron Hendel,
Reinhard G. Kratz and Markus Witte

Volume 464

Daisy Yulin Tsai

Human Rights in Deuteronomy

—

With Special Focus on Slave Laws

DE GRUYTER

ISBN 978-3-11-036320-3
e-ISBN 978-3-11-036442-2
ISSN 0934-2575

Library of Congress Cataloging-in-Publication Data
A CIP catalog record for this book has been applied for at the Library of Congress.

Bibliographic Information published by the Deutsche Nationalbibliothek
The Deutsche Nationalbibliothek lists this publication in the Deutsche Nationalbibliografie;
detailed bibliographic data are available in the Internet at http://dnb.dnb.de.

© 2014 Walter de Gruyter GmbH, Berlin/Boston
Printing and binding: CPI books GmbH, Leck
♾ Printed on acid-free paper
Printed in Germany

www.degruyter.com

MIX
Papier aus verantwor-
tungsvollen Quellen
FSC
www.fsc.org   FSC® C003147

To David Ding-Hwang (定煌, 小ㄷㄷ), my younger brother, who passed away during the pursuit of this study

Preface

This volume presents a new approach to the comparative legal study of the biblical and the ANE slave laws. It adopts a multidimensional examination that compares not only laws with similar subject matter of slavery, but also their rhetorical techniques, methods of law grouping, arrangements of law collections, and the rationale of legal philosophy behind the law books. By this examination, one is able to compare degrees of similarity and dissimilarity between the biblical and the ANE slave laws.

The biblical laws examined present two diverse rationales of legal philosophy in contrast to the ANE ones: (1) *all* agents (e.g., slaves, captives, and criminals) are regarded as *persons* and should be treated accordingly, and (2) *all* legal subjects are seen as *free*, *dignified*, and *self-determining* human beings. In addition to these two extraordinary legal philosophies, the biblical laws often distinguish an offender's "criminal intent," by which a criminal's rights are also considered. Based on these two distinctive legal philosophies and also the distinction of criminal intent, the biblical laws are able to articulate YHWH's humanitarian concerns and the basic concepts of human rights presented in Deuteronomy.

Via these approaches, Deuteronomy is found to be purposefully constructed to reflect the legal position that laws should carry the function of morality shaping. YHWH is identified as that *personal* monarch that establishes a covenantal relationship so that he can interact with his legal subjects relationally to shape their peoplehood and promote the ethical values of his humanitarian concerns. Deuteronomy proclaims that the one who reveres YHWH by obeying his words under his covenantal relationship could assume moral strength and convictions, because YHWH and his words are the universal origins and norms of righteousness and justice. In this way, by obeying his words and laws, Israel would also learn of God's character and in turn be shaped not only in their moral development and betterment of interpersonal relationships with the slaves in Israelite society, but as to function as whole moral persons in *spirit* and in *deed*. This monograph is a revised version of my dissertation which was examined in 2011.

To my husband Lewis and my daughter Katherine, my parents and other family members in Taipei I owe a debt greater than can be reckoned. I have been encouraged in my work by Dr. Richard E. Averbeck, a humble and rigorous scholar, and Dr. Willem A. VanGemeren, a father-like and wise advisor. Special thanks to Dr. Choon-Leong Seow for his recommendation so that this work can be published in the series of the Zeitschrift für die alttestamentliche Wissenschaft. My gratitude also goes to several couples, who supported me with their generosity and prayers. They are Hueiling and Chengyu Chen, Patrick and Joyce Chen, Linda and Percy Deng, Chunju and Jichong Liu, and Zijuan and Jinmu Yang.

Contents

Abbreviations

CAD   The Assyrian Dictionary of the Oriental Institute of the University of Chicago. Chicago, 1956-

Dt 15   Hebrew Manumission Slave Laws in Deut 15:12–18

Ex 21   Hebrew Manumission Slave Laws in Exod 21:2–11 as a whole

HL   Hittite Laws

Jr 34   Hebrew Manumission Slave Laws applied in Jer 34:8–22

Lev 25 Hebrew Manumission Slave Laws in Lev 25:39–55 (in chapter one's review of literature, for some scholars, the slave laws in Leviticus 25 may include different scopes of verses, e. g., vv. 39–43, or 39–46)

LE   Laws of Eshununna

LH   Laws of Hammurabi

LL   Laws of Lipit-Ishtar

LNB   Neo-Babylonian Laws

LU   Laws of Ur-Namma

MAL   Middle Assyrian Laws

SLEx   Sumerian Laws Exercise Tablet

1 Introduction and Methodological Considerations

Hebrew slaves and the slave manumission laws in the Pentateuch elucidate something that rarely has been touched upon. The Hebrew slave manumission laws (Exod 21:2–11; Lev 25:39–55; Deut 15:12–18) contain various rhetorical techniques that mark a strong call for the listeners' attention. Slavery was a significant issue from the very beginning of Israelite history. Originally, Israel was mainly composed of escaped Egyptian Hebrew slaves. The very first law of the ordinances from the Covenant law book[1] that the Lord set before these fugitives concerns the manumission of a Hebrew slave (Exod 21:2–11).[2] R. Averbeck notes

---

1 Instead of the use of the term "code," this study will use "law collection" or "law book" to designate the biblical and ANE legal corpus. Traditionally, scholars often referred to biblical and cuneiform law collections as "codes," but today many scholars refer to them as "collections" instead of *codes*. S. Greengus indicates that the modern term "code" can be misleading: "The collections are not 'codes' in the modern, comprehensive sense of that term, because they convey only a part of all the operative laws at that time." The convention of referring to these law collections as 'codes' goes back to J. V. Scheil, whose *edition princeps* is entitled *Code des Lois (droit privé) de Hammurabi*. However, it is believed that Driver and Miles's reservations about the label 'code' are typically influential. R. Westbrook subscribes to the view that these documents are not legislation in the modern sense, but rather academic treatises on law expressed in casuistic form. Recently, M. T. Roth published an essay arguing that "codification" and "code" are labels that can only be applied to ancient compilations anachronistically. She believes that the Law of Hammurabi is not a codification of laws and legal practices, but that it is a *text* with a textual and manuscript history. See discussions such as Samuel Greengus, "Legal and Social Institutions of Ancient Mesopotamia," in *Civilizations of the Ancient Near East, I* (ed. Jack M. Sasson; New York: Charles Scribner's Sons, 1995), 471; V. Scheil, *Code des Lois (droit privé) de Hammurabi*, (Paris, 1902); G. R. Driver and John C. Miles, *The Babylonian Laws* (vol. 1; Oxford: Clarendon; 1952), 45 n.1; Jean Bottéro, *Mesopotamia: Writing, Reasoning, and the Gods* (trans. Zainab Bahrani and Marc Van De Mieroop; Chicago: University of Chicago Press, 1992), 156–184; Raymond Westbrook, "The Development of Law in the Ancient Near East: Slave and Master in Ancient Near Eastern Law," *Chicago-Kent Law Review* 70 (1995): 1632; Martha T. Roth, "The Law Collection of King Hammurabi: Toward an Understanding of Codification and Text," in *La Codification des Lois dans L'Antiquité: Actes du Colloque de Strasbourg 27–29 Novembre 1997* (ed. Edmond Lévy; Paris: De Boccard, 2000), 9–31. Concerning the discussion of the terminology, see also Russ VerSteeg, *Early Mesopotamian Law* (Durham: Carolina Academic Press, 2000), 13–14.

2 For example, the Law of Hammurabi (hereafter LH) sets the major section of slave laws at the last (pars. 278–282). Such a unique opening, for some scholars, is regarded as an addition that does not belong to the original section of Exod 21:12–22:16. See J. P. M. van der Ploeg, "Slavery in the Old Testament" in *Congress Volume: Uppsala*, 1971 (Leiden: E. J. Brill, 1972), 78. For A. Phillips, Exod 21:2–11 should have originally belonged to the second section of the book of the Covenant, 22:20–23:19, a mixture of humanitarian and cultic injunctions. Philips believes that Exod 21:2–4 owes nothing to biblical law; rather, it is a statement of belief. Anthony Phillips,

that "[t]he *placement* of Exodus 21:2–11 is striking. For the debt-slave laws to be at the beginning of this very important section of laws is conspicuous both historically and theologically."[3] The Covenant law book is the only ancient law collection that opens with this topic. The last legal regulation regarding slaves in the Pentateuch is in Deut 23:16–17 [Eng. 23:15–16], which is a petition to protect escaped slaves. This petition finds no correspondence among the ANE slave laws, and the law is one of the most humane appeals in the entire repertoire of biblical and ANE laws.[4]

Scholars in human rights and anthropology have often reckoned these biblical laws to be an integral pedestal for early ethical contributions.[5] Unfortunately, biblical scholars have not given commensurate attention to the relationship between their theological significance and humanitarian concerns. In striking contrast to their ANE counterparts, Israelite slave laws in the Pentateuch, especially in Deuteronomy, demonstrate a strong humanitarian overtone.[6]

"The Law of Slavery: Exodus 21:2–11," *JSOT* 30 (1984): 51–66. P. C. Craigie and N. M. Sarna both agree that the priority given to this subject by the Torah has a historical explanation: Having recently experienced liberation from bondage, the Israelites were commanded to be particularly concerned about slavery. Peter C. Craigie, *The Book of Deuteronomy* (Grand Rapids: Eerdmans, 1976), 79–83; Nahum M. Sarna, *Exodus* (New York: The Jewish Publication Society, 1991), 118.

3 Richard E. Averbeck, "Law," in *Cracking Old Testament Codes* (ed. D. Brent Sandy and Ronald L. Giese, Jr.; Nashville: Broadman & Holman, 1995), 133.

4 On the contrary, most slave laws call for the return of escaped slaves. Robert I. Vasholz, "A Legal 'Brief' on Deuteronomy 23:16–17," *Presbyterion* 17 (1991): 127.

5 Micheline R. Ishay, *The History of Human Rights: From Ancient Times to the Globalization Era* (Berkeley and Los Angeles: University of California Press, 2004), 17–61. Gillian Feeley-Harnik, "Is Historical Anthropology Possible? The Case of the Runaway Slave," in *Humanizing America's Iconic Book: Society of Biblical Literature Centennial Addresses 1980* (ed. Gene M. Tucker and Douglas A. Knight; Chico: Scholars, 1982), 95–126; René Cassin, *Amicorum discipulorumque liber. IV, methodologie des droits de l'homme* (Paris: Pédone, 1972), 98.

6 According to M. Weinfeld, "The book contains many ethical laws which have no counterpart elsewhere in the Pentateuch, and those which do have Pentateuchal parallels appear in Deuteronomy with divergent and more humanistic overtones." Moshe Weinfeld, *Deuteronomy and the Deuteronomic School* (Winona: Eisenbrauns, 1992), 282. Likewise, Craigie states, "The concern for the resident aliens finds more compassionate expression in Deuteronomy than anywhere in Pentateuch." See Craigie, *The Book of Deuteronomy*, 59. Topics regarding social justice and a utopian social response especially in Deuteronomy 15 have gained a broad discussion. See works such as Jeffries M. Hamilton, *Social Justice and Deuteronomy: The Case of Deuteronomy 15* (Atlanta: Scholars, 1992); Eckart Otto, "Programme der Sozialen Gerechtigkeit: die Neuassyrische (an-)durāru-Institution Sozialen Ausgleichs und das Deuteronomische Erlassjahr in Dtn 15," *ZABR* 3 (1997): 26–63; Martin J. Oosthuizen, "Deuteronomy 15:1–18 in Socio-Rhetorical Perspective," *ZABR* 3 (1997): 64–91; Heinz-Josef Fabry, "Deuteronomium 15: Gedanken zur Geschwister-Ethik im Alten Testament," *ZABR* 3 (1997): 92–111. See also Guy Lasserre, "Lutter

Review of Literature

Cuneiform law collections were first discovered in the beginning of the twentieth century. With this discovery came a growing interest of comparative study between biblical and cuneiform law collections, as well as intertextual legal comparison.[7] As a result, scholars began comparing *similar* laws in the biblical and cuneiform law collections. In general, they paid attention to analogous subject matters. For example, in 1902, D. H. Müller compared some resemblances between the Law of Hammurabi, Covenantal, and Deuteronomic law collections in his book *Die Gesetze Hammurabis*, while later in 1935 C. Gordon published a book showing a parallel between LH 23–24 and some Nuzi tablets that reflected a custom similar to Deut 25:11–12.[8] In the past few decades, comparative legal study has become a newly energized area of biblical law research.[9] The investi-

---

contre la paupérisation et ses conséquences: Lecture rhétorique de Dt 15/12–18," *Études théologiques et religieuses* 70 (1995): 481–492 ; Haroldo Reimer, "Un Tiempo de Gracia para Recomenzar: el año Sabático en Exodo 21, 2–11 y Deuteronomio 15, 1–18." *Revista de interpretación bíblica latino-americana* 33 (1999): 31–47; Jean Marie van Cangh, "Le Jubilé biblique: un Temps Marqué Ouvrant un Temps Neuf," *Science et esprit* 53 (2001): 63–92.

7 See David Heiner Müller, *Die Gesetze Hammurabis und ihr Verhältnis zur mosaischen Gesetzgebung sowie zu den XII Tafel* (Wien: Alfred Hölder, 1904), 275–284.

8 Cyrus Herzl Gordon, *A New Akkadian Parallel to Deuteronomy 25:11–12* (Jerusalem, 1935).

9 For some biblical scholars, apparent correspondences (i.e., casuistic formulated laws, similar subject matters) do not necessarily provide satisfactory reasons for the comparative study of biblical and ANE laws. See Samuel Greengus, "Some Issues Relating to the Comparability of Laws and the Coherence of the Legal Tradition," in *Theory and Method in Biblical and Cuneiform Law: Revision, Interpolation and Development* (ed. Bernard M. Levinson; Sheffield: Sheffield Academic Press, 1994), 60–87. A number of scholars have called to question the academic disciplines regarding biblical comparative study. For example, in order to provide the framework in the comparative studies, S. Talmon segregates four major principles: proximity in time and place, the priority of inner biblical parallels, correspondence of social function, and the holistic approach to texts and comparisons. See Shemaryahu Talmon, "The 'Comparative Method' in Biblical Interpretation—Principles and Problems," in *Essential Papers on Israel and the Ancient Near East* (ed. Frederick E. Greenspahn; New York: New York University Press, 1991), 320–356. M. Malul suggests two comparative methods: historical and typological comparative approaches. On this, see M. Malul, *The Comparative Method in Ancient Near Eastern and Biblical Legal Studies* (Kevelaer: Butzon & Bercker; Neukirchen-Vluyn: Neukirchener Verlag, 1990). See also the debates between D. P. Wright and B. Wells. David P. Wright, "The Laws of Hammurabi as a Source for the Covenant Collection," *MAARAV* 10 (2003): 11–87; Bruce Wells, "The Covenant Code and Near Eastern Legal Traditions: A Response to David P. Wright," *MAARAV* 13, no. 1 (2006): 85–118; David P. Wright, "The Laws of Hammurabi and the Covenant Code: A Response to Bruce Wells," *MAARAV* 13, no. 2 (2006): 211–260. D. P. Wright, *Inventing God's Law: How the Covenant Code of the Bible Used and Revised the Laws of Hammurabi* (New York: Oxford University Press, 2009). R. Westbrook, affirms that the biblical law is based upon the same concepts as those of

gation of biblical slave laws has focused on the literary relation between the three slave manumission laws in the Pentateuch: Exod 21:2–11 (hereafter Ex 21), Lev 25:39–55 (hereafter Lev 25), and Deut 15:12–18 (hereafter Dt 15).[10]

The first stage of hermeneutics on these slave laws, according to B. M. Levinson, is the "standard source critical model" which was pervasive until the 1960's.[11] This model diachronically regards Ex 21, Lev 25, Dt 15, and Jer 34:8–22 (hereafter Jr 34), as a developing series of the manumission laws. It assumes that the apparent discrepancy between the laws indicates that the later legislator was modifying or repealing the earlier law. According to this view, Ex 21 that requires the release of male slaves in the seventh year was chronologically first. Then from it Dt 15 stemmed out, with the same numerical scheme but with a series of revisions. Next was the prophetic narrative of Jr 34, which recounts how Zedekiah sought to implement the law as the Babylonians besieged Jerusalem, presumably so as to abortively add soldiers to the militia. Finally, the author of the Holiness Code deferred the slave law to the jubilee in the fiftieth year in Lev 25, desperately hoping somehow to retrieve the institution. In view of the standard source critical model, the development of the sources can be summarized as follows: Ex 21→ Dt 15→ Jr 34→ Lev 25.[12]

---

the other ANE legal system and thereby draws comparisons between them. Raymond Westbrook, *Studies in Biblical and Cuneiform Law* (Paris: J. Gabalda, 1988). A. Watson, one of the world's foremost authorities on comparative law, jurisprudence, and law in the Gospels, has suggested some principles in this study: Alan Watson, *Legal Transplants: An Approach to Comparative Law* (Athens: University of Georgia Press, 1993).

10 The adjective עִבְרִי *Hebrew* occurs in Exod 21:2–6, Deut 15:12–18, and Jer 34:8–22. The phenonmenon makes these laws similar in the eyes of some scholars. For them, these laws dealt with *any Israelite* who might have become a slave of *an Israelite* master, whatever the cause or circumstances. The sabbatical institutions and the lack of the adjective *Hebrew* are two distinctive elements that make the Leviticus slave law different from the other three. See H. L. Ellison, "The Hebrew Slave: A Study in Early Israelite Society," *EvQ* 45 (1973): 30–35.

11 B. M. Levinson, "The Manumission of Hermeneutics: The Slave Laws of the Pentateuch as a Challenge to Contemporary Pentateuchal Theory" in *Congress Volume Leiden 2004* (ed. André Lemaire; Boston: E. J. Brill, 2006), 283–284. The model is conventionally regarded as initiated by the Graf-Kuenen (1886)-Wellhausen (1963) school, proposing the hypothesis that H (Lev 25) is later than D (Dt 15). The "standard source critical model" was held by those such as S. R. Driver, *A Critical and Exegetical Commentary on Deuteronomy* (Edinburgh: T. & T. Clark, 1965), 185; R. de Vaux, *Ancient Israel: Its Life and Institutions* (trans. John McHugh; Grand Rapids: Eerdmans, 1961), 82–90. A. Phillips, *Ancient Israel's Criminal Law: A New Approach to the Decalogue* (Oxford: Basil Blackwell, 1970), 73–78.

12 Levinson, "The Manumission of Hermeneutics," 283–284. See also M. Leuchter's discussion on Lev 25's dependence on Jer 34, Mark Leuchter, "The Manumission Laws in Leviticus and Deuteronomy: The Jeremiah Connection," *JBL* 127, no. 4 (2008): 635–653.

Subsequently, various theories about the literary relation between these slave laws surfaced and challenged what was then the consensus on the standard source critical model.[13] The Israeli scholar Y. Kaufmann (1889–1963) may be the earliest forerunner who denied any literary relation between biblical and cuneiform laws, as well as among any of the Pentateuchal legal collections.[14] Three decades later, R. P. Merendino incorporated Kaufmann's position into the form critical approach. Precluding any literary dependence between biblical and cuneiform laws, he proposed a theory similar to the two-source hypothesis for the synoptic problem by appealing to an unknown independent literary source like the hypothetical Q.[15] Others such as S. Japhet argue for Dt 15's dependence on Lev 25. Her view has become a building block for a number of scholars including C. J. H. Wright, J. Weingreen, and J. Milgrom.[16] In addition to establishing literary relation, Japhet has noted that the human so-

---

13 This does not mean that recent scholarship has completely overturned the earlier model. In terms of the relationship between the slave laws of Dt 15 and Lev 25, some recent scholars, such as A. Cholewiński, I. Cardellini, R. Gnuse, S. A. Kaufmann, C. Bultmann, and B. M. Levinson etc. still follow the early regnant standard source critical model, proposing that Lev 25 (H) is later than Dt 15 (D). See Alfred Cholewiński, *Heiligkeitsgesetz und Deuteronomium : Eine vergleichende Studie* (Rome: Biblical Institute Press, 1976), 217–251; Innocenzo Cardellini, *Die biblischen Sklaven-Gesetze im Lichte des keilschriftlichen Sklavenrechts: Ein Beitrag zur Tradition, Überlieferung und Redaktion der alttestamentlichen Rechtstexte* (Königstein: Peter Hanstein Verlag, 1981), 280–286; Robert Gnuse, *You Shall Not Steal* (Maryknoll: Orbis, 1985), 21–28; S. A. Kaufmann, "A Reconstruction of the Social Welfare Systems of Ancient Israel," in *In the Shelter of Elyon* (ed. W. Boyd Barrick and John R. Spencer; Sheffield: JSOT, 1984), 277–286; C. Bultmann, *Der Fremde im antiken Juda* (Göttingen: Vandenhoeck & Ruprecht, 1992). Levinson, "The Manumission of Hermeneutics," 293–324.
14 Yehezkel Kaufmann, *The Religion of Israel: From Its Beginnings to the Babylonian Exile* (trans. M. Greenberg; New York: Schocken, 1972), 205. The original Hebrew work was published in 1937.
15 See R. P. Merendino, *Das deuteronomische Gesetz: Eine literarkritische, gattungs-und überlieferungsgeschichtliche Untersuchung zu Dt 12–26* (Bonn: P. Hanstein, 1969), 401–402. In addition, while M. Weinfeld agrees with Kaufmann that Dt 15 and Lev 25 are independent compositions, yet he believes that they are related in content. Moshe Weinfeld, *Deuteronomy and the Deuteronomic school* (Winona Lake: Eisenbrauns, 1992), 223 n.3.
16 Sara Japhet, "The Relationship between the Legal Corpora in the Pentateuch in Light of Manumission Laws," in *Studies in Bible* (ed. Sara Japhet; Jerusalem: Magnes, 1986), 63–89. See also Christopher J. H. Wright, "What Happened Every Seven Years in Israel? Old Testament Sabbatical Institutions for Land, Debts and Slaves Part II," *EvQ* 56 (1984):193–201; Jacob Weingreen, *From Bible to Mishna: The Continuity of Tradition* (New York: Holmes & Meier, 1976); 134–142. Jacob Milgrom, *Leviticus 23–27: A New Translation with Introduction and Commentary* (New York: Doubleday, 2001), 2254–2257.

cial implications of the slave laws in Deuteronomy reveal additional aspects of thought and worldview.[17]

In recent decades (from the 1980's to present), biblical scholars have paid more attention to the emphatic tone of human rights in Deuteronomy. However, many of them explained this humanitarian overtone by their dating of the book. G. Braulik's article, "Das Deuteronomium und die Menschenrechte" in 1986, illustrated how the Deuteronomic statutes demonstrate the compassionate spirit of human rights.[18] Braulik explained that such humanitarian sympathy was a plan for a just society which Josiah pledged to the Israelite people in 621 B.C.[19] Later in 1993, C. Chirichigno proposed a synchronic reading of these slave laws from a socio-economic perspective. However, he paradoxically dated these legal corpora diachronically.[20] Another variation appeared in 2002 with E. Otto's *Gottes Recht als Menschenrecht: Rechts und literaturhistorische studien zum Deuteronomium* that placed Deuteronomy in a pre-exilic period (most likely in the time of Josiah).[21] Here, Otto believed that Deuteronomy created a complementary relationship between ethics and law in response to Mesopotamian economic problems and the occasional debt-release decrees.[22] In identifying the ideal political freedom of Deuteronomy, he asserts that the concept comes from the threat of the Neo-Assyrians.[23] J. Van Seters maintains that Dt

---

17 Japhet, "The Relationship between the Legal Corpora in the Pentateuch in Light of Manumission Laws," 89.

18 George Braulik, "Das Deuteronomium und die Menschenrechte," *TQ* 166 (1986): 8–24. Also English translation, George Braulik, "Deuteronomy and Human Rights," *Skrif en kerk* 19 (1998): 207–229.

19 Braulik, "Das Deuteronomium und die Menschenrechte," 9.

20 Chirichigno maintains that the three manumission laws constitute a synchronically coherent system. He suggests that the law collection of Deut 12–26, which was promulgated by Moses, coincides with the present literary framework of Deuteronomy, but the final compilation of the slave law in Dt 15 should be dated to the time of Josiah or Hezekiah. Gregory C. Chirichigno, *Debt-Slavery in Israel and the Ancient Near East* (Sheffield: JSOT, 1993), 343, 356–357.

21 Otto believes that the way to begin dating Deuteronomy, as well as the Pentateuch as a whole, is not with the customary connection to Josiah's reforms in 2 Kings, but in light of key extra-biblical texts of the loyalty oaths (*SAA* 2, 6) and to the Neo-Assyrian material. Otto, *Gottes Recht als Menschenrecht*, 219–239.

22 Z. G. Glass recapitulates and agrees with several scholars' similar studies about how Deuteronomic slave laws reflect the economic situation in the eighth century B.C. in ancient Israel. Zipporah G. Glass, "Land, Slave Labor and Law: Engaging Ancient Israel's Economy," *JSOT* 91 (2000), 27–39. See also Henri Cazelles, "Droit Public dans le Deutéronome," in *Das Deuteronomium: Entstehung, Gestalt und Botschaft* (ed. Norbert Lohfink; Leuven: University Press, 1985), 102. Eckart Otto, *Gottes Recht als Menschenrecht: Rechts und literaturhistorische Studien zum Deuteronomium* (Wiesbaden: Harrassowitz, 2002), 12.

23 Otto, *Gottes Recht als Menschenrecht*, 176–177, 184–186.

15 comes first and Ex 21 last in his 2003 work *A Law Book for the Diaspora*,[24] asserting that the emphasis of humanitarian "brotherly" ethics of Dt 15 is an earlier presentation and that Ex 21 should be understood as "a window on the exilic and postexilic conditions of Hebrew enslavement."[25]

Independent from the source hypothesis, C. Carmichael's historical analysis suggests a different theory for the three release laws.[26] Based on a synchronic reading, he asserted that the texts themselves provide accounts of their authors and dates. Each slave law in Ex 21, Dt 15 and Lev 25 reflects a recent slave experience and provides directions for the future life of the Israelite people.[27] Carmichael contends that attempting "to date the texts must end in frustration because the historical data necessary for the task are simply not available to us."[28]

In addition to the intertextual focus in the Hebrew Bible, ANE socio-economic investigations provide a contextual panorama to understand the institutions of ancient slavery. A socio-economic approach concentrates on issues such as the sources of slaves, the legal status of slaves, the economic roles of slavery, and the manumission of slaves.[29] A plethora of studies show that since variegated factors

---

24 Van Seters dates Pentateuchal legal corpora in a rather different perspective from the majority of scholars. For Van Seters, the literary sequence would be Dt 15→Jr 34→Lev 25→Ex 21. J. Van Seters, "The Law of the Hebrew Slave," *ZAW* 108 (1996): 534. See also J. Van Seters, *A Law Book for the Diaspora: Revision in the Study of the Covenant Code* (Oxford: Oxford University Press, 2003), 8–18, 82–95.

25 Van Seters, *A Law Book for the Diaspora*, 94–95.

26 Calum M. Carmichael, "The Three Laws on the Release of Slaves," *ZAW* 112 (2000): 509–525. C. Carmichael is not the first to interpret these slave laws in light of their prior narratives in order to find the concomitant legal conceptions of the early Hebrews. See other scholars and their works, such as, David Daube, *Studies in Biblical Law* (New York: Ktav Publishing House, 1969); Franz Steiner, "Enslavement and the Early Hebrew Linage System: An Explanation of Genesis 47:29–31; 48:1–16," in *Anthropological Approaches to the Old Testament* (ed. Bernhard Lang; Philadelphia: Fortress, 1984), 21–25.

27 For example, "in giving his Exodus slave law, Moses looks back to Jacob's problems described in the Book of Genesis, when serving the Aramean Laban. In giving his Leviticus law, he takes stock of the experience of the economic situation in Egypt, again in the Book of Genesis, when Joseph enslaves the Egyptians but before the Israelites themselves experience slavery in Egypt. For Deuteronomic law, he considers Israel's experience of slavery during his own lifetime as recounted in the Book of Exodus." Carmichael, "The Three Laws on the Lease of Slaves," 510.

28 Ibid., 509.

29 See Muhammad A. Dandamayev, "Slavery," *ABD* 6:58–65; Isaac Mendelsohn, *Slavery in the Ancient Near East: A Comparative Study of Slavery in Babylonia, Assyria, Syria, and Palestine from Middle of the Third Millennium to the End of the First Millennium* (Westport: Greenwood Press, 1978); idem, "Slavery in the OT," *IDB* 1:383–391; Raymond Westbrook, "The Character of Ancient Near Eastern Law," in *A History of Ancient Near Eastern Law* (ed. Raymond Westbrook; vol. 1; Leiden: E. J. Brill, 2003), 40–44.

affect the status and circumstances around slaves,[30] the emphasis on human rights in Deuteronomy should not be simply attributed to mere redaction or studies of dates.

In a comparison of biblical slave laws to ANE slave laws, S. Greengus notes that laws dealing with slave trade are absent in the Hebrew Bible.[31] In terms of the sale of chattel slaves, indeed Greengus is correct; however, such a phenomenon does not mean that the Israelites had never owned chattel slaves. The cases in Exod 21:20 – 21, 26 – 27 imply that chattel slaves did exist in the society. Furthermore, Lev 25:45 allowed the Israelites to buy chattel slaves from foreigners.

Until the end of the twentieth century, discussions on biblical slave laws have been primarily limited to the three release laws. The fact that the *subject matter* of debt slavery remains the same for the three laws favors the use of comparative studies that are characterized by source and dating issues. Other slave regulations, such as Exod 21:20 – 21, 26 – 27, 32; Lev 19:20 – 22; and Deut 23:16 – 17, have been inadvertently ignored, possibly due to the fact that these laws are rarely categorized as *slave laws*.[32] They are more commonly recognized under the categories of "bodily injury," "adultery," "ox goring," or "runaway slaves." Such grouping appears to be subjective.[33] To detect the overarching logic behind these ancient laws and categorize them with similar subject matters remain a significant challenge in this field.[34]

---

30 Dandamayev points out that "although in view of the law the slave was mere chattel, the actual position of slaves varied greatly even in a single society in the same historical period." Dandamayev, "Slavery," 60. Recent scholarship, however, suggests that ancient Hebrew slaves were not chattel slaves, but mostly indentured servants, who are redeemable after seven year servitude. See Jeffrey H. Tigay, *Deuteronomy* (Philadelphia: Jewish Publication Society of America, 1996), 147–148; Tikav Frymer-Kensky, "Israel," in *Security for Debt in Ancient Near Easter Law* (Leiden: E. J. Brill, 2001), 251–263.
31 Greengus suggests that the omission of slave trade may reflect the moral, religious, or political policies that have been paramount for the scriptural writers and editors. Ideologically, the absence reflects an understandable resistance to the imposition of "foreign laws" by the conquering and occupying powers. His suggestion is based on prevalent belief that the Pentateuch was still in forming state during the long period of Assryo-Babylonian plus Aramean cultural domination. Samuel Greengus, "The Selling of Slaves: Laws Missing from the Hebrew Bible?" *ZABR* 3(1997): 1–11. See also Samuel Greengus, "Biblical and ANE Law," *ABD* 4: 243.
32 VerSteeg, *Early Mesopotamian Law*, 5.
33 R. Haase probably was the first to classify most of the ANE laws into 95 categories, presenting them in German alphabetic order. R. Haase, *Keilschriftrechtliches* (Leonberg: Im Selbstverlag des Verfassers, 1998), 43–56.
34 In *A History of Ancient Near Eastern Law*, Westbrook concisely excludes sacral law and classifies the ANE laws into six major categories: personal status, family law, property, contracts,

Meanwhile, issues regarding human rights in the Hebrew Bible, and Old Testament ethics in general, have received increased attention in recent years.[35] Numerous scholars (e. g., H. C. Brichto, G. Braulik, E. Otto, and J. H. C. Wright) have observed that the treatment of slaves in the Hebrew Bible illustrates a certain shade of human rights. Otto professes, "[t]he Hebrew Bible and especially the book of Deuteronomy as the 'cradle' of the modern world (Max Weber) had an important impact on the conceptualization of these fields of human rights."[36]

Problem Statement

The preceding survey shows that a full-blown understanding of human rights in Deuteronomy is still ongoing. More often than not, scholars have neglected the

---

crime and delict, and international law. Westbrook, "The Character of Ancient Near Eastern Law," 2–4, 35–88.

35 See works such as Herbert Chanan Brichto, "The Hebrew Bible on Human Rights," in *Essays on Human Rights: Contemporary Issues and Jewish Perspectives* (ed. David Sidorsky; Philadelphia: Jewish Publication Society of America of America, 1979); idem, "Religion Is about Freedom, Human Rights, and Individual Autonomy," *ABQ* 19, no. 4 (2000): 307–308; James Limburg, "Human Rights in the Old Testament," in *The Church and the Rights of Man* (ed. Alois Müller and Norbert Greinachherceds; New York: Seabury, 1979), 20–26; Walter Harrelson, *The Ten Commandments and Human Rights* (Philadelphia: Fortress, 1980); James Barr, "Ancient Biblical Laws and Modern Human Rights," in *Justice and the Holy: Essays in Honor of Walter Harrelson* (ed. Douglas A. Knight and Peter J. Paris; Atlanta: Scholars, 1989), 21–33; Douglas A. Knight, "The Ethics of Human Life in the Hebrew Bible," in *Justice and the Holy: Essays in Honor of Walter Harrelson* (eds. Douglas A. Knight and Peter J. Paris; Atlanta: Scholars, 1989), 65–88; Moses Greenberg, "Biblical Attitudes toward Power: Ideal and Reality in Law and Prophets," in *Religion and Law: Biblical-Judaic and Islamic Perspectives* (ed. Edwin B. Firmage, Bernard G. Weiss, John W. Welch; Winona Lake: Eisenbrauns, 1990), 101–112; E. Otto, *Theologische Ethik des Alten Testaments* (Stuttgart: W. Kohlhammer, 1994); idem, "Human Rights: the Influence of the Hebrew Bible," *JNSL* 25 (1999): 13; idem, *Das Deuteronomium: Politische Theologie und Rechtsreform in Juda und Assyrien* (Berlin: De Gruyter, 1999); Wolfgang Huber, "Human Rights and Biblical Legal Thought," in *Religious Human Rights in Global Perspective* (ed. John Witte, Jr. and Johan D. van der Vyver; Hague: Martinus Nijhoff, 1996), 47–63; Cyril S. Rodd, *Glimpses of a Strange Land: Studies in Old Testament Ethics* (Edinburgh: T & T Clark, 2001); J. W. Rogerson, ed., *Theory and Practice in Old Testament Ethics* (New York: T & T Clark, 2004); Bernard M. Levinson and Eckart Otto, eds., *Recht und Ethik im Alten Testament: Beiträge des Symposiums 'Das Alte Testament und die Kultur der Moderne' Anlässlich des 100. Geburtstags Gerhard von Rad (1901–1971) Heidelberg, 18.–21. Oktober 2001* (Münster: Lit Verlag, 2004); J. H. Christopher Wright, *Old Testament Ethics for the People of God* (Downers Grove: InterVarsity Press, 2004), 333–337; Joe M. Sprinkle, *Biblical law and Its Relevance: A Christian Understanding and Ethical Application for Today of the Mosaic Regulations* (Lanham: University Press of America, 2006).

36 Otto, "Human Rights: the Influence of the Hebrew Bible," 13.

humanitarian aspect of the book, focusing instead on establishing the literary relation among the three slave manumission laws in the Pentateuch.

Slave laws in Deuteronomy, however, reflect much more than documentary dependence, possible historical settings, or slave release regulations. The Deuteronomic slave laws in fact go far beyond manumission.[37] The injunction of Deut 15:12–18 to furnish a slave with material rewards and heartfelt blessings by a master demands more than granting liberty. The command of Deut 23:16–17 to protect a freed slave finds no other social or historical equivalence in biblical times. One cannot but think of the theological connection between the One and Only God that Deuteronomy emphatically proclaims and the human rights it sympathetically portrays.[38] The two major themes of Deuteronomy, monotheism and humanitarian concerns, have been separately appreciated by scholars, but their relationship is often overlooked.[39] This study thus will attest that in Deuteronomy, the One and Only God YHWH, who has great compassion for the rights of human beings, identifies himself with a proper worldview for true human rights that can ultimately be defined and executed.

Research Methodology

Rather than following a source critical agenda, this research will pursue a text-oriented reading, dealing with the final form of these slave laws. Likewise, instead of tackling their contentious functions and purposes, an attempt to ask what *values* the laws promoted or what *interests* they protected will be the ultimate goal in understanding the idiosyncratic spirit of human rights presented in Deuteronomy.[40]

---

37 "It was not sufficient to give a man-servant and maid-servant their liberty after six years of service...if they had nothing with which to set up a home of their own; but love to the poor was required to do more than this, namely, to make some provision for the continued prosperity of those who were set at liberty." C. F. Keil and F. Delitzsch, *The Pentateuch* (trans. James Martin; vol. 3; Grand Rapids: Eerdmans, 1949), 372.
38 J. G. McConville contends that theology influenced the terminology and style of Deuteronomic laws, an opinion against M. Noth's proposal that the laws of Deuteronomy wielded influence upon its theology. J. G. McConville, *Law and Theology in Deuteronomy* (Sheffield: Sheffield Academic Press, 1984).
39 N. McDonald indicates, "Deuteronomy's right to a place in the discussion of 'monotheism' is beyond dispute, even its exact role is controversial." N. McDonald, *Deuteronomy and the Meaning of 'Monotheism'* (Tübingen: J. C. B. Mohr, 2003), 59.
40 This follows R. Versteeg's suggestion. Versteeg, *Early Mesopotamian Law*, 22. On this point, K. J. Vanhoozer states that "[s]ince the Enlightenment, most biblical scholars in the university

This study is essentially interdisciplinary, involving comparative legal study, legal sociology, biblical law exegesis, and ethics. Therefore, it will involve knowledge of both comparative law and legal sociology. R. Cotterrell indicates that "comparative law and sociology of law have been said by comparatists to be inseparable;" however, he also points out that the nature of this relationship has seldom been examined in detail. Rarely do scholars have a "sufficient interest in both fields to motivate such an inquiry," and even fewer are capable of such research.[41] As a note, it will be beyond this author's ability to discuss the slave laws with comprehensive knowledge in both fields. This study will discuss certain sociological perspectives, along with the theological ideas expressed in these slave laws, and not rely heavily upon or lean toward these two disciplines.

In the past several decades, at least five main approaches have been used in comparative legal study of biblical law, some of which can be used in various combinations in this study:

(1) Redactional reconstruction: This approach focuses on comparing biblical and cuneiform laws in order to discern identical sources and the periods in which they were edited. Scholars ascribe most of the so-called illogical and inconsistent arrangements of biblical law collections to redaction, revision, or interpolation. For example, in Exod 21:37–22:3 [Eng. 22:1–4], 22:1 appears to be an abrupt insertion into the law relating to the theft of an ox.[42]

(2) Canonical: In contrast to the standard source critical model, synchronic readings had a minor voice in the past century.[43]

---

adopted a strictly historical approach to the biblical texts in order to concentrate on the 'facts' rather than 'values'." Kevin J. Vanhoozer, *Is There a Meaning in This Text? The Bible, the Reader, and the Morality of Literary Knowledge* (Grand Rapids: Zondervan, 1998), 284–285. See also Jeffries M. Hamilton, *Social Justice and Deuteronomy: The Case of Deuteronomy 15* (Atlanta: Scholars, 1992), 2, 8.

41 Roger Cotterrell, "Comparatists and Sociology," in *Comparative Legal Studies: Traditions and Transitions* (ed. Pierre Legrand and Roderick Munday; New York: Cambridge University Press, 2003), 131.

42 For similar discussions, see Bernard M. Levinson, "The Case for Revision and Interpretation within the Biblical Legal Corpora," and Sophie Lafont, "Ancient Near Eastern Laws: Continuity and Pluralism," in *Theory and Method in Biblical and Cuneiform Law: Revision, Interpolation and Development* (ed. Bernard M. Levinson; Sheffield: Sheffield Academic Press, 1994), 37–59 and 91–118. J. M. Powis Smith, *The Origin and History of Hebrew Law* (Westport: Hyperion, 1990); J. J. Finkelstein, *The Ox That Gored* (Philadelphia: The American Philosophical Society, 1981); Van Seters, *A Law Book for the Diaspora*; and David P. Wright, "The Laws of Hammurabi as a Source for the Covenant Collection," *MAARAV* 10 (2003): 11–87.

43 R. Westbrook is often thought to be the leading representative of this approach. However, it is little known that his dating to the Pentateuch differs from most scholars in this camp. He dates the Covenant law book, "essentially Exod 21:1–22:16," at the ninth century with reservation, and

(3) Classification of legal patterns: This approach develops B. Gemser's study of motive clauses and A. Alt's two legal categories—apodictic and casuistic legal formulation. According to R. Sonsino, Gemser was the first scholar who seriously devoted himself to the issue of motive clauses in biblical laws.[44] Despite the strong challenge by E. Gerstenberger, Alt's classification of biblical law was picked up and revised by D. Patrick and is deemed as the point of departure for all subsequent form criticism of the laws.[45]

(4) Treaty framework: G. E. Mendenhall was the first to recognize the resemblance between the Israelite covenant and the ANE treaties—As early as 1954, his famous work called attention to this issue with reference to the Hittite vassal-treaties.[46] Thereafter, "more and more scholars accepted both the antiquity and significance of 'covenant' in early Israel, arguing in its favour under fresh impulses."[47] Although some remain skeptical about this observation,[48] two pop-

---

the Deuteronomic law book at the seventh century. In "The Development of Law in the Ancient Near East: Slave and Master in Ancient Near Eastern Law," he asserts that "the early centuries of the first millennium were marked by Assyria's rise to universal dominion. At its zenith in the eighth and seventh centuries, the Assyrian Empire controlled the entire Fertile Crescent. Sources from this period are referred to as Neo-Assyrian. Most of biblical law can be dated to this and the subsequent period." Raymond Westbrook, "The Development of Law in the Ancient Near East: Slave and Master in Ancient Near Eastern Law," n.p. [cited 4 November 2009]; idem, "What Is the Covenant Code?" in *Theory and Method in Biblical and Cuneiform Law: Revision, Interpolation and Development* (ed. Bernard M. Levinson; Sheffield: Sheffield Academic Press, 1994), 15–36. B. M. Levinson implies that J. G. McConville and G. C. Chirichigno, who completed their dissertations under the tutelage of Gordon J. Wenham, tend to read the biblical legal texts synchronically. B. M. Levinson, "The Manumission of Hermeneutics," 288–289.

44 See Rifat Sonsino, *Motive Clauses in Hebrew Law: Biblical Forms and Near Eastern Parallels* (Chico: Scholars, 1980), xv.

45 See Dale Patrick, "Casuistic Law Governing Primary Rights and Duties," *JBL* 92, no. 2 (1973): 180–184, and Dale Patrick, *Old Testament Law* (Atlanta: John Knox, 1985). Proponents of this approach include: Berend Gemser, "The Importance of the Motive Clause in Old Testament Law," *VTSup* (1953): 50–66. Rifat Sonsino, *Motive Clauses in Hebrew Law: Biblical Forms and Near Eastern Parallels* (Chico, Scholars, 1980), and Roger William Uitti, "The Motive Clause in Old Testament Law" (Ph.D. diss., Lutheran School of Theology at Chicago, 1973). Albrecht Alt, "The Origins of the Israelites," in *Essays on Old Testament History and Religion* (trans. R. A. Wilson, Sheffield: JSOT, 1989), 79–132. See also Fred L. Horton, "A Reassessment of the Legal Forms in the Pentateuch and Their Functions," in *One Hundred Seventh Annual Meeting Seminar Papers* (Atlanta: SBL, 1971), 347–396.

46 George E. Mendenhall, "Covenant Forms in Israelite Tradition," *BA* 17, no. 3 (1954): 50–76; idem, "Ancient Oriental and Biblical Law," *BA* 17, no. 2 (1954): 26–46; *Law and Covenant in Israel and the Ancient Near East* (Pittsburgh: The Biblical Colloquium, 1955).

47 K. A. Kitchen, "The Fall and Rise of Covenant, Law and Treaty," *TynBul* 40 (1989): 119. See also discussion in Margaret Elizabeth Bellefontaine, "A Study of Ancient Israelite Laws and Their Function as Covenant Stipulations" (Ph.D. diss., University of Notre Dame, 1973), 61–83.

ular datings of Deuteronomy stem from the increasingly recognized pattern between the overall structure of the book of Deuteronomy and that of the ANE vassal treaty. The first is that the treaty structure points to the Mosaic period or shortly thereafter (e. g., P. C. Craigie, M. G. Kline, and K. A. Kitchen).[49] The second is that Deuteronomy is a composition of the eighth or seventh century B.C. (e. g., D. McCarthy, M. Weinfeld, and R. Frankena).[50] In the past four decades, Kitchen has endeavored to establish "an outline history of treaty, law, and covenant through some two thousand years, from circa 2500 down to circa 650, in six distinct phases, using between eighty to ninety documents."[51] According to his research on the ANE treaty patterns, the suzerainty-treat format of Deuteronomy belongs "squarely within phase V, within 1400–1200, and *at no other date*. The impartial and very extensive evidence (thirty Hittite-inspired documents and versions!) sets this matter beyond any further dispute."[52] Kitchen's argument

---

48 See works such as Erhard S. Gerstenberger, "Covenant and Commandment," *JBL* 84, no. 1 (1965): 38–51; Ernest W. Nicholson, *God and His People: Covenant and Theology in the Old Testament*, (New York: Oxford University Press, 1986) and G. Beckman, "Hittite Treaties and the Development of the Cuneiform Treaty Tradition." in *Deuteronomistischen Geschichtswerke* (ed. Markus Witte, et al.; Berlin: Walter de Gruyter, 2006), 298.

49 See discussion in Craigie, *The Book of Deuteronomy*, 24–29. See also M. G. Kline, *The Structure of Biblical Authority* (Grand Rapids: Eerdmans, 1972), 9–14, 43–44.

50 Dennis J. McCarthy, *Treaty and Covenant: A Study in Form in the Ancient Oriental Documents and in the Old Testament* (Rome: Biblical Institute, 1981), 157–187, 287; R. Frankena, "The Vassal-Treaties of Esarhaddon and the Dating of Deuteronomy," in *25:1940–1965; Oudtestamentlich Werkgezelschap in Nederland* (Leiden: E. J. Brill, 1965), 122–154. M. Weinfeld, *Deuteronomy 1–11* (New York: Doubleday, 1991), 2–9; idem, *Deuteronomy and Deuteronomic School* (Winona Lake: Eisenbrauns, 1992), 59–157.

51 Kitchen, *On the Reliability of the Old Testament*, 283–284. Kitchen emphasizes that "[w]e do *not* possess an official copy or formal text of the actual covenant itself, but only presentations of the *enactment* of that covenant (with considerable sections of its contents) at Sinai (in Exodus-Leviticus), and of the *enactment* of renewals of it both in the plains of Moab forty years later (extensively in Deuteronomy) and in Canaan soon afterward (Josh. 8, mention only; and 23, summary). This distinction is of very great importance, because external evidence on treaties and covenants shows that (e. g.) the order of enactment does *not* always correspond to the final order of items in formal written copies of such a document. Nevertheless, the congruity of contents and the main order amply suffices to establish with utmost clarity that close correspondences and what contrasting differences actually exist between our biblical and external material." Kitchen, *On the Reliability of the Old Testament*, 283. See also his works, "Ancient Orient, 'Deuteronism,' and the Old Testament" in *New Perspectives on the Old Testament* (ed. J. Barton Payne; Waco: Word, 1970), 1–24; idem, *The Bible in Its World: The Bible and Archaeology Today* (Exeter: Paternoster, 1977), 79–85; idem, "The Fall and Rise of Covenant, Law and Treaty," *TynBul* 40 (1989): 118–135.

52 Kitchen, *On the Reliability of the Old Testament*, 287–288. Kitchen notes, "It is *not* my creation, it is inherent in the mass of original documents *themselves*, and so cannot be gained, if the brute facts are to be respected." Kitchen, *On the Reliability of the Old Testament*, 288.

and methodology have not led to a firm consensus at this time. Scholars argue vigorously from both sides. Nonetheless, one thing we can be sure of is that Deuteronomy is about the covenant bond between God and his people.

(5) Social and judicial institutions: In this approach, scholars are devoted to distinguishing social and judicial institutions in the ANE world.[53]

Lastly, rhetorical analysis is significant for understanding Deuteronomic laws, given that the laws in Deuteronomy are lavishly rhetorical with modes of persuasion. The most outstanding feature of the Deuteronomic style, notes M. Weinfeld, is its use of rhetoric not only in the introductory discourses but also in the laws.[54] At the present, though a rhetorical study of the Deuteronomic laws is still in germination,[55] three traditional rhetorical modes of argumentation can be easily found in the discourses and laws of Deuteronomy: ethos, pathos, and logos.[56] T. A. Lenchak perceives that all three aspects are in play in Moses' third discourse (Deut 28:69–30:20). The ethos is dominated by both YHWH and his agent Moses. The pathos is revealed by figures of presence (especially devices of repetition, amplification, and accentuation) and the use of emotional words and techniques. The logos can be discovered in several rational argumentations, such as, YHWH being the One and Only God, who is solely to be revered, who initiates redemption, who elects his people, and who establishes his covenant.[57] The same is also true for Deut 15:12–18, as this study will disclose in detail. Most recent approaches from legal semiotics, studies of legal discourse, and narrative reading of laws in Pentateuchal legislative texts will also be considered in this research.[58]

---

53 Moshe Weinfeld, *Social Justice in Ancient Israel and in the Ancient Near East* (Minneapolis: Fortress, 1995); K. D. Irani, and Morris Silver, eds. *Social Justice in the Ancient World* (Westport: Greenwood, 1995). See also a number of scholars' monographs on legal and social institutions in the biblical and ANE world in the volume 1 of Jack M. Sasson, ed., *Civilizations of the Ancient Near East*, 2 vols. (Peabody: Hendrickson, 2000), 517–603.
54 Moses Weinfeld, *Deuteronomy and the Deuteronomic School* (Winona: Eisenbrauns, 1992), 3, 51–58, 171–178.
55 See works such as Martin J. Oosthuizen, "Deuteronomy 15:1–18 in Socio-Rhetorical Perspective," *ZABR* 3 (1997): 64–91. Timothy A. Lenchak, *Choose Life! A Rhetorical-Critical Investigation of Deuteronomy 28,69–30,20* (Roma: Editrice Pontificio Istituto Biblico, 1993), 1–37; James W. Watts, "Rhetorical Strategy in the Composition of the Pentateuch," *JSOT* 68 (1995): 18–19.
56 Richard McKeon, ed., *The Basic Works of Aristotle* (New York: Random House; 1941), 1329–1336.
57 See Lenchak's discussion particularly in chapter 4. Lenchak, *Choose Life! A Rhetorical-Critical Investigation of Deuteronomy 28,69–30,20*, 119–169.
58 Bernard S. Jackson, *Studies in the Semiotics of Biblical Law* (Sheffield: Sheffield Academic Press, 2000); Assnat Bartor, "The Representation of Speech in the Casuistic Laws of the Pen-

This study, however, proceeds with the assumption that neither dates nor historical settings of biblical laws are critical for explaining the underlying concept of human rights. The reason for this assumption is threefold:

(1) The questioning of current dating methods: In recent years, an increasing number of comparative legal studies have disputed the adequacy of dating methods. R. Westbrook reminds his readers that "apparent inconsistencies should be ascribed to the state of our ignorance concerning the social and cultural background to the laws, not necessarily to historical development and certainly not to an excess of either subtlety or incompetence on the part of their compiler."[59]

(2) That law often shapes social and economic factors, not vice versa. A. Watson advises that "similarities between a few individual legal provisions are not particularly significant, nor necessarily are statements from a much later writer that a certain provision was the result of direct borrowing."[60] The slave laws that stress humanitarian concerns in Deuteronomy could be legislated purposely to shape Israel's culture.

(3) Speculative theories about the function and purpose of the ANE and biblical laws.[61] Considering that these ancient laws were theoretical documents in essence, Westbrook argues that it is difficult to know how much they represent the law in practice.[62] It is also quite possible that some of these laws might

---

tateuch: the Phenomenon of Combined Discourse," *JBL* 126, no. 2 (2007): 231–249; idem, *Reading Law as Narrative: A Study in the Casuistic Laws of the Pentateuch* (Atlanta: Society of Biblical Literature, 2010); Chaya Halberstam, "The Art of Biblical Law," *Prooftexts* 27, no. 2 (2007): 345–364, see specially 360–361, n. 6.

59 Westbrook, "What Is the Covenant Code?" 36.

60 Watson, *Legal Transplants*, 25. By focusing on the role of law as a culture-shaping force, F. Deng shows how distorting it is to treat law as a mirror and register of social power. Francis Mading Deng, *Tradition and Modernization: A Challenge for Law among the Dinka of the Sudan* (New Haven: Yale University Press, 1986).

61 In answering the questions of the nature and purpose of law collections, J. M. Hamilton gives three theories—first, as an addendum to or revitalization of common law; second, as an enumeration of case decisions around a series of themes with the purpose of serving as a guide to judges (i.e., the law collections as practical application of legal theory); and third, as the self-justification of the king to posterity concerning the just character of his reign (the law collections as royal apology). Hamilton, *Social Justice and Deuteronomy*, 35–36. See also Finkelstein, *The Ox That Gored*, 16–17. In her recent essay, M. T. Roth is convinced that the ancient legal compositions were copied and recopied, used to teach scribes the proper way of writing and phrasing documents, and even used to instill into the scribal class a unified vision. Roth, "The Law Collection of King Hammurabi," 31.

62 Westbrook, "The Character of Ancient Near Eastern Law," 70–71.

serve the purpose of royal propaganda.[63] In R. Cotterrell's *The Sociology of Law: An Introduction*, he points out that many jurisprudential writings tend to confuse the concepts of function and purpose. For him, the function of the law may well have no relation at all to its original purpose.[64] Arbitrarily imposing *function* or *purpose* on these ancient laws (e. g., to solve the Josianic social and economic problems or to reflect the enslavement of exilic or postexilic people) by arguing a specific historical scene as a prerequisite is not only questionable but also fruitless.

We should note that this study does not intend to bypass the historical setting of these laws to mean that they arose *sui generis*. They were potentially borrowed. Law borrowing, or in a more technical term, legal transplant, was common in ancient societies as "societies largely invent their constitutions, their political and administrative systems, even in these days their economies; but their private law is nearly always taken from others."[65]

Watson champions the term "legal transplants" to designate the moving of a rule or a system of law from one country/people to another.[66] According to him,

---

63 A similar case can also be found in the account of 2 Kgs 14:5–6, which applied the law of Deut 24:16 to promulgate Amaziah's virtue as becoming a *function* of the law.

64 Cotterrell states, "The purpose of laws may be seen differently at different times and they exist for reasons quite different from those contained in explicit legislative or judicial justifications. Further, many laws may have no discernible purpose, existing perhaps only, for example, because of tradition, legislative inertia, or the need to compromise radically different purposes of interest groups." Roger Cotterrell, *The Sociology of Law: An Introduction* (London: Butterworths, 1992), 72. E. Rostow summarizes Montesquieu's view: "The principal function of law is to serve as one of the educational and formative influences of the culture, not merely in bringing the law in action up to the standard of the existing goal of law, but in perfecting the goal of the law." Eugene Rostow, *The Sovereign Prerogative: The Supreme Court and the Quest for Law* (Westport: Greenwood, 1962), 141.

65 Watson, *Legal Transplants*, 8, quoting S. F. C. Milsom, *Historical Foundations of the Common Law* (London: Butterworths, 1969), ix.

66 Some comparative law scholars disagree with Watson's theory of legal transplants, while many still embrace and develop Watson's proposal. See Pierre Legrand, "The Impossibility of 'Legal Transplants'," *Maastricht J. European and Comparative Law* 4 (1997): 111–124. See also Pierre Legrand and R. J. C. Munday, eds., *Comparative Legal Studies: Traditions and Transitions* (Cambridge: Cambridge University Press, 2003). A. Watson's response to Legrand's criticism, see Alan Watson, "Legal Transplants and European Private Law," *Electronic Journal of Comparative Law* 4, no. 4 (2000): n.p. [cited 17 February 2009]. Online: http://www.ejcl.org/44/art44–2.html. See also David A. Westbrook, "Theorizing the Diffusion of Law: Conceptual Difficulties, Unstable Imaginations, and the Effort to Think Gracefully Nonetheless," *Harvard International Law Journal* 47 (2006): 489–505; John W. Cairns and Olivia F. Robinson, eds., *Critical Studies in Ancient Law, Comparative Law and Legal History: Essays in Honour of Alan Watson* (Oxford: Hart,

legal transplants have been common since the earliest records of human history.[67] Most changes in legal systems result from borrowing. He further contends that legal transplants are the major contributors of legal development, as laws were commonly inspired by foreign policies and experiences.[68] Therefore, "it is in fact remarkable how different in important detail even two closely related systems might be."[69] For Watson, law is a reflection of the spirit of a people, a sign of people's identity.[70]

In the recent edited work, *A History of Ancient Near Eastern Law*, Westbrook follows his earlier position and ventures that all the ANE systems belong to a common legal culture in varying degrees, sharing a legal ontology.[71] Moreover, a law transformation may take place during the process of transmission, when those who take up the law infuse a disparate spirit into it. The private laws in the Pentateuch might have adopted similar legal scopes and rules from other ancient sources, or from a common legal ontology, yet they definitely claim their own *Volksgeist*.

Likewise, D. Patrick urges biblical scholars to go beyond form criticism and critical historical methods, to study biblical law as a humanistic literature, as a coherent and comprehensive system of thoughts, and to reconstruct the intellectual system *behind* it.[72] The Deuteronomic slave laws articulated an innovative identity for a newborn society regardless of how, when, or where these laws were modified and/or transformed from other law collections. To understand how such an innovative identity is transformed in terms of the theological thinking behind it will be important in the study of slave laws.

From a synchronic reading, the establishment of this innovative identity may be assumed as a divine oracle given by YHWH through his meditator Moses to the new born God's people on the brink of their entering the Promised Land.[73] J. G. McConville suggests that the book of Deuteronomy or at least a form of it is the document of a real political and religious constitution of Israel from the

---

2001); E. Örücü and David Nelken eds., *Comparative Law: A Handbook* (Oxford and Portland: Hart, 2007).

67 Watson, *Legal Transplants*, 21.

68 Ibid., 21–30; idem, *Society and Legal Change* (Edinburgh: Scottish Academic Press, 1977), 98–114; idem, *Sources of Law, Legal Change, and Ambiguity* (Philadelphia: University of Pennsylvania Press, 1984).

69 Watson, *Legal Transplants*, 21.

70 Ibid., 21.

71 Westbrook, "The Character of Ancient Near Eastern Law," 4.

72 Dale Patrick, "Studying Biblical Law as a Humanities," *Semeia* 45 (1989): 27–47.

73 Craigie, *The Book of Deuteronomy*, 28.

pre-monarchal period.[74] Of course, in the historical critical study of the Pentateuch since De Wette it has been argued that Deuteronomy is the law book created in connection with Josiah's reforms in the third part of the seventh century
B.C.[75] Given that the book of Deuteronomy is highly structured and known for its
suzerainty-treaty frame and the three valedictory speeches of Moses,[76] this study
will treat synchronic and diachronic readings as complimentary to each other.
The book of Deuteronomy is surely an edited work, as McConville indicates,
"there is no reason to suppose that the content of the book may not have
changed over time."[77] To explore the origin and development of the text through
analysis of its sources is a legitimate scholarly pursuit,[78] yet the hypotheses concerning the growth of the book of Deuteronomy do not really help explain the
humanitarian spirit that the Deuteronomic laws reflect, which is what this research is all about.

---

74 McConville, *Deuteronomy*, 34.

75 In R. G. Kratz's recent work, *One God, One Cult, One Nation: Archaeological and Biblical
Perspectives*, he provides a concise summary and analysis on the scholarly development of the
idea of cultic centralization, from J. Wellhausen, De Wette, M. Weinfeld, to E. Otto. See Reinhard
G. Kratz, *One God, One Cult, One Nation: Archaeological and Biblical Perspectives* (Berlin: Walter
de Gruyter, 2010).

76 Scholars usually divide Deuteronomy into three Mosaic addresses, see e.g., R. Polzin, D. L.
Christensen, and C. J. Labuschagne, M. Weinfeld, and J. H. Tigay etc. However, N. Lohfink
exceptionally divides Moses' oration into four separate speeches, based on the superscriptions
found in Deut 1:1, 4:44, 28:69, and 33:1. Robert Polzin, *Moses and the Deuteronomist: A Literary
Study of the Deuteronomic History* (New York: Seabury 1980), 25–72; D. L. Christensen, "Form
and Structure in Deuteronomy 1–11," in *Das Deuteronomium: Entstehung, Gestalt und Botschaft*
(ed. N. Lohfink; Leuven: University Press, 1985), 135–144; C. J. Labuschagne, "Divine Speech in
Deuteronomy," in *Das Deuteronomium: Entstehung, Gestalt und Botschaft* (ed. N. Lohfink; Leuven: University Press, 1985), 111–126; Weinfeld, *Deuteronomy 1–11*, 4–9; Tigay, *The JPS Torah
Commentary: Deuteronomy*, ix. Norbert Lohfink, *Das Hauptgebot: Eine Untersuchung Literarischer Einleitungsfragen zu Dtn 5–11* (Roma: Pontificio Instituto Biblico, 1963), 3.

77 McConville, *Deuteronomy*, 39.

78 See such as Horst Dietrich Preuss, *Deuteronomium* (Darmstadt: Wissenschaftliche Buchgesellschaft, 1982); Eckart Otto, *Das Deuteronomium im Pentateuch und Hexateuch* (Tübingen:
Mohr Siebeck, 2000); Timo Veijola, "Deuteronomismusforschung zwischen Tradition und Innovation (I)," *Theologische Rundschau* 67 (2002): 273–327; idem., "Deuteronomismusforschung
zwischen Tradition und Innovation (II)," *Theologische Rundschau* 67 (2002): 391–424; idem.,
"Deuteronomismusforschung zwischen Tradition und Innovation (III)," *Theologische Rundschau*
68 (2003): 1–44; Erik Aurelius, "Der Ursprung des Ersten Gebots," *Zeitschrift für Theologie und
Kirche* 100.1 (2003): 1–21; Reinhard G. Kratz, *The Composition of the Narrative Books of the Old
Testament* (London: T&T Clark, 2005). Ernst Axel Knauf, "Observations on Judah's Social and
Economic History and the Dating of the Laws in Deuteronomy," *The Journal of Hebrew Scriptures*
9, a.18 (2009): n.p. [cited: 17 November 2013]. Online: http://www.jhsonline.org/Articles/article_
120.pdf.

For example, based on three criteria, R. G. Kratz believes that the basic document of Deuteronomy, so-called "Ur-Deuteronomy" is a novella of the book of the Covenant in Exodus 20 – 23 and originally contained only the centralization laws in Deuteronomy 12– 21. He proposes that Deut 6:4 – 5 and 26:16 form a more or less independent framework around Ur-Deuteronomy and everything else in Deuteronomy 12– 25 that falls outside of the criteria should be regarded as secondary and supplemental.[79] Finally, he suggests two possibilities: The idea of centralization and the unusual call of "Hear, Israel" in Deut 6:4f is a reaction to either the downfall of Samaria or the downfall of the kingdom of Judah.[80] With this suggestion, the basic part of the book of Deuteronomy could be produced at the time around 720 – 586 B.C., and the rest, at a later time. The problem is that, for example, this dating creates an anachronism between the historical narrative of 2 Kgs 14:5 – 6 and the legislative text of Deut 24:16. In the account of 2 Kgs 14:5 – 6, the narrator claims that Amaziah's merciful act of avoiding vendetta is due to his obedience to "what is written in the Book of *the Torah of Moses*" (כַּכָּתוּב בְּסֵפֶר תּוֹרַת־מֹשֶׁה), boasting the king's humanitarian concern based on the law of Deut 24:16. According to Kratz, Deut 24:16 belongs to an appendix of Deut 21:10 – 25:19, a later supplement.[81] As for the account of 2 Kgs 14:5 – 6, he suggests that 2 Kgs 14:6, a supplement that belongs to the secondary Deuteronomistic revision (Dtr[S]), is quoted literally from Deut 24:16.[82] The account of 2 Kgs 14:5 – 6 implies that in Amaziah's time, people could be familiar with this law; otherwise this promulgation is nonsensical. There must have been at least some version of the *Torah of Moses* that contains this law before the time of Amaziah's reign, which is ca. 796 – 767 B.C.[83] If not, one has to assume that the compiler of the book of Kings adds and fakes the legal basis for the king's act, because Deut 24:16 is a later law that does not exist in Amaziah's time according to Kratz's compositional theory. But then, one has to further explain why the compiler does this to favor to Amaziah, who does not keep Moses' commands

---

79 The three criteria are: change of number in the form of address, the relationship to the book of the Covenant in Exod 20:22– 23:33, and the notion of the centralization of the cult. Kratz, *The Composition of the Narrative Books of the Old Testament*, 114– 133.
80 Ibid., 132.
81 Ibid., 132.
82 Ibid., 163, 168, 185.
83 Edwin R. Thiele, *The Mysterious Numbers of the Hebrew Kings* (Grand Rapids: Zondervan, 1983), 113.

to destroy the high places (e. g., Deut 16:1–8, 21–22). And then, a more profound question should be brought up, "How do we date ideologies?"[84]

Put aside the possible dates of both books, the account of 2 Kgs 14:5–6 reveals a lucid message: The author of the account or the compiler of the book must acknowledge the humanitarian spirit that the law of Deut 24:16 connotes and assume that its readers would appreciate this positive *value*. None of these factors, the origins of sources, the purposes of insertions, the functions of supplements, or the motives of writings, etc., can change the ethical *value* that both passages intend to share with their readers. This is what this study intends to focus on. Rather than surmising dates from critical historical methods, our study looks at biblical law as humanistic literature. Nevertheless, Kratz has made some good and useful observations and Deuteronomy should not be interpreted in isolation from the so-called Deuteronomistic History (DtrH), as suggested by McConville.[85] The author of Kings is undeniably influenced by Deuteronomy.[86] As Kratz observes, both books share the same concern for the place of worship and the high reverence for the Oneness of YHWH, which strongly represents the spirit of the First Commandment.[87] In the scholarly discussion the "land" has rarely been discussed along with the covenant, the cult, and the humanitarian spirit of the laws. In Deuteronomic law, however, the land is presented in an indirect but very important way: the agrarian products (grain, new wine, and herd/flock). These are blessings from YHWH and should be used to revere him and to share with the socially weak. The so-called "Ur-Deuteronomy" carries not only the idea of cultic centralization, but also the scheme of sharing agrarian products with the underprivileged.[88] This study will therefore discuss

---

84 See Richard D. Nelson, "A Response to Thomas C. Römer, The So-Called Deuteronomistic History," *The Journal of Hebrew Scriptures* 9, a.17 (2009): n.p. [cited: 17 November 2013]. Online: http://www.jhsonline.org/Articles/article_119.pdf.

85 McConville, *Deuteronomy*, 32–33.

86 Scholars have different perspectives on the so-called "Deuteronomistic History." The recent monograph published by Thomas Römer, *The So-Called Deuteronomistic History: A Sociological, Historical, and Literary Introduction*, while presents a proposal of both descriptive and prescriptive approaches, does not settle the battle of this debate. Thomas Römer, *The So-Called Deuteronomistic History: A Sociological, Historical, and Literary Introduction* (London: T. & T. Clark, 2005). Four other representatives of thoughts and discussions from R. D. Nelson, S. L. McKenzie, E. Otto, and Y. Amit can be found in Raymond F. Person, Jr. et all., "In Conversation with Thomas Römer, *The So-Called Deuteronomistic History: A Sociological, Historical, and Literary Introduction* (London: T. & T. Clark, 2005)," *The Journal of Hebrew Scriptures* 9, a.17 (2009): n.p. [cited: 17 November 2013]. Online: http://www.jhsonline.org/Articles/article_119.pdf.

87 Kratz, *The Composition of the Narrative Books of the Old Testament*, 162–163. See also Aurelius, "Der Ursprung des Ersten Gebots," 1–21.

88 Deut 12:17–19; 14:28–29; 26:11–14.

the theological connection of the land theme, the reverence of YHWH, and the humanitarian concern in the Deuteronomic laws.

This study will seek to follow an inductive examination, and face squarely the different details of legal changes on the other. Scholars in comparative law, legal sociology, and biblical comparative studies have recently called attention to distinguishing *differences* from similarities.[89] M. Malul maintains that "a good methodology must take into account all the possible data, the differences and similarities as well as the wider context on both sides of the equation, and study them in an objective manner with the criterion of coincidence *versus* uniqueness as a main guiding rule."[90] In the past, many comparative legal studies between biblical laws and their ANE counterparts have ignored their contrastive elements and focused merely on resemblance. W. W. Hallo in his "Compare and Contrast: The Contextual Approach to Biblical Literature" proposes a "contrastive approach" to pay equal attention to possible contrasts between biblical phenomena and their ANE counterparts, whether in the realm of institutions or literary formulation.[91]

"In a number of instances," according to K. L. Younger, Jr., "scholars have been too quick in attempting to do comparative study without allowing time to fully establish the proper reading and understanding of the newly discovered text."[92] He explains the past phenomena in biblical comparative studies,[93]

The fact is that presuppositions often shape the comparative evaluation. Some scholars emphasize the Old Testament's similarity to and continuity with ancient Near Eastern literature. In this way they seek to demonstrate that the Old Testament is authentic or, on the other hand, that it is merely a product of its environment. Other scholars emphasize the Hebrew Bible's divergence from and contrast with its background. In this, they seek to demonstrate that it is absolutely different or, on the other hand, that each of the ancient Near

---

89 Cotterrell, "Comparatists and Sociology," 135; Pierre Legrand, "The Same and the Different," in *Comparative Legal Studies: Traditions and Transitions* (ed. Pierre Legrand and R. J. C. Munday, Cambridge: Cambridge University Press, 2003), 271–272; Lawrence Rosen, "Beyond Comparison," in *Comparative Legal Studies: Traditions and Transitions* (ed. Pierre Legrand and R. J. C. Munday, Cambridge: Cambridge University Press, 2003), 503; David A. Westbrook, "Theorizing the Diffusion of Law," 491.

90 Malul, *The Comparative Method in Ancient Near Eastern and Biblical Legal Studies*, 159.

91 W. W. Hallo, "Compare and Contrast: The Contextual Approach to Biblical Literature," in *The Bible in the Light of Cuneiform Literature: Scripture in Context III* (ed. William W. Hallo, Bruce William Jones, and Gerald L. Mattingly; Lewiston: E. Mellen, Pickwick, 1990), 1–30.

92 K. Lawson Younger, Jr. "The 'Contextual Method': Some West Semitic Reflections," in *The Context of Scripture III* (ed. William W. Hallo, and K. Lawson Younger, Jr.; New York: E. J. Brill, 2003), xxxvi.

93 Younger, "The 'Contextual Method': Some West Semitic Reflections," xxxvii.

Eastern literatures should be appreciated on its merits, not just in comparison with the others.

Younger suggests that balance in the evaluation of evidence is achieved through assessing propinquity along four lines: linguistic, geographic, chronological, and cultural.[94] He draws from three ANE texts, which parallel the curse formula in Lev 26:26, and concludes that it would be wrong to argue either for a direct borrowing on the part of the Hebrew Bible, or for a particular date for the biblical text.[95] Hence, the comparative legal study in this study will utilize a balanced approach, as Hallo proposes, of a "contextual method" to observe comparisons as well as contrasts between ANE laws and biblical laws.[96] It will seek to not only carefully follow an inductive examination, but also explore epistemological answers about the different details of legal changes.

In addition to the main passages in Deut 15:12–18; 23:16–17, this study will also examine other passages that touch on slave laws, such as: Exod 21:2–11, 20–21, 26–27, 32; Lev 19:20–22; 25:39–55, and Jer 34:8–16, as well as other ANE laws that mention slavery (LU 4, 5, 8, 17, 24–26; LL f, 12–14, 25–26; LE 22–23, 31, 33–35, 40, 49–52, 55, 57; LH 7, 15–20, 114–119, 146–147, 199, 205, 213–214, 226–227, 231, 252, 278–282; MAL A 39, A 44, A 48, C+G 1, C+G 2, C+G 3, C+G 7; HL 22–24) etc.[97] Some other biblical regulations related to slaves, for instance the right to observe feasts and sabbatical rests with Israelite people

---

94 Ibid, xxxvii. He notes that it is not necessarily in this order. Younger explains, "A parallel that is closer to the biblical material in language, in geographic proximity, in time, and culture is a stronger parallel than one that is removed from the biblical material along one or more of these lines."

95 Ibid, xxxix. Younger says, "It appears that there were some stock West Semitic curse formulae that could be drawn from in the composition of curse passages and that these could be adapted to the particular needs of the ancient writers, the apodosis of the curse is modified."

96 William W. Hallo, "Biblical History in Its Near Eastern Setting: the Contextual Approach," in *Scripture in Context: Essays on the Comparative Method* (ed. Carl D. Evans, William W. Hallo, and John B. White; Pittsburgh: Pickwick, 1980), 1–26; idem, "Compare and Contrast: The Contextual Approach to Biblical Literature," in *The Bible in the Light of Cuneiform Literature: Scripture in Context III* (ed. William W. Hallo, Bruce William Jones, and Gerald L. Mattingly; Lewiston: E. Mellen, Pickwick, 1990), 1–30. K. Lawson Younger, Jr. "The 'Contextual Method': Some West Semitic Reflections," in *The Context of Scripture III* (ed. William W. Hallo, and K. Lawson Younger, Jr.; New York: E. J. Brill, 2003), xxxv-xlii.

97 LE, Laws of Eshnunna; MAL, Middle Assyrian Laws. The abbreviations used are commonly accepted in recent scholarship. See also Martha T. Roth, *Law Collections from Mesopotamia and Asia Minor* (Atlanta: Scholars Press, 1997); William W. Hallo and K. Lawson Younger, eds., *Context of Scripture* (3 vols.; New York: E. J. Brill, 2003).

(Exod 20: 8 – 11; 23:12; Lev 25:6; Deut 5:12 – 15; 16:9 – 15), and ancient legal documents with slave issues, will also be incorporated into discussions.[98]

Following similar research by R. Haase, this study will tabulate biblical and ANE law collections to provide a more inclusive base for comparative studies of ancient slave laws.[99] In order to discern the degrees of analogy, this study will suggest a legal categorizational system to distinguish laws in three levels of similarities and differences—*topics*, *issues*, and *situations*. Based on these tabulations and the legal categorizational system, biblical and ANE slave laws will be categorized and compared to see whether the traditionally assumed *similarities* between these laws are analogous due to merely similar subject matter, or if there are close parallels, differences, contrasts, or a mix of these in their legal topics and issues.[100] Laws that share the same subject matter of slave release may differ fundamentally in their legislative spirits, ethical values, social-economic motivations, political intentions, or theological rationales.[101] This study will also explore the different cosmologies, worldviews, and positions on morality shaping in laws between the ANE and the Bible to seek the rationales that influence the humanitarian concerns present in the laws. Rather than evaluating each category of human rights, this study will observe human rights in Deuteronomy by the fundamental theme—liberty, equality, and fraternity.[102] This tripartite set will help direct examination of human rights in Deuteronomy.

---

98 W. Hallo and K. Lawson Younger, eds., *Context of Scripture:* "A Lawsuit Over a Syrian Slave," 31 – 32; "Sale of Three Slaves," 258 – 259; "Sale of Slave Woman," 259 – 260; "A Slave Redemption," 260 – 261; "Sale of a Slave," 261 – 262. "Slave Sale," 299, 315.

99 R. Haase, *Keilschriftrechtlichesrs*, 43 – 56.

100 The two volume work *A History of Ancient Near Eastern Law* discusses the topic of slavery by individual period and geographic area in twenty six separate essays by thoroughly surveying ANE laws. However, it does not make any particular comparison between similar subject matter. Raymond Westbrook, ed., *A History of Ancient Near Eastern Law* (2 vols.; Leiden: E. J. Brill, 2003).

101 As anthropologist Gill Feeley-Harnik indicates, slavery is not merely an academic concern, but a very sensitive political, religious, and social issue in which it has proved extremely difficult for both anthropologists and biblical scholars to disentangle the data from the passions of every successive age. Gillian Feeley-Harnik, "Is Historical Anthropology Possible?" 100.

102 These concepts and the categories of human rights have gained a common consensus. On Dec 10, 1948, the General Assembly of the United Nations adopted and proclaimed Universal Declaration of Human Rights. It consists of 30 articles that outline the view of the General Assembly on the human rights guaranteed to all people. See also Fraser Watts, "Human Dignity: Concepts and Experiences," *in God and Human Dignity* (ed. R. Kendall Soulen and Linda Woodhead; Grand Rapids: Eerdmans, 2006), 247 – 262; Winfried Brugger, "The Image of the Person in the Human Rights Concept," *Human Rights Quarterly* 18 (1996): 594 – 611; A. Belden

Projection of Research Significance

This study hopes to contribute to the field of biblical legal studies in at least three ways. First, through the above methodology, it proposes to develop a new way of reading biblical laws. It works to move beyond the long-established conjectures regarding date and function to an understanding of the values and the interests that the biblical laws aim to promote and protect, and toward a reading which takes in view theological, rhetorical, jurisprudential, and socio-logical considerations in Deuteronomy. Second, this study seeks to help people contemplate the relationship between God's love and his commandments. People have long held misconceptions about biblical laws.[103] Some argue that biblical laws are tools of social control wielded by one stronger party against weaker groups,[104] and some even preclude the possibility that biblical laws promote true human rights properly defined.[105] All these are due to the stereotypical thinking that slavery and human rights as two incompatible topics. This study will show that God's gracious love goes beyond manumission to include prospering the freed ones with equality, dignity, and fraternity. Third, this study hopes to answer the question raised by recent scholarship in theology, philosophy, ethics, and re-ligion—"Does human rights need God?"[106]If slavery is one of the fundamental tests of human rights, then what is God, the legislator of the slave laws, trying to promote in regard to human rights?

Fields and Wolf-Dieter Narr, "Human Rights as a Holistic Concept," *Human Rights Quarterly* 14 (1992): 1–20.

103 Such as "The law is all about works; there is no grace in the law;" "the law is only a set of rules and does not call for genuine heart devotion to the Lord." A private communication with Richard E. Averbeck.

104 Harold V. Bennett, *Injustice Made Legal: Deuteronomic Law and the Plight of Widows, Strangers, and Orphans in Ancient Israel* (Grand Rapids: Eerdmans, 2002).

105 Such as "the law is only for ancient Israelites." See Barr, "Ancient Biblical Laws and Modern Human Rights," 21–33.

106 Given the pervasiveness of human rights talk in contemporary society, one might be tempted to conclude that the world has finally reached an undisputed consensus on human rights. Why, then, do human rights abuses continue to occur all around the world? In order to provide solutions, during 2002 to 2003, a lecture series at the University of Chicago, entitled "Does Human Rights need God?" was presented by a number of scholars from diverse areas. E. M. Bucar and B. Barnett challenged, "Perhaps one way to gain purchase on this paradox is to consider what the Universal Declaration of Human Rights (UDHR) is to consider not what the UDHR sought to accomplish, but what it failed to address." Elizabeth M. Bucar and Barbra Barnett, eds., *Does Human Rights Need God?* (Grand Rapids: Eerdmans, 2005), 1.

2 Exegesis of Deuteronomic Slave Laws

Before launching into any exegetical analysis on the two slave laws in Deut 15:12–18 and Deut 23:16–17 [Eng. 23:15–16], one critical question must be addressed: Why do seven chapters separate them in spite of the shared *subject matter* of slavery?[1] At first glance, the two passages appear to be in two different pericopes: Deut 15:12–18 is part of the seven-year debt remission unit in Deut 15:1–18, while Deut 23:16–17 seems to be randomly interpolated into a bunch of miscellaneous laws.[2] The arrangement appears to be at odds with the traditional view that the grouping of ancient laws is primarily based upon their subject matters. This chapter will first survey and critique past studies on the arrangement of Deuteronomic laws in order to account for the placements of the two slave laws and the theological significance for this arrangement. Then an exegesis will be conducted on the slave law passages to lay a foundation for the following chapters.

The Arrangement of Deuteronomic Slave Laws

There are two primary approaches to outlining the Deuteronmic laws.[3] One may be referred to as the "association of elements," for it makes use of the associative elements, e.g., sounds, words, phrases, topics, and abstract concept, as well as transitional logic. The other approach may be titled "Decalogue correspondence," for it draws from the structure of the Decalogue.

Association of Elements Approach

This approach is considered to be one of the most arresting approaches in the study of how Deuteronomic laws and other Old Testament books are arranged.

---

1 Scholars commonly classify Deut 12–26 as the central section of laws, with Deut 26:16–27:16 being the conclusion of the ceremony of blessings and curses of Gerizim and Ebal. See Moshe Weinfeld, *Deuteronomy 1–11* (New York: Doubleday, 1991), 10.
2 J. H. Tigay divides the Deuteronomic law collection into five sections from Deut 12:2 to Deut 26:16–17. Deut 23:16–17 belongs to the fourth section, miscellaneous laws, where the laws primarily deal with private matters concerning individuals, their family and their neighbors. Jeffrey H. Tigay, *The JPS Torah Commentary: Deuteronomy* (Philadelphia: Jewish Publication Society, 1996), 446–459.
3 Here we call these two methods as "approaches," which are actually categories that include variations that share major features.

This approach was founded by H. M. Weiner,[4] and followed by U. Cassuto and A. Rofé.[5] Rofé considers the present arrangement of the laws in Deuteronomy to be well-planned, systematic, and unitary in accordance with various associations.[6] He points out that the law of the triennial tithe in Deut 14:28–29 and the law of remission of the poor in Deut 15:1–11 are associated with similar openings (14:28—מִקְצֵה שָׁלֹשׁ שָׁנִים, *at the end of every* third *year*; 15:12 מִקֵּץ שֶׁבַע שָׁנִים *the end of every* seven *year*). In his view, the slave law of Deut 15:12–18 is linked with the next section by the numeral "seven." Deut 15:15 "Bear in mind that you were a slave in the land of Egypt and YHWH your God redeemed you" is a transitional statement that brings up the dedication of the firstborn (Deut 15:19–23).[7] As for Deut 23:16–17 [Eng. 23:15–16], Rofé argues that the wordplay of *l'twnnw* and *'tnn* (לֹא תוֹנֶנּוּ, do not mistreat him in Deut 23:17 and אֶתְנַן, the wage of a harlot in Deut 23:19) links the fugitive slave laws to the prohibition of prostitution.[8] The two slave laws are separated from each other, according to Rofé's perspective, due to associative elements.

Decalogue Correspondence Approach

Decalogue correspondence was first suggested by S. Kaufman,[9] and later embraced and developed by J. H. Walton and G. Braulik.[10] This approach contends

---

4 Harold M. Wiener, "The Arrangement of Deuteronomy XII-XXVI," in *Posthumous Essays* (ed. Herbert Loewe; London: Oxford University Press, 1932), 26–36.

5 Rofé credits Wiener of being the predecessor of the theory. For him, the great merit of Cassuto is to point out that alternatives existed besides the universally recognized topical arrangement. A. Rofé, "The Arrangement of the Laws in Deuteronomy," *Ephemerides theologicae lovanienses* 64, no. 4 (1988): 269.

6 Ibid., 282–283.

7 Rofé, "The Arrangement of the Laws in Deuteronomy," 279–280.

8 Ibid., 282.

9 Kaufman gives all due credit to H. Schulz, whom he assumes to be the first modern scholar who identified the Decalogue-structure of the Deuteronomic Law. Interestingly, Schulz's study itself was only mentioned in an excursus of his dissertation, which was omitted in the final published form. Stephen A. Kaufman, "The Structure of the Deuteronomic Law," *MAARAV* 1, no. 2 (1978–1979): 112 and n. 43. See also Hermann Schulz, *Das Todesrecht im Alten Testament: Studien zur Rechtsform der Mot-Jumat-Satze* (Berlin: A. Topelmann), 1969. A brief summary of Schulz' position is available in Otto Kaiser, *Introduction to the Old Testament: A Presentation of Its Results and Problems* (trans. John Sturdy; Minneapolis: Augsburg, 1975), 121.

10 John H. Walton, "Deuteronomy: An Exposition of the Spirit of the Law," *Grace Theological Journal* 8, no. 2 (1987): 213–215; George Braulik, "The Sequence of the Laws in Deuteronomy 12–26 and in the Decalogue," in *A Song of Power and the Power of Song: Essays on the Book of*

that the major topical units of Deuteronomic legal corpus correspond in an orderly manner to those of the Decalogue. At first glance, this prevailing idea brings to light the logic of the Deuteronomic structure. However, supporters of this theory diverge on the extent one finds any correspondence and in addition, how the Deuteronomic laws should be exactly divided.

Kaufman suggests that the laws in Deuteronomy 12 reflect the spirit of the first two commandments which he deems as an inseparable whole.[11] For him, Deut 24:1–4 is the only single law which may seriously be considered out of place.[12] Unlike him, Walton asserts that the First Commandment focuses on the authority of God and is closely aligned with Deuteronomy 6–11, as the laws in Deuteronomy 12 reproduce the idea of the Second Commandment.[13] He matches Deut 19:1–21:23 to the Sixth Commandment, even though he admits that Deut 19:14 and 21:10–17 do not match this commandment.[14] In comparison, Braulik is more reserved on the structural parallelism. He advocates that "it is only beginning with chapter 19 that one can discern most correspondences to the fifth through tenth commandments." For him, Deuteronomy 12–18 corresponds to the Decalogue only in some vague and general respect.[15]

Regarding the arrangement of two slave laws in Deut 15:12–18 and 23:16–17, these three scholars agree that the indebted slave law in Deut 15:12–18 belongs to the rules for Sabbath observance.[16] However, they part ways from that point onwards. For example, Kaufman includes the fugitive slave laws (Deut 23:16–17) within the larger unit of Deut 22:9–23:19, which for him reflects the ethical virtue of the Seventh commandment—"You shall not commit adultery." He indicates that Deut 23:16–17 is universally recognized as applicable to a fugitive in Israel from abroad, arguing that the law only takes effect during wartime. Based on this, he finds its connection with the commandments on sexual purity

---

Deuteronomy (ed. Duane L. Christensen; Winona Lake: Eisenbrauns, 1993), 313–335. See also Walter C. Kaiser, "The Law of Deuteronomy," in *Toward Old Testament Ethics* (Grand Rapids: Zondervan, 1983), 127–137.

11 Kaufman, "The Structure of the Deuteronomic Law," 118–122.

12 Ibid., 144.

13 Walton, "Deuteronomy: An Exposition of the Spirit of the Law," 214–215, 217–218.

14 Ibid., 218–219.

15 Braulik suggests that "[o]nly within chaps. 19–25 are the so-called *biʿarta* laws correctly arranged in relation to the respective commandments of the Decalogue." Braulik, "The Sequence of the Laws in Deuteronomy 12–26 and in the Decalogue," 333. *biʿarta* laws refer to laws with the verbal form עֵרְתָּ (you shall purge) in Deut 19:13, 19; 21:21; 22:21, 22; 24:7.

16 Kaufman, "The Structure of the Deuteronomic Law," 129–132; Walton, "Deuteronomy: An Exposition of the Spirit of the Law," 223–224; Braulik, "The Sequence of the Laws in Deuteronomy 12–26 and in the Decalogue," 321.

and cleanliness in the military camp in Deut 23:10 – 15. Kaufman thereby contends that Deut 23:16 – 17 functions as an important transition to the Eighth commandment—"You shall not steal," since failure to return an escaped slave was the most serious kind of theft.[17] With this kind of rationale, he argues that a law which opposes all the ancient laws and treaties came into being. Braulik holds the similar opinion that Deut 23:16 – 24:5 bridges from "sexuality" to "property,"[18] while Walton ascribes 23:16 – 24:7 to the prohibition against stealing.[19] For Walton, the runaway slave regulation serves to prevent slaves who were deprived from also losing their freedom (which was an issue of dignity). On this, therefore he asserts that 23:16 – 24:7 belongs to the prohibition against *stealing*.[20] Subsequently, 23:16 – 17 is to be viewed as a law against the commandment "do not steal."

The Limits and Problems of the Two Approaches

The elements association approach is a good way to explain how individual laws could be linked. For example, Rofé addresses its linguistic features and its ability to link laws which were thought to be irrelevant in the earlier studies with associative elements. However, this method does not do so much in analyzing the grouping of law nor provide an adequate explanation to the entire structure of the Deuteronomic laws in the book.

On the other hand, the Decalogue correspondence approach attempts to do what the elements association cannot, which is to explain the entire structure of the law book. However, what is unsatisfactory about this approach is that it raises more questions than it answers as well as inevitably introducing contradictions. For example, if (according to Kaufman and Braulik), the location of the fugitive slave law in Deut 23:16 – 17 is better viewed as a transition between the Seventh and the Eighth commandments, there is no satisfactory explanation why the compiler would invent a new law that is opposed to the custom of the entire ANE world in order to provide a transition between two commandments. In addition, it is startling to classify this law as a prohibition against stealing since not returning a fugitive slave is considered to be a crime of theft

---

17 Kaufman, "The Structure of the Deuteronomic Law," 137–138.
18 Braulik, "The Sequence of the Laws in Deuteronomy 12–26 and in the Decalogue," 322.
19 Walton, "Deuteronomy: An Exposition of the Spirit of the Law," 219.
20 Ibid., 219.

in the entire ANE world (cf. LE 50, "..., the palace shall bring a charge of *theft* against him." *šurqam*, "theft, stolen property").[21]

The Decalogue is mostly comprised of prohibitions. These prohibitions, (especially those that are negatively-formulated) in various degrees invoke positive values such as the protection of others. However, to extract positivity from prohibitions runs the risk of being subjective. For example, "Do not steal" virtually means "to protect others' property or surviving supports." If (according to Walton) denying freedom from a runaway slave is to *steal* dignity from him/her, can we also argue that if a master does not release the slave in the seventh year he also commits the same crime of larceny? In this manner, Dt 15 can also be deemed as a law that reflects the virtue of the Eighth commandment; meanwhile, Deut 23:16–17 can be regarded as glorifying the Sabbath, since the law concerns the physical and mental rest of a fugitive slave.

In addition, the so-called correlations between the laws and ethical values may be multi-faceted. For example, according to Braulik's evaluation, Deut 15:12–18 corresponds to more than the eight articles of virtue that the Universal Declaration of Human Rights (hereafter referred to as UDHR) upholds.[22] As a result, reading the Deuteronomic laws through the lens of the Decalogue creates many frustrations. As F. Crüsemann comments, "[i]nterpreting deuteronomic law on the basis of the overall structure of Deuteronomy and the role of the Decalogue within it, as a kind of commentary on the Decalogue or provisions for its implementation is here made into a literary structural principle to which the texts do not yield."[23]

---

21 See also LU 17; LL12–16; LE 22–23, 49, 51–52; LH 15–20; HL 22–24.

22 Braulik points out that Deut 15:12–18 directly or indirectly relates to Art. 2 (the prohibition of discrimination), Art. 3 (the right to life and liberty), Art. 4 (the prohibition of slavery), Art. 6 (the entitlement to be recognized as a person before the law), Art. 12 (protection of the privacy of the individual), Art. 16 (freedom to marry and protection of the family), and Art. 22 (the right to social security). George Braulik, "Das Deuteronomium und die Menschenrechte," *TQ* 166 (1986): 8–9. Also English translation, George Braulik, "Deuteronomy and Human Rights," *Skrif en kerk* 19 (1998): 208.

23 Crüsemann rejects Braulik's view, "[t]o be sure, there are substantive parallels between the prohibition against killing and Deut 19:1–21:23 (preserve life) 26 or between the prohibition against adultery and 22:13–23:15 (protect the honor of man and woman), but to try to connect Deut 23:16–24:7 with the prohibition against theft by putting them under the heading 'placing human needs and relationships above property' shows that, apart from 24:7, there is no real connection. The corresponding passages in the Book of the Covenant, which are a concretization of the prohibition against theft (Ex 21: 37–22:14), are not continued in Deuteronomy. It is even less precise and rather arbitrary to regard 24:8–25:4 (denying the poor, the socially weak and debtors their rights) as corresponding with the prohibition against bearing false witness, or in 25:5–12 (not hindering the begetting of descendants) as corresponding to the first half of the prohibition against coveting, and

These two approaches that ostensibly differ do share some common ground.[24] Both approaches seek to show that the Deuteronomic law book is remarkably structured, even when they have different sets of checking points. Both of them also assume that a motif is prominent for law grouping.[25]

The associative principles of organization for Deuteronomic laws is, as J. H. Tigay (citing quotes from Kauffman) states,

> The individual law and larger sub-units of each topical unit are arranged according to the ancient Near Eastern method of 'concatenation of ideas, key words and phrases, and similar motifs' so as to form what for the ancient eye and ear were smooth transitions between sub-units and frequently, between the various topical units themselves. This procedure has frequently been characterized as 'free association,' but in reality it is a carefully planned procedure that is anything but free.[26]

Kauffman and Rofé do contribute significantly to how individual biblical and ANE laws may be linked and grouped. However, their approaches on the arrangement of the Deuteronomic laws provide no satisfying explanations as to how this entire law book is structured, nor do they resolve the question raised at the beginning—

25:13–16 to the second half. It is not possible to demonstrate more than a very weak connection from the first to the second table." Frank Crüsemann, *The Torah: Theology and Social History of Old Testament Law* (Minneapolis: Fortress, 1996), 206.

24 Rofé disapproves of Kaufman and C. M. Carmichael's explanations for the arrangement of the laws in Deuteronomy and asserts that they both have disregarded Cassuto's contribution to this question. Rofé, "The Arrangement of the Laws in Deuteronomy," 269–270, n 21. Rofé does not give details about his opinion against Carmichael. However, it is apparent that Kaufman and Rofé understand Carmichael's approach on the arrangement of Deuteronomic laws differently. Kaufman thinks that Carmichael's argument can be reduced to the principles of free associations and expansions advocated by Weiner. See Kaufman, "The Structure of the Deuteronomic Law,"108. In fact, Carmichael's position is closer to thematic associations in terms of the linked method of arrangement. Carmichael considers that the literary setting of Jacob's farewell speech in Gen 49, as well as the style of wisdom literature, greatly influences the presentation of the Deuteronomic laws. His analysis supposes that the law book was written by a single author, a seventh century teacher, who attempted to present his viewpoint in Mosaic form. According to Carmichael, the law book was based upon a series of repetitions of the author's own material, combined with allusions, Israelite prophetic, revolutionary morality with traditional proverbial teaching. See C. M. Carmichael, *The Laws of Deuteronomy* (Ithaca: Cornell University Press, 1974), 17–67, 68–69, 255–259.

25 Both approaches agree that "Deuteronomic family laws" in Deut 21:10–25:10 shows that Deuteronomy was aware of the similar topics pertaining to marriage and family. Rofé, "The Arrangement of the Laws in Deuteronomy," 282–283; Kaufman, "The Structure of the Deuteronomic Law,"115. See also Carolyn Pressler, *The View of Women Found in the Deuteronomic Family Laws* (Berlin: W. de Gruyter, 1993), 1–8.

26 Jeffrey H. Tigay, "The Arrangement of the Laws in Deuteronomy," in *The JPS Torah Commentary: Deuteronomy* (Philadelphia: Jewish Publication Society, 1996), 449–450.

Why are the two slave laws set apart from each other despite the shared *subject matter?* Is there an explanation for the arrangement of the Deuteronomic law book? Here we examine a third approach—the "chiastic framework"—to better resolve these issues.

Chiastic Framework Approach

The previous two approaches fail to appreciate the internal coherence of Deuteronomic law book. A chiastic framework approach pays attention to two overlooked features in the structure of the Deuteronomic law: First, the laws in Deuteronomy are abundantly rhetorical in modes of persuasion. Second, the Deuteronomic laws (especially in Deut 14:22–26:15) form an internal chiastic framework (Hereafter, this section of laws in Deut 14:22–26:15 will be referred to as "the chiastic framework").[27] This chiastic framework, first suggested by Crüsemann and then further developed by M. J. Oosthusizen, satisfactorily accounts for the separation of the two slave laws and the arrangement of this law book.[28] The framework can be illustrated as follows:[29]

A 14:22–29 Tithe
   B 15:1–16:17 Protection laws for the socially weak (by periodically sacral times)
      C 16:18–18:22 Public institutions and offices
         D 19:1–21:9 Preservation of life
      C′ 21:10–23:15 Private institutions for family, sexuality
   B′ 23:16–25:19 Protection laws for the socially weak[30]
A′ 26:1–15 Tithe

---

27 D. L. Christensen outlines numerous passages and the entire book of Deuteronomy with chiastic frameworks. However, adopting Lohfink's position, he does not take the law collection (Deut 12–26) as a literary unit. Instead, he divides the book of Deuteronomy into two sections according to the triennial lectionary system of Palestinian Judaism. Duane L. Christensen, *Deuteronomy 1:1–21:9* (Nashville: Thomas Nelson, 2001); idem, *Deuteronomy 21:10–34:12* (Nashville: Thomas Nelson, 2002.)

28 Crüsemann, *The Torah*, 206–207; Martin J. Oosthuizen, "Deuteronomy 15:1–18 in Socio-Rhetorical Perspective," *ZABR* 3 (1997): 64–91. See also Eckart Otto, "Vom Bundesbuch zum Deuteronomium: Die deuteronomische Redaktion in Dtn 12–26," in *Biblische Theologie und gesellschaftlicher Wandel: für Norbert Lohfink SJ* (ed. George Braulik OSB, Walter Groß, and Sean McEvenue; Herder: Freiburg, 1993), 260–278.

29 This framework stems from and refines Crüsemann and Oosthuizen's proposals. Oosthuizen argues that the tithe law in Deut 26 is from vv. 1–15, not merely 12–15. Oosthuizen, "Deuteronomy 15:1–18 in Socio-Rhetorical Perspective," 79.

30 Deut 25:18 gives the motivation for the law upon the defeat of the Amorites (Deut 25:17–19): the Amorites attacked "among you all the stragglers at your rear when you were faint and weary; and he did not fear God." The law seems to imply that to attack weak people is regarded as an immoral deed against fearing God.

There are three sets of parallel themes in this passage. Both 14:22–29 and 26:1–15 (A and A', hereafter referred to as the "tithe" sections) begin with a theme of tithing (Deut 14:22–29a and 26:1–14) and end with that of blessing (Deut 14:29; 26:15). In the second parallel (B and B', hereafter referred to as the "protection laws for the socially weak" sections), Deut 23:16–25:19 starts with the fugitive slave law, which echoes the indebted slave law in Deut 15:1–16:17. The third symmetrical pair (C and C', hereafter referred to as the "administrational institutions" sections) stipulates public and private institutions for protecting the socially weak. The core section, 19:1–21:9 (D), begins and ends with the same cautious note on judgment. The two slave laws in Deut 14:22–26:15 are symmetrically structured in the second stratum of this chiastic framework.

In view of this framework, the Deuteronomic laws demand a social network to protect and provide *anyone* who lives in the land, with basic rights of liberty, equality, and fraternity. The central theme of Deut 14:22–26:15 is preserving human life. At Deut 19:1–21:9, where the text is enveloped by the protection of socially deserted murder suspects, the passage reaches its culmination. Deut 21:9 claims YHWH's determination of protecting all human life on his promised *land*. Nevertheless, this protection is by no means unconditional: The prerequisite is to identify YHWH as the One and Only God. If anyone on the *land* worships other gods, instead of being socially protected, he/she shall face the death penalty.[31]

The chiastic framework approach suggests that the section of Deut 12:1–14:21, which precedes the chiastic framework, is a prologue for the law book.[32] The cultic and religious themes dealt in Deut 12:1–14:21 manifests the crucial and the upmost purpose for the law book: The Israelites are to ultimately enjoy life on the land and carry out these social protection laws in faithfulness to the One and Only God, YHWH. In addition to Deuteronomy, the other two Pentateuchal law books also precede such a cultic and religious section with a number of stipulations (Exod 20:22–26, and Lev 17:1–16). For example, both Lev 17:1–16 and Deut 12:1–28 start with issues regarding the altar—sanctuary sacrifices and a prohibition against blood eating. The fact that all the three law books in the Pentateuch contain altar-centered sections in their prologues is by no

---

31 Deut 6:13–15; 7:1–5; 8:19–20; 9:2–5; 11:16–17, 28; 12:2–32; 13:1–18; 17:2–7; 18:9–13. See also Moshe Weinfeld, *Deuteronomy and Deuteronomic School* (Winona Lake: Eisenbrauns, 1992), 320–322.
32 The issue about the single altar and centralization is beyond the scope of this study. As P. T. Vogt concludes, "the overall lack of consensus regarding the nature of centralization has led to tremendous diversity in the interpretation of the book as a whole." Peter T. Vogt, *Deuteronomic Theology and the Significance of Torah: A Reappraisal* (Winona Lake: Eisenbrauns, 2006), 70.

means coincidental or a redactional insertion.[33] Their function is to uphold the premise of reverence for YHWH by the observation of such laws.[34]

The chiastic framework reveals that the "tithe" sections (14:22–29 and 26:1–15) are thematically, verbally, and conceptually linked with each other.[35] When Oosthuizen combines the socio-rhetorical perspective with the chiastic framework, he concludes that there are clear links at thematic and terminological levels between the "protection laws for the socially weak" sections (15:1–16:17 and 23:16–25:19).

At the thematic level, both sections deal with the problems of economic deprivation. In addition to the slave issues (e.g., 15:12–18 and 23:16–17), the law against usury in 23:20–21 reflects the distinction between the "brother" and the "foreigner," just as with the *Shemittah* law (15:1–11).[36] Moreover, both sections claim to protect the poor[37] and to provide justice and basic living rights for the alien, the fatherless, and the widows. These are themes that are present in both sides of the parallel in 15:1–16:17 and 23:16–25:19.

At the terminological level, these two sections contain recurrent formulas that convey the lawgiver's clear social concern. The formula "to bless the enterprise of" appears in connection with the triennial tithe (14:29), the *Shemittah* law (15:10), the indebted slave laws (15:18), the observation of the festival of Booths (16:15), the prohibition against usury (23:21), and the gracious gleanings from the harvest (24:19).[38] Another formula is the remembrance of Israel's slavery in Egypt.[39] The exact formula "remember that you were a slave in the land of Egypt" (וְזָכַרְתָּ כִּי־עֶבֶד הָיִיתָ בְּאֶרֶץ מִצְרַיִם) are found in Deut 15:15;16:12; 24:18, 22.[40] In a

---

33 H. J. Boeker suggests that the altar section is a redactional insertion. Hans Jochen Boecker, *Law and the Administration of Justice in the Old Testament and Ancient East* (Minneapolis: Augsburg 1980), 145.

34 J. I. Durham suggests that the altar issue in the beginning of the Covenant law books signifies a place where YHWH chose to "dwell" in their midst (cf. Exod 25:8) to recall the similar metaphor in Deuteronomy 12. John I. Durham, *Exodus* (Waco: Word, 1987), 319.

35 Oosthuizen, "Deuteronomy 15:1–18 in Socio-Rhetorical Perspective," 79–80.

36 Ibid., 80. Oosthuizen remarks that "the fact that Deut 23:21 uses a blessing formula which stands the closest to Deut 15:10, by using the words בכל משלח ידך, does not seem accidental."

37 Ibid., 80. אֶבְיוֹן (the poor) occurs in 15:4, 7(x2), 9, 11(x2) vs. 24:15 and עָנִי in 15:11vs. 24:12, 14, 15.

38 Ibid., 81. See also Weinfeld and Crüsemann's discussion on this blessing formula. Moshe Weinfeld, *Deuteronomy and the Deuteronomic school* (Winona Lake: Eisenbrauns, 1992), 345, and Crüsemann, *The Torah*, 206–207.

39 Ibid., 81.

40 The mentions of the Egyptian experience prevail throughout the entire book of Deuteronomy. See also 1:27; 5:6.

similar manner, reminiscences of Egyptian experience occur more than twenty times with diverse phraseology.[41]

These formulas invoke a persuasive pathos that promotes social care for the socially weak—the poor, slaves, sojourners, fatherless, widows, and the Levites. All of them are outside of the normal Israelite social protection and the support of חֶלְקָה.[42] J. M. Hamilton notes that "Deuteronomy displays a particular concern for those who have none of the built-in supports which Israelite society normally provided—specifically those supports provided by one's tribe and family."[43] Similarly, Oosthuizen suggests that "[t]he fact that these blocks of material in Deut 15:1–16:19 and Deut 23:16–25:19 have been incorporated within the framework which rests upon a theology of divine privilege, [and] indicates that the call for various acts of social care is motivated by the recognition of God's authority over every aspect of Israel's life."[44]

In these ways then the chiastic framework approach demonstrates how the Deuteronomic laws are structured for its social concern and the humanitarian spirit. Through this approach, the authorial intent and rationale behind the arrangement of the Deuteronomic laws becomes clear. In the following section, we shall see that in Deuteronomy, the divine privilege is presented by YHWH's sovereignty over the Promised land (as well as things in the land).

The Land and Agrarian Symbols in Deuteronomy with Reference to Its Slave Laws

The land theme is inseparable from the laws in Deuteronomy. The Deuteronomic laws are presumptively to be implemented *only* in the "land" of Israel.[45] In the beginning of the legal corpus, Deut 12:1 claims that the whole law book is stipulated in relation to the land.[46]

---

41 Deut 1:27; 5:6, 15; 6:12; 7:8, 15, 18; 8:14; 9:7; 10:19; 11:3, 4, 10; 13:6, 11; 16:3, 20:1; 28:27, 60, 68; 29:1, 15, 24; 34:11, etc. See also Weinfeld, *Deuteronomy and the Deuteronomic School*, 326–327.
42 Revised from Oosthuizen's idea. Oosthuizen, "Deuteronomy 15:1–18 in Socio-Rhetorical Perspective," 81.
43 Jeffries M. Hamilton, *Social Justice and Deuteronomy: The Case of Deuteronomy 15* (Atlanta: Scholars, 1992), 2.
44 Oosthuizen, "Deuteronomy 15:1–18 in Socio-Rhetorical Perspective," 82.
45 Moshe Weinfeld, *Deuteronomy 1–11*, 57–60.
46 Patrick D. Miller, "Gift of God: Deuteronomic Theology of the Land," *Int* 23, no. 4 (1969): 459–465.

The land plays a central role in Deuteronomic theology, as G. von Rad, P. D. Miller, and A. D. H. Mayes have all observed.[47] From its earliest mentioning in 1:8 to the final words of YHWH to Moses in 34:4, the land is frequently reiterated throughout Deuteronomy. Without the land, there is neither life nor rest for the Israelites.[48] YHWH, land, and law form the indivisible central theological theme in Deuteronomy. W. Brueggemann points out,

> Israel's involvement is always with land and with Yahweh, never only with Yahweh as though to live only in intense obedience, never only with land, as though simply to possess and manage; always with land and with Yahweh, always receiving gifts from land, always being addressed by Yahweh, always being assured and summoned, always being both nourished and claimed, always being of the family of earth, but always and at the same time Yahweh's peculiar listening partner in historical covenant.[49]

It is commonly believed that Deuteronomy has an exceptional perspective on the promises concerning the land among the Pentateuch. While from Genesis to Numbers, the land is a perpetual and unconditional gift to Israel, Deuteronomy speaks of the promise of the land as a motivation for Torah observance.[50] Brueggemann asserts that although the Deuteronomic tradition is replete with references to the land, it *revises* the land promise. The land which was a free gift is now conditional. Disobedience will lead to the loss of the land.[51]

Though the thesis is attractive, Brueggemann however fails to appreciate the inner coherence of the Pentateuch. The concept of reception and retention of the land remains intact throughout the Pentateuch. The principle of living on YHWH's land is always associated with obeying his laws. In the beginning of Genesis, YHWH unconditionally provided a living place, but when Adam disobeyed YHWH's commands, he was expelled from the land (Gen 1–3; cf. Leviticus

---

47 Gerhard von Rad, *The Problem of the Hexateuch and Other Essays* (New York: McGraw-Hill, 1966), 90–93. Miller, "Gift of God: Deuteronomic Theology of the Land," 452. A. D. H. Mayes, *Deuteronomy* (Grand Rapids: Eerdmans, 1981), 79.
48 Von Rad, *The Problem of the Hexateuch and Other Essays*, 95.
49 Walter Brueggemann, *The Land: Place as Gift, Promise, and Challenge in Biblical Faith* (Minneapolis: Fortress, 2002), 49.
50 Weinfeld, *Deuteronomy 1–11*, 58–59. Brueggemann, "The transposition of the *land promise* into a motivation for *Torah obedience* became central to Old Testament theology and would become the ground for prophetic speeches of judgment. Land joined to Torah now becomes crucial for Israel's faith and provides a context for the formulation of exilic theology." Walter Brueggemann, *Old Testament Theology: An Introduction* (Nashville: Abingdon, 2008), 273; Mayes, *Deuteronomy*, 78–79. See also J. G. McConville, *Law and Theology in Deuteronomy* (Sheffield: Sheffield, Academic Press, 1984), 11–13.
51 Brueggemann, *Old Testament Theology*, 272.

25 – 26). Towards the end of the Pentateuch, Deuteronomy resumes the same thought that no man can subsist on YHWH's land in disobedience. In this aspect, Deuteronomy is in harmony with the rest of the Pentateuch. It is however important to distinguish the land loss in a theological sense from the socio-economic one. The former results from the collective sin of Israel against YHWH, while the latter from sales of individual property.

YHWH, land, and law are inseparate themes consistently being reiterated in the Pentateuch. In Old Testament ethical studies, *God, Israel*, and the *land* are often recognized as "the three pillars of Israel's worldview." They are the primary factors of Israel's theology and ethics.[52] C. J. H. Wright conceptualizes these three as a relational triangle to demonstrate their interdependency.[53] Drawing from Wright and supplementing it with the central role of law, the following figure illustrates Deuteronomy's theology and ethics.

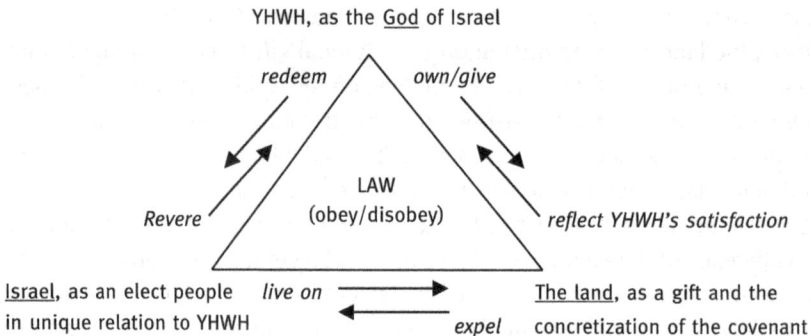

Within this framework, the key to understanding how the relational triangle functions in Deuteronomy is one's relationship towards the *law*— הַדְּבָרִים (the words), הַמִּצְוֹת (the commandments), הַחֻקִּים (the statutes), and הַמִּשְׁפָּטִים (the judgments) given by YHWH. If this is interpreted correctly, one's relationship to the land acts as a covenantal gauge of Israel's standing before YHWH.[54] The land functions as a sociological symbol of divine care, rather than merely a free gift from God. Deuteronomy carries out the land promise by characterizing the

---

52 Christopher J.H. Wright, *Old Testament Ethics for the People of God* (Downers Grove: InterVarsity, 2004), 19.

53 Ibid., 19.

54 Wright, *Old Testament Ethics for the People of God*, 96.

land and *law* together with a combined theological and sociological meaning:[55] Thus, the land is the concretization of the covenant, a reminder of YHWH's covenant with the Israelites, and a motivator for law obedience.

The law and the land in the chiastic framework present a combined theological and sociological meaning. In the "tithe" sections (A-A', 14:22–29 and 26:1–15), the firstborn, the first of the produce, and the tithe symbolize the blessings of the land. They have to be brought to YHWH and be shared with the socially weak. In the "protection laws for the socially weak" sections (B-B', 15:1–16:17 and 23:16–25:19), the land is mentioned as the vehicle of YHWH's blessing for the Israelites to be generous to the underprivileged in accordance with his law. However, in the sections that concern the administrative institutions (C-C', 16:18–18:22 and 21:10–23:15), the laws appear to be weakly associated to the land. A closer look reveals that the sections are immediately adjacent to the laws for protection of the socially weak, to remind the administrative authorities to practice justice so as to prevent the people from being expelled out of the land. In this manner, Deuteronomy presents the combined theological and sociological meaning of land and law.

The Israelites who freely receive the land and everything in it are to give freely. The usage of נתן (give) in Deuteronomy illustrates this thought. J. G. McConville observes that among the 167 occurrences of נתן in Deuteronomy, 113 times it has YHWH as its subject—evidence of the primacy of YHWH's action in Israel's possession of the land. The use of נתן with the land theme embodies the need for Israel to be generous to everyone who live in the land.[56] Brueggemann notes that "[t]here is no more radical word than that in Deut 8:18,[57]... Israel is offered a covenantal understanding of power, power that is not vested in Israel but in the other One who meets Israel at the point of need."[58] Wealth is a powerful sign of divine blessing;[59] therefore, it should be shared with the *powerless*.

M. Weinfeld notes that the concept of reward and blessing is prominent in Deuteronomy. The criterion for reward and blessing is obedience to YHWH's laws.[60] The agricultural products and their resources (livestock, threshing

---

55 A. Phillips sees the connection between the law and the land, but he interprets it with the historical and social background of the seventh century B. C. Anthony Phillips, "The Attitude of Torah to Wealth," in *Essays on Biblical Law* (New York: Sheffield Academic Press, 2002), 148–163.

56 McConville, *Law and Theology in Deuteronomy*, 12.

57 Deut 8:18 "Remember that it is YHWH your God, for it is he who is giving you *power* (כח) to get wealth, that he may confirm the covenant which he swore to your fathers, as it is today."

58 Brueggemann, *The Land*, 53.

59 Phillips, "The Attitude of Torah to Wealth," 148.

60 Weinfeld, *Deuteronomy and Deuteronomic School*, 310–312.

floor, wine vat) symbolize blessings of the land from YHWH, as a result of his satisfaction with the covenantal people's obedience to his laws (e.g., compare Deut 7:12–13 to Deut 28:51). The three terms, firstborn (בְּכֹרָה), grain (דָּגָן), and new wine (תִּירוֹשׁ)/oil (יִצְהָר), form a series of agrarian yields that contrast to their corresponding resources—herd/flock (בָּקָר /צֹאן), threshing floor (גֹּרֶן), and wine vat (יֶקֶב). These are the principal products of ancient Israelite agriculture that describe fertility.[61] At the same time, they are the embodiments of YHWH's blessings and power that expound the relationship between "land" and "covenant."[62] They are frequently mentioned in the first half of the chiastic framework, i.e., 14:22–18:22, as the following chart demonstrates.[63]

7:13 Agrarian products are YHWH's blessings: "grain (דָּגָן), new wine (תִּירוֹשׁ)/oil (יִצְהָר), and herd/flock (בָּקָר /צֹאן)" etc.	
Ch.12 Revere YHWH and rejoice them with others	12:6–7, 11revere YHWH with "the firstborn of your herd and of your flock (וּבְכֹרֹת בְּקָרְכֶם וְצֹאנְכֶם)" etc, and rejoice with one's household and the socially weak 12:17–19: rejoice them with one's household and the socially weak people —includes most of the items in 7:13 and 12:6–7, 11—"grain, new wine/oil + the firstborn of herd/flock + sacrifices and offerings
14:22–29 Tithe	14:22–23 revere YHWH with tithe of "the firstborn of your herd and of your flock (וּבְכֹרֹת בְּקָרְכֶם וְצֹאנְכֶם)" etc. *14:28 provision for the socially weak through the tithe of* תְּבוּאָה *in every three years.*
15:1–16:17 Laws for protection of the socially weak	15:14 **provision YHWH's blessings for the powerless people, slave, from "flock (צֹאן), threshing floor (גֹּרֶן), and wine vat (יֶקֶב)."** 15:19 revere YHWH with "the firstborn of your herd and of your flock (וּבְכֹרֹת בְּקָרְכֶם וְצֹאנְכֶם)." 16:2 revere YHWH and rejoice blessings "standing grain (קָמָה)" with one's household and the socially weak

61 Scholars note that the terms for grain (דָּגָן), wine (תִּירוֹשׁ), offspring (שֶׁגֶר), and lambs (עַשְׁתְּרוֹת) in Deut 7:13 are also the names of Canaanite deities. However, Tigay dissents, "Most Israelites were probably as unaware of the etymology of these terms as English speakers are when they speak of cereal." Jeffrey H. Tigay, *Deuteronomy* (Philadelphia: Jewish Publication Society of America, 1996), 89.
62 J. G. McConville, *Deuteronomy* (Downers Grove: InterVarsity 2002), 159.
63 The three mentions of the agrarian products outside the framework (Deut 7:13, 28:51, and Deuteronomy 12) are used to be the introductory and concluding emphases of the idea that these agrarian products symbolize YHWH's blessings.

	16:13 revere YHWH and rejoice blessings "threshing floor (גֹּרֶן) and wine vat (יֶקֶב)" with one's household and the socially weak.
16:18 – 18:22 public institutions and offices	18:4 **provision YHWH's blessings for the Levites, the priests, and all the tribe of Levi, who have no power (portion and inheritance) to produce living essentials for themselves**—the first fruits of your "grain (דָּגָן), new wine (תִּירוֹשׁ)/oil (יִצְהָר), and the first sharing of your flock (צֹאן)"
26:1 – 15 tithe	*26:12 provision for the socially weak through the tithe of תְבוּאָה in every three years.*

28:51 Agrarian products are YHWH's blessings: "grain (דָּגָן), new wine (תִּירוֹשׁ)/oil (יִצְהָר), and herd/flock (צֹאן/בָּקָר)" etc.

The above chart shows that in order to continuously receive YHWH's blessings, the Israelites are supposed to use them to revere YHWH, to share with his household (including slaves/servants), the socially weak (the Levite, the alien, the orphan, and the widow), and to provide for the socially weak periodically (the Levite, the alien, the orphan, and the widow, but excluding slaves/servants at triennial tithe).

The chart also illustrates why the two slave laws, Deut 15:12–18 and 23:16–17 are included in Deuteronomy. The Hebrew slave manumission law (Deut 15:12–18) emphasizes the necessity of supplying manumitted Hebrew slaves and setting them free without hardship. The fugitive slave law (Deut 23:16–17) commands providing escaped slaves with residential freedom instead of extraditing them back to their masters who probably mistreated or abused them. These two slave laws address the most basic human rights—to live freely without fear and to live with substantial provision—regardless of one's status, gender, and ethnicity. These two slave laws can be regarded as the prominent representatives of the combined theological and sociological theme of the law book. At the core of the value system for YHWH's people is human life. They are to unconditionally protect the marginal peoples in YHWH's land. The arrangement of the two slave laws in the chiastic structure signifies the Deuteronomic concerns of social justice and protection of basic rights for the most powerless people in the society.

Indebted Hebrew Slave Law (Deut 15:12 – 18)

With regard to the stipulations in Deut 15:12–18, several problematic issues must be addressed. The following discussion will study the structure of

Deut 15:1–16:17 and the most disputed terms in the Hebrew slave manumission laws— אָחִיךָ הָעִבְרִי אוֹ הָעִבְרִיָּה and חָפְשִׁי.[64] Thereafter, we will examine issues concerning the identification of enslaved members in the indebted family, the provision for the manumitted slaves in Deut 15:13–14, the motive clauses in Deut 15:15, 18b and their relationship with the exceptional case in Deut 15:16–17.[65]

The Structure of Deut 15:1–16:17

In view of the chiastic framework, Deut 15:1–16:17 does not start with a slave law to match with the beginning slave law of Deut 23:16–25:19. This asymmetry invites some explanation. One good reason for the presence of the slave law in Deut 15:1–16:17 is that this is a purposeful and meaningful arrangement: Placing the *Shemittah* law ahead of the indebted slave law introduces a series of time sequences for this entire section.

Each regulation in Deut 15:1–16:17 contains a temporal adverbial phrase that informs the rhetorical structure of the passage.

Deut 15:1–6 מִקֵּץ שֶׁבַע־שָׁנִים at the end of every seven year (15:1)
Deut 15:7–11 שְׁנַת־הַשֶּׁבַע the seventh year (15:9)
Deut 15:12–18 וּבַשָּׁנָה הַשְּׁבִיעִת but in the seventh year (15:12)
   Deut 15:19–23 שָׁנָה בְשָׁנָה every year (15:20)
Deut 16:1–8 שִׁבְעַת יָמִים seven days (16:3); בַּיּוֹם הַשְּׁבִיעִי in the seventh day (16:8)
Deut 16:9–12 שִׁבְעָה שָׁבֻעֹת seven weeks (16:9)
Deut 16:13–15 שִׁבְעַת יָמִים seven days (16:13, 15)
   Deut 16:16–17 שָׁלוֹשׁ פְּעָמִים בַּשָּׁנָה three times in a/every year

Each law in this pericope designates a sacral time for a blessed Israelite to respond to recurrent duties. The outline above makes it clear that the repetition of the numeric pattern 7, 3, and 1 noticeably stands out.[66] The eight laws manifest

---

64 These terms occur both in Ex 21 and Dt 15, except Ex 21 does not use הָעִבְרִיָּה and אָחִיךָ.
65 Issues related to the resemblance and divergence between Ex 21 and Dt 15 (including viewpoints of buyer's or seller's, released action verbs, female slaves, leaving conditions, and permanent slave ceremony) will be examined in chapter three, as well as the comparative studies with Lev 25. The rest of the slave laws pertaining to slave's injury death, martial/sexual rights, and situational redemption (Exod 21:20–21, 26–27, 32; Lev 19:20–22, etc.) will be discussed in chapter four with their related issues and their ANE correspondences.
66 Tigay notes that "these laws are about periodic obligations performed at intervals of a certain number of years or a certain number of times each year." He suggests the law of firstlings is practiced annually and thus should join the group of the periodic laws in Deut 14:22–16:17.

an easy mnemonic pattern of sacral times: Twice of [(every 7 x 3) +1 every year (and finally three times a year)]. These laws set forth the passage of Deut 15:1–16:17 with the strongest humanitarian spirit in Deuteronomy.

Deut 15:1 leads this series of laws with a fixed due time—at the *end* of every seventh year. It reminds the listeners of a time of being gracious and thankful. The indebted Hebrew slave law in Deut 15:12–18 is thus a natural sequel to the *Shemittah* law in Deut 15:1–11. Both laws deal with loans and poverty,[67] and they both extend grace to the socially weak by periodic repetitions of such sacral times. The starting points for the seven-year-period in Deut 15:1 and 15:12 are different—the former is based on a universal cycle, while the latter begins with a debt service. Among all the OT books, only Deuteronomy links these two kinds of seven-year release.[68] From the above analysis, it is apparent that the *Shemittah* law and the indebted slave laws are purposefully linked together in the current setting.

חָפְשִׁי and אָחִיךָ הָעִבְרִי אוֹ הָעִבְרִיָּה

אָחִיךָ הָעִבְרִי אוֹ הָעִבְרִיָּה

Often used in contrast to non-Israelites, עִבְרִי is understood as the oldest designation for the Israelites. This designation would not have been used before the time of Israel (Jacob).[69] Early scholars note the possible phonetic connection between עִבְרִי and *ḫapiru* of certain cuneiform texts.[70] The *ḫapiru* dwelt in Babylon, Mari, Nuzi, and Alalakh as a half-settled group. They earned their living by performing

---

Tigay, *Deuteronomy*, 452–453. D. P. Wright regards Deut 14:22–16:17 as a pericope of "calendar and cycles." D. P. Wright, *Inventing God's Law: How the Covenant Code of the Bible Used and Revised the Laws of Hammurabi* (New York: Oxford University Press, 2009), 113.Oosthuizen notes that Deut 15:1–16:17 extends the rhythm of sacral cycles from 14:22–29. "Deuteronomy 15:1–18 in Socio-Rhetorical Perspective," 80.

67 Tigay, *Deuteronomy*, 148; Christensen, *Deuteronomy 1:1–21:9*, 319.

68 McConville, *Deuteronomy*, 262.

69 C. Mark McCormick, "Hebrew People," *The New Interpreter's Dictionary of the Bible* 2:778; N. P. Lemche, "Hebrew," *ABD* 3:95–96. Tigay, *Deuteronomy*, 148.

70 See M. Weippert's review of scholarship and discussion. Manfred Weippert, *The Settlement of the Israelite Tribes in Palestine: A Critical Survey of Recent Scholarly Debate* (trans. James D. Martin; London: SCM, 1971), 63–101. See also N. Freeman and B. E. Willough, "עִבְרִי," *TDOT* 10:430–445; Herni Cazelles, "the Hebrews," in *Peoples of Old Testament Times* (ed. D. J. Wiseman; London: Oxford University, 1973), 1–28. Nadav Na'aman, "Ḫabiru and Hebrews: The Transfer of a Social Term to the Literary Sphere" *JNES* 45, no. 4 (1986): 271–279.

labor and military duties.[71] The identity of *ḥapiru* raises the question of whether עִבְרִי is a gentilic noun or an appellative.[72]

M. G. Kline, J. H. Tigay, and M. Weippert all suspect the phonetic equation of עִבְרִי and *ḥapiru*.[73] Kline and Tigay view עִבְרִי as an ethnic identity for the Israelite. For Tigay, עִבְרִי and *ḥapiru* are not necessarily related. He remarks that in all contexts עִבְרִי clearly refers to an ethnic group, whereas *ḥapiru* refers to a social class. He translates אָחִיךָ הָעִבְרִי into "fellow Hebrew," and he paraphrases the same phrase in Jer 34:9 as "Judean Kinsman."[74] Weippert suggests a much more complex solution. For him, the status of the עֶבֶד עִבְרִי in Exod 21:2 is comparable with that of the *ḥapiru*-people in the *wardūtu*-contracts of Nuzi, whereas the Deuteronomic phrase "your brother, the Hebrew" (Deut 15:12; cf. Jer 34:14) refers to an Israelite who sold himself into "slavery." As for Jer 34:9, the "brother" refers to a Judean.[75] In his recent publication, W. H. C. Propp also asserts that עִבְרִי is the normal ethnic adjective for an Israelite.[76]

Many others, however, read עִבְרִי through a sociological lens. On this, there are two different views: One of them regards עִבְרִי as a Hebrew in a destitute status; the other regards the term as a reference to a social class, such as a lower class or landless class. For N. P. Lemche, חָפְשִׁי is a social designation which ranges somewhere between a slave and a freeman,[77] while עִבְרִי is an ethnic designation which means "a countryman" or "an Israelite." Lemche argues that עִבְרִי means a חָפְשִׁי who had become destitute in a foreign land, having to work his full six year term in order to regain his mortgaged land and חָפְשִׁי status.[78]

---

71 L. Koehler and W. Baumgartner, "עִבְרִי," *HALOT* 1:782–783.

72 D. N. Freeman and B. E. Willough believe that "[a]lthough no definite etymology and solution to these semantic problems can be presented, philological findings regarding the historical use of the word suggest that *'ibrî* and *ḥapiru* (*'apiru*) are not etymologically or semantically related." However, they assert that "the probability does exist that some relationship obtains insofar as the biblical gentilic noun is a postmonarchical development of the word that once referred to an 'outlaw' or *ḥapiru*." D. N. Freeman and B. E. Willough, *TDOT* 10:433.

73 Weippert, *The Settlement of the Israelite Tribes in Palestine*, 74–101. M. G. Kline, "Hebrews," *NBD* 457; Tigay, *Deuteronomy*, 452–453.

74 Tigay, *Deuteronomy*, 148.

75 Weippert, *The Settlement of the Israelite Tribes in Palestine*, 83–84.

76 William H. C. Propp, *Exodus 19–40: A New Translation with Introduction and Commentary* (New York: Doubleday, 2006), 186–188.

77 The term חָפְשִׁי occurs in Exod 21:2, 5, 26, 27; Deut 15:12, 13, 18; and Jer 34:9, 10, 11, 14, 16 etc. N. P. Lemche, "The Hebrew Slave: Comments on the Slave Law Ex 21:2–11," *VT* 25.2 (1975): 140.

78 In this regard, Lemche's exact position causes confusions. In his article, "The Hebrew Slave: Comments on the Slave Law Ex 21:2–11," he argues for a sociological meaning of עִבְרִי. However, in "The Manumission of Slaves—the Fellow Year—the Sabbatical Year—the Jobel Year," he claims that the term means an ethnic synonym of "countryman," "Israelite." N. P. Lemche, "The

V. H. Matthew follows Lemche and contends that when a slave is released, he/she is restored to full citizenship status as a חָפְשִׁי.[79] A. Alt suggests that עִבְרִי refers to the social standing of one who sells himself as a slave.[80] N. Na'aman considers the term to denote Israelites who are in exceptional and precarious situations, such as migrants or slaves.[81] Likewise, C. Pressler understands it as referring to economically marginalized Israelites.[82] On the other hand, עִבְרִי is also understood as a social class. W. Helck, A. H. J. Gunneweg, and E. Lipinski understand עִבְרִי as a lower class Israelite in the pre-exilic community.[83] For H. L. Ellison, C. J. H. Wright, and S. A. Kaufman, עִבְרִי refers to a landless class who sells himself for a living.[84]

Upon closer examination, a sociological understanding of עִבְרִי is not convincing. There are two reasons for calling it into question. First, no biblical evidence supports this understanding. Second, the Deuteronomic laws consistently highlights and identifies those who are in the lower level of its social stratification—the poor, the slave, the sojourner, the fatherless, the widow, and the Lev-

---

Manumission of Slaves—the Fellow Year—the Sabbatical Year—the Jobel Year," *VT* 26, no. 1 (1976): 44. Furthermore, in the résumé of "The Hebrew Slave," he explains that "[t]he thought that the Hebrew of Ex. xxi 2 was necessarily an Israelite must be ruled out, but this does not exclude the possibility that he might have been. It is quite possible that impoverished Israelites or groups from the now resident Israelite tribes joined the *ḫapiru*, and for the original inhabitants it must sometimes have been difficult to distinguish between Hebrews and Israelites among the roaming gangs of robbers." See Lemche, "The Hebrew Slave," 144.

79 Victor H. Matthews, "The Anthropology of Slavery in the Covenant Code," in *Theory and Method in Biblical and Cuneiform Law: Revision, Interpolation and Development* (ed. Bernard M. Levinson; Sheffield: Sheffield Academic Press, 1994), 128 – 129.

80 Albrecht Alt, "The Origins of the Israelites," in *Essays on Old Testament History and Religion*. (trans. R.A. Wilson; Sheffield: JSOT, 1989), 93 – 95.

81 Nadav Na'aman, "Ḫabiru and Hebrews: The Transfer of a Social Term to the Literary Sphere," *JNES* 45, no. 4 (1986): 288.

82 Carolyn Pressler, "Wives and Daughters, Bond and Free: Views of Women in the Slave Laws of Exodus 21:2 – 22," in *Gender and Law in the Hebrew Bible and the Ancient Near East* (ed. Victor H. Matthews, Bernard M. Levinson, and Tikva Frymer-Kensky; Sheffield: Sheffield Academic Press, 1998), 151– 152.

83 Wolfgang Helck,"Die Bedrohung Palästinas durch einwandernde Gruppen am Ende der 18 und am Anfang der 19 Dynastie," *VT* 18, no. 4 (1968): 479 – 480. Antonius H. J. Gunneweg, *Geschichte Israels bis Bar Kochba* (Stuttgart: Verlag W. Kohlhammer, 1972), 37; Edward Lipiński, "L''esclave Hébreu'," *VT* 26, no. 1 (1976): 123.

84 H. L. Ellison, "The Hebrew Slave: A Study in Early Israelite Society," *EvQ* 45 (1973): 33.Christopher J. H. Wright, "What Happened Every Seven Years in Israel: Old Testament Sabbatical Institutions for Land, Debts and Slaves," *EQ* 56 (1984): 129 – 138. Kaufman, Stephen A. "A Reconstruction of the Social Welfare Systems of Ancient Israel," in *In the shelter of Elyon* (ed. Boyd Barrick and John R; Spencer: Sheffield: JSOT, 1984), 282.

ites. These are the kinds of people who are powerless and vulnerable in the ancient agrarian society that the laws in Deut 14:22–26:15 are meant to protect. These people are, as S. Bendor suggests, out of the protection of their *beit 'ab* (the institution of family, or the kinship group).[85] Understood in this manner, עִבְרִי never refers to a sociological inferior in the ancient Israelite society; instead, the Pentateuchal laws clearly claim the poor, the slave, the sojourner, the fatherless, the widow, and the Levites are the underprivileged.

The fact that עִבְרִי is generally spoken by non-Israelites is taken by many commentators to assume a derogatory nuance.[86] However, we have no evidence to go beyond the fact that the term always denotes ethnicity.[87] In the Pentateuchal narratives, עִבְרִי typically occurs in the Egyptian stories and contrasts ethnically with the Egyptians (Gen 39:14, 41:12, and Exod 2:11). It is also the case with the plural form עִבְרִים (Gen 40:15, 43:32; Exod 1:15, 16, 19; 2:6, 7, 13; 3:18; 5:3, 7:16; 9:1,13; 10:3). The formula יְהוָה אֱלֹהֵי הָעִבְרִים (YHWH, the God of *the Hebrews*) occurs six times in Exodus 3–10,[88] where this divine epithet is always coupled with a request for the release of the Hebrews to worship YHWH.[89] Given the uniform use of the word in the Pentateuch, it would be more pertinent to regard עִבְרִי/עִבְרִים (Hebrew/Hebrewess) as a term bearing the Israelite slave experience in Egypt.

Rhetorically, עִבְרִים/עִבְרִי also resonates with the enslaved memories in the story of Joseph in Genesis 37–50 and brings to mind the history of Israel in Egypt in Exodus 1–10.[90] Likewise, the phrase עִבְרִים/עִבְרִי in Ex 21 and Dt 15 is to remind Israel of their Egyptian enslavement and YHWH's new role as their

---

85 Shunya Bendor, *The Social Structure of Ancient Israel: The Institution of the Family (beit 'ab) from the Settlement to the End of the Monarchy* (Jerusalem: Simor, 1996), 229–241.

86 Kline, "Hebrews," *NBD* 458.

87 B. S. Childs also notes that in Exod 21:2 the term Hebrew was losing its wide connotation and became identified with the Israelite. Brevard S. Childs, *The Book of Exodus: A Critical, Theological Commentary* (Philadelphia: Westminster 1974), 468. See also D. Patrick's discussion on the contrast between a Hebrew and a foreigner. Dale Patrick, *Old Testament Law* (Atlanta: John Knox, 1985), 70.

88 Exod 3:18; 5:3; 7:16; 9:1, 13; 10:3.

89 Nahum M. Sarna, *Exodus* (New York: the Jewish Publication Society, 1991), 19.

90 Apart from these major narratives and slave laws in the Pentateuch, "the Hebrew" is mentioned in Gen 14:13 as a designation of Abraham, in 1 Samuel as a designation of the Israelite from the mouths of the Philistines and in Jonah 1:9 as the prophet's self-designation. See Lemche, *ABD* 3:95. J. Van Seters notes that עִבְרִי is a gentilic adjective which occurs in Joseph and the exodus accounts. These occurrences show that the term is evenly distributed in both J and E sources. John Van Seters, "The Law of the Hebrew Slave," *ZAW* 108, no. 4 (1996): 539–540.

master.[91] Propp suggests that עֶבֶד עִבְרִי (a Hebrew slave) in Exod 21:2 echoes Moses' demand of liberation, and this allusion is heightened and made explicit in the slave law of Deut 15:12 – 18.[92] The memory of slavery must have left a vivid impression as the Israelites had just departed Egypt. This may presumably explain why the first law to them opens with the subject of the manumission of עֶבֶד עִבְרִי (a Hebrew slave) in Exod 21:2. Instead of the pharaoh, now YHWH is the master of all Hebrew people. They are no longer servants of pharaoh but only YHWH's (cf. Lev 25:42, 55).[93] Under YHWH's governing sovereignty, there will be no more *involuntary* permanent Hebrew slaves.[94]

In view of the context, the term אָחִיךְ (literally: your brother) is clearly defined in Deuteronomy. Most often in Deuteronomy, אָחִיךְ is used as an ethnic designation as "an Israelite." S. Japhet understands אָחִיךְ as a reference to the nation of Israel or the covenant community.[95] McConville concurs that "[t]he term *'āḥîm*, 'brothers', is Deuteronomy's characteristic expression for referring to fellow-Israelites, regardless of social status or tribal divisions."[96]

The context of Deuteronomy 15 also makes an ethnic distinction between אָחִיךְ and הַנָּכְרִי (the foreigner, cf. Deut 17:15). In Deut 15:3, אָחִיךְ is contrasted with הַנָּכְרִי in ethnic sense. In general, גֵּר (sojourner) refers to a social status and נָכְרִי denotes a non-Israelite. According to *HALOT*, גֵּר (sojourner) denotes "a man who (alone or with his family) leaves his village and tribe because of war, famine, epidemic, blood guilt etc. and seeks shelter and residence at another place, where his right of landed property, marriage and taking part in jurisdiction, cult and war has been curtailed."[97] Any Israelite can be a גֵּר (sojourner) inside or outside the promised land, as long as he is living out of his hometown (cf. Exod 2:22 and 2 Sam 4:3). A נָכְרִי living in the Israelite society is doubtless a גֵּר

---

91 Exod 4:23; 7:16, 26; 8:16; 9:1, 13; 10:3 claim that the request of release is so that the Hebrew people may worship YHWH.

92 Propp, *Exodus 19 – 40*, 188.

93 Lev 25:42—For they are my servants whom I brought out from the land of Egypt; they are not to be sold in a slave sale. Lev 21:55—For the sons of Israel are my servants; they are my servants whom I brought out from the land of Egypt. I am YHWH your God.

94 J. H. Tigay and C. L. Meyers both assess that this is a law that concerns debt-servitude. They suggest that the term עֶבֶד should be translated as "servants." "Slave" has a negative connotation that may not be justified in an English rendering. Tigay, *Deuteronomy*, 147–148, and Carol L. Meyers, *Exodus* (Cambridge: Cambridge University Press, 2005), 190–191.

95 Sara Japhet, "The Relationship between the Legal Corpora in the Pentateuch in Light of Manumission Laws." in *Studies in Bible* (ed. Sara Japhet; Jerusalem: Magnes, 1986), 77.

96 McConville, *Law and Theology*, 19.

97 Koehler and W. Baumgartner, "גֵּר" *HALOT* 1:201.

(sojourner), but a גֵּר (sojourner) is not necessarily a נָכְרִי. In view of this, אָחִיךָ is without a doubt an ethnic term that conveys a sense of sociological empathy.

Therefore, the expression in 15:12, אָחִיךָ הָעִבְרִי אוֹ הָעִבְרִיָּה (your fellow Hebrew, male or female), is for rhetorical emphasis. The definite עִבְרִי (Hebrew) and עִבְרִיָּה (Hebrewess) are the appositions of the subject אָחִיךָ. As M. Weippert notes, "[h]ere the 'Hebrew' is described as the 'brother' of the person addressed in the legal text and is, therefore, defined as an Israelite."[98]

The use of עִבְרִי/עִבְרִיָּה and אָחִיךָ indicates that the expression which includes both them is not tautologous even though both words are essentially ethnic in meaning.[99] The Deuteronomic formula אָחִיךָ הָעִבְרִי אוֹ הָעִבְרִיָּה conveys a deep-rooted fraternity. It brings out Israel's harrowing memory and appeals to the sense of fraternal intimacy. It appeals to the sympathy of its audience, swaying their rational (logos) and emotional (pathos) reception into compliance with the law.

חָפְשִׁי

In addition to עִבְרִי, the use of חָפְשִׁי (lit., free) is also significant to slave manumission laws. Ex 21 and Dt 15 both use חָפְשִׁי to express the meaning of "release," though they are phrased somewhat differently.[100] In the Old Testament, חָפְשִׁי primarily refers to the emancipation of Hebrew (Israelite/Judean) slaves who are released from their debts and obligations (Exod 21:2, 5, 26–27; Deut 15:12–13, 18; and Jer 34:9, 11, 14, 16). חָפְשִׁי is for some scholars (e. g., Lemche and Matthews), a designation of a social low class.[101]

N. Lohfink disputes the claim that חָפְשִׁי designates a low social stratum, for he finds no evidence for such a class in the history of Israel.[102] R. de Vaux remarks that the word is used almost always in the context of liberation of slaves except in Job 39:5 and 1 Sam 17:25. He thus opposes equating חָפְשִׁי to a specified

---

98 Weippert, *The Settlement of the Israelite Tribes in Palestine*, 87.
99 As questioned by C. J. H. Wright. Christopher J. H. Wright, "What Happened Every Seven Years in Israel? Old Testament Sabbatical Institutions for Land, Debts and Slaves Part II," *EQ* 56 (1984): 196–197.
100 יֵצֵא לַחָפְשִׁי חִנָּם (he shall go out *free* without payment) in Exod 21:2 and תְּשַׁלְּחֶנּוּ חָפְשִׁי (You shall sent him *free*) in Deut 15:12. Weinfeld notes that the difference of verbal forms is indicative of the humanistic approach of Deuteronomy. A detailed discussion on the differences of these two verbs will be expounded in chapter three. See Weinfeld, *Deuteronomy and Deuteronomic School*, 283.
101 Lemche, "The Hebrew Slave: Comments on the Slave Law Ex 21:2–11," 140; Matthews, "The Anthropology of Slavery in the Covenant Code," 128–129.
102 N. Lohfink, "חָפְשִׁי," *TDOT* 5:114–118.

social class.[103] For Th. C. Vriezen, the fact that "the Book of the Covenant (Exod xxi) starts with the demand for the release of the Hebrew slave after six years,"[104] speaks volumes. "The legislator is anxious to protect the *liberty* of those who are socially weak."[105] Vriezen's view is accepted by J. P. J. Olivier, who suggests that the first law with the demand of חׇפְשִׁי for the Israelite debt slaves underlines the prominence of human freedom in the Old Testament. This drive for freedom should be connected with the most dominant tradition in the history of Israel, the Exodus. The divine deliverance from servitude in the past serves as a paradigm of liberty. As a result, no Israelite will be deprived of his freedom indefinitely.[106] Olivier further proposes that the release of the indentured Hebrew slave simply entails the slave's return to his/her ordinary life as a free citizen.[107]

Meanwhile, Olivier believes that a political interpretation of the Exodus event is a much later development (by Philo, and modern textual theologians, esp. in Latin America and Africa). For this reason, he defines the Exodus event as a redemptive act rather than a liberation or an emancipation from slavery (Deut 7:8). The concept of freedom implied in redemption in its full sense is lacking in the Old Testament.[108]

Though Olivier's observation is an important point, it is irrelevant to the issue at hand. Later interpretations and applications do not affect the meaning of words in their original contexts. The political interpretation of the Exodus event by no means alters חׇפְשִׁי in the Hebrew slave manumission laws that originally speak about human freedom. In Deuteronomy, as well as in the Pentateuch, slavery is in opposition to freedom both sociologically and soteriologically. Moreover, ethics is fundamentally *theological* in the Old Testament. Ethical teachings are related to God—to his character, his will, his actions, and his purpose.[109] E. D. Radmacher provides a similar theological concept of freedom that is in present from the beginning of Genesis. Ever since Adam forfeited the obedience-oriented way of life and replaced it with the rebel-oriented way of lust (Gen 3:6), humankind has been constantly struggling for freedom. Since the fall, these two orientations, obedience and rebellion, have marked all human behavior and thus determined human freedom. These two orientations

---

103 Roland de Vaux, *Ancient Israel: Its Life and Institutions* (Grand Rapids: Eerdmans, 1997), 88.
104 Th. C. Vriezen, *An Outline of Old Testament Theology* (Newton: C. T. Branford, 1970), 420 – 421.
105 Ibid., 421.
106 J. P. J. Olivier, "חפשׁ," *NIDOTTE* 2:238 – 242.
107 Olivier, *NIDOTTE* 2:240.
108 Olivier, *NIDOTTE* 2:239.
109 Wright, *Old Testament Ethics for the People of God*, 22.

or ways of life lead to two utterly different destinies—obedience that leads to liberty and freedom, and rebellion that leads to slavery and imprisonment. At any given time, a person, state, or a nation must place their allegiance either to what God commands (his word), or to what man desires (his sin).[110]

Therefore, the meaning of freedom conveyed in חָפְשִׁי is both theological and sociological. The release ought to be understood as restitution for an Israelite slave who can (1) return to his/her hometown, (2) regain an unbounded ordinary life,[111] and (3) worship YHWH freely.

The Identification of Enslaved Members in the Indebted Family

ANE slave laws usually and explicitly identify the family members sold into debt servitude or to be a debt pledge. For example, LH 117 plainly lists the family members who could be sold into debt servitude—a man's wife, son, or daughter. Interestingly, Deut 15:12–18 does not provide such explicit information. G. C. Chirichigno argues that the verb יִמָּכֵר in Deut 15:12 is a clue that identifies the ones who are sold. He deems that the law most likely deals with the manumission of Israelite debt-slaves who are *dependents* of the debtor who sells them.[112] For him, מכר in *niphal* form signifies that the dependents are *forced* to be sold by the head of the family, the father/debtor. Chirichigno's understanding of יִמָּכֵר is based on two assumptions: First, the slave laws in Ex 21 and Dt 15 are similar to LH 117, which mentions only the sale of family dependents. Second, the debtor who makes a pledge is excluded from being a pledge. He can give his dependents as a pledge, but not himself. Otherwise it would only increase the difficulty for him to repay the loan.[113]

In the general rules of Hebrew grammar, יִמָּכֵר can be rendered either reflexively ("sells himself/herself"), or passively ("is sold"). If it is rendered reflexively, it refers to an indigent person who sells himself/herself for sustenance. If it is

---

110 Earl D. Radmacher, "Liberty and Freedom in the Old Testament," in *America in History and Bible Prophecy* (ed. Thomas S. McCall; Chicago: Moody 1976), 129.
111 Moshe Weinfeld, "Freedom Proclamations in Egypt and in the Ancient Near East," in *Pharaonic Egypt: The Bible and Christianity* (ed. Sarah Israelit-Groll; Jerusalem: Magnes, 1985), 317–319.
112 Gregory C. Chirichigno, *Debt-Slavery in Israel and the Ancient Near East* (Sheffield: JSOT, 1993), 216, and see also his discussions from pages 200–217, 272–278.
113 Ibid., 269–282. LH 117—"If an obligation is outstanding against a man and he sells or gives into debt service his wife, his son, or his daughter, they should perform service in the house of their buyer or of the one who holds them in debt service for three years; their release shall be secured in the fourth year."

rendered passively, it refers to the sale of a son, a daughter, or a wife by an indigent father/husband, or the sale of a thief by the court (as is the case in Exod 22:2 [Eng. 22:3]). Chirichigno interprets יִמָּכֵר in Deut 15:12 with a passive meaning, which is primarily based on his assumption that Dt 15 is a parallel law with LH 117; but the same יִמָּכֵר in Lev 25:39 he renders into a reflexive meaning because the context of Leviticus 25 is different. According to A. Schenker and J. Milgrom, מכר in *niphal* always conveys a passive meaning. Had a reflexive meaning been intended, the *hithpa'el* would have been used, as is in Deut 28:68.[114] With Schenker and Milgrom's suggestion and the case in Lev 25, it demonstrates that even יִמָּכֵר carries a passive meaning; its usage in the slave laws does not necessarily mean that it must be a compulsory sale. יִמָּכֵר is most likely used to indicate the destitute situation so that one is sold.

Chirichigno's view that an Israelite can *only* be sold by his father has also been rebutted by Schenker and McConville. Schenker points out that such a restriction is not supported by the Bible.[115] McConville argues that there does not seem to be a reason to suppose that those who enter service are only the dependants of the impoverished person, given that Deut 15:16–17 is not applicable to the debtor's wife.[116] Tigay inclines to leave the two possibilities open, "as long as the debt servitude is permitted, the aim in either case would be to satisfy a debt or raise the fund to do so."[117] It is not necessary to limit the enslaved members only to the debtor's dependents.

The Provision for the Manumitted Slave in Deut 15:13–14

The scope of the manumission slave law in Dt 15 goes far beyond that of Ex 21. Whereas the latter merely regulates releases under different marital situations (cf. Exod 21:3–4), the former requires generously supplying the freed Hebrew slave with agrarian products. Tigay, Christensen, and Nelson believe that the provision intends to prevent the newly released fellow Hebrew/Hebrewess from starting off penniless, lest the slave soon becomes needy for basic substance and reverts to the same condition that led him/her to servitude in the first

114 Adrian Schenker, "The Biblical Legislation on the Release of Slaves: The Road from Exodus to Leviticus," *JSOT* 78 (1998): 31–32; Jacob Milgrom, *Leviticus 23–27: A New Translation with Introduction and Commentary* (New York: Doubleday, 2001), 2219.
115 Schenker, "The Biblical Legislation on the Release of Slaves, 27.
116 McConville, *Deuteronomy*, 262–263.
117 Tigay, *Deuteronomy*, 149.

place.[118] Mayes suggests that the supplement will provide the fellow Hebrew/He-brewess with the means of establishing himself/herself as a full and independ-ent member of the Israelite society.[119] These proposals are probable; however, Deut 15:13–14 speaks with a deeper humanitarian spirit.

Deut 15:13 commands the owner not to send slaves away empty-handed (רֵיקָם). Scholars, such as C. Carmichael and Chirichigno, observe that Gen 31:42 and Exod 3:21 also share similar wording of רֵיקָם with Deut 15:13. They then argue that the stipulation of provisioning is most likely due to Deuterono-my's literary dependency on Genesis and Exodus.[120]

The overall use of רֵיקָם in the Old Testament points to a profound sociolog-ical relationship. In its sixteen occurrences, רֵיקָם regularly pairs with action verbs, including שׁלח (send away, Gen 31:42; Deut 15:13; 1 Sam 6:3; Job 22:9), הלך (go/walk away, Exod 3:21), ראה (appear, Exod 23:15; 34:20; Deut 16:16), שׁוב (return, Ruth 1:21), and בוא (come/go in, Ruth 3:17; 2 Sam1:22; Isa 55:11; Jer 14:3; 50:9).[121] Whenever the context relates to a social issue, these action verbs are fol-lowed by the adverb רֵיקָם to articulate grace extending beyond action to humani-tarianism (see Gen 31:42; Exod 3:21; Deut 15:13; Ruth 1:21; and Job 22:9).[122]

In these cases, the formula "action verb + adverb רֵיקָם" brings up humanitar-ian concerns. The direct objects of the action verbs are usually the socially weak. An Israelite who returns home empty-handed is described to be in a miserable situation. Ruth 1:21 and Jer 14:3 portray the feeling of those who return home empty-handed in a state of humiliated situation lacking YHWH's blessing. Mean-while, for those who are prosperous, releasing a social-economic inferior and providing them with provisions is not only a praise-worthy gesture but also a representation of humanitarian concerns. For example, Laban and Boaz are so-cially and economically powerful in relation to Jacob and Ruth/Naomi. All of those who were socio-economically powerful (e.g., Laban, the Egyptians, the

---

118 Peter C. Craigie, *The Book of Deuteronomy* (Grand Rapids: Eerdmans, 1976), 238; Tigay, *Deuteronomy*, 149; Christensen, *Deuteronomy 1:1–21:9*, 320; Richard D. Nelson, *Deuteronomy: A Commentary* (Louisville: Westminster John Knox, 2002), 199.
119 Mayes, *Deuteronomy*, 251. See also Walter Brueggemann, *Deuteronomy* (Nashville: Ab-ingdon Press, 2001), 166–167.
120 Calum M. Carmichael, "The Three Laws on the Release of Slaves," *ZAW* 112 (2000): 519–523; Chirichigno, *Debt Slavery in Israel and the Ancient Near East*, 288–289.
121 The only two exceptions occur in Ps 7:5 [Eng. 7:4]; 25:3. See J. Shepherd's discussion about the distinctive usage in these two places in Psalm. Jerry Shepherd, "ריק," *NIDOTTE* 3:1106–1109.
122 Other than the formulas in social contexts, similar formulas are used in the contexts of presenting gifts to YHWH (Exod 23:5, 34:20; Deut 16:16; 1 Sam 6:3) and in describing, abstractly, one with such might will surely not make mistakes (Saul's sword in 2 Sam 1:22, warrior's arrow in Jer 50:9, and YHWH's word in Isa 55:11). L. Koehler and W. Baumgartner, "רֵיקָם," *HALOT* 2:1229.

slave owner, and Boaz) could have released the powerless (e. g., Jacob, the Israelites, the slave, and Ruth) in empty-handed terms. None of them would have
been punished had they simply done so. In view of these, Dt 15 purposely
makes the humanitarian concern that flows out of the biblical narrative into a
stipulation of a slave manumission law.

Moreover, Deut 15:14a suggests that Deuteronomy intends to go beyond material supplement: The verbal usage there is instructive in at least two ways:
First, Deuteronomy chooses the rare verb ענק instead of the common נתן,
which occurs in similar contexts in Deut 15:9, 10, 14.[123] ענק literally means to
adorn the neck of someone with a necklace.[124] It expresses celebration rather
than merely giving supplement. Second, Deut 15:14 starts the request with
the collocation of the infinitive absolute with the imperfect, הַעֲנֵיק תַּעֲנִיק (generously furnish). The verbal usage demonstrates that not only does the law ask
for providing substance to solve the newly released slave's needs, but also encourages the master to be as generous as he/she could. Furthermore, the three
agrarian resources (livestock, threshing floor, wine vat) referred in Deut 15:14a
are also terms used for the joyful feast scenario found in Deut 15:19 – 16:17. They
perfectly correspond with the three agrarian items for the three annual season-
al sacrifices—firstborn male of "your herd and of your flock" (Deut 15:19),
"standing grain" (Deut 16:9), and "what you have gathered from wine vat
and threshing floor" (Deut 16:13). In addition to the agricultural products in
15:19 – 16:17, Deut 16:16 also uses the formula "action verb ראה + adverb רֵיקָם."
These elements together depict a scene of sharing exhilaration in a celebratory
ambiance with others in front of YHWH. In short, Deut 15:13 – 14a does not only
request the master to give material substance,[125] but also implicitly demands the
master to send the slave away joyfully, hosting a farewell party with banquet and
gifts.

The אֲשֶׁר clause in 15:14b may accordingly be rendered as כַּאֲשֶׁר (just as, according to) and be translated to "just as YHWH your God has blessed you." This
reading is also supported by textual witnesses including the SP and some LXX
manuscripts, as well as the possible haplography suggested by the *kaph* at the
end of the preceding word.[126] Moreover, the similarity between 15:14b and
Deut 16:17b also supports this reading.

---

123 Chirichigno, *Debt Slavery in Israel and the Ancient Near East*, 290.
124 Malcolm J. A. Horsnell, "ענק," 3:466.
125 It is commonly assumed that the verb echoes the curious feature about jewelry in the
Exodus narrative. See Chirichigno, *Debt Slavery in Israel and the Ancient Near East*, 290;
McConville, *Deuteronomy*, 263. Carmichael, "The Three Laws on the Release of Slaves," 522.
126 Christensen, *Deuteronomy 1:1 – 21:9*, 318.

Deut 15:14b אֲשֶׁר בֵּרַכְךָ יְהוָה אֱלֹהֶיךָ תִּתֶּן־לוֹ (you shall give to him just as YHWH your God has blessed you)

Deut 16:17b כְּבִרְכַּת יְהוָה אֱלֹהֶיךָ אֲשֶׁר נָתַן־לָךְ (just as the blessing of YHWH your God which He has given you)

Hamilton argues that Masoretes also understood this concept in the same way in the clause of v.14. The *'atnāḥ* beneath וּמִיִּקְבֶךָ breaks the flow of the sentence. "This means that the blessing of YHWH is understood not as being conferred *upon* the owner's property (in which case the verse would read 'you should liberally provide for that one from your flock and threshing-floor and vineyard with which YHWH your God has blessed you'—no break) but that the blessing of YHWH is understood to belong to the latter part of the verse."[127] The three agrarian resources must not only mean material supplements in a literal sense,[128] but also depict a mirthful and festival scene that the master should bid farewell to a slave, sharing the good things and having feast with him/her as part of the master's reverence for YHWH. Therefore, Deuteronomy does not consider the stipulation merely as a humanitarian gesture, but as a theological command which must be obeyed if Israel is to continue in receiving God's blessing (s).[129] The sympathy embedded in Deut 15:13–14 is at the heart of the Deuteronomic law, as McConville indicates.[130] The spirit of the law stresses the dignity of the released slave.

The Motive Clauses in Deut 15:15, 18 and Their Relationship with Deut 15:16–17

Three issues pertaining to the motive clauses of Dt 15 have long been debated. One debate centers on the function of the motive clause in Deut 15:15. The second debate has been whether G. Seitz and Mayes are correct in their claim that v. 18 is a later addition due to its awkward placement.[131] The third is over the ambiguous

---

127 See discussion in Hamilton, *Social Justice and Deuteronomy*, 25 n. 35.
128 If the list means merely material provision, questions concerning feasibility surface. For instance, "it is impossible for the owner to give the slave wine from his wine vat, since the slave would have to drink the wine right away"; and "if the released slave would have somewhere to store the wine." See Chirichigno, *Debt Slavery in Israel and the Ancient Near East*, 290.
129 Chirichigno, *Debt Slavery in Israel and the Ancient Near East*, 292. See also McConville, *Law and Theology in Deuteronomy*, 16–17.
130 McConville, *Deuteronomy*, 263.
131 Gottfried Seitz, *Redaktionsgeschichtliche Studien zum Deuteronomium* (Stuttgart: Verlag W. Kohlhammer, 1971), 172; Mayes, *Deuteronomy*, 252. See also Hamilton, *Social Justice and Deuteronomy*, 19–20 n. 26.

meanings of מִשְׁנֶה (double, copy, and second) and מִשְׁנֶה שְׂכַר שָׂכִיר (double the serv-ice of a hired man). Each of these issues will be examined in the following dis-cussion.

The motive clause of Deut 15:15 carries the memory of Israel's historical ex-perience. According to B. Gemser's category, it "can be defined as of *historicao-religious* character."[132] Such clauses "urge the fulfilling of the commandment by reference to and on the ground of 'die grossen Heilstaten Jahwes in der Ge-schichte,' especially the deliverance from Egypt and the granting of the land of Canaan."[133] McConville indicates that the call for Israel to remember slavery is to invoke empathy for the needs of slaves that should lead to their generosity towards the latter.[134] Others believe that its main purpose is to remind Israel of YHWH's redemption and kindness (e. g., Daube, Craigie, Mayes, Chirichigno, Tigay, and Christensen).[135] These interpretations do not satisfactorily explain the meaning and function of this motive clause, for they relate the recollection to *Exodus* (be brought out of the slave house of Egypt) rather than to *the enslaved experience in Egypt*. The latter is what Deut 15:15a points to. The following discus-sion about the usage of the Deuteronomic pattern language in the motive clauses of Deut 15:15 and 18 will show that they intend to describe sufferings experienced in enslavement rather than victory in the Exodus deliverance. The proposal of the Deuteronomic pattern language sheds light to the interpretation of the twofold motive clauses in this slave law.

The Motive Clause in 15:15 in View of the Deuteronomic Pattern Language
Deuteronomy makes use of various formulated phrases. Unfortunately, few have ever discussed the heavy use of repetition and distinctive phraseology in the book.[136] Other than Weinfeld who relegates Deuteronomic phraseology to the ap-

---

132 Berend Gemser, "The Importance of the Motive Clause in Old Testament Law," *VTSup* (1953): 60.

133 Ibid., 60.

134 McConville, *Deuteronomy*, 263.

135 David Daube, *Studies in Biblical Law* (New York: Ktav Publishing House, 1969), 49 – 50; Craigie, *The Book of Deuteronomy*, 239; Mayes, *Deuteronomy*, 251; Chirichigno, *Debt Slavery in Israel and the Ancient Near East*, 292; Tigay, *Deuteronomy*, 149; Christensen, *Deuteronomy 1:1 – 21:9*, 320.

136 M. K. Deeley argues in her doctoral dissertation that part of those abundant calls to remember the past are a late or post-exilic redaction. This redaction changed the law book "from a book of promulgation with a heavy emphasis on covenant to a book of possibilities which re-rooted the exilic Jews in their beginnings as a slave nation." Mary Katharine Deeley, "The Rhetoric of Memory: A Study of the Persuasive Function of the Memory Commands in Deute-

pendix in his *Deuteronomy and the Deuteronomic School*,[137] no scholar has tried to investigate the nuance of this Deuteronomic formularization.

Weinfeld regards these formulated phrases as idioms and classifies them into thirteen categories, such as "the struggle against idolatry," "centralization of worship," "Exodus, covenant, and election," etc.[138] However, the Deuteronomic formulation goes beyond merely a classification of phrases. Another manner of understanding these phrases in Deuteronomy is to see these formulated phrases that consist of specific vocabularies as renovating a pseudo language that may be termed as a "pattern language."[139]

In its basic makeup, the prime unit of a formulated phrase is a set of specific vocabularies which expresses a similar concept (such as, "in Egypt" and "in the land of Egypt"). A classical illustration of Deuteronomic formularization can be found in the motive clause of Deut 15:15, which consists of three formulated phrases, וְזָכַרְתָּ כִּי עֶבֶד הָיִיתָ בְּמִצְרַיִם/בְּאֶרֶץ מִצְרַיִם "remember that you were a slave in Egypt," וַיִּפְדְּךָ יְהוָה אֱלֹהֶיךָ "YHWH your God redeemed you," and עַל־כֵּן אָנֹכִי מְצַוְּךָ אֶת־הַדָּבָר הַזֶּה הַיּוֹם "therefore I am commanding you this today." The three Deuteronomic formulated phrases—"remember that you were a slave in Egypt/in the land of Egypt," "YHWH your God redeemed you," and "therefore I am commanding you this today,"—occur frequently throughout Deu-

---

ronomy 5–26" (Ph.D. diss., Northwestern University, 1989). See also Timothy A. Lenchak, Timothy A. Lenchak, *Choose Life! A Rhetorical-Critical Investigation of Deuteronomy 28,69–30,20* (Roma: Editrice Pontificio Istituto Biblico, 1993); and McConville, *Deuteronomy*, 19.

137 Weinfeld, *Deuteronomy and the Deuteronomic School*, 320–365.

138 Ibid., 324.

139 In the late 1970s, C. Alexander and his coworkers published *A Pattern Language: Towns, Buildings, Construction*, in which they championed the framework and philosophy of the "pattern language" in architecture. Upon the publication of the book, patterns and pattern languages were soon applied to other fields, such as software design, user interface design, sociology, and so forth. A *pattern* in architecture is a description of a solution to a recurring problem, denoting a configuration which brings life to a building. A *pattern language* is a network of patterns that call upon one another. Patterns characterize the insights and knowledge of a design and can be used in combination to manifest an organized mind behind the design of a building. The use of keywords and formulaic phrases in Deuteronomy reflect authorial intent, just as the pattern and the pattern language to buildings. Hereafter in this study, "pattern" is adopted to refer to the combinations of the recurrent keywords and formulaic phrases, and "pattern language" is used to describe the overarching phraseology the author/compiler utilizes to convey his/her purpose. See Christopher Alexander, Sara Ishikawa, and Murray Silverstein, *A Pattern Language: Towns, Buildings, Construction* (New York: Oxford University Press, 1977), and Christopher Alexander, *The Timeless Way of Building* (New York: Oxford University Press, 1979).

teronomy.[140] When more than one formulated phrases are combined in a sentence, they form a *pattern*. For instance, the three formulated phrases in Deut 15:15 form a pattern: "Remember that you were a slave *in the land of Egypt*, and YHWH your God redeemed you; therefore I am commanding you *this today*."

The pattern in Deut 15:15 later occurs in Deut 24:18 again: "Remember that you were a slave *in Egypt* and YHWH your God redeemed you *from there*; therefore I am commanding you *to do this*." Note that minor differences do exist between Deut 15:15 and 24:18, *"in Egypt"* and *"in the land of Egypt," "redeemed you"* and *"redeemed you from there," "this today"* and *"to do this."* These slight discrepancies do not, however, skew the fact that Deuteronomy repeatedly invokes specific combinations of linguistic constructions.

Likewise, when the formulated phrase "so that one may learn to fear YHWH" (Deut 4:10; 14:23; 17:19; 31:12, 13) is attached to "assemble the people" (Deut 4:10, 31:12) and "that they may hear my words/words of this law" (Deut 4:10, 31:12),[141] they form another pattern, "[a]ssemble the people...to hear my words so that they may learn to fear me/YHWH your God." (Deut 4:10 and Deut 31:12). The proverbial expression "so that you may prolong your days" can be combined with "keep/listen/walk in his statutes/his commandments/his ordinances/ every commandment/his voice/his ways/his words/these words" and "which I am commanding you today." Together they form another recurrent pattern in the Deuteronomic pattern language: "[k]eep his statues and his commandments/every commandment/his voice, which I am commanding you today, that you may prolong your days." (Deut 4:10; 6:2; 11:8 – 9; 30:20).[142]

In the same way, the collocation of תּוֹעֵבָה (abomination) and יהוה merits more attention than it was given in the past. In Deuteronomy, תּוֹעֵבָה (which generally denotes the persons, things, or practices that offend against one's ritual or moral

---

140 "Remember that you were a slave in Egypt/in the land of Egypt" in Deut 5:15; 15:15; 16:12; 24:18, 22; cf. also 7:8; 24:9; 16:3, "YHWH your God redeemed you," in Deut 15:15; 24:18; cf. also 7:8; 9:26; 13:6; 15:15; 21:8, and "therefore I am commanding you this today," in Deut 15:15; 24:18, 22; cf. 15:11; 19:7.
141 Weinfeld notes that "to learn to fear YHWH" is always attached to "walk in his ways, listen to his voice, observe truth, keep and do" and other phrases. Weinfeld, *Deuteronomy and the Deuteronomic School*, 332.
142 Phrases that involve this pattern include "so that you may prolong your days" (Deut 4:40; 5:16; 6:2; 11:9; 22:7; 25:15; 30:20); "keep/listen/walk in his statutes/his commandments/his ordinances/every commandment/his voice/his ways/his words/these words, etc." (Deut 4:40; 5:1, 10, 29, 31; 6:1, 2, 3, 17, 20, 24, 25; 7:9, 11, 12; 8:2, 6, 11; 10: 12, 13; 11:1, 8, 13, 22, 27, 28, 32; 12: 1, 28; 13:4, 19 [Eng. 13:3, 18]; 16:12; 17:10, 19; 19:9; 26:14, 16, 17, 18; 27:1, 10; 28:1, 2, 13, 15, 45; 29:9; 30:10, 11, 16; 31:12, 13; 32:46; 33:9 etc.), and "which I am commanding you today" (Deut 4:40; 6:6; 7:11; 8:1, 11; 10:13; 11:8; 13:19; 15:5; 19:9; 27:10; 28:1, 13, 15; 30:2, 8, 11, 16).

order)[143] is often joined with יהוה (תּוֹעֲבַת יהוה, Deut 7:25; 12:31; 17:1; 18:12; 22:5; 23:19; 25:16; 27:15).[144] Other than Deuteronomy, this collocation only occurs elsewhere in the book of Proverbs.[145] When it is further combined with other phrases to form a pattern such as "for it is an abomination to YHWH your God" (כִּי תוֹעֲבַת יְהוָה אֱלֹהֶיךָ הוּא), the resultant pattern functions as a motive clause that warns about straying from God ("for it is an abomination to the LORD your God" Deut 7:25 and 17:1).[146]

By no means is this design of patterns coincidental or purposeless. As an example, the reiteration of such patterns apparently makes the content recognizable and memorable. However, the didactic function of the pattern language is not limited to it.[147]

There are three major features one can observe from the Deuteronomic pattern language. The first feature is its constant relatedness to YHWH. The pattern language is designed to stress a relationship on YHWH himself with respect to—his redemption, nature, instructions, and good-will for his people. The three patterns shown above reinforce these themes—(1) "Remember that you were a slave in the land of Egypt, and YHWH your God redeemed you; therefore I am commanding you this today," (2) "Keep his statues and his commandments/every commandment/his voice, which I am commanding you today, that you may prolong your days," and (3) "for it is an abomination to the LORD your God." There

---

143 Michael A. Grisanti, "תעב," *NIDOTTE* 4:314–318.

144 Deut 7:25; 12:31; 17:1; 18:12; 22:5; 23:19; 25:16; 27:15; Prov 3:32; 11:1, 20; 12:22; 15:8, 26; 16:5; 17:15; 20:10, 23.

145 M. Weinfeld is convinced that law and wisdom existed as two separate disciplines until the seventh century. "The author of Deuteronomy and the Deuteronomist" who conceived wisdom in an entire novel manner and amalgamated these two disciplines in the book, so that the laws of the Torah are now identified with wisdom. Weinfeld, *Deuteronomy and the Deuteronomic School*, 254–256.

146 A thorough discussion of various other combinations in the Deuteronomic pattern language is beyond the scope of this study. Issues that would be explored in such a study would include L. J. de Regt's observation that "the traditional distinction between principle clause and subordinate clause is difficult to maintain for Deuteronomy 1–30 as far as the word order is concerned." It is thus possible that the device of pattern language is an influential factor that causes this difficulty. See L. J. de Regt, "Word Order in Different Clause Types in Deuteronomy 1–30," in *Studies in Hebrew and Aramaic syntax: Presented to Professor J Hoftijzer on the Occasion of His Sixty-Fifth Birthday* (ed. H L. Murre-Van den Berg K. Jongeling, and Lucas Van Rompay; Leiden: E. J. Brill, 1991), 152–172.

147 Weinfeld and Lenchak both view that such phrases mainly serve a didactic purpose. Weinfeld, *Deuteronomy and the Deuteronomic School*, 298–306; Timothy A. Lenchak, *Choose Life! A Rhetorical-Critical Investigation of Deuteronomy*, 8–10.

are more patterns that reflect this feature of relatedness to YHWH, but the limits of this study do not allow for a complete presentation here.

The second feature is that a pattern in Deuteronomy often serves as a motive clause that usually carries strong persuasive modes with the pathos, ethos, and logos. In the past, Gemser has pointed out the startling contrast between the ANE law collections and biblical laws. The latter contains abundant motive clauses with various contents and forms, while a motive clause is in complete absence in the former.[148]

The formulated phrases in Deuteronomy often represent an insightful opinion, proverbial wisdom, or historical truth that draws the listener's attention, such as, "so that you may learn to fear YHWH," "that you may prolong your days," "you were a slave in Egypt," and "YHWH your God redeemed you." To the audience, the recollection of the motive clause in Deut 15:15 reflects and recalls their experiences as slaves in Egypt, appealing directly to their emotions. As W. Brueggemann summarizes this idea:[149]

> the memory of Exodus makes clear that the entitlements of creditors is recent, that what creditors have is gift and not possession, that creditors and debtors have more in common than what may distinguish them. Finally, Exodus memory recalls that a cry to YHWH (as in v. 9, on which see Exod 2:23 – 25) evokes divine action that causes redress. It is this specific memory that creates a context and pressure for visible, substantive, prompt, durable redress of social inequity. Creditors are called not to act like Pharaoh, but to replicate the action of YHWH who overcame debt-slavery in Egypt.

The reappropriation of the Egyptian sufferings as an element of both the people's collective biography and personal experiences, as Oosthuizen indicates, is to facilitate a perceptional change.[150] By identifying with the Egyptian persecution as a foundational event, the audience is challenged to associate with the socially vulnerable.[151] In this light, the mention of YHWH's redemption in Deut 15:15 therefore serves a deeper purpose than merely motivating Israel towards material generosity or obeying the law.

Third, the Deuteronomic pattern language conceptually links similar laws and commandments together. Such a link often intends to highlight its humanitarian concerns. The motive clauses in Deut 5:15; 15:15; 16:12; 24:18, 22, which are

---

148 Gemser. "The Importance of the Motive Clause in Old Testament Law," 62.

149 Brueggemann, *Deuteronomy*, 167.

150 Oosthuizen, "Deuteronomy 15:1–18 in Socio-Rhetorical Perspective," 75.

151 Ibid., 75.

associated with various "remembrance" patterns, are humanitarian in nature.[152] Among them, the same pattern in Deut 15:15 occurs again only in Deut 24:18, where it serves as the motive clause for forbidding the perversion of justice towards an alien or orphan and prohibiting the taking of a widow's garment in pledge (Deut 24:17). It is of great significance that the same pattern occurs in the symmetrical sections of "laws for the protection of the socially weak" (Deut 15:1–16:17 and Deut 23:16–25:19). The fact that Deut 15:15 and Deut 24:18 share this pattern suggests that it serves as a rhetorical device in pleading empathy for the socially weak.[153]

In summary, the Deuteronomic pattern language is a deliberate design which relates YHWH to his people and his humanitarian concerns. The pattern that Deut 15:15 employs demonstrates that this slave manumission law is essentially humanitarian. This motive clause reflects the idea of a YHWH oriented equality: Only when one has experienced God's redemption and has understood that all he/she has is from God can one truly treat one another with equality.

The Relationship between the Motive Clauses in 15:15, 18 and the Exceptional Case in 15:16–17

For some scholars, Deut 15:18 fits better as a continuation of v.15 which concludes the preceding section. If so, it follows then that 15:16–17 may be an insertion.[154] However, with the discovery of the Deuteronomic pattern language, we could have a more satisfactory reason for this scenario where the literary relationship between vv. 16–17 and the motive clauses in vv. 15 and 18 could be explained by the pattern language.

V. 18b also contains a pattern: "So YHWH your God will bless you in all that you do" (וּבֵרַכְךָ יְהוָה אֱלֹהֶיךָ בְּכֹל אֲשֶׁר תַּעֲשֶׂה) is made of two formulated phrases "YHWH your God will bless you" and "in all that you do."[155] The idea of divine reward upon corporate Israel for their obedience is found throughout the book of

---

152 N. E. Andreasen observes that these regulations are humanitarian in nature. Niels Erik Andreasen, "Festival and Freedom: A Study of an Old Testament Theme," *Int* 28, no. 3 (1974): 286.

153 Gemser notices that in the Covenant law book, as well as in the Deuteronomy law, many of their motive clauses are particularly for the protection of the underprivileged and the socially weak. Gemser. "The Importance of the Motive Clause in Old Testament Law," 63.

154 Gottfried Seitz, *Redaktionsgeschichtliche Studien zum Deuteronomium* (Stuttgart: Verlag W. Kohlhammer, 1971), 172; Mayes, *Deuteronomy*, 252. See also Hamilton, *Social Justice and Deuteronomy*, 19–20 n. 26.

155 Deut 2:7, 14; 14:29; 15:10, 18; 16:15; 23:21 [Eng. 21:20]; 24:19; 28:8, 12. See Weinfeld, *Deuteronomy and the Deuteronomic School*, 345.

Deuteronomy. Conversely, rebellion comes with privation. This dual consequence is the main theme of Deuteronomy 28. Other than the occurrences in Deuteronomy 28 (28:8, 12), this pattern in v. 18 (sometimes added with יָדֶךָ "of your hands") takes place only in the context of laws for protecting the socially weak (the poor in Deut 15:10; 23:21 [Eng. 23:20]; the slave in Deut 15:18; the sojourner, the orphan, and widow in Deut 24:19). Thus, the pattern in v. 18 demonstrates again that Deuteronomy uses the same patterns to link similar commandments to call for extra attention for protection of the socially weak. In view of the Deuteronomic patterns, these two verses stand out, since no other law in Deuteronomy contains twofold motive clauses with two distinctive patterns that particularly plead for the socially powerless.

In addition, the symmetrical structure of the manumission law in Deut 15:12 – 18 and the *Shemittah* law in Deut 15:1 – 11 can further explain the function of the twofold motive clauses. This structure is suggested by Hamilton.[156] Both laws follow the same sequence: heading-law→ warrant→ call to obedience→positive consequence.

15:1	Heading-law	15:12
15:2 – 3	warrant	15:13 – 14
15:4 – 6	call to obedience	15:15
15:7 – 11	Consequence in specific situation	15:16 – 18

According to Hamilton, this flow of logic does not only correspond to an observable arrangement in wisdom literature, but also follows the description of an argumentation proposed by S. E. Toulmin.[157] It is particularly remarkable that both laws in Deut 15:10b and Deut 15:18b adopt the same pattern as motive clauses to issue a concluding exhortation. The rhetoric is exquisite and aims to strive towards an understanding that goes beyond merely releasing a loan or a slave. While v. 16 starts with וְהָיָה כִּי to indicate that vv. 16 – 17 is a new departure in the discourse,[158] it does not necessarily signify an additional literary strata.[159]

---

156 Hamilton, *Social Justice and Deuteronomy*, 26.

157 Cited from Hamilton, *Social Justice and Deuteronomy*, 26. See also Stephen Edelston Toulmin, *The Use of Argument* (London: Cambridge University Press, 1958), 97 – 107.

158 Paul Joüon, and T. Muraoka, *A Grammar of Biblical Hebrew* (Roma: Editrice Pontificio Istituto Biblico, 2008), 589, (§ 166 p), 592 (§ 167 g); Innocenzo Cardellini, *Die biblischen Sklaven-Gesetze im Lichte des keilschriftlichen Sklavenrechts: ein Beitrag zur Tradition, Überlieferung und Redaktion der alttestamentlichen Rechtstexte* (Königstein: Peter Hanstein Verlag, 1981), 274; William S. Morrow, *Scribing the Center: Organization and Redaction in Deuteronomy 14:1 – 17:13* (Atlanta: Scholars, 1995), 113; Oosthuizen, "Deuteronomy 15:1 – 18 in Socio-Rhetorical Perspective," 76.

Hamilton argues that vv.7–11 and 16–18 both introduce a situation contrary to what has been expected by its heading-law.[160] In a sense, the behavior described in Deut 15:7–11 is not related to the heading-law as it is the case for vv. 2–3. Therefore, as Hamilton remarks,

> it is not the release of loans which is in view but the continued willingness to lend to the poor despite release. By analogy, it is not manumission which is in view in Deut 15:16–18a but the restricted conditions under which manumission can be forfeited and the way in which that restriction affects the attitude of the owner.[161]

The thrust of the law—*all* slaves should go out of service in the seventh year—is never lost.[162] Nothing but the willingness of the slave can negate this intention (vv. 16–17), and no one is supposed to be retained in bondage. The latter half of the slave law in vv. 16–17 and the motive clause in verse 18b are not awkward insertions, but an explication of the intrinsic value that the law intends to promote: i.e., liberty is an indispensible moré for all who are under YHWH's redemption and covenant.[163]

The Meaning of מִשְׁנֶה and the Somatic Vocabulary in 15:18

In 1958, M. Tsevat called into question the traditional understanding of מִשְׁנֶה (twice, double, copy, or second). Tsevat asserted that this term should be understood on the basis of the Akkadian cognate *mištannu* whose meaning is "equivalent, *quid pro quo*." Therefore, מִשְׁנֶה should be understood as "equivalent" rather than "double."[164] In 1991, J. M. Lindenberger refuted Tsevat on the basis of M. Mayrhofer's semantic and etymologic study. Mayrhofer argued that *mištannu* in this text is possibly Hurrian in origin. If *mištannu* is not a Semitic word at all, his

159 R. P. Merendino and G. Seitz suggest that Deut 15:12–18 contains two or more literary strata. Rosario Pius Merendino, *Das deuteronomische Gesetz: eine literarkritische, gattungs-und überlieferungsgeschichtliche Untersuchung zu Dt 12–26* (Bonn: P. Hanstein, 1969), 114–115; Seitz, *Redaktionsgeschichtliche Studien zum Deuteronomium*, 171–172.
160 Hamilton, *Social Justice and Deuteronomy*, 20.
161 Ibid., 21.
162 Ibid., 21.
163 H. W. Wolff suggests, "The basis for giving slaves equal status with their masters is the recognition that Israel's God liberated the slaves in Egypt; a supplementary basis is rooted in the acknowledgement that all men have one and the same Creator." Hans Walter Wolff, "Masters and Slaves: On Overcoming Class-Struggle in the Old Testament," *Int* 27, no. 3 (1973): 271.
164 Matitiahu Tsevat, "Alalakhiana," *HUCA* 29 (1958): 109–134.

finding rules out its connection with the Hebrew מִשְׁנֶה.[165] In response to Lindenberger, Tsevat maintained that the meaning "equivalent" stands, even if a Semitic etymology for *mištannu* does not support his proposed meaning of מִשְׁנֶה in
Deut 15:18.[166]

In most biblical usage, מִשְׁנֶה refers to quantity or frequency.[167] It is most likely that, as Tigay puts it,

> the servant has given twice the service that a hired man would have performed for the same
> cost. The point may be that the wages of a hired man would have been twice what the serv-
> ant cost (room and board, and perhaps a loan on which he defaulted), or that a hired man
> would have worked only during the day, while the servant was available day and might.[168]

However, even if the meaning of מִשְׁנֶה cannot be certain and the phrase
מִשְׁנֶה שְׂכַר שָׂכִיר (double the service of a hired man) is obscure, the clause clearly
intends to make a contrastive and affective argument, particularly when associated with v.18.

V. 18a uses the negative adverb לֹא to make the clause an exhortative commandment. The verse follows the adverb with a sentimental description of the
listener's sensory organ (in your eyes) and then an explanatory כִּי clause. The sequence of argumentation—לֹא with exhortation + sentimental description with
somatic vocabulary (hand, heart, and hand) + כִּי with sensible reality—vividly
conveys both affective and sensate metaphors. The same symmetrical structure
can also be found in Deut 15:7 – 9. In Deuteronomy 15, heart is explicitly paired
with eyes in v. 9 and implicitly with eyes in v. 10. These occurrences of somatic
terminology serve a similar function in the argument of the *Shemittah* and manumission laws which Hamilton terms as "Further Instruction with Reference to
Act and Attitude."[169]

The somatic vocabulary (e. g., hand, heart, and eye) is not unusual in Deuteronomy, and they often delineate the anticipated attitudes of the listeners be it
inappropriate or appropriate.[170] For example, the clause that contains somatic
vocabulary in the current passage expresses a description rather than a regula-

---

165 James M. Lindenberger, "How Much for a Hebrew Slave? The Meaning of Mišneh in Deut
15:18," *JBL* 110, no. 3 (1991): 479 – 498.
166 Matitiahu Tsevat, "The Hebrew Slave According to Deuteronomy 15:12 – 18: His Lot and the
Value of His Work, with Special Attention to the Meaning of מִשְׁנֶה," *JBL* 113, no. 4 (1994): 587 –
595.
167 Richard S. Hess, "מִשְׁנֶה," *NIDOTTE* 2:1138 – 1139.
168 Tigay, *Deuteronomy*, 150.
169 Hamilton, *Social Justice and Deuteronomy*, 33 – 34.
170 Ibid., 31 – 34.

tion. It is as if the lawgiving God could see the listener's/master's heart or expose his/her innermost feeling. Either attempts to strike a grudging heart. The motive clause in v. 18b provides another impetus for the master to obey the law: The master will in reality lose nothing financially, since YHWH's blessing will make up any possible loss.[171]

The use of twofold patterns as motive clauses in Deut 15:15 and 18 is unique. It significantly reinforces the legal writing by also making it convincing in affections. Not only does the argumentation in Deut 15:15, 16 – 17, and 18 reflect classical rhetorical elements of pathos, ethos, and logos, it is also logically arranged. All these highly structured settings touch the hearts of the listeners to raise their affections into compliance with the law, as well as utter the spirit of human rights in its ethics. The vernacular in Deut 15:12 – 18 in fact challenges a listener's heart to be released from the bondage of egocentricity and antipathy rather than just a mere surface compliance to the law to liberate slaves. Human rights in this sense can only be executed with a heart truly relying on YHWH and an attitude of selflessness.

Exegesis of Fugitive Slave Law (Deut 23:16 – 17)

For a regulation like Deut 23:16 – 17 [Eng. 23:15 – 16] that finds no precedence in the ANE laws, probing its motivation and rationale is a convoluted issue. Neither conjectures in source criticism nor studies in its historical setting leads to a satisfactory interpretation. A further difficulty is that this unique law goes *against* all other comparative laws. ANE laws *forbid* harboring fled slaves, and international treaties during those times habitually required allies to extradite fled slaves. Weinfeld thus suggests, "[t]he deuteronomic prescription is not to be taken, then, as a legal ordinance but rather as an appeal to the conscience of the individual of the type met with in wisdom literature-exhorting the free Israelite to give asylum to the fugitive slave who has fled from his oppressive master (cf. Gen. 16:6)."[172] Carmichael concurs, stating that, "[t]he law can be explained as a D creation based on the Genesis tradition about Esau's reception of Jacob."[173]

With this background in mind, we are now ready to examine Deut 23:16 – 17. For the book of Deuteronomy, virtually all commentators hold that 23:16 – 17 re-

171 Nelson, *Deuteronomy*, 200.
172 Weinfeld, *Deuteronomy and the Deuteronomic School*, 272.
173 Carmichael, *The Laws of* Deuteronomy, 186.

fers to slaves who escape from foreign countries to Israel.[174] For them, the law would have described the slave as "your brother" if the law had meant to refer to a Hebrew slave (cf. Deut 15:12 – 18). In addition, the phrase "in your midst" seems to imply that the slave is in a foreign territory.[175] Tigay proposes that the only practice that may be considered as remotely related to this law in the ANE world is the asylum granted to slaves fleeing from harsh treatment to certain temples. Instead of being permanent, such asylum provides protection for the slave until the slave could come to terms with the master or be sold to another master. In light of this, Deut 23:16 – 17 arguably treats the whole land of Israel as a sanctuary offering permanent asylum.[176]

T. Work puts it well that "Israel is a place where YHWH holds jurisdiction, an earthly sign of heaven's kingdom."[177] In view of this, protection for a foreign escaped slave is a delicate design that coincides with the combined theme of YHWH, the land, and law in Deuteronomy. The three incredibly benevolent requests for the runaway slave in Deut 23:17 demonstrate their correspondence with the combined theme: First, the slave can stay in the midst of Israel. Second, the slave may dwell in a town of his/her choice. Third, the slave is not to be mistreated.

The phrase בְּקִרְבְּךָ (in your midst) implies no discrimination against the new comers. The verb בחר (choose) is also significant to the issue at hand. It occurs thirty one times in Deuteronomy, which is more than in any other Old Testament book. Twenty-three times it occurs in the *qal* imperfect, five times in the *qal* perfect, and three times in the *qal* waw-consecutive imperfect (Deut 4:37; 7:7; 10:5). In terms of the subject, apart from Deut 23:17 (*qal* imperfect) and 30:19 (*qal* perfect),[178] the subject of the verb is always YHWH. Most of the time, the verbal forms express YHWH's choice of the place of worship.[179]

---

174 Tigay, *Deuteronomy*, 387 n. 58.
175 This is a long standing interpretation, going back at least to Ibn Ezra and Rashi. Joseph Reider, *Deuteronomy* (Philadelphia: JPS, 1937), 217. See also Craigie, *The Book of Deuteronomy*, 300; Georg Braulik, *Deuteronomium II, 16, 18 – 34*, 12 (Wurzburg: Echter, 1992), 173; Tigay, *Deuteronomy*, 215; McConvilles, *Deuteronomy*, 351.
176 Tigay, *Deuteronomy*, 215.
177 Telford Work, *Deuteronomy* (Grand Rapids: Brazos, 2009), 210.
178 P. A. Baker notices that in Deut 30:19 בחר occurs in the *qal* perfect, where it is clearly an imperative in meaning. This usage draws attention to the seriousness of the decision to obey or disobey YHWH's laws. However, Baker ignores the uniqueness of the *qal* imperfect form used in Deut 23:16 and provides no further discussion on it. Paul A. Baker, *The Triumph of Grace in Deuteronomy: Faithless Israel, Faithful Yahweh in Deuteronomy* (Carlisle: Paternoster, 2004), 201.

While all other occurrences of בחר in the *qal* imperfect form in Deuteronomy consistently have YHWH as the subject, in Deut 23:17 a fugitive slave is the subject. The *qal* imperfect of בחר in Deut 23:17 invokes YHWH's choosing of the place of worship, calling to mind the *sanctuary* where YHWH would place his name.[180] Therefore, the law conveys a deep theological resonance. It implies that the slave is likely to replicate YHWH in the free choice of a "place." They may *choose* to live and have a fully integrated presence in Israel's midst just as YHWH does (Deut 6:15; 7:21).[181] In this sense, the text gives the escaped slave almost approximating "YHWH-like" power.[182] In other words, it requests dignity for the runaway slave. Though the idea may be extremely utopian, this is the ideal that the law intends to promote.

Deut 23:16 – 17 also goes beyond slave manumission. It presumes that when a slave ran away from his/her bounded land and entered into the land of YHWH, his/her status was thereby changed: He/she would no longer be regarded as a slave, but as an alien. The phrase לֹא תוֹנֶנּוּ "do not oppress him" underpins this concept. לֹא תוֹנֶנּוּ also occurs in the two laws which spell out regulations against mistreatment to aliens (Exod 22:21 [Eng. 22:20] and Lev 19:33). Therefore, the verb ינה (oppress) in Deut 23:17 recalls not only the Egyptian enslavement but also the transition of Israel's status as a result of divine redemption. In the same way, when a non-Hebrew slave enters into the land of YHWH, he/she should be regarded as a resident alien rather than a slave, who is allowed to legally reside in the land of Israel.[183] In this sense, this law intends to protect the interest of the resident alien. The law demonstrates that the land is a permanent asylum not only for the Hebrew slaves who escaped from Egypt, but also for all escaped slaves. The land promise includes freedom from involuntary enslavement, free choice of a living place, and dignity.

---

179 It occurs either in the basic form of "the place YHWH your God will choose," or with a further descriptive phrase, such as "in one of your tribes." See discussion in Emile Nicole, "בחר," *NIDOTTE* 1:638 – 642.

180 Christopher J. H. Wright, *Deuteronomy* (Peabody: Hendrickson 1996), 250.

181 Nelson, *Deuteronomy*, 280.

182 Hamilton, *Social Justice and Deuteronomy*, 118.

183 Gerhard von Rad, *Deuteronomy: A Commentary* (Philadelphia: Westminster, 1966), 147; Mayes, *Deuteronomy*, 319; Eugene H. Merrill, *Deuteronomy* (Nashville: Broadman & Holman, 1994), 312; Nelson, *Deuteronomy*, 280.

Inner-Comparative Study between Deut 15:12 – 18 and Deut 23:16 – 17

The spirit of human rights is present in the two slave laws in Deut 15:12 – 18 and Deut 23:16 – 17. Nonetheless, as Hamilton notes, these two laws create tension. The former appears to retain slavery as a part of the economy of Israel's society, and the latter seems to undermine the authority of a master over a slave.[184] Some commentators attempt to relieve this tension by saying that the slave in view of Deut 23:16 – 17 is a foreign slave; however, the two laws appear to have contrary views on the justness of slavery.[185] Others suggest that there could also have been Israelite slaves who were enslaved involuntarily or were ill-treated causing them to end up as runaways.[186] Yet if such is the case, how can these two laws be taught at the same time?

Two important observations help us resolve the tension between these two Deuteronomic slave laws. First, both laws require the granting of liberation. 15:12 – 18 precisely regulates releasing the slave in the seventh year. Retaining a slave is a legal exception when the slave has voluntarily consented to remain so under slavery. One has to know that the legal topic of this law is "debt-servitude." Its main subject is about a Hebrew debtor who enters a temporary bondage (six years) to pay off his debt by working for his fellow creditor. Although this law sides with the master's interest (having six year's servitude), it cares for the slave's right of release (in the seventh year). The issue of interest protected will be further discussed in chapter three. Second, 23:16 – 17 does not explicitly mention who shall be hosting the runaway slave. Anyone who happens to meet this fugitive? Are the elders, the rich, or the judges of this town obliged to help? Deut 23:16 – 17 reminds the entire community to recognize that YHWH is the real Master of the Land who commands all listeners to heed the law.

In addition, these two slave laws aim at protecting human life in YHWH's land (Deut 19:1 – 21:9). The whole land is considered to be *a sanctuary*—offering permanent asylum is the idea behind the law in Deut 23:16 – 17. According to numerous mainstream scholars, the concept of sanctuary as a place of YHWH's choice is contradictory if the reference of "YHWH's chosen place" implies a *sole* sanctuary for all Israel. בחר is not necessarily related to the physical worship place that YHWH chose. In terms of the combined theological and sociological theme of YHWH, land, and law, Deuteronomy may well have in mind a broader

---

184 Hamilton, *Social Justice and Deuteronomy*, 118.
185 Ibid., 119.
186 Tigay, *Deuteronomy*, 215.

sense of sanctuary. Both slave laws reveal the same significant message that the whole land belongs to YHWH and it is *the sanctuary* where life is to be preserved with security and dignity.

Summary and Conclusion

In this chapter, five significant contributions have been presented. First, the chiastic framework approach demonstrates how the Deuteronomic laws are structured to expound YHWH's humanitarian concerns and protective care for the socially weak. The central theme of the chiastic framework is his determination to protect all human life on his promised land. The prerequisite of enjoying this protection is to identify YHWH as the One and Only God. This approach explains the placement of the two slave laws in their current settings: They illustrate YHWH's concern for human rights.

Second, within this framework, Deuteronomy presents YHWH's concern for human rights with a combined theological and sociological theme. The most important feature of this theme is that YHWH, land, and law are inseparable. Deuteronomy does not view the land promise as unconditional, but carries out the promise by characterizing the *land* and *law* together with a combined theological and sociological meaning: i.e., the land is the concretization of the covenant, a reminder of YHWH's covenant with the Israelites. The agrarian products thus are symbols of YHWH's blessings rather than merely material provisions. To continue receiving YHWH's blessings and protection is to always obey his laws. The two slave laws are representative of the combined theological and sociological theme of the law book: They aim to unconditionally protect the underprivileged in YHWH's land and address the most basic human rights—to live freely without fear and to live with substantial provision regardless of one's status, gender, and ethnicity.

Third, the exegesis of Deut 15:12–18 shows that the collocation of עִבְרִיָּה/עִבְרִי and אָחִיךָ are not tautologous even though both terms are ethnic in sense. The phrase אָחִיךָ הָעִבְרִי אוֹ הָעִבְרִיָּה reflects Israel's harrowing memory but also appeals to the intimate community. It speaks of an inherent concept of fraternity. The phrase evokes listeners' strong affection of sympathy and sways their rational (logos) and emotional (pathos) reception into compliance with the law. The idea of equality that the law promotes in Deut 15:12–18 is this: Only when one has experienced God's redemption and selflessness can he/she truly treat others with equality. While the latter half of the law and the motive clause in verse 18b may read like awkward insertions at first, the intrinsic value it promotes is to explicate liberty for all those who are under YHWH's redemption and covenant: *all* slaves should go out of service in the seventh year unless the slave is willing to stay.

Fourth, the Deuteronomic pattern language is a deliberate design which relates YHWH to his people and his humanitarian concerns. It has three major features: (1) It is YHWH-related. (2) A pattern often serves as a motive clause and this motive clause usually carries strong persuasive modes with the pathos, ethos, and logos. (3) The Deuteronomic pattern language conceptually links similar laws and commandments together. Such a link often intends to highlight its humanitarian concerns. The legal writing of Dt 15 is unique among ANE laws, in particular showcased by the Deuteronomic pattern language. The law is reinforced by twofold patterns as motive clauses, which makes the law affectionately convincing to the listeners. The rhetoric in the law on the one hand intends to emotionally move the audience to willingly comply with it while on the other hand it rationally advocates human rights.

Fifth, the exegesis of Deut 23:16–17 shows that the land promise includes freedom and human dignity for anyone who enters into this land. It is an asylum not only for the Hebrew slaves who escaped from Egypt, but also for any other non-Hebrew slave fugitives. Deut 23:16–17 challenges the entire community to recognize that YHWH is the real Master of the Land. Slavery, for any Israelite, is a means of requiting debt, not a destiny. The expressions of the two slave laws stress the dignity of a released person and demands letting him/her go with extravagant honor.

3 Comparative Studies of Biblical Slave Manumission Laws

This chapter will focus on the similarities and differences between Deut 15:12–18 and its two biblical correspondents, Exod 21:2–11 and Lev 25:39–55. This study will follow the basic principles of the contextual method proposed by W. W. Hallo and K. L. Younger, Jr., previously mentioned in chapter one.[1]

Deut 15:12–18 and Exod 21:2–11

In comparative legal study of biblical texts, Deut 15:12–18 and Exod 21:2–11 are usually regarded as *parallel* slave laws. However, apart from having the same subject matter of Hebrew slave release, they are *different* in at least four ways:[2] (1) Although both are presented in a typical ANE casuistic fashion, they use different verbs with different persons in mind (Exod 21:2 תִּקְנֶה, you buy; Deut 15:12 יִמָּכֵר he/she sells himself/herself is sold) that seemingly take the different points of view. For example, Ex 21:2 takes *ex latere emptoris* [from the buyer's point of view], while Deut 15:12 takes *ex latere venditoris* [from the seller's point of view]).[3] (2) The verbs for the released action are יצא in Exod 21:2 and שלח in Deut 15:12, respectively. (3) Exod 21:7 regulates that a daughter sold as a slave does not go free in the same way a male slave does; however, such distinction is missing in Deut 15:12–18. This omission in Dt 15 suggests an equal release right of male and female slaves. (4) For some scholars, the Deuteronomic version appears to abolish the stipulation in Exod 21:3–4, as the former requests that the master gives provision to the manumitted slave (Deut 15:13–15). On the other hand, the qualification in Exod 21:3–4 immediately affects the way in which the slave's retention in service should be understood in Exod 21:5–6. Further-

---

1 K. Lawson Younger, Jr. "The 'Contextual Method': Some West Semitic Reflections," in *The Context of Scripture III* (ed. William W. Hallo, and K. Lawson Younger, Jr.; New York: E. J. Brill, 2003), xl.

2 J. Van Seters suggests a fifth difference—that Deuteronomic law devotes a longer discussion of humanitarian concerns to strengthen religious motivation (Deut 15:14–15, 18). However, since this has already been discussed in chapter two, we will only focus on the four differences here. J. Van Seters, *A Law Book for the Diaspora: Revision in the Study of the Covenant Code* (Oxford: Oxford University Press, 2003), 85.

3 Raymond Westbrook, "What Is the Covenant Code?" in *Theory and Method in Biblical and Cuneiform Law: Revision, Interpolation and Development* (ed. Bernard M. Levinson; Sheffield: Sheffield Academic Press, 1994), 35.

more, the ceremonies for a permanent slave are somewhat different between Deut 15:16 – 17 and Exod 21:5 – 6.

These differences between the slave laws in Dt 15 and Ex 21 invite certain questions: When scholars assume they are parallel, similar, or different, what are the essential elements to determine the degree of analogy? On what methodological bases are these two laws deemed to be parallel, similar, or different? In the pages to follow, these two questions will be answered with the discussion of the four differences between Ex 21 and Dt 15.

Changes of Persons and Verbs from the Buyer's to the Seller's Point of View

The fact that the second-person voice in Exod 21:2a differs from other casuistic laws of the Covenant law book and cuneiform laws has been at the center of a heated debate. One resolution to this debate is that some have sought to revise the verb to the third person.[4] For J. Van Seters, the second person verb תִקְנֶה in Exod 21:2 is a "redactional" change by assuming its dependence on Deuteronomy and the Holiness Code. On this basis, Van Seters seeks to redefine the prevailing scholarly consensus vis-à-vis the literary sequence of the Pentateuchal manumission laws.[5] In his reading of the protasis "if you purchase a Hebrew slave" (Exod 21:2a), Van Seters suggests that the most obvious and direct meaning of this statement implies two things: (1) The person is already a slave for whatever reason and has been purchased from another owner. (2) The seller must be a foreigner, rather than a member of the Israelite community.[6] The reason for Van Seters' identification of the seller as a foreigner is "because that would be contradictory and make void the law if an Israelite could sell his fellow Hebrew within the six-year period."[7] In the ensuing discussion, Van Seters' view will first be critiqued and then an alternative interpretation that explains the use of the second person and the polyvocality of combined discourses in the legislative texts will be attempted by reading the law in its own context.

---

4 Owing to the predominant third-person formulation, A. Jepsen advocates to correct כִּי תִקְנֶה to כִּי יִקָּנֶה אִישׁ. A. Alt proposes to emend the verb יִמָּכֵר in correspondence with Deut 15:12a and Lev 25:39a. Alfred Jepsen, *Untersuchungen zum Bundesbuch* (Stuttgart: W. Kohlhammer, 1927), 56; Albrecht Alt, "The Origins of Israelite Law," in *Essays on Old Testament History and Religion* (trans. R. A. Wilson; Sheffield: JSOT, 1989), 93 – 94.

5 Van Seters, *A Law Book for the Diaspora*, 84 – 90; idem, "Law of the Hebrew Slave: A Continuing Debate," *ZAW* 119 (2006): 169, 177.

6 Van Seters, *A Law Book for the Diaspora*, 87.

7 Ibid., 87.

Response to Van Seters' Point of View

Several scholars have challenged Van Seters' reading. Among them, E. Otto indicates that Van Seters' reading would mean that the Covenant law book also addresses foreigners, which is rather unfathomable for an exilic author.[8] Otto maintains that Exod 21:2a includes a performative speech act to express the fact that the purchase of a free person makes one into a debt-slave.[9] B. S. Jackson thinks that the choice of the verb קנה corroborates the scenario that the initiative may be taken by the creditor when a debtor is in default. For example, there are more materials in the ancient Near East on the institution of "distraint" in these kinds of circumstances. In addition, Exod 21:7 provides a cross reference to Exod 21:2—just as the daughter was not an אָמָה before, so the temporary Hebrew slave was not an עֶבֶד עִבְרִי before.[10]

Another scholar, B. M. Levinson has remarked that Van Seters provides no linguistic and textual supports to verify his claim. Based on the distinction between "affected object" and "effected object" of grammatical patients (as status, category, or thing, depending upon context) and from his redefined recognition,[11] Levinson suggests that an effected object is a prototypical seman-

---

8 Eckart Otto, review of Van Seters, *A Law Book for the Diaspora: Revision in the Study of the Covenant Code*, *RBL* (2004): n.p. [cited 17 January 2010] Online: http://www.bookreviews.org/pdf/3929_3801. This review also has a German version in *Biblica* 85 (2004): 272–277.

9 E. Otto gives an example of understanding how the performative speech act functions: When one says, "ein Präsident sei gewählt," that does not mean that he was a Präsident before he was elected. Eckart Otto, *Das Deuteronomium: Politische Theologie und Rechtsreform in Juda und Assyrien* (Berlin: De Gruyter, 1999), 303–311, esp., 305 n. 451; and idem, "Exkurs: Das Deuteronomium als Quelle des Bundesbuches? Zu einer These von John Van Seters," in *Gottes Recht als Menschenrecht: Rechts und literaturhistorische Studien zum Deuteronomium* (Wiesbaden: Harrassowitz, 2002), 22–23. However, B. M. Levinson considers that the speech-act theory is irrelevant in this context. Bernard M. Levinson, "The 'Effected Object' in Contractual Legal Language: The Semantics of 'If You Purchase a Hebrew Slave' (Exod xxi 2)" *VT* 56, no. 4 (2006): 487, n. 8.

10 Bernard S. Jackson, "Revolution in Biblical Law: Some Reflections on the Role of Theory in Methodology," *JSS* 50 (2005): 88.

11 Traditionally, biblical Hebrew textbooks acknowledge that an effected object is produced by the action itself, whereas the affected object is understood as existing prior to the action. For instance, Gen 1:29 זֶרַע זֹרֵעַ (cf. Gen 1:11, 12) *producing seed*, זֶרַע is an effected object, whereas it is an affected object in זֶרַע to scatter and sow seed of Deut 11:10, 22:9 etc. P. Joüon, and T. Muraoka suggest, "the effected object, thus as defined, is rather rare; we find it with verbs such as בָּנָה to build, בָּרָא to create, יָלַד to bear, יָצַר to form, כָּתַב to write, עָשָׂה to make, but otherwise it is hardly ever found except with a verb of the same root." See Paul Joüon, and T. Muraoka, *A Grammar of Biblical Hebrew* (Roma: Editrice Pontificio Istituto Biblico, 2008), 420 (§ 125 p), and also 410 (§ 125 a). B. K. Waltke and M. O'Connor conclude that "[t]he verb and the effected object are often derived from the same root; such an object is called a *cognate effected accusative*." See

tic patient that results from the verbal action. An affected object is much less.[12] He concludes that Van Seters' argument assumes that the protasis refers to an "affected object" and thereby fails to consider the semantic category of "effected object."[13] The slave of the protasis is not necessarily in enslaved status but instead may acquire that status through the verbal action.[14]

In his recent article "Law of the Hebrew Slave: A continuing Debate," Van Seters responds to Otto, Jackson, and Levinson to defend his identification of the foreigner as the seller but not the purchaser.[15] The view that the law addresses foreigners is certainly not the case he intends to make.[16]

In assuming these arguments, one conclusion is that Van Seters' assertion goes far beyond the law and is based on questionable assumptions. Three critical points may be raised here against Van Seters. First, there is no constraint on the Israelites holding other Israelites as slaves, nor restrictions regarding the *sale* of a Hebrew slave within six years. As Levinson indicates, "the only basis for claiming that an Israelite cannot hold an Israelite as a slave is the prohibition found in the Holiness Code (Lev 25:39 – 46), but if the explanation of the protasis of the manumission law of the Covenant Code is controlled by the distinctive requirements of the Holiness Code, then the priority of the Holiness Code to the Covenant is assumed a *priori*."[17]

Second, one's social status could be changed according to circumstances. For example, Joseph was bought as a slave by Potiphar from the Ishmaelites (Gen 39:1). Under the Ishmaelites' custody, Joseph is considered as a slave before he was sold to Potiphar, but not so before he was sold by his brother. In Eccl 2:7, the Preacher boasts of having bought many male and female slaves. He perhaps

---

Bruce K. Waltke, and M. O'Connor, *An Introduction to Biblical Hebrew Syntax* (Winona Lake: Eisenbrauns, 1990), 166 (§ 10.2.1 f). However, B. M. Levinson challenges the accustomed view and asserts that "restricting the effected object to verbs of the same root overlooks that certain verbs almost by definition take an effected object." He lists as an exemple in Gen 1:27, God creates humankind. Here, an effected object in this case results in a logical and theological absurdity. He believes that verbs of creation and appointment (such as Gen 1:27 and Exod 21:2 etc.) are frequently ditransitive. Such verbs may also leave the affected object implicit while specifying only the effected object. Bernard M. Levinson, "The 'Effected Object' in Contractual Legal Language: The Semantics of 'If You Purchase a Hebrew Slave' (Exod xxi 2)" *VT* 56, no. 4 (2006): 491– 504.

12 Ibid., 491.

13 Levinson, "The 'Effected Object' in Contractual Legal Language," 491.

14 Ibid., 488.

15 Van Seters, "Law of the Hebrew Slave: A Continuing Debate," 169 – 183. See also Van Seters, *A Law Book for the Diaspora*, 191, n. 28 and 193, n. 54.

16 Van Seters, "Law of the Hebrew Slave: A Continuing Debate," 171.

17 Levinson, "The Manumission of Hermeneutics," 296.

acquired him/her who was, as Van Seters alleges, "already a slave for whatever reason and has been purchased from another owner," or a freeman who was forced to enter slavery on account of debt-servitude. However, there is no point to surmise situations that the text does not provide and shows no interest of.

Third, the use of קנה and מכר "in legal usage does not necessarily indicate a purchase/sale but applies also to the obtainment of property as a gift or other legal titles."[18] Contrary to Van Seters' view, the slave transaction in Exod 21:2 does not essentially *assume* slave trade. It is a law of debt-servitude. The verb קנה is often used to describe acquisition;[19] acquisition can be, however not limited to, *trade by money*. In his investigation of קנה and its antonym מכר in legal usage, Z. W. Falk suggests that the omission of the reference to silver in the protasis in Exod 21:2 does not preclude an acquisition other than purchase (e. g., Exod 22:2; cf. Ruth 5:5, 10).[20] Most importantly, the choices of using מכר or קנה suggest nothing about a slave/a person's status. For example, Joseph's story uses both verbs to describe the transactions of Joseph. מכר is used to refer to the sale from his brothers to the Ishmaelites (Gen 37:28; cf. Deut 15:12); קנה is employed to indicate the purchase from the Ishmaelites to Potiphar (Gen 39:1; cf. Exod 21:2). These different verbs may simply be the writer's choice of words to enrich the narrative.

In summary, the usage of these verbs gives no essential clues to identify the nationality of the seller, the social status of the acquired people, nor any social background (such as monarchic, exilic, post-exilic, etc.). Such information must be determined from other contextual clues (e. g., Lev 25:47–51, to buy back/redeem an indebted Hebrew fellow slave from foreigners or sojourners). Meanwhile, the issue at hand is not whether the object is an affected or effected one as the verbal forms do not intrinsically refer to social status.[21] Instead, as Å. Viberg suggests, "the fact that the text of Exod 21:2 states that a slave was bought does not necessarily mean that the person was a slave before the so-

---

18 When the context speaks of the acquisition of slaves for a price, mention is made of the כֶּסֶף (silver). See examples such as Gen. 17:12, Exod 12:44, and Lev 22:11 etc. Z. W. Falk, "Hebrew Legal Terms: II," *JSS* 12, no. 2 (1967): 241.

19 Izak Cornelius, and Raymond C. Van Leeuwen, "קנה," *NIDOTTE* 3:940–942.

20 In Ruth 4:5, קנה denotes the purchase of a field from its possessor, but in Ruth 4:10 it refers to the acquisition of a dead kinsman's widow by the redeemer. Falk, "Hebrew Legal Terms: II," 241–243.

21 Levinson is right in arguing that with some exceptions (e. g., Gen 1:27), the effected object should not be restricted within verbs of the same root. However, the standard grammatical rules on the distinction between affected object and effected object do not rebut the condition when the objects and the verbs are not the same root, the objects would become an affected one.

called purchase, where the status to which the person is transferred is used by the author to describe him even before he became a slave."[22] In a legal document, the protasis should most likely be considered as a case of prolepsis.[23]

The Second Person Addressed in the Legislative Texts

Laws codified using the second person voice in Exodus has long been regarded as secondary additions or deuteronomistic.[24] For example, much energy has been expanded in trying to glean the number of the second person references in Exodus, Leviticus, and Deuteronomy in order to support the theories they impose upon the texts.[25] However, the outcomes of such efforts tend to be forced or imposed on the text, and it is hard to reach a satisfactory conclusion.[26]

---

22 Å. Viberg, Åke Viberg, *Symbols of Law: A Contextual Analysis of Legal Symbolic Acts in the Old Testament* (Stockholm: Almqvist & Wiksell International, 1992), 84.

23 Ibid., 84. See also B. M. Levinson, "The Manumission of Hermeneutics: The Slave Laws of the Pentateuch as a Challenge to Contemporary Pentateuchal Theory," in *Congress Volume Leiden 2004* (ed. André Lemaire; Boston: E. J. Brill, 2006), 294; Lemche, "The Hebrew Slave," 135.

24 Crüsemann, *The Torah*, 109 n. 2. Since J. Wellhausen, a part of the statements formulated in the second person plural have been regarded as secondary and deuteronomistic. Most recently, E. Otto, N. Lohfink, and Schwienhorst-Schönberger still purport the idea. See Julius Wellhausen, *Die Composition des Hexateuchs und der historischen Bücher des Alten Testaments* (Berlin: W. de Gruyter, 1963), 89 – 90; Norbert Lohfink, "Gibt es eine deuteronomistische Bearbeitung im Bundesbuch?" in *Pentateuchal and Deuteronomistic Studies* (Louvain: Leuven University Press, 1990), 91 – 113; Ludger Schwienhorst-Schönberger, *Das Bundesbuch, Ex 20:22 – 23:33: Studien zu seiner Entstehung und Theologie* (Berlin: Walter de Gruyter, 1990), 284 – 286.

25 In general, the singular is used to address a definite individual, and the plural is assumed as a collection of persons before the speaker. However, in the speeches and legal corpora in Exodus, Leviticus, and Deuteronomy, the plural is sometimes employed when the people are addressed as a whole, and the singular, when they are regarded as individuals (cf. Deut 4:20 and Deut 7:6, the plural and singular forms are interchangeable in the sense that both denote the Israelite people as a whole and simultaneously as individuals.

26 In 1899, H. G. Mitchell devoted almost 50 pages to specifically investigate the second person singular and plural in law books of Deuteronomy, as well as in Exodus and Leviticus. In doing so, he came up with only suppositions of the probable diversity of authorship for each law books. For Exodus, he suggests that "[t]he only supposition that accounts for the change in number is that the passages in which the plural occurs have been added to the original text by some person or persons to whom the singular was not a natural or customary mode of expression." As for Deuteronomy, Mitchell suggested that two or more writers contributed to the book and that one of the authors used the singular of the second person whereas the other (or others) habitually employed the plural. H. G. Mitchell, "The Use of the Second Person in Deuteronomy," *JBL* 18 (1899): 61 – 109.

Building theories upon the layers of the second person singular and plural voice in biblical law inevitably engenders more problems. One of the problems has to do with the exceptions of the rules. For example, it is commonly said that Deuteronomy 12 contains two parallel prescriptions about the centralization of the cult in vv. 1–12 and 13–25. These two sets are distinguished by their styles.[27] In the former the people are addressed mainly in the second person plural, while in the latter the address is primarily in the second person singular. However, the exceptions in the former section are numerous: Deut 12:1a "the God of your [sg.] fathers has given you [sg.]"; Deut 12:5b, "and there you [sg.] shall go," and Deut12:7b, "YHWH your [sg.] God"), and the latter also contains an exceptional case in Deut 12:16a, "you [pl.] shall not eat."[28] Some ancient witnesses therefore seek to smooth the texts, changing these abnormities to conform to the presumed style.[29]

On the other hand, some have argued that the interchanges of second person singular and plural should not be explained merely on the grounds of literary criticism alone. In the early 70's, F. L. Horton's assessment of the legal forms in the Pentateuch had already detected that "a shift in person does not necessarily imply a shift of form. The 'casuistic' category contains rules in the second person which are quite at home in surroundings which contain third-person casuistic formulations."[30]

For Weinfeld, the change may simply be a pedagogical device, or it may reflect the urge for literary variation.[31] Crüsemann also doubts whether the differentiation of styles may be made into the only principle for literary-critical partition. He observes that Exod 21:12–36 is consciously shaped as a linguistic unity.

---

27 M. Weinfeld, *Deuteronomy 1–11* (New York: Doubleday, 1991), 15.

28 M. Weinfeld mistakenly notes the only exception for vv. 13–25 is verse 24a. There is no second person plural style in verse 24. Ibid., 15. See also H. G. Mitchell's list. Mitchell, "The Use of the Second Person in Deuteronomy," 67.

29 A small group of the Alexandrinus and Vaticanus codex reads Deut 12:1 "*your* [sg.] fathers" first person plural. Other witnesses, such as the LXX, Syr. and Tg. Ps.-J, read the second person plural pronominal suffix. In addition, the LXX, Syr., and Tg. Ps.-J also suggest "given *you* [sg.]" in the second person plural pronominal suffix. In Deut 12:5b, most LXX witnesses, SP, Syr., and Tg. Ps.-J read "*you* [sg.] shall go" in the second person plural ובאתם. For Deut 12:7b, Syr., Tg. Ps.-J, and Vg. also has a similar suggestion. The tendency here is to harmonize the paragraph with second person plural.

30 Fred L. Horton, "A Reassessment of the Legal Forms in the Pentateuch and Their Functions," in *One Hundred Seventh Annual Meeting Seminar Papers* (vol. 2; Atlanta: SBL, 1971), 356.

31 He suggests that certain changes in the stylistic addresses can be explained by the supposition that an expression is being quoted (e.g., Deut 11:19b). The author shifts to the plural in order to create a contrast between Israel and the nations (e.g., Deut 4:19–20) Weinfeld, *Deuteronomy 1–11*, 15–16.

Crüsemann suggests that the switch of number signifies a change of the target: The singular form of the second person address in Exodus 21 casuistic laws refers to the authority who administers justice, rather than the plaintiff or defendant.[32]

D. Patrick proposes to distinguish the casuistic laws where apodoses do not prescribe compensation or relation for the person found liable from other casuistic laws. This kind of law is typically remedial in nature. He describes the type of law as "casuistic law governing primary rights and duties." [33] Hereafter this study will refer to the "casuistic law governing primary rights and duties" as "casuistic primary law," and the other type of law that prescribes compensation as "casuistic remedial law." Exod 21:2 – 6 and Deut 15:12 – 18 belong to "casuistic primary law." Patrick indicates that the personal address at the beginning of Exod 21:2 refers to the stronger party of the relationship.[34] He thereby further suggests that in the remainder of the Covenant law book, examples of this class of casuistic law are aimed at the higher rank of the legal relation or the party who has authority.[35] Since many of these casuistic primary laws in the Pentateuch morph into moral injunctions on matters completely beyond the competence of positive law, he concludes that these laws concern the "social" rather than the "legal" relation between people.[36]

Another approach is D. P. Wright who theorizes that the Covenant law book is "closely, consciously, and almost entirely modeled on the Laws of the Hammurabi."[37] He claims that Exod 21:2 uses קנה with the second person pronominal suffix to transition from the preceding altar laws in Exod 20:24 – 26 and to continue the address to the audience. Wright explains, "[t]he use of a verb of acquisition instead of selling allows the law to be addressed to the economically able and thus the presumed majority in society, rather than to the weak and minority members of the society."[38] C. Halberstam observes that unlike most narratives, the biblical law provides the richest characterization not of a third-person protagonist, but of the second-person "you." He enumerates the "you" in Deut 30:3 – 4 and asserts that the passage designates the "you" as involved members of the community. These members become integrated into the logic of the narra-

32 Crüsemann, *The Torah*, 144 – 145.
33 Dale Patrick, "Casuistic Law Governing Primary Rights and Duties," *JBL* 92, no. 2 (1973): 180 – 181.
34 Ibid., 181.
35 Ibid., 181 – 182.
36 Patrick, "Casuistic Law Governing Primary Rights and Duties," 183.
37 D. P. Wright, *Inventing God's Law: How the Covenant Code of the Bible Used and Revised the Laws of Hammurabi* (New York: Oxford University Press, 2009), 124.
38 Ibid., 124.

tive and thoroughly characterized as one who protects, restores, and acts with compassion like YHWH.[39]

It is therefore crucial to reconsider the connotation and importance of the second person addressed in these and other Pentateuchal laws. At first glance, most readers would assume that the second person "you" being addressed in speeches and laws within the Pentateuch is primarily "the Israelite," the Covenant people, as its audience in either individual or collective sense. In the relationships where there are legal obligations, the second person may seemingly address specific event characters, such as the creditor (e. g., the "you" in Exod 21:2, Deut 15:1–11, 12–18), or the legal administrator (e. g., the "you" in Exod 21:13, 23, Deut 16:18–20). Hamilton writes that "the rhetoric and thrust of the legislation in Deuteronomy dealing with issues of social justice are aimed at the powerful, at those who have the capacity to shape society in this regard."[40] In a legal sociological sense, the prominence of the second person in these laws often addresses the more affluent or powerful people blessed by YHWH in an attempt to evoke their empathy and sympathy toward the underprivileged. They intend to connote a sublime ethical expectation on the listeners as well as shape the readers' morality. Last but not least, the combination of all of these discourses also directly speaks to the readers of any era, even today.

The Polyvocality of Combined Discourses in the Legislative Texts

In the past thirty years, studies on the interchange of addressed persons in the casuistic laws of the Pentateuch have interested some scholars and has spawned engagement via a method of narrative reading of law (reading law as story), rather than the traditional investigations from the approach of form-criticism. A. Bartor proposes a narratival reading of law as a method in dealing with legislative texts, by adopting and applying techniques from the disciplines of literature and narratology.[41]

According to Bartor, the common rules and conventions for narratives may inform our understanding of laws significantly. Reading a law as a narrative could directly evoke emotions and induce listeners' involvement with regulations

---

39 Chaya Halberstam, "The Art of Biblical Law," *Prooftexts* 27, no. 2 (2007): 359.

40 Hamilton, *Social Justice and Deuteronomy*, 150.

41 Assnat Bartor, "The Representation of Speech in the Casuistic Laws of the Pentateuch: the Phenomenon of Combined Discourse," *JBL* 126, no. 2 (2007): 231, 231 n.1, 2, 3, and 232 n. 5; idem, *Reading Law as Narrative: A Study in the Casuistic Laws of the Pentateuch* (Atlanta: Society of Biblical Literature, 2010).

that are ostensibly dreary and matter-of-fact.[42] Halberstam observes that in the Hebrew Bible "law" and "narrative" share many rhetorical techniques. In some biblical legislative texts, various narrative skills and structural elements are combined not only to provide dramatic tension, emotional reverberation, and possibility of restoration and resolution, but also to provide rich characterization, as all good narratives do.[43]

Similar to the case of biblical narratives, speech events within the casuistic laws tend to have the lawgiver using direct discourses. When God, the lawgiver, exposes a particular character's consciousness—his/her thoughts, views, desires, decisions—they are represented as direct speeches, as an internal monologue.[44] This rhetorical technique is employed in the slave laws in Ex 21 and Dt 15 where they both illustrate the lawgiver's "penetration" into the slave's psyche (e. g., Exod 21:5—"But if the slave plainly says, '*I* love *my* master, *my* wife and *my* children; *I* will not go out free.'" Deut 15:16—"But if he says to you, '*I* will not go out from you,' because he loves you and your household, since he fares well with you.").[45] The lawgiver's utterance reflects the slave's personal style and voice. These motive clauses, Exod 21:5 "But if *the slave* plainly says, *I* love..." and Deut 15:16 "But if *he* says to you..., *I* love...." are called combined discourse.[46] The use of such technique in Pentateuchal laws enhances the polyvocality (or bivocality) of the text with a plurality of speakers and attitudes. It imitates reality, vividly describing events and characters in the laws, and thereupon leaves the listeners/readers with an intense impression.[47]

In laws that concern the socially powerless, this technique is exclusively used to evoke sympathy and camaraderie. Through combined discourse the lawgiver helps shape the readers' attitude toward the underprivileged. In Exod 22:21 – 27, God does not only enact the law but also acts as the patron of the socially powerless.[48] In both slave laws of Exodus and Deuteronomy, the first person discourse (Exod 21:5; Deut 15:16) speaks of the thoughts, emotion, and deci-

---

42 Bartor, "The Representation of Speech in the Casuistic Laws of the Pentateuch: the Phenomenon of Combined Discourse," 232 – 233.

43 Halberstam, "The Art of Biblical Law," 359.

44 Bartor, "The Representation of Speech in the Casuistic Laws of the Pentateuch," 234.

45 Ibid., 235. Bartor explains, "Combined discourse is one of the methods a narrative text represents an utterance—spoken discourse or unspoken thoughts. More discussion on Exod 21: 5 – 6 and Deut 15: 16 – 17 will be provided later in this chapter.

46 Ibid., 238 – 239.

47 Ibid., 248.

48 Ibid., 236 – 237. In Bartor's study, she examines the poor only in Exod 22:24 – 26. However, the entire paragraph uses the combined discourse in verses 24 and 28 applied to all the underprivileged—the sojourner, the widow, the orphan, and the poor.

sion from within the slave's mind and therefore, inspires the listener to envisage the social relation and actions between masters and slaves.[49]

To sum up, the combined discourses illustrate God's intervention and his concern of wellbeing, justice, and human rights for the socially powerless persons. These combined discourses color the lawgiver's speech with the inferiors' feeling, stimulating readers' empathy, and evoking sympathy and solidarity toward the underprivileged.[50]

Reading the Law in Its Context
Many proponents of source critical model interpret Ex 21 and Dt 15 superficially by their wordings (e. g., persons, or verbal forms) and consider them as speaking from different distinctive perspectives or social backgrounds. They understand the two laws out of one single clause (Deut 15:12 or Exod 21:2), instead of the entire paragraph (Deut 15:12–18 or Exod 21:2–6) as a whole or as *a* law. This practice illustrates a fundamental fallacy—reading individual laws out of context, rather than appreciating the integrity of the whole paragraph. Deut 15:12–18, like Exod 21:2–6, is a law that addresses the second person singular listener. Moreover, as shown in the previous discussion, the two slave laws both use a combined discourse to evoke a listeners' emotional resonance. The differences of persons and verbs are used for rhetorical effect rather than reflecting a different spirit embodied in the laws. In a real sense, the two slave laws address the same legal topic: They both demand the release of a Hebrew indebted slave after a servitude of six year. And they promote in readers the same ethical value that the Israelites were to note, i. e., to heed the powerless people's needs, for YHWH is the patron of the socially weak.

The Distinction of Verbs on Released Action

The verb that denotes manumission in Exod 21:2 is יצא, which differs from the verb שלח used in Deut 15:12. Weinfeld suggests that the use of שלח is "indicative of the humanistic approach of the Deuteronomic author."[51] He argues that יצא in Ex 21 establishes the right of the slave to go free, whereas שלח in Dt 15 states that the slave owner is *obliged* to manumit his slave. The use of the verb demonstrates

---

49 Ibid., 238–239.
50 Revise and expand Bartor's idea and sentences in the last paragraph of page 237. Ibid., 237.
51 Moshe Weinfeld, *Deuteronomy and the Deuteronomic School* (Winona Lake: Eisenbrauns, 1992), 283.

that the author of the Covenant law book is aware of the difference in meaning between the two verbs, given that שלח is used in Exod 21:26 – 27.[52] According to Weinfeld, יצא deals with debt-slave manumission (Exod 21:2 – 11), while שלח refers to the release of the slave due to an injury caused by the master. [53] Weinfeld's proposal is plausible; however it is more important to see that the entire rhetoric in Deut 15:12 – 18 is humanitarian, and that the regulations reflect an overarching theological concern of the passage.

The Differences Regarding Female Slaves Manumission

The entry and release of female slaves is the most dissimilar point between these two slave laws that stirs the most debate. Deut 15:12, 17 clearly expresses equalization between the releasing of male and female slaves, which appear to be completely different from the manner stated in Exod 21:7. In addition, structural and syntactical analyses which consensually agree that Exod 21:2 – 6 echoes Exod 21:7 – 11. They have similar formulations and contain analogous regulations, cohering as a literary and conceptual unit,[54] thus making it easy to perceive that a male slave can be released after his six-year service. However, the terminable period cannot be similarly applied to a female slave. This asymmetry has caused dispute among scholars: Deut 15:12 – 18 abrogates the regulations regarding a female slave release in Exod 21:7 – 11 and discards gender discrimination implied in Ex 21.[55]

Two major solutions have been suggested by scholars: The first is to take Deuteronomy late (which is the most common conjecture), while the second is to assert that the debt slave manumission in Ex 21 is gender inclusive.

For the first, proponents suggest that at the time of the Deuteronomic surroundings (be it Josiah's reform, or the post-exilic period), social disruptions in divergent social, historical, and theological milieus changed women's status.

---

52 Weinfeld refers to the occurrences of שלח in Exod 21:27 – 28. Weinfeld, *Deuteronomy and the Deuteronomic School*, 283 n. 1.

53 Ibid., 283 n.1.

54 Yair Zakovitch, *For Three... and for Four: The Pattern of the Numerical Sequence Three-Four in the Bible* (Jerusalem: Makor, 1979), xxv-xxvi; Gregory C. Chirichigno, *Debt-Slavery in Israel and the Ancient Near East* (Sheffield: JSOT, 1993), 198 – 199; and Levinson, "The Manumission of Hemeneutics," 297.

55 M. Noth finds his answer in the presumed gender discrimination. He proposed that the gender difference "may rest on the view that only the male is a person, while the woman on the other hand is a possession." Martin Noth, *Exodus: A Commentary* (trans. J. S. Bowden; Philadelphia: Westminster, 1962), 177.

The change caused the author of Deuteronomy to hold an egalitarian position modifying the rule of Ex 21 to that of Dt 15 as the present style.[56]

The second solution is to assert Exod 21:2–6 as a general principle where עֶבֶד עִבְרִי does not specially refer to only *male* slave but gender-inclusively covers all labor-servitude. In the late 1890's, S. R. Driver provided the presumed harmonization of the two laws: (1) That the law of Exod 21:2 tacitly intends to include women; (2) That the law of Deut 15:12–18 does not abrogate Exod 21:7, but includes the extension implied in Exod 21:2. However, when he observed that in Exod 21:3–4 even a female slave who married to a bondman during his period of service is not to go free with her husband, Driver rendered it improbable that this extension of Exod 21:2 can be designed. He concluded that Deut 15:12–18 has abrogated the stipulations regarding the debt-slave who is given to a male slave (Exod 21:3–4) and an Israelite daughter who is sold as a wife or concubine (Exod 21:7–11).[57]

This study supports the proposal that the Hebrew slave manumission law is gender inclusive in both contexts of Ex 21 and Dt 15, but not in full agreement with previous proposals that the term עֶבֶד עִבְרִי is gender-inclusive. In the ensuing paragraphs, previous proposals of gender-inclusiveness will be examined, and then, a new proposal will be made. Then, two perplexing problems within Ex 21 itself will be studied in detail: (1) Whether Exod 21:2–11 contains one law or two laws, i.e., should Exod 21:7–11 be regarded as a sub-case of Exod 21:2–6, or another independent law regulating a different scenario, as Driver suggested, a law concerning an Israelite daughter to be sold as a wife or concubine

---

56 Niels Peter Lemche, "Manumission of Slaves—the Fallow Year—the Sabbatical Year—the Jubilee Year," *VT* 26, no.1 (1976): 44–45; Christopher J. H. Wright, "What Happened Every Seven Years in Israel? Old Testament Sabbatical Institutions for Land, Debts and Slaves Part II." *EQ* 56 (1984): 199–201; Carolyn Pressler, "Wives and Daughters, Bond and Free: Views of Women in the Slave Laws of Exodus 21:2–22," in *Gender and Law in the Hebrew Bible and the Ancient Near East* (ed. Victor H. Matthews, Bernard M. Levinson, and Tikva Frymer-Kensky; Sheffield: Sheffield Academic Press, 1998), 170–171; Eckart Otto, "False Weights in the Scales of Biblical Justice: Different Views of Women from Patriarchal Hierarchy to Religious Equality in the Book of Deuteronomy," *Gender and Law in the Hebrew Bible and the Ancient Near East* (ed. Victor H. Matthews, Bernard M. Levinson, and Tikva Frymer-Kensky; Sheffield: Sheffield Academic Press, 1998), 142–144; J. Van Seters, *A Law for Diaspora*, 90–91; Haroldo Reimer, "A Time of Grace in Order to Begin Anew: The Sabbatical Year in Exodus 21:2–11 and Deuteronomy 15:1–18," in *God's Economy: Biblical Studies from Latin America*. (ed. F. Ross Kinsler, and Gloria Kinsler; Maryknoll: Orbis Books, 2005), 79–80; Levinson, "The Manumission of Hermeneutics," 302–304.
57 S. R. Driver, *A Critical and Exegetical Commentary on Deuteronomy* (Edinburgh: T.& T. Clark, 1896), 182–183. See also Chirichigno, *Debt Slavery in Israel and the Ancient Near East*, 279–280.

(Exod 21:7–11)? (2) Is the term אָמָה (female slave) in Exod 21:7 the female equivalent of עֶבֶד (male slave) as in Exod 21:2?

These issues will be the key factors that will assist us in determining the idea of gender inclusiveness in Ex 21. Lastly, the regulations regarding female slave in Ex 21 and Dt 15 will be compared.

Reading Exod 21:2 – 6 as a Gender-Inclusive Law

U. Cassuto was the pioneer in defining the idea of gender-inclusiveness for Exod 21:2– 6 in the 1960's. He asserted that "the term Hebrew slave in Exod 21:2 includes the bondswomen, and the law in regard to her is the same as that for the male slave."[58] Cassuto's revolutionary standpoint is upheld by several recent scholars.

Based on the ANE customs, Jackson and Crüsemann both suggest that daughters are usually sold first and are actually taken as debt-slaves for general, non-sexual services more often than and prior to men. Therefore, the rule in Exod 21:2 should be applied to female slaves.[59] C. Pressler also challenges the once-pervasive opinion that עֶבֶד in Exod 21:2 is exclusively male. She argues that the writing of the laws, both in cuneiform and in the Bible, is couched in masculine language. The contexts of these ancient laws often show that the male language is generic rather than exclusive.[60] Pressler finds support for her view from several other slave laws in Exod 21:20 – 21, 26 – 27, 32; Deut 23:16 – 17; Jer 34:8 – 16.[61] In Exod 21:20 – 21, 26 – 27, and 32, while the protases all mention male and female respectively, their following statements and apodoses take up the third person masculine singular to include both genders. Pressler reveals a similar context and usage in Jer 34:8 – 16, where an explicit reference is made to both bondsmen and bondswomen, even though the law cited in Jer 34:14

58 Umberto Cassuto, *A Commentary on the Book of Exodus* (Jerusalem: Magnes, 1967), 266.
59 Bernard S. Jackson, "Some Literary Features of the Mishpatim," in *"Wünschet Jerusalem Frieden": Collected Communications to XIIth Congress of Int'l Org for Study of the Old Testament, Jerusalem, 1986* (ed. Matthias Augustin and Klaus D. Schunck; Frankfurt am Main: Peter Lang, 1988), 235; idem, "Gender Critical Observations on Tripartite Breeding Relationships in the Hebrew Bible," in *A Question of Sex? Gender and Difference in the Hebrew Bible and Beyond* (ed. Deborah W. Rooke; Sheffield: Sheffield Phoenix Press, 2007), 41; Bernard S. Jackson and Trevor F. Watkins, "Distraint in the Laws of Eshnunna and Hammurabi," in *Studi in onore di Cesare Sanfilippo* (Rome/Miland: Giuffrè, 1982), 418. See also Crüsemann, *The Torah*, 157.
60 Pressler, "Wives and Daughters, Bond and Free: Views of Women in the Slave Laws of Exodus 21:2– 22," 168– 170.
61 Ibid., 168.

uses masculine language. Deut 23:16–17 refers only to the male slave, but it is unlikely that the law only applies to them.[62]

A closer examination reveals that although עֶבֶד specifies a male slave in Exod 21:20–21, 26–27, 32 in its entire context (of masculine language), these laws present the idea of gender equality on slave release. Likewise, in the context of Jer 34:8–16, especially with regard to Jer 34:9, עֶבֶד is used in both gender inclusive and exclusive senses. The first half of the verse has a male Hebrew slave in view, but the second half speaks of a gender-inclusive idea that all Hebrew male and female slaves should be freed in the same manner. In Deut 23:16–17, עֶבֶד also appears as a generic term. These texts thus demonstrate that slave release, whether at the end of debt-servitude or due to incidental situations of body injury, are gender inclusiveness.

On the other hand, A. Phillip notes that the slave laws with emphatic ethnic terms עִבְרִיָּה/עִבְרִי and אָחִיךָ in Exod 21:2–6, Lev 25:39–45, and Deut 15:12–18 are distinctive from other slave laws that are without such a stress (e. g., Exod 21:20–21, 26–27, 32 etc. as mentioned above). He thus suggests that the slave provisions in Exodus applied to all slaves (both male and female) whatever their origins (house-born, war captive, or chattel slaves purchased from foreigners), but that Exod 21:2 should be understood to be limited to *male Israelite slaves.*[63] He supports his view with the notion that the Book of the Covenant (Exod 21:2–23:19) is dated at the time of the united monarch, and possibly the time of David.[64] He believes that the recognition of the Israelite nationality of the male slaves in Exod 21:2–6 provides the only satisfactory explanation for the present position of the law of slavery (Exod 21:2–11) in the Book of the Covenant. For him, the dating also explains why this law, unlike the other slave provisions of the Book of the Covenant, remains of interest to the Deuteronomists.[65]

While Phillips' interpretation is agreeable,[66] his presumption is questionable. The slave laws without emphasis on ethnic identity are, as Phillips suggests, rules that are applicable to various slaves regardless of their origins. Nevertheless, the stress of the ethnic identity could also come from the newly inaugurated nation in the present context of Sinai, soon after Israel gained its own national identity via the redemption of YHWH (Exod 19:5–6). To surmise a postdated his-

---

62 Ibid., 168–169.

63 Anthony Phillips, "The Law of Slavery: Exodus 21:2–11," *JSOT* 30 (1984): 61.

64 Ibid., 53.

65 Ibid., 61.

66 R. Averbeck also suggests that the laws in Exod 21:20–21, 26–27, 32 "apparently apply to property slave, not debt-slaves." See Richard E. Averbeck, "Law," in *Cracking Old Testament Codes* (ed. D. Brent Sandy and Ronald L. Giese, Jr.; Nashville: Broadman & Holman, 1995), 133.

torical and specific social setting is not necessary for the interpretation of the differences between laws. One solution is to reconsider the understanding of the phrase עֶבֶד עִבְרִי in Exod 21:2. While the term most likely refers to *only* a male Hebrew slave (especially with its following context in Exod 21:3 – 5 that mentions wife and children), it does not necessarily mean that the Hebrew debt-slave manumission law regulates *only* a male slave. Thus, while *the phrase* עֶבֶד עִבְרִי in the near context of Exod 21:2 – 5 may denote a male slave, but the surrounding context of Ex 21 in which vv. 2 – 5 is embedded in *the law* does not restrict the debt slave manumission only on male slaves. This idea can be illustrated by arguing that Exod 21:2 – 11 should be divided into two laws.

Separating Exod 21:2 – 6 and 7 – 11 as Two Different Laws

There are two units in Exod 21:2 – 11—verses 2 – 6 and 7 – 11. In the past, these two units have been regarded as structurally and syntactically interlocked with each other. They have similar formulations and contain analogous regulations, cohering as a literary and conceptual unit,[67] which easily leads to the conclusion that a male slave can be released after his six-year service, but the terminable term cannot be applied to a female slave. Recently, more scholars have reckoned Exod 21:2 – 6 and 7 – 11 to be two different laws, where the latter distinctively regulates an exceptional sale of a daughter into a contract marriage, concubinage, or sexual services.[68]

Syntactical analysis can also be furthered to argue that these two units should be regarded as two different laws. For example, the introductory conjunc-

---

67 Yair Zakovitch, *For three... and for Four: The Pattern of the Numerical Sequence Three-Four in the Bible* (Jerusalem: Makor, 1979), xxv-xxvi; Gregory C. Chirichigno, *Debt-Slavery in Israel and the Ancient Near East* (Sheffield: JSOT, 1993), 198 – 199; and Levinson, "The Manumission of Hemeneutics," 297.

68 Most earlier commentators who propose Exod 21:2 – 6 and 21:7 – 11 as two separated laws do not explicitly assert that עֶבֶד עִבְרִי includes women slaves. They mostly emphasize that Exod 21:7 – 11 is a special sale of daughters to become concubines. See such as Bunyan Davie Napier, *The Book of Exodus* (Richmond: John Knox, 1963), 94 – 95; H. L. Ellison, *Exodus* (Philadelphia: Westminster, 1982), 124 – 125; Willem Hendrik Gispen, *Exodus* (trans. Ed van der Maas; Grand Rapids: Zondervan, 1982), 204 – 209. Others, such as H. J. Grimmelsman, G. H. Davies, R. A. Cole, B. Childs, G. Bush, and R. Averbeck, etc., though do not clearly set Exod 21:2 – 11 apart as two laws, agree that Exod 21:7 – 11 expressly deals with a concubine marriage. H. Joseph Grimmelsman, *The Book of Exodus: A Study of the Second Book of Moses with Translation and Concise Commentary* (Cincinnati: The Seminary Book Store, 1927), 144 – 146; Gwynne Henton Davies, *Exodus* (London: S.C.M. Press, 1967), 175 – 176; Robert Alan Cole, *Exodus: An Introduction and Commentary* (Downers Grove: InterVarsity, 1973), 164 – 167; Childs, *The Book of Exodus*; George Bush, *Notes on Exodus* (Minneapolis: James and Klock, 1976), 7 – 14. Averbeck, "Law," 131 – 132.

tion וְכִי that leads this clause to be understood with a contradictory meaning making the rules in Exod 21:7–11 stand in stark to contrast to the preceding law in Exod 21:2–6. T. J. Turnham suggests that the preposition כִּי with an infinitive construct should be read as temporally. His understanding is supported by a large Pentateuchal legal context where an introductory structure does not necessarily refer to a contrast situation against its foregoing rule (e. g., Exod 21:14 indeed uses וְכִי in contrast to its foregoing law in Exod 21:12–13).[69] Furthermore, it is not unusual for a Pentateuchal regulation that initiates with וְכִי to be an independent law. For instance, every law in the group pertaining to "body injury" in Exod 21:18–27 starts with וְכִי.[70] Therefore, Exod 21:7–11 is not a sub-case of Exod 21:2–6, but an independent law concerning a sale of an Israelite daughter into a marital contract. They are grouped and linked together for its logic that will continue to be explored in the following discussion.

The Term אָמָה in Exod 21:7

The term אָמָה (female slave) in Exod 21:7 is often regarded to be the female equivalent of עֶבֶד (male slave) in Exod 21:2.[71] Indeed, in many biblical laws (e. g., Exod 21:20–21, 26–27, 32), אָמָה is contrasted with עֶבֶד as its female counterpart.[72] This is one of the reasons that one would easily grant Exod 21:7–11 as a regulation regarding female slave in contrast to the male slave law in Exod 21:2–6. However, even though אָמָה is a term often used to contrast עֶבֶד, it does not mean that this אָמָה is the same kind of female slave as in Exod 21:20–21, 26–27, 32. The other term בַּת in Exod 21:7 and the clause itself defines that this is a special female slave sale.

The most obvious meaning of בַּת in legal contexts and narratives is "daughter," particular referring to *one's daughter*.[73] In the Pentateuchal laws, it often designates someone's stay-at-home daughter who is under the protection and authority of her father (betrothed or unbetrothed). However, on no account does it serve as a generic term for any women. Generic designations of any woman in

69 Timothy John Turnham. "Male and Female Slaves in the Sabbath Year Laws of Exodus 21:1–11," *SBLSP* 26 (1987): 545.
70 Exod 21:18–19, 20–21, 22–25, and 26–27 are *four* laws under the same group that can be categorized as laws regarding "body injury."
71 Richard Schultz, "אָמָה," *NIDOTTE* 1:418–421.
72 In Genesis, עֶבֶד frequently pairs with שִׁפְחָה, a synonym of אָמָה (Gen 12:6; 20:14; 24:35; 30:43; 32:5). However, שִׁפְחָה and אָמָה are sometimes interchangeably used (e. g., Gen 30:3–4). In Exodus and Deuteronomy, עֶבֶד mostly mates with אָמָה (Exod 21:10, 17; Deut 5:14,21; 12:18; 16:11,14).
73 Chrys C. Caragounis, "בַּת," *NIDOTTE* 1:779–781.

Pentateuchal laws (e. g., Lev 20: 13, Deut 17:2, 5; 20:14; 22:5) constantly use אִשָּׁה.[74] As Pressler indicates, בַּת in Exod 21:7 does not include *all* female slaves, but only *daughters*, namely, unbetrothed girls.[75] Tigay agrees with Pressler and argues that the prohibition of releasing bondswomen in Exod 21:7 is speaking of a *daughter* sold as a slave who does not go free in the same way male slaves do. A daughter *is sold back* to her father or *released* if her master fails to fulfill certain obligations, such as providing her with a husband.[76]

Tigay and Pressler correctly point out that Exod 21:7 does specify בַּת, not just *any* woman. It is highly possible that she is an unbetrothed girl,[77] given the fact that in biblical and ANE laws to seduce and deflower one's virgin wife (betrothed girl) is regarded as the violation of her fiancé's right and the seducer would be put to death.[78] Therefore, whereas in other slave laws אָמָה refers to a general female slave, in Exod 21:7 this term is specifically used to denote an unbetrothed girl that is in a special marital case of sale.

The Special Marital Sale and Redemption in Exod 21:7 – 11

Exod 21:7 – 11 is a special marital sale of one's stay-at-home daughter. Some scholars challenge that nothing in the terminology suggests that marriage was meant in Exod 21:7 – 11. For example, Westbrook, E. Levine, and Jackson question that Exod 21:7 – 11 indeed enacts a law on marriage or concubinage.[79] However,

---

74 The occurrences of בַּת in Pentateuchal laws: Exod 21:4, 7, 9, 31; Lev 18:9, 10, 11, 17; 19:29, 20:17; 21:2, 9; 22:12, 13; 24:11; Deut 13:7; 16:11, 14; 18:10; 22:16, 17; 23:18. In Deut 22:13 – 21 although the story shows that this daughter has married, in ancient customs, the parents have the responsibility to keep the evidence of their daughter's virginity, if a newly married daughter encounters such slander, the father is his daughter's legal agent in this situation.

75 Pressler, "Wives and Daughters, Bond and Free: Views of Women in the Slave Laws of Exodus 21:2 – 22," 168.

76 Tigay, *Deuteronomy*, 148. A. Phillips argues that this opportunity to redeem is not to be understood as restricted to the girl's father or near kinsman (cf. Lev 25:48 – 54). Phillips, "The Law of Slavery: Exodus 21:2 – 11," 60. However, the girl's father should have the first prior right to redeem her.

77 See also Matthews, "The Anthropology of Slavery in the Covenant Code," 133; James K. Bruckner, *Exodus* (Peabody: Hendrickson, 2008), 200.

78 See the laws of Deut 22:23 – 27, LU 6, LE 26, and LH 130.

79 While Westbrook is suspicious about the relationship between the girl and the purchaser, he still accepts the status of the girl in Exod 21:7 to be that of concubinage. See Raymond Westbrook, "The Female Slave," in *Gender and Law in the Hebrew Bible and the Ancient Near East* (ed. Victor H. Matthews, Bernard M. Levinson, and Tikva Frymer-Kensky; Sheffield: Sheffield Academic Press, 1998), 218 – 219. Etan Levine, "On Exodus 21,10 'onah and Biblical Marriage," in *ZABR* (ed. Echart Otto; vol.5.; Wiesbaden: Harrassowitz, 1999), 160; Bernard S. Jackson, "Gender

the exegesis shows that there is actually a technical terminology of marriage in the protasis of Exod 21:10, אִם־אַחֶרֶת יִקַּח־לֹו (if he takes to himself another woman). The verb לקח (take) means "to take in marriage" in marital and legal contexts,[80] and thus this protasis "if he takes *another* woman" implies that the girl was also taken into a form of marriage, maybe a second wife or a concubine (cf. Gen 16:3). In addition, the two verbs יעד and בגד in Exod 21:8 also imply that this is a marital enactment. S. M. Paul points out that יעד (determine, designate, appoint) is most likely the technical term designating this type of marriage.[81] Lexically, while most of the time the object of the verb בגד (act or deal treacherously) is God, it is also used in cases where human beings commit acts of faithlessness or treachery against one another, including infidelity in marriage.[82]

These wordings suggest that the law has in mind notions of a marital sale. Therefore, since Exod 21:7–11 deals with a girl being sold for a marriage contract (which creates a permanent relationship), there would not be any *ex lege* release after six years. However, due to the marital relationship, the girl is entitled to the rights of a concubine or a second wife. What must be kept in mind is that this is a special marital contract where Exod 21:8–11 further suggests conditions and protection for the girl's rights.

W. H. C. Propp proposes that the female is in a status of a prospective wife. In this case, he takes יעד as meaning "to make a commitment;" that is, the owner is obliged to elevated the girl into a concubine or wife. For him, יעד refers to the action of her guardian, who has the right to bestow her on whom he pleases, in-

---

Critical Observations on Tripartite Breeding Relationships in the Hebrew Bible," in *A Question of Sex? Gender and Difference in the Hebrew Bible and Beyond* (ed. Deborah W. Rooke; Sheffield: Sheffield Phoenix Press, 2007), 44. I. Mendelsohn compares Deut 21:7–11 with Nuzi documents that describe a commercial transaction where the adopter acquires a girl from her parents as a daughter, with the explicit right to give the girl in marriage and receive her bridal payment. R. Westbrook, however, disagrees with Mendelson's comparison and translation of the Nuzi texts. See I. Mendelsohn, "The Conditional Sale into Slavery of Free-Born Daughters in Nuzi and the Law of Ex. 21: 7–11," *JAOS* 55, no. 2 (1935): 190–195 and R. Westnrook, "The Female Slave," 218–219.

80 As a martial technical terminology in Pentateuch, Gen 4:19; 6:2; 11:29; 19:14; 21:21; 24:3, 4, 7, 37, 38, 40, 67; 25:1, 20; 26:34; 27:46; 28:1, 2, 6, 9; 31:50; 34:9, 16, 21; 36:2; 38:2, 6; Exod 2:1; 6:20, 23, 25; 21:10; 34:16; Lev 18:17, 18; 20:14, 17, 21; 21:7, 13, 14; Num 21:1; Deut 7:3; 20:7; 21:11; 22:13, 14; 23:1; 24:1, 3, 4, 5; 25:5, 7, 8. See also P. J. J. S. Els, "לקח," *NIDOTTE* 2:812–817.

81 Shalom M. Paul, *Studies in the Book of the Covenant in the Light of Cuneiform and Biblical Law* (Leiden: E. J. Brill, 1970), 54.

82 Robin Wakely, "בגד," *NIDOTTE* 1:582–595. See also Chirichigno, *Debt Slavery in Israel and the Ancient Near East*, 249–250.

cluding the option of marrying her himself.[83] The owner should assure her marriage right.

One should note that Propp's understanding is essentially based on his following of the MT Kethib—אִם־רָעָה בְּעֵינֵי אֲדֹנֶיהָ אֲשֶׁר־לֹא יְעָדָהּ, while he remarks that the textual situation in Exod 21:8a is far more complex than what the *BHS* notes suggest.[84] Scholars who follow the Kethib reading have to take יעד as an action of decision and v. 8 as dealing with a "first opinion," occurring *before* any assignment to a man, and render it "if she does not please her master, who has not yet made a decision regarding her."[85] On the other hand, commentators who stay with the Qere reading אִם־רָעָה בְּעֵינֵי אֲדֹנֶיהָ אֲשֶׁר־לוֹ יְעָדָהּ, interpret יעד euphemistically, and translate it as "if she does not please her master who designated her for himself." Considerations supporting this reading are: The Qere reading offers a parallel to verse 9 and is found in LXX, Targ., Vg., and several Hebrew MSS.[86]

Westbrook suggests that, in terms of the girl's redemptive right, there is little difference with either reading. He indicates that the father normally has the right to redeem his daughter, but that right is lost when her enslavement is for the purpose of concubinage.[87] Westbrook suggests that this is exactly the rationale behind Exod 21:8:[88]

The right of redemption revives only if the purchaser fails to abide by the special purpose of the contract—if he fails either to consummate the assignment himself (*qere*) or to assign her

---

83 Propp, *Exodus 19 – 40*, 197.

84 Ibid., 119.

85 Crüsemann, *The Torah*, 157–158. See also James Gracey Murphy, *A critical and Exegetical Commentary on the Book of Exodus: With a New Translation* (Andover: Warren F. Draper, 1881), 249; Jacob Hoftijzer, "Exodus 21:8." *VT* 7, no. 4 (1957): 390. R. E. Clements, *Exodus* (Cambridge: Cambridge University Press, 1972), 131; Adrian Schenker, "Affranchissement d'une Esclave selon Ex 21:7 – 11." *Bib* 69, no. 4 (1988): 550 – 551; and Carmichael, *The Laws of Deuteronomy*, 58 n.7. Carmichael suggests that the Qere reading should not be dismissed altogether; however, it is possible that verse 11 represents a coda that has been added, not after the ruling in verse 8, where logically it should have appeared, but at the end of the existing code of provisions on the release of slaves, slave concubines, etc.

86 Jackson, "Gender Critical Observations on Tripartite Breeding Relationships in the Hebrew Bible," 43. Childs, *The Book of Exodus*, 448. Childs judges that the Kethib reading "he does not take the decision about her" is unconvincing. See also Durham, *Exodus*, 311–312; Pressler, "Wives and Daughters, Bond and Free," 158 n.26; Sarna, *Exodus* (New York: the Jewish Publication Society, 1991), 121; Chirichigno, *Debt-Slavery in Israel and the Ancient Near East*, 247; Thomas B. Dozeman, *Commentary on Exodus* (Grand Rapids: Eerdmans, 2009), 515, 520. Childs judges that the Kethib reading, "he does not take the decision about her" is unconvincing.

87 Westbrook, "The Female Slave," 219.

88 Ibid., 219.

for concubinage altogether (*ketib*). In either case, the purchaser has treated the contract as one of ordinary servitude, not concubinage, and has denied the slave-woman the possibility of gaining the protection available to a concubine through motherhood. In those circumstances, it is logical that the ordinary right of redemption should apply notwithstanding the fact that the slave is female.

That is, when a young woman enters this marital relationship, she is not allowed to be released or redeemed as the debt slave, as announced in Exod 21:7. However, when a master fails to fulfill the special purpose of this marital contract, the female's redemptive right is revived to the same *legal status* as the ordinary servitude of a non-marital one. This revived legal status implied in Exod 21:11 means that she becomes in a *redeemable* status like a debt slave but not limited to a six years' servitude term or with any payment. Namely, the daughter's redemption under such a circumstance becomes unconditional.

A. Schenker reaches the same conclusion with an insightful observation on the antithetical parallel structure of the liberation theme in Exod 21:2–6 and 7–11, which also demonstrates such a thought behind the law: Exod 21:2–3 starts with the liberation of a male servant after six-year indentured service, and then in Exod 21:4–6 where the exceptional situation of non-liberation is provided. Conversely, Exod 21:7 begins with a case of non-liberation after six-year service, followed by Exod 21:8–11 presenting the exceptional situation when a female slave can be liberated.[89] Working from the same perspective with Schenker, Propp adds the rabbinic view that a female slave is generally promoted to a wife or concubine.[90] The rationale behind Ex 21 is thus that a Hebrew woman is redeemable as a Hebrew man. In ANE, both types of female marital sale and female debt servitude exist simultaneously.[91] For Ex 21, since females are often sold into this kind of marital sale, it then juxtaposes this law along with the debt slave manumission law, which is thought to be applicable for the male. In this kind of marital sale the Hebrew woman does not have to wait for six years or so to be released and cannot be sold to a foreigner by the master. She can leave freely as long as the basic rights of a wife or concubine are deprived.

---

89 Schenker, "Affranchissement d'une Esclave selon Ex 21:7–11," 550. R. Averbeck also observes a similar chiastic structure in Exod 21:2–6 and 7–11, "the laws are shaped into a chiasm with freedom at the beginning and end and permanent status in the middle (at the end of the first section and beginning of the second)." Averbeck, "Law," 131.
90 Propp, *Exodus 19–40*, 198.
91 Tigay, *Deuteronomy*, 149.

The above discussion raises another question: Is it possible that a father may sell his daughter into a marriage contract due to case of insolvency? Such cases exist in the ANE, such as in Middle Babylonian period. In one case, for example, a Babylonian man purchases a young girl as a wife for his second son, and part of her purchase price was food to be given to her parents.[92] In cases like this, financial difficulty was the primary motivation for people to sell their family members into slavery or a marital relationship.[93] However, the female sold into a marriage due to financial difficulty does not enter an indentured servitude. When one reads the ANE laws, it is easy to see that these ancient people knew how to account for various situations, prices, and contracts accordingly.[94] Thus, while the possibility that a father may sell his daughter into a marriage contract due to cases of insolvency in Israel cannot be definitely proven, its plausibility exists when one compares the many other similarities already discussed within the Deuteronomic slave laws. Thus, within the social setting of other ANE laws, though there is currently no evidence of the Israelite practice, one cannot assume it does not exist.

The Term עִבְרִיָּה in Dt 15 and the Terms בַּת and אָמָה in Ex 21 Denote Different Situations

The previous discussion reveals two significant points. (1) With the specified clarification of בַּת, אָמָה in Ex 21 means a young female who is sold into a special marital relationship. Thus, אָמָה is not the counterpart of עִבְרִיָּה in Dt 15, which refers to a Hebrew woman who is temporarily sold into non-sexual services.[95] (2) The marital technical terms demonstrate that Exod 21:7 – 11 is not a sub-case of Exod 21:2 – 6 under the same legal topic of Hebrew debt slave manumission, nor a parallel law with Dt 15. Tigay remarks that, [96]

> Some scholars view Deuteronomy's law as superseding that of Exodus, by granting equal treatment to females instead of permitting their manumission only in a limited number of circumstances. This view assumes that the Hebrew woman of Deuteronomy 15 is the same as the daughter in Exodus 21. However, it is possible that the two laws refer to differ-

---

92 Kathryn Slanski, "Mesopotamia: Middle Babylonian Period," in *A History of Ancient Near Eastern Law* (ed. Raymond Westbrook; vol. 1; Leiden: E. J. Brill, 2003), 499.
93 Further ANE cases will be seen in chapter four.
94 LU 15; LL11, 29; LE 17 – 18, 25 – 28; LH 128, 156, 159 – 161; MAL A 30, 31, 32, 43, 48; HL 28 – 30.
95 Jackson, "Revolution in Biblical Law: Some Reflections on the Role of Theory in Methodology," 89.
96 Tigay, *Deuteronomy*, 148 – 149.

ent cases. Exodus refers to a minor sold conditionally by her father for the purpose of marriage; such a sale would naturally not be terminated after six years. Sales of this type, by poor families, are known from the ancient Near East. Deuteronomy, on the other hand, may refer only to a girl or woman who becomes indentured because of insolvency or debt—her own or that of a husband or father with no intention of marriage.

Therefore, the daughter's marital sale in Exod 21:7–11 and the female debt slave sale in Deut 15:12–18 are not comparable, and to assert that the author of the latter law holds a different position and abrogates the former one is groundless. It is more convincing that Tigay's point that the debt slave manumission law of Exodus 21:2–6 regarding male slave also applies to the indentured women in Deuteronomy.[97] Furthermore, it is better to conclude that, "Deuteronomy would have recognized the Exodus law about sale for marriage as a special case."[98] In this manner, Deuteronomy may have well adopted the thought behind Ex 21 that, a Hebrew woman is redeemable as a Hebrew man, and also understood that the debt-slavery termination after six years was also applicable to women.[99] This may be the precise reason that Deuteronomy employs a different term עִבְרִיָּה with respect to Hebrew female debt slaves to make it clear that those in a non-concubinage arrangement would have exactly the same legal status as a male.[100]

Reading the Law in Its Context

As a literary and conceptual unit, Exod 21:2–6 and 7–11 relate to the issue of liberation vs. non-liberation under one *theme*, but not as one coherent *law*.[101] Here, one can consider reading Exod 21:2–6 and 7–11 as *two* laws, as they deal with different legal topics: the general manumission of a debt slave and the special manumission of a marriage female slave. Meanwhile, the issue of female slaves in Dt 15 and Ex 21 are both conceptualized as different legal topics.[102] However, the release of an indentured Hebrew female slave should

---

97 Tigay, *Deuteronomy*, 149.
98 Ibid., 149.
99 Jackson, "Gender Critical Observations on Tripartite Breeding Relationships in the Hebrew Bible," 41.
100 Ibid., 219 n.14.
101 See also B. S. Jackson's discussion. Bernard S. Jackson, "Slavery," in *Wisdom-Laws: A Study of the Mishpatim of Exodus 21:1–22:16* (Oxford: Oxford University Press, 2006), 79–119.
102 Tikav Frymer-Kensky, "Anatolia and the Levant Israel," in *A History of Ancient Near Eastern Law* (ed. Westbrook, Raymond; Leiden: E. J. Brill, 2003), 2: 1006.

be considered in the same terminable manner as a male slave. In this sense, Deut 15:12–18 is *parallel* to Exod 21:2–6.

Dissimilar Accounts and Ceremonies for a Permanent Slave

Dt 15 has no concern for the marital status of the released slave, but Exod 21:3–4 regards the marital status as the most crucial component of the slave's emancipation:
-   If he comes alone, he shall go out alone.
-   If he has a wife, his wife shall leave with him.
-   If his master gives him a wife and she bears him children, the wife and her children shall belong to her master and he shall go out alone.
-   If the slave declares, "I love my master, my wife, and my children, I do not wish to go free," then the slave will become a perpetual slave through a ceremony of ear piercing.

When one examines Exod 21:3–4, two problematic issues are in view: First, considering that a wife and her children have to be separated from her husband or children's father, this law appears to destroy the concept of marriage and the value of family ties taught in Scripture. B. S. Childs writes that "[t]he sense of cruel inconsistency between this stipulation and the concept of marriage found in Gen 2:24—not to speak of Matt 19:6—would finally destroy this law within Israel, but only after considerable passage of time."[103] In response, W. Janzen argues that "here ownership is placed *above* marriage and family ties."[104] Second, the "love" for his wife and children would be a major factor for the slave to reluctantly stay. This causes a debate among scholars—whose interest does this law intend to protect? As there is considerable support for both views in the following discussion, these different positions will be surveyed and evaluated and an alternative solution will be proposed.

The Value and the Interest That the Law Promotes and Protects
For Paul, Phillips, Otto, Pressler and D. K. Stuart, the law seeks to protect the manumitted slave. For example, in comparing this practice at Nuzi, Paul ob-

103 Brevard S. Childs, *The Book of Exodus: A Critical, Theological Commentary* (Philadelphia: Westminster 1974), 468.
104 Waldemar Janzen, *Exodus* (Waterloo: Herald, 2000), 291.

serves that the slave can leave at the end of six years, neither having to pay for his release nor to provide a replacement.[105] Exod 21:2–4, in Phillips' opinion, is a statement of belief about the true nature of Israelite society, which is assumed to be composed of free men.[106] By considering that the law contains no severe sentences, Otto is convinced that this law is interested in social protection.[107] Due to its representative efforts to prevent bondage from being permanent, Pressler understands Exod 21:2–6 as protecting the manumitted slave.[108] "This law protects the worker from a rash decision or from being pressured by his employer into staying on permanently," Similarly, Stuart remarks that "[i]t also protects an employer from the possibility of being charged with failing to honor the six-year time limit for a servant's contract labor."[109]

The opposite conclusion is held by Noth, Crüsemann, and Jackson who argue that the law "sides with the owner." Considering that the marriage law is only valid for the free Israelite, Noth presents the idea that this is an exceptional case that the children follow the mother not the father. The interest of the owner is carried out at the expense of the slave.[110] Likewise, Crüsemann perceives that the majority of the law treats the modalities that facilitate a transition into permanent slavery in the interest of the owner's position, rather than discussion manumission. Only in the first case (where a married slave entered service together with his wife) would he be released without complications. In all other cases, familial ties would hold him back from leaving. Thus, Crüsemann explains that Ex 21:2–6 is not a provision for protection, but a regulation that in the majority of cases must force male slaves into permanent slavery.[111] Supporting the idea that the law favors the master, Jackson argues that the owner may use his male slave for breeding purpose to reproduce corveé labor.[112]

---

105 Paul, *Studies in the Book of Covenant in the Light of Cuneiform and Biblical Law*, 47.
106 Phillips, "The Law of Slavery: Exodus 21:2–11," 62.
107 Eckart Otto, *Wandel der Rechtsbegründungen in der Gesellschaftsgeschichte des antiken Israel: eine Rechtsgeschichte des "Bundesbuches" Ex XX 22-XXIII 13* (Leiden: E. J. Brill, 1988), 36.
108 Pressler, "Wives and Daughters, Bond and Free: View of Women in the Slave Laws of Exodus 21:2–11," 151.
109 Douglas K. Stuart, *Exodus* (Nashville: Broadman & Holman, 2006), 480–481.
110 Noth, *Exodus*, 178. All biblical evidences suggest that in Israelite time ethnic identity passed through the father. See Propp, *Exodus 19–40*, 191. Crüsemann supposes that Noth's agreement to the view that the regulation serves as protection for the slave's side is incorrect. See Crüsemann, *The Torah*, 143 n.174, and 156 n.241.
111 Crüsemann, *The Torah*, 156.
112 Jackson, "Some Literary Features of the Mishpatim," 236; idem, "Revolution in Biblical Law: Some Reflections on the Role of Theory in Methodology," 89 n.14; idem, "Gender Critical Observations on Tripartite Breeding Relationships in the Hebrew Bible," 40.

In evaluating these above arguments, the assertion that this law downgrades the value of marriage and family ties is however unconvincing. Here, two points can be raised in objection: (1) It ignores the fact that the slave's wife can go out with him if she entered the debt service with him. Although the law does not address the children born prior the father's enslavement, common sense would suggest that, like his wife, any children the man brought into servitude would be released along with him.[113] (2) This law also does not mention other situations, e. g., if the wife does not bear any children for the slave, if he loves only his wife but not children can the wife go with him?[114] The answers to these questions are likely "no." The principle of the law may better be interpreted this way: "What he has brought into slavery he shall take out; what he has acquired while within his master's household, he shall leave."[115] This should be the core essence of the rules expressed in Exod 21:3 – 4.

This is not to say that this law may completely evade abuse. If a man on the basis of this law claims that he can leave his wife, he may. However, if this does happen, the problem lies in the man, not in the law. In Matt 19:3 – 10, Jesus clarifies to the Pharisees on the divorce issue and indicates that the value behind Moses' marriage law should be examined in the whole context of Scripture. The problem is not about legislation but the hardness in a person's heart (Matt 19:8). The law should be read in the entire context, as well as within the entire Scripture. One should refrain from extracting the values of the law merely by one verse, Exod 21:4.[116] The issue in view also speaks directly to a significant point that this research intends to highlight in biblical legal study: Some scholars commit a categorical mistake when they assume that the applications of a law indicates its purpose or function.

How a law is used does not essentially represent the intention or the essence of its design. It is certainly possible that an owner could abuse this law and treat the male slave as a vehicle of reproduction to gain a large workforce. However, if Onan has the knowledge to come up with the idea of avoiding giving offspring to his brother (Gen 38:9), could not a slave do the same thing to his abusive master?

---

113 Propp, *Exodus 19 – 40*, 191.
114 D. Patrick proposes an assumption behind this rule: "[t]he slave could not contract a marriage while enslaved unless his master provides a woman, and the law assumes that the master would give a slave, for a free woman would not have been his to give." D. Patrick, *Old Testament Law* (Atlanta: John Knox, 1985), 70.
115 Janzen, *Exodus*, 291.
116 Undeniably, some instances of ANE laws still confuse scholars as to where one "law" concludes and the next "law" begins. Consequently, interpretations of the legal import of the text at such junctures may vary considerably. See J. J. Finkelstein, *The Ox That Gored* (Philadelphia: The American Philosophical Society, 1981), 14 – 15.

In addition, unlike Onan, there is no punishment for the slave if he does not beget children for the master. As Propp comments, "it is unclear whether the master is simply breeding slaves like cattle, or whether this is a real marriage with the owner acting *in loco parentis*."[117] R. Averbeck suggests that the reason that the wife given by the master is not allowed to leave with the slave is possibly because the slave has not yet paid the brideprice.[118] This suggestion is agreeable, given that brideprice (מֹהַר in Hebrew and *terḫatum* in Akkadian) is a common custom in the ancient societies (e.g., Gen 34:12; Exod 22:15 – 16 [Eng. 22:16 – 17]; 1 Sam 18:25; LH 138 – 139; MAL 30 – 31; also cf. Gen 24:53).[119]

Indeed, the latter part of the law (Exod 21:5 – 6) focuses on outlining the procedures for the man to become a permanent slave and thus remain with his family.[120] However, given that the law devotes more portions on the retention of a permanent slave, it is apparent that Crüsemann wrongly asserts that the law does not discuss manumission. Here Crüsemann commits the same injustice as mentioned above—reading the law in verses 3 – 6 in isolation, rather than appreciate *the entire law* in the context of Exod 21:2 – 6. As one examines in further detail the procedure of becoming a permanent slave, there is neither any hint that the law favor for the master, nor does the law imply that the master could lure his slave into permanent slavery. On the contrary, both Deut 15:16 – 17 and Exod 21:5 – 6 require the slave's own voice to determine his own fate. The first person discourse (Exod 21:5; Deut 15:16) speaks from the slave's stance. Both slave laws maintain the same thrust—*all* debt-slaves should go out of service in the seventh year, except when the slave desires otherwise. To remain in bondage is an exception, requiring a solemn and public declaration—his own statement and an ear-piercing ritual. The slave has to declare his intention openly and make his formal renunciation of returning to a status of freedom.[121] Furthermore, the entire procedure of the formal declaration and the public ceremony safeguards the rights of the slave, that he would not be illegally retained.

---

117 Propp, *Exodus 19 – 40*, 191.
118 A private talk with R. Averbeck.
119 Regarding the brideprice, see discussions in Reuven Yaron, "Matrimonial Mishaps at Eshnunna," *JSS* 8, no. 1 (1963): 3; Isaac Mendelsohn, "The Family in the Ancient Near East," in *The Biblical Archaeologist Reader* (ed. David Noel Freedman and Edward F. Campbell; vol. 3; Garden City: Anchor, 1970), 146 – 156; Katarzyna Grosz, "Bridewealth and Dowry in Nuzi," in *Images of Women in Antiquity* (ed. Amélie Kuhrt and Averil Cameron; Detroit: Wayne State University Press, 1983), 193 – 206.
120 Dozeman, *Exodus*, 528.
121 Durham, *Exodus*, 321; Sarna, *Exodus*, 119. Walter Brueggemann, *Deuteronomy* (Nashville: Abingdon Press, 2001), 168; Richard D. Nelson, *Deuteronomy: A Commentary* (Louisville: Westminster John Knox, 2002), 199.

The conjecture that the "love" for his wife and children was a major factor for slaves to reluctantly decide to stay ignores the prominence of the "love" for the slave's master. In this respect, Deut 15:16 shares the same emphasis with Exod 21:5. The love for the master is painted in the first place in both passages. The fact that the law assumes that it is possible that the slave would love the master encourages the treatment of debt-slave in an expectation of benign treatment.[122] Rarely would anyone voluntarily stay with an abhorrent master. But if a slave is treated well during his service, he probably wants to take advantage of the security and comfort within the mater's household over an insolvent future or lonely liberty.[123] In this manner, the law there implicitly promotes a virtue. However, even if the benign treatment facilitates the man's willingness to remain as a permanent slave, the law is still far away from protecting the master's interest. The chances that a master would abuse the law and force his slave to make a fake oath, refuse to free the slave, or regret the release (as the case in Jer 34:8 – 11), are not entirely impossible, but that is not the intended purpose of the law.

Similar Ceremonies with Different Expressions

The ceremonies of becoming a permanent slave described in Deut 15:17 and Exod 21:6 are similar, except that Deut 15:17 skips the action of bringing the slave to/ before אֶל־הָאֱלֹהִים (the term הָאֱלֹהִים could be translated as "God," "judges," and "gods"). To properly understand this verse requires an examination of two issues: (1) The omission in Deut 15:17 is ascribed by Falk, Mayes, Braulik, and Christensen to the changes in social backdrop and theological comprehension. (2) Its connection to the assumption that הָאֱלֹהִים is to be interpreted in light of Israelite society within a single sanctuary.[124]

With regard to the first issue, the reference of הָאֱלֹהִים is debatable. Historically, all three interpretations (i.e., God, judges, and gods) have found theological support from various interpreters. In 1935, C. H. Gordon argued that the literal translation of *gods* (plural) found in the Vulgate *(ad deos)* and Luther's version *(vor die Götter)* better suited the passage instead of *God*, as the LXX translates. He also disagreed with the translation of *judges,* which is the construal of the Peshitta and Targum Onkelos, followed by Rashi and Ibn Ezra, and by several Eng-

---

122 Tigay, *Deuteronomy*, 149.
123 Saran, *Exodus*, 119; Janzen, *Exodus*, 291; Propp, *Exodus*, 192; Stuart, *Exodus*, 480.
124 Ze'ev W. Falk, "Exodus 21:6," *VT* 9, no. 1 (1959): 86; A. D. H. Mayes, Deuteronomy (Grand Rapids: Eerdmans, 1981), 252; Georg Braulik, *Deuteronomium 1 – 16, 17* (Würzburg: Echter Verlag, 1986), 115; Duane L. Christensen, *Deuteronomy 1:1 – 21:9* (Nashville: Thomas Nelson, 2001), 321.

lish versions.[125] In 1959, Z. W. Falk argued that the term refers to "in the presence of God," because God is concerned with the manumission of slaves and the fact that particularly, God had liberated the people from the serfdom of Egypt.[126] In the same year, F. C. Fensham published his article "New Light on Ex 21:6 and 22:7 from the Laws of Eshnunna." There, he argues that הָאֱלֹהִים denoted *YHWH, the God of Israel.*[127] Elsewhere, N. M. Saran regarded "before *elohim*" as an echo of pre-Israelite legal terminology, and it should simply mean "in the sanctuary," denoting the location for the ceremony.[128]

With regard to the issue of the single sanctuary, the understanding of הָאֱלֹהִים consequentially affects the reference of the phrase אֶל־הָאֱלֹהִים (to God, to judges, to gods) and the location of the door/doorpost: the master's house, the city gate, and the temple. Since the symbols of gods were placed by the doorways of private home and also by the portals of temples in Mesopotamia,[129] those who regarded the phrase as "to gods," (e. g., Mayes), suggest that the ceremony is held at the door of the master's house. Mayes believes that because the idea of a single sanctuary is implied behind Deuteronomy and that הָאֱלֹהִים probably refers to the household gods found at the home entrance, Dt 15 intentionally omits the phrase.[130] Phillips suggests that since no oath is required, the expression הָאֱלֹהִים in Exod 21:6 does not mean that this ceremony is held in the sanctuary. Instead, this is a nonreligious ceremony held before the household gods, which signifies that the slave now is part of the master's property. For him, there is no religious content to this ceremony. However, Phillips further proposes that אֶל־הָאֱלֹהִים and "to the door/doorpost" is to be taken as the same procedure.[131] Propp suggests that if the present law does not originate in an ultra-religious monotheistic context, the phrase אֶל־הָאֱלֹהִים may be considered divine, as it refers to household gods or ancestral deities. However, this phrase would only bear an ordinary meaning: The master and slave resort to *YHWH* to swear the commitment to voluntary lifelong servitude.[132]

---

125 Cyrus Herzl Gordon, "ELOHIM in Its Reputed Meaning of Rulers, Judges," *JBL* 54, no. 3 (1935): 140. Such a translation is agreed by T. B. Dozeman, *Commentary on Exodus*, 528.
126 Falk,"Exodus 21:6." 88. Falk's interpretation is espoused by J. I. Durham. See Durham, *Exodus*, 321.
127 F. Charles Fensham, "New Light on Ex 21:6 and 22:7 from the Laws of Eshnunna," *JBL* 78, no. 2 (1959): 161.
128 Sarna, *Exodus*, 120.
129 See the discussions in Propp, *Exodus 19–40*, 193, and McConville, *Deuteronomy*, 264.
130 Mayes, *Deuteronomy*, 252.
131 Anthony Phillips, *Ancient Israel's Criminal Law: A New Approach to the Decalogue* (Oxford: Basil Blackwell, 1970), 74–75.
132 Propp, *Exodus 19–40*, 193.

In considering the above views, although Deuteronomy omits אֶל־הָאֱלֹהִים, it does not mean that Dt 15 intends to desacralize the ceremony, McConville suggests the following reason:[133]

> The reason for this omission is the deuteronomic address to the whole people as such, omitting any special references to judicial procedures (cf. on 13:9; also Chirichigno 1993:299). The act may well have required witnesses to give it legal standing, and indeed, it is unclear whether 'the door' is at the owner's house or at the sanctuary. In any case, Deuteronomy passes over the circumstances of the procedure, focusing instead on its meaning for the master and the slave.

The more important thing is that Dt 15 and Ex 21 both express the concern about the slave's own willingness to stay as a permanent slave and demand a similar public ceremony. In this view, they are concordant to the stance of retaining a permanent slave.

Discerning the Similarities and Differences between Dt 15 and Ex 21 with the Legal Categorizational System

The above discussion shows that although these two slave laws share similar thoughts and values, they are also dissimilar in other ways. In order to discern the degrees of similarities and differences and answer the questions raised in the beginning of this chapter,[134] this study suggests a legal categorizational system to distinguish the laws in three levels of similarities and differences: *topic* (sometimes with vague or opposite *positions*, which mostly occur in biblical laws with theological connotations),[135] *issues*, and *situations*.[136] For example, the biblical and ANE slave laws can be classified into three major *legal topics:* (1) *Slave Escape*, (2) *Slave Purchase and Management*, and (3) *Debt-servitude*

---

133 McConville, *Deuteronomy*, 264.
134 The two questions raised were the following: "What are the essential elements to determine the degree of analogy?" and "On what methodological bases are two laws deemed as parallel, similar, or different?"
135 Most of the ANE and biblical laws share similar topics in various degrees. The only legal topic that contains laws with two opposite positions is *Slave Escape*. The single case that holds a completely different position against its ANE counterparts is Deut 23:16 – 17. Since these kinds of opposite cases are very rare, the category of *position* is not used in this current proposal.
136 This legal categorizational system and the three major legal topics of slave laws will be continuely applied in chapter four.

and Other Forms of Human Bondage.[137] Laws within the same legal topic are further distinguished into different legal issues. Under one legal issue, laws will be additionally divided into various *situations*. With this legal categorizational system, one could distinguish the degrees of similarity and difference in comparative legal studies for casuistic laws: Whether two laws are *closely parallel*, or they merely have the same *legal topic*, yet differ in *positions* or deal with different *legal issues* and diverse *situations*. This legal categorizational system suggests the standard of analogy as such: Laws in the same legal topic and under a similar legal issue can be considered as *parallel*. Laws that have a similar situation can be regarded as *closely parallel*. Outside of this standard, laws may have only *similar* legal topics or *similar* legal issues.

Accordingly, Deut 15:12–15 and Exod 21:2–6 possess the same legal topic concerning *Debt-servitude*. They also share three legal issues: (1) Both laws demand the release of a Hebrew debt slave after six years. (2) To retain a slave permanently is viewed as an exception—only through a public ceremony in which the slave professes his/her own voluntariness can the master legally and perpetually acquire the slave. (3) Both laws use the polyvocality of combined discourses, and in both passages the slave has to verbally express his "love" for the master. This encourages a benign treatment to slaves. In view of these, Deut 15:12–18 and Exod 21:2–6 are *parallel* laws pertaining to the same *legal topic* and *issue* on Hebrew debt slave manumission. At the same time, Exod 21:7–11 is regarded as an independent law with the legal topic about *Marriage*, and can be further categorized into the legal issue of *slave marriage*.

In spite of these similarities, these two laws seem to hold vague positions and emphasize different issues. Dt 15 is silent on the issue concerning female slave marriage sales and debt slave's marital status. Likewise, regarding the provision to the released slave and female debt slave's liberty, these issues are absent in Ex 21. As the earlier section had previously discussed, it does not mean that Dt 15 supersedes Ex 21, or that Ex 21 holds a different view on the release of a Hebrew female debt slave. There is no indication that Dt 15 and Ex 21 contradict each other. Therefore, we may still suggest that they are *parallel* to the same legal topic in the discussion of *Debt-servitude* that links to the same issues on Hebrew indebted slave release. Whatever the linkage, they do not *closely parallel* one another.

---

137 The methodology of this classification will be further explained and discussed in chapter four.

Deut 15:12 – 18 and Lev 25:39 – 55

Here, the nature of how long the status of a Hebrew perpetual slave could be retained is examined. At the outset, both Dt 15 and Ex 21 provide no further clues on this matter. Rabbinic interpretations often bring in Lev 25 in discussion of permanent slavery: the "perpetuity" may mean that the new term of service ends at the next Jubilee year (as prescribed in Lev 25) or at the death of the master (whichever comes first).[138] According to Milgrom, Rabbis also indicate that with regard to Ex 21 and Lev 25, two different kinds of slave-servitude are in view—seven years if he is sold by the court (Ex 21), and fifty years if he sells himself (Lev 25).[139] Ironically, in a source critical perspective, Lev 25 seems to speak for the opposite view: that Lev 25 is regarded as a sophisticated citation and lemmatic reworking of Dt 15 and Ex 21 to supersede or to reject the notion that an Israelite can become a slave, by allowing only permanent foreign slaves.[140]

A comparison of Lev 25 and Dt 15 shows some common elements: (1) They adopt similar linguistic features (e. g., "your brother," the *niphal* נמכר, "be sold," and the second person addresses). (2) They both deal with the impoverishment and use the exodus experience as a motivation for treating the debtor humanely.[141]

With these similarities, scholars have been drawn to establishing literary dependence between Lev 25 and Dt 15. Ever since A. Cholewiński's literary analysis, the scholarly consensus is that (1) H's literary and conceptual dependence upon D is most evident in Leviticus 17, 23, and 25. (2) The slave law in Lev 25 has its

---

138 See Sarna, *Exodus*, 120; Tigay, Deuteronomy, 150. Christensen, *Deuteronomy 1:1 – 21:9*, 321. However, Christensen notes, "We do not know when the Year of Jubilee was established in ancient Israel, nor if it was ever anything more than a utopian ideal."
139 Jacob Milgrom, *Leviticus 23 – 27: A New Translation with Introduction and Commentary* (New York: Doubleday, 2001), 2224.
140 Christophe Nihan, "The Holiness Code between D and P: Some Comments on the Function and Significance of Leviticus 17 – 26 in the Composition of the Torah," in *Das Deuteronomium zwischen Pentateuch und deuteronomistischem Geschichtswerk* (ed. Eckart Otto and Reinhard Achenbach. Göttingen: Vandenhoeck & Ruprecht, 2004), 81 – 122; Bernard M. Levinson, "The Birth of the Lemma: The Restrictive Reinterpretation of the Covenant Code's Manumission Law by the Holiness Code (Leviticus 25:44 – 46)," *JBL* 124, no. 4 (2005): 617 – 639; Mark Leuchter, "The Manumission Laws in Leviticus and Deuteronomy: The Jeremiah Connection," *JBL* 127, no. 4 (2008): 635 – 653.
141 Van Seters, *A Law Book for the Diaspora*, 83 – 84; idem, "Law of the Hebrew Slave: A Continuing Debate," 177.

closest parallels with Exod 21:2–6 and 23:10–11, as well as Deut 15:1–11 and 12–18.[142]

Yet, further examination also show that the differences between Lev 25 and Dt 15 point to the opposite direction, which have perplexed scholars of biblical comparative legal study. There exist at least three major problems on which scholars have not yet been able to reach a consensus: (1) The two passages regulate the terms for the debt-servitude in different lengths (six years versus forty-nine years). (2) Lev 25 may refer to a different kind of debt-servitude from that in Dt 15 and Ex21. (3) Lev 25 appears to supersede its precursors, for it allows acquiring slaves only from foreigners.

The Different Length of Term in Lev 25

If a Hebrew slave would be freed every seventh year, why is there a need for the regulation for the release at the year of Jubilee (יוֹבֵל)? Historically, various approaches have attempted to answer this question with various conjectures.[143]

There are at least eight solutions proposed to the issue at hand.

(1) S. R. Driver suggests that it is to reform the older laws in Deuteronomy, which might have proved to be impractical and unenforceable.[144]

(2) E. Ginzberg is convinced that this is to help the rich by providing a longer and steady supply of labor.[145]

---

142 Alfred Cholewiński, *Heiligkeitsgesetz und Deuteronomium: Eine vergleichende Studie* (Rome: Biblical Institute Press, 1976), 217–251. See also Nihan, "The Holiness Code between D and P," 83–84; Eckart Otto, "Vom Bundesbuch zum Deuteronomium: Die deuteronomische Redaktion in Dtn 12–26," in *Biblische Theologie und gesellschaftlicher Wandel: für Norbert Lohfink SJ* (ed. George Braulik OSB, Walter Groß, and Sean McEvenue; Herder: Freiburg, 1993), 260–278; N. Lohfmk, "Fortschreibung? Zur Technik von Rechtsrevisionen im deuteronomischen Bereich, erörtert an Deuteronomium 12, Ex 21,2–11 und Dtn 15,12–18," in *Das Deuteronomium und seine Querbeziehungen* (ed. T. Veijola; Helsinki: Göttingen 1996), 151–152.

143 J. E. Hartley synthesizes a summary of these approaches from 1890's to 1990's (including his own approach). John E. Hartley, *Leviticus* (Dallas: Word, 1992), 431–433.

144 Driver, *A Critical and Exegetical Commentary on Deuteronomy*, 185.

145 Eli Ginzberg, *Studies in the Economics of the Bible* (Philadelphia: Jewish Publication Society of America, 1932), 48–53.

(3) I. Mendelsohn proposes that Lev 25 deals with a different social circumstance that leads one into slavery (i. e., Ex 21 and Dt 15 speaks of those who are forced into service, while the debtors of Lev 25 sell themselves into bondage).[146]

(4) Lemche interprets the term יֹבֵל as the "manumission year," "the year of release," or something otherwise similar. Consequently, there may be a connection between the celebration of the Sabbatical Year every seventh year and the יֹבֵל year. In this view, a service period lasting up to 50 years would mean lifelong slavery, and the offer of manumission would accordingly be nominal.[147]

(5) C. J. H. Wright assumes that the *Hebrew* in Ex 21 and Dt 15 is a class of landless people who supported themselves by working for others, while an Israelite in Lev 25 has patrimony but due to debts he has to submit himself to be a hired labor.[148]

(6) That the three laws have distinctive social agendas. J. E. Hartley explains that Ex 21 and Dt 15 govern the length of servitude of each individual slave, whereas Lev 25 concurrently proclaims liberty for all slaves, particularly for those who chronically fall into heavy debt.[149]

(7) G. C. Chirichigno indicates the possibility that Leviticus may be trying to introduce a new kind of family member sold into servitude. For him, Ex 21 and Dt 15 refer to a family dependent sold by his/her father, whereas Lev 25 speaks of a *pater familias*, the head of the household selling himself into debt-service, and thus must be treated as a resident alien and a hired worker.[150]

(8) Building on Chirichigno's suggestion, A. Schenker believes that Lev 25 is meant to be a supplement to Ex 21 and Dt 15. Ex 21 and Dt 15 focuses on unmarried cases, while Lev 25 complements them with the regulation for married Israelites who have (male) children.[151]

Among these views, Wright and Chirichigno's (which ascribe the different lengths of term to diverse social classes or family roles), have been shown to be unconvincing in chapter two.[152] Mendelsohn's distinction of forced and volun-

---

146 Isaac Mendelsohn, *Slavery in the Ancient Near East: A Comparative Study of Slavery in Babylonia, Assyria, Syria, and Palestine from Middle of the Third Millennium to the End of the First Millennium* (Westport: Greenwood Press, 1978), 89 – 90.
147 Lemche, "The Manumission of Slaves," 50.
148 Wright, "What Happened Every Seven Years in Israel," 195 – 200.
149 Hartley, *Leviticus*, 433.
150 Chirichigno, *Debt-Slavery in Israel and the Ancient Near East*, 330 – 336.
151 Adrian Schenker, "The Biblical Legislation on the Release of Slaves: The Road from Exodus to Leviticus," *JSOT* 78 (1998): 31 – 33.
152 A. Schenker and C. Nihan both have challenged Chirichigno's argument. See Schenker, "The Biblical Legislation on the Release of Slaves," 27 – 29; Nihan, "The Holiness Code between D and P," 86 n. 25.

tary slavery and Hartley's classification of individual and chronic types of debtors are groundless. Lemche's reading of יוֹבֵל as a manumission year is also implausible, given that Lev 25:8–10 has defined the יוֹבֵל as the fiftieth year.

To resolve the deadlock, Lev 25 must be read in the context of the whole chapter.[153] The primary theme of Leviticus 25 is the ultimate *rest* for all in the Sabbatical year. In order to receive this ultimate rest, the land and the lives of people in it have to be restored to their original *free* status—free from any kinds of *bondage* of labor, loan, and debt. The free status for an Israelite is to return to his *land/possession* (אֲחֻזָה) and his *family* (מִשְׁפָּחָה) as claimed in Lev 25:10.[154]

Therefore, there should be no *perpetual* separation from one's land and family, but only impoverishment on account of debt would *temporarily* lead a man to become alienated from his land and family, and eventually to the enslavement of the entire family.[155] This idea is illustrated by the three successive stages of destitution,[156] which are all characterized by the formula—"if your brother becomes poor" (כִּי יָמוּךְ אָחִיךְ, vv. 25, 35, 39, and with a change dictated by the case in v. 47).[157] The first stage describes an Israelite becoming so poor that he has to sell part of his inherited land (vv. 25–34). The second stage and lower stage concerns a landless Israelite who comes into financial difficulty and finds himself in need of support (vv. 35–38). The third stage (and bottom of all the previous stages) envisages an Israelite who has no other choice but to

---

153 J. Milgrom asserts that Leviticus 25 flows logically and coherently because it is no longer possible to identify the separable stages of compositional growth of the chapter. Milgrom, *Leviticus 23–27*, 2149–2150.

154 The common denominator of all the sections of chapter 25 is "land." It occurs twenty times. The associated words *possession* (אֲחֻזָה) appears twelve times; *redeem* (גאל), fifteen times; *jubilee* (יוֹבֵל), ten times; *sabbath* (שַׁבָּת) of land, nine times. Ibid., 2151.

155 Robert North, *Sociology of the Biblical Jubilee* (Rome: Pontifical Biblical Institute, 1954), 187–188; Raymond Westbrook, "Jubilee Laws," *ILR* 6 (1971): 213–214; Gordon J.Wenham, *The Book of Leviticus* (Grand Rapids: Eerdmans, 1979), 317; Patrick, *Old Testament Law*, 183. See also Tikva Frymer-Kensky, "Israel," in *Security for Debt in Ancient Near Eastern Law.* (ed. Raymond Westbrook and Richard Lewis Jasnow; Boston: E. J. Brill, 2001), 251.

156 Sara Japhet, "The Relationship between the Legal Corpora in the Pentateuch in Light of Manumission Laws," in *Studies in Bible* (ed. Sara Japhet; Jerusalem: Magnes, 1986), 74–75.

157 In the 1960's H. G. Reventlow had suggested the use of this formula. See Henning Graf Reventlow, *Das Heiligkeitsgesetz formgeschichtlich Untersucht* (Neukirchen: Neukirchener Verlag, 1961), 125, 135–142.

sell himself into debt-service (vv. 39 – 43),[158] or even worse, to foreigners (vv.47 – 55).[159]

An overview of these three stages of laws indicates an inner advocacy of a protective system for the poor. Each apodosis provides an antidote to *prevent* the poor from entering the next stage, presumably worse than the current one. In stage one, the law asks the poor's nearest kinsman to buy back what this relative has sold (Lev 25:25b). If the nearest kinsman did buy back the land, the poor then would return to his original status, allowing him to repossess and dwell again in his land. If no kinsman is able to purchase the land, then his fellow Israelites, or even, the listeners, are obligated to sustain him, with money or food (Lev 25:35b, 36 – 37). If he could gain provision from his fellow Israelite, he would escape the threat of slavery. If it is an even worse scenario (i.e., that there is no sustenance provided) where the Israelite has to sell himself (along with possibly his family) into slavery, he should not be treated as a slave, but as כְּשָׂכִיר כְּתוֹשָׁב. (lit., "as a hireling, as a sojourner"). Finally, even if the worst situation happens and the poor Israelite is sold to foreigners, the law in Lev 25:48 – 54 calls for actions from all possible close relatives, whoever has the ability to redeem.

The laws that aim at these three stages form a protective system to prevent an Israelite from entering the next worse situation. The presumption that lies underneath the legislation is that only impoverishment would lead a man to become alienated from his land and family, and eventually to the enslavement of entire families.[160] The rationale behind this social protective system is explicitly stated at the end of Leviticus 25—"For the sons of Israel are my servants; they are my servants whom I brought out from the land of Egypt. I am YHWH your God." (Lev 25:55). Therefore, the interpretation of Lev 25 should consider the logic of this idealistic protective system. The manumission law here expresses nothing about a forty-nine year long debt-service, because it holds this assumption—if the situations (land redemption and sufficient supplement) in the first two stages had been resolved, the successive third stage would not have to

---

158 G. C. Chirichigno and J. Milgrom both categorize only three stages, combining the third and fourth as the worst situation, in which an Israelite enters into enslavement. See Chirichigno, *Debt-Slavery in Israel and the Ancient Near East*, 323; Milgrom, *Leviticus 23 – 27,* 2191 – 2241.

159 Japhet, "The Relationship between the Legal Corpora in the Pentateuch in Light of Manumission Laws," 75; "The Biblical Legislation on the Release of Slaves," 37. See also Nobuyoshi Kiuchi, *Leviticus* (Downers Grove: InterVarsity, 2007), 460 – 462.

160 Robert North, *Sociology of the Biblical Jubilee* (Rome: Pontifical Biblical Institute, 1954), 187 – 188; Raymond Westbrook, "Jubilee Laws," *ILR* 6 (1971): 213 – 214; Wenham, Gordon J. *The Book of Leviticus* (Grand Rapids: Eerdmans, 1979), 317; Patrick, *Old Testament Law*, 183.

take place. The Jubilee is the last *recourse* of this social protective system. No one should be retained in bondage in the Jubilee year.

The Types of Debt Slave in Lev 25

With the context of Lev 25 in mind, the next question can be examined: Whether Lev 25 is a law for a different type of debt slave from Ex 21 and Dt 15. The law in Lev 25 starts with וְכִי יָמוּךְ אָחִיךָ (when your brother becomes poor, Lev 21:39), which is used in all the protases to initiate the first three stages of destitution (Lev 21:23, 35, and 39). That is, Lev 25 explicitly depicts the situation that this slave service is due to poverty, similar with the situations in Dt 15 and Ex 21. However, Lev 25 outlines more details about the treatment of a debt slave.

Lev 25 demands gentle and proper treatment of the debt slave (e. g., Lev 25:39a, 40, and 42–43). The slave should not work like a slave or corveé, but כְּשָׂכִיר כְּתוֹשָׁב (lit., "as a hired man, as a sojourner"). In addition, he should not be treated with severity. In Dt 15 and Ex 21, a benign treatment is indirectly promoted, but Lev 25 directly guides the treatment. These principles, representing strong humane concern, find no parallels in ANE slave laws.

The phrase כְּשָׂכִיר כְּתוֹשָׁב consists of the preposition כְּ and two nouns, שָׂכִיר (a hireling) and תוֹשָׁב (a sojourner), yet without the conjunction אוֹ that connects them. The two nouns are often rendered as two different referents, such as, "like an employee or a settler,"[161] "as a hired worker or a temporary resident,"[162] "like a wage earner or a temporary resident,"[163] and "as a hired servant and as a sojourner."[164] While both B. A. Levine and Milgrom render this phrase with a single referent, they understand this composite phrase differently. Levine translates it "as a hired or bound laborer."[165] Milgrom interprets it "as a resident hireling."[166] Levine and Milgrom thus have different understandings of this composite term.

Levine indicates that these two terms are subject to varying interpretations according to the context. For example, שָׂכִיר usually refers to a labor who works for wages, whereas תוֹשָׁב often designates a foreign "resident," a merchant

---

161 Wenham, *The Book of Leviticus*, 315.

162 Mark F. Rooker, *Leviticus* (Nashville: Broadman & Holman, 2000), 309. See also Roy Gane, *Leviticus, Numbers* (Grand Rapids: Zondervan, 2004), 431.

163 Hartley, *Leviticus*, 419.

164 Kiuchi, *Leviticus*, 447.

165 Baruch A. Levine, *Leviticus* (Philadelphia: Jewish Publication Society, 1989), 179.

166 Milgrom, *Leviticus 23–27*, 2221.

or a labor. In Lev 25:6, with the phrase הַגֵּרִים עִמָּךְ (the sojourner who lives with you), these two words should be rendered as two different people groups, "the hired and bound labors."[167] In Lev 25:35, when תּוֹשָׁב is jointed with גֵּר, גֵּר וְתוֹשָׁב should be rendered as "a resident alien," who mortgaged or sold his land and became a tenant on his own land.[168] Similar to Lev 25:23, Lev 25:40 also contains the collocation of תּוֹשָׁב and שָׂכִיר. Here, the phrase should mean "a hired or bound laborer."[169]

Milgrom explains that תּוֹשָׁב is never attested independently, but always in tandem with either גֵּר (alien) or שָׂכִיר (hireling). Besides, כְּשָׂכִיר כְּתוֹשָׁב takes a singular verb יִהְיֶה here (cf. Exod 12:25; Lev 22:10). The phrase as a whole should be understood as a hendiadys, in which the addition of תּוֹשָׁב is significant. He indicates that a *resident hireling* is not a שָׂכִיר (hireling, day-laborer; Lev 19:13; Deut 24:14 – 15). That is, a *resident hireling* is not one who returns to his family every evening, but a long term employee who lives with his family on the master's property. The resident hireling receives room and board from his employer.[170]

HALOT views שָׂכִיר as a designation for a landless waged labor, working under a short-term contract (e. g., Exod 20:14; Lev 19:13; 25:50, 53; Deut 15:18; 24:14; Isa 16:14; 21:16, etc.). Socially, such laborers are deemed to be freemen, even though their job or duty is the same as that of slaves.[171] As for the term תּוֹשָׁב, *HALOT* agrees with Levine, considering it a denotation of a citizen who does not have full civic rights. Likewise, when תּוֹשָׁב is put together with שָׂכִיר in Lev 25:40, it means "resident alien."[172]

In summary, the above survey shows that כְּשָׂכִיר כְּתוֹשָׁב is better understood as a hendiadys that denotes a single referent. The phrase כְּשָׂכִיר כְּתוֹשָׁב may be translated to "as a resident hireling," as Milgrom proposes. Furthermore, a broader context of Leviticus 25 may inform our understanding of the phrase. In Lev 25:23b, when YHWH explains the prohibition of the permanent sale of a land, he proclaims, "for the land is mine; for you are but *resident alien* (גֵּרִים וְתוֹשָׁבִים) *with me* (עִמָּדִי)." In front of YHWH, the real Master of the Land, all the Israelites are resident aliens. The hendiadys reminds the slave owner of his own status before YHWH that he may be humble and merciful to his slave brother. As N. Kiuchi observes in Lev 25:39 – 41 the prepositional phrase עִמָּךְ (with you) occurs four times (vv. 39a, 40a, 40b, 41a),

---

167 Levine, *Leviticus*, 170 – 171.

168 Ibid., 178.

169 Ibid., 179.

170 Milgrom, *Leviticus 23 – 27*, 2221.

171 L. Koehler and W. Baumgartner, "שָׂכִיר," *HALOT* 2:1327 – 1328.

172 L. Koehler and W. Baumgartner, "תּוֹשָׁב," *HALOT* 2:1712 – 1713.

which is not only noticeable but apparently with the nuance of "together with," just as YHWH treats his fellow Israelite.[173] The term עִמָּדִי (with me) in Lev 25:23b, when contrasted with the repeated occurrences of עִמָּךְ in the slave laws reveals a clear theological message of empathy and graciousness. With the preposition בְּ, כְּשָׂכִיר כְּתוֹשָׁב, Israel is taught not only about *understanding* legal concerns of the types of labor, but about *acting* as graciously as YHWH does towards them.

The Gender Inclusive Release in Lev 25

Lev 25:40b-41 provides two principles about the release. In addition to the command of manumission in the Jubilee year, the other principle requests that "he and his son with him shall go back to his family" (Lev 25:41). Taken at face value, this statement declares that this law is *only* for a male slave who enters slavery with *sons*. However, since a Sabbatical rest suggests all should return to his/her family, the law definitely has both genders in view for debt slave release.[174] More importantly, this expression should be read under the three-stage social protective system previously discussed within the context of Leviticus 25 where אָחִיךְ is a keyword that links these three destitute stages to this expression. It has already been shown that אָחִיךְ repeatedly appears as the subject in each beginning clause of every destitute stage (vv. 25, 35, 39, and 47). As chapter two previously discussed this, אָחִיךְ conveys sociological empathy. These intensive appearances of אָחִיךְ turns the audience's attention to consider how "*my* brother" could arrive at his present predicament with the listener ("*you*") having one's arms folded. Lev 25 thus emphasizes a strong bonding of "brotherhood." The same idea of fraternity is also presented in Dt 15. As Averbeck puts, "Deuteronomy 15:12–18 points to its benevolent nature and Leviticus 25:39–43, 47–55 emphasizes the lack of harshness with which the institution was to be characterized in Israel."[175]

The Acquisition of Permanent Slaves in Lev 25

Due to the negation of Israelite slaves in Lev 25:42, some scholars (e. g., Nihan, Levinson, and Leuchter) have challenged that this is a prohibition to acquire a

---

173 Kiuchi, *Leviticus*, 462.
174 See also Levinson's discussion. Levinson, "The Birth of the Lemma," 631.
175 Averbeck, "Law," 132.

Hebrew brother as a slave.[176] However, Lev 25:42 does not forbid acquiring a Hebrew brother as a *debt* slave, but presents an idea that no Israelite will be sold as a slave if his fellows could have provided assistance in time. Therefore, the three-fold repetition of admonishment in vv. 43, 46, and 53 highlights the significance of the prohibition—one shall not rule over him with hardness. It reminds the master to treat his Hebrew slave with kindness. The Israelite could become a slave *in status*, but cannot be treated like a slave/corveé.

S. Japhet remarks that the slave law of Lev 25 mirrors the land law. Just as only the usufruct of the land, but not the land itself, may be sold, only the labor of the Israelite, not the Israelite himself, may be sold.[177] Israelite slaves are merely *nominal* slaves, as Milgrom conceives that "the Israel slave is not a slave."[178] The concept that an Israelite permanent slave is the master's property should be redressed. An Israelite slave should never be treated as a property per se, but only as belonging to YHWH. As a result, Lev 25:44 – 46a clarifies that if one wants to possess permanent slaves as their *inherited property* that may be bequeathed to his children,[179] he can acquire aliens or the sojourners among Israel.

Milgrom asserts that "the assumption here is that the alien is a chattel-slave, not a debt-slave,"[180] which is confirmed by the verb קנה (purchase). However, Milgrom's interpretation is incorrect, for Ex 21 uses the same verb קנה to express the purchase of the Hebrew debt-slave. Here, the significance lies in the verbal expression, וְהִתְנַחֲלְתֶּם. The *hithpael* form of נחל is mostly used in the context of taking possession of land (e.g., Num 32:18; 33:54; and 34:13). In Isa 14:2, it is used to make the point that Israel will again acquire the aliens as their male and female slaves. Here the verbal expression conveys the same meaning: If an Israelite wants to obtain a permanent slave as an *inheritable property* for their children, he can *only* buy it among the non-Israelite!

---

176 Christophe Nihan, "The Holiness Code between D and P: Some Comments on the Function and Significance of Leviticus 17–26 in the Composition of the Torah," in *Das Deuteronomium zwischen Pentateuch und deuteronomistischem Geschichtswerk* (ed. Eckart Otto and Reinhard Achenbach. Göttingen: Vandenhoeck & Ruprecht, 2004), 81–122; Bernard M. Levinson, "The Birth of the Lemma: The Restrictive Reinterpretation of the Covenant Code's Manumission Law by the Holiness Code (Leviticus 25:44–46)," *JBL* 124, no. 4 (2005): 617–639; Mark Leuchter, "The Manumission Laws in Leviticus and Deuteronomy: The Jeremiah Connection," *JBL* 127, no. 4 (2008): 635–653.
177 Cited from Milgrom, *Leviticus 23–27*, 2217.
178 Ibid., 2216.
179 Kiuchi, 463.
180 Milgrom, *Leviticus 23–27*, 2230.

From his understanding of the syntax of Lev 25:46, B. M. Levinson also provides that Lev 25 allows the permanent indentured applying only to foreigners, which is a reinterpretation of Ex 21 and Dt 15.[181] He argues that the term אֲחֻזָּה לְעֹלָם has long been misread, as if they were an idiom that לְעֹלָם modifies אֲחֻזָּה and thus is translated "as a possession forever." Levinson indicates that the absolute noun אֲחֻזָּה is never constructed with or modified by the adverbial phrase לְעֹלָם, except for this disputed case here. He suggests that "[m]ore accurately, the absolute noun אֲחֻזָּה should *conclude* the clause in which it is found," and that the translation of Lev 25:46 should be: "You may transfer them as hereditary to your children after you, to inherit as property. Forever—them—may you make work as slaves."[182] Levinson considers that the adverbial phrase לְעֹלָם is supposed to mark the beginning of a new clause, structured as a *casus pendens*. This parsing of the syntax is preserved by the Masorah,[183]

> "The disjunctive accent *zāqep qātôn*, which is placed over אֲחֻזָּה, recognizes it as the end of the clause and clarified that the new phrase should begin with לעלם. Although infrequent, there are other cases where לע(ו)לם serves as the first word of a clause or verse, especially to create rhetorical emphasis."

In summary, Lev 25 should not be regarded as a new law that intends to deny the possibility of a Hebrew debt slave, or to abolish the permanent Hebrew debt slave. In ancient Israel, Hebrew slaves are usually acquired as a result of their destitution, and loans are seen as a device by which the poor stave off disaster. Hence, loans are mentioned with a positive valence and the institution of protection for the debtors is considerable.[184] In light of the legal topic, the three slave laws, Ex 21, Dt 15, and Lev 25, all deal with the sale of an Israelite fellow on account of poverty. With respect to humanitarian treatments to a fellow Israelite who enters into the debt-service then, Lev 25 presents the consistent spirit expressed in Ex 21 and Dt 15 where both implicitly uphold a benign handling of the slave. There exists no discrepancy between these three laws regarding the identity of the enslave person. They all speak of undifferentiated Israelites.[185] With the above interpretation, one can agree with the Rabbinic interpretation that the term of "permanent" for an Israelite slave in Ex 21 and Dt 15 properly

181 The purpose is to abolish the permanent Israelite slave. Levinson, "The Birth of the Lemma," 617–623, 637–639.
182 Ibid., 624–625.
183 Ibid., 625.
184 Frymer-Kensky, "Anatolia and the Levant Israel," 2:1003; idem, "Israel," 251, 254–256.
185 Milgrom, *Leviticus 23–27*, 2253.

means "for the rest of the master's life" and that the new term of service ends *at the next Jubilee year* or *at the death of the master*, whichever comes first.

Problems Concerning the Claim of Supersession between the Laws

Concerns over whether Lev 25 supersedes Dt 15 and Ex 21, or as mentioned earlier, whether Dt 15 abolishes Ex 21 regarding the female slave release, necessarily leads to the following question: When scholars claim that biblical law *A* supersedes or abolishes biblical law *B*, are there any references that indicates what or how this so-called *supersession* or *abolishment* takes place? For example, does it refer to a historical legal practice in accordance with the changes of social context? Or, does it refer to the intention of the so-called "Deuteronomists," "the reformer," or "the H compiler" for the sake of their own plotted political, sociological, or religious agenda? Taken as a whole, most scholars who conclude with judgments of supersession or abolishment rarely clarify the connotations of supersession or abolishment.

Perhaps the only scholar who has detailed his opinion on abolishment and abrogation is Levinson. On this, he has argued that there is no change in topic between theses slave laws and thus suggests that the legal hermeneutics involved are dialectical in nature. Therefore, there is no abrogation, except that dialectically, Lev 25 reinterprets its precursors with a restriction that permanent slaves can *only* be acquired from the foreigner.[186] He is convinced that the process of any legal amendment(s) "began with Deuteronomy's revision of the Covenant Code's law of manumission, which avoided the terms 'master' and 'slave' altogether."[187] If Levinson is understood correctly, he means that there is *no abrogation* between Lev 25, Ex 21 and Dt 15 in terms of the legal topic *per se*. Properly viewed, Levinson then sees Lev 25 amending Ex 21 and Dt 15 to *abolish* the enslavement of the Israelites, replacing the previous laws with a restrictive reinterpretation. However, as previously indicated, the Israelite could become a temporary debt slave due to insolvency but cannot be treated like a slave, which is the spirit that Lev 25 intends to stress.

Another difficulty in assessing the problem is that for most biblical laws, how they had been historically and experimentally applied or how they were regulated remained unknown.[188] Weinfeld contends the following,

---

186 Levinson, "The Birth of the Lemma," 639.
187 Ibid., 635–636.
188 The accounts in 2 Chr 8:7–9, Jer 34 and Neh 5 are the cases related to the manumission law and the indentured issue, which may provide partial and fragmental pictures.

> "In Israel, as in Mesopotamia, the collections of laws were edited by scribes whose object was to present the *desirable* rather than the actual and hence the gap between the laws and the legal documents, which reflected the actual reality. However, one cannot repudiate the real historical basis reflected in the pentateuchal laws of the Sabbatical year and the year of Jubilee, just as one cannot deny the actual reality standing behind the Mesopotamian laws."[189]

If these biblical laws are principally theological, didactic, idealistic, and utopian, the assertion that a later law *supersedes* or *abolishes* the former one is superfluous and questionable, unless there is evidence of such a legal edict which declares this is an amendment of supersession or abolishment. One should note that the challenge here lies on the assertion of a so-called *later law* which *supersedes* or *abolishes* a former law, not on the entire scholarly endeavors of literary transmission. As chapter one has previously discussed, legal transplants and revisions already prevailed in ancient legal writings, so that a law that is revised, reworked, or innovated could occur at any time for a community to voice its new or supplemental perspective.

Discerning the Similarities and Differences between Dt 15 and Lev 25 with the Legal Categorizational System

Lev 25 adopts similar linguistic features with Dt 15 and also emphasizes humanitarian concerns and fraternity for Hebrew/Israelite indebted slaves. The rationale behind Lev 25 is built upon a social protective system for the poor Israelites, rather than a forty-nine years long debt-service. Lev 25 emphasizes that the Jubilee is the final recourse of this social protective system. Based on the Sabbatical rest in the Jubilee year, it is not necessary to assume that the release meant only for male slaves. The intent of the regulation concerning the acquisition of permanent slaves in Lev 25 is not to abolish that of Dt 15 and Ex 21, but to stress that permanent slaves that the Israelites desire to bequeath to their children as *inherited property* can only be acquired from non-Israelites. Conclusively, Lev 25 does not denote a different type of debt-slave, but the same as that of Dt 15 and Ex 21.

In summary, the legal topic of Lev 25 remains the same with Dt 15 and Ex 21, *Debt-servitude*, as Lev 25 shares some basic legal issues with them—demanding

---

189 Moshe Weinfeld, "Sabbatical Year and Jubilee in the Pentateuchal Laws and Their Ancient Near Eastern Background," in *Law in the Bible and in Its Environment* (ed. Timo Veijola; Göttingen: Vandenhoeck & Ruprecht, 1990), 42–43.

the release of Hebrew/Israelite debt slaves as well as benign treatments to them. Similarly, Lev 25 appears to have vague positions (the release upon seven years is unmentioned, and only the case of the male slave with his children is mentioned) and certain issues are emphasized (the Hebrew indebted slave should work as a *resident hireling*, and permanent slaves of *inherited property* should be acquired from non-Israelites). Lev 25, Dt 15, and Ex 21 parallel one another in terms of the legal topic of *Debt-servitude* and the legal issue of Hebrew indebted slave manumission. However, they are not *closely* parallel with one another.

Summary and Conclusion

From the above assessment, several significant points about reading and interpreting biblical laws can be made.

First, the second person in legislative texts represents multiple levels of referents. In the Mosaic speech context, the second person, singular or plural, mostly indicates the "Israelite" as the Covenant people. In a legal relationship, the second person may be addressed to specific event characters, such as the creditor and the legal administrator. In a social relationship, the second person often addresses those who are blessed by YHWH with more power, in an attempt to arouse empathy and sympathy for the less privileged. Rhetorically, an address in the second person enhances the laws to speak directly to audiences of any era.

Second, the polyvocality of the combined discourses demonstrate that Dt 15 and Ex 21 maintain the same attitude concerning regulations of permanent slaves. By reading the biblical laws as narratives, we read the underprivileged's attitudes and minds as the lawgiver speaks. The combined discourses expound the lawgiver's intention to help readers understand his attitude toward the underprivileged and his concern about human rights. Likewise, Lev 25 uses another rhetorical skill to present the same concern. The three destitute stages begin with the persuasive mode of pathos, (when your brother becomes poor) and the four occurrences of "with you" that repeatedly sways a listener's heart, to share the sympathy with the lawgiver toward the poor brother.

Third, the female slaves indicated in Exod 21:7–11 and Deut 15:12–18 are different. In light of this, the female release should not be compared as parallel between these two passages. A better approach may be to read Exod 21:2–6 and 7–11 as two separate laws but under the same group of subject matter of slavery.

Fourth, misinterpretations of the laws result from partially studying the law with merely one verse, rather than appreciating the law with its entire context. This is seen in the discussions concerning the change of viewpoints from buyer to seller, assertions that the laws destroy the marriage concept and family ties, that male slaves can be used for reproduction, or that the laws protect only the owner's profit, etc. A biblical law should be read as a whole.

Fifth, the legal categorizational system provides a tangible way to demarcate the degrees of similarity and difference, which contributes to the field of comparative legal study. With a measurement of the similarities and differences between laws, what value one law promotes and what interest it protects may be understood in the law's own terms, which enables us to objectively evaluate the argument of duplication or abolishment. To assert abolishment or abrogation by merely scholarly consensus without any clear or standard criterion is questionable. The definition of such an assertion has rarely been clarified. Mostly, when scholars presume literary dependency between the laws or posit specific historical setting behind them, this assertion appears to be the only way to resolve the differences. However, based upon comparative studies with the legal categorizational system, these three laws can be understood in another manner: (1) That they have the same *legal topic* of *Debt-servitude*, (2) That their primary *legal issue* concerns the same one regarding Hebrew debt slave manumission, and (3) That their *legal style* (casuistic primary law) and *substance* (release with various conditions) are similar. They are parallel in certain aspects but in their different details, they are not closely parallel.

This section has attempted to distinguish and explain the differences and similarities within the context of each law/passage in Ex 21, Dt, 15, and Lev 25. Not only do these three laws aim to protect the socially weak, they also connote strong humanitarian concerns that are neglected in the similar ANE slave laws, which will be the subject of exploration in the next chapter.

4 Comparative Studies of ANE Slave Laws

Stipulations concerning the slave in ANE law collections are more plentiful and complicated than the biblical variety. The previous two chapters have shown that all three biblical slave laws share one common legal issue: the manumission of a Hebrew debt-slave (except Exod 21:7–11). In comparison, a broad range of ANE laws touch upon slave matters with regard to social class, personal status, property, trading, loan, and pledge.

This chapter will explore and submit that, the concept and situation of ANE laws in contrast to the biblical data are completely different. When examples of legal topics, issues, and situations are compared between the ANE and biblical slave laws one recognizes that the humanitarian concerns emphasized in the biblical slave laws is absent in their ANE counterparts.

At the outset, the investigation here will introduce the terminology for *slave* in various ANE languages and the slave systems in the ANE to avoid misinterpreting different legal conditions. Thereafter, it will proceed to investigate the grouping methods of ANE laws. The second section will survey and sort out a variety of ANE slave laws and laws related to slave issues in order to distinguish debt-slave laws from other slave provisions. The third step will compare the matter of slavery between the ANE and the modern worlds. Lastly, the fourth section will then compare and contrast biblical and ANE slave laws with the legal categorizational system.

Before examining the ANE laws, some comparative considerations between ANE and biblical laws should be briefly illustrated. J. J. Finkelstein's monograph *The Ox that Gored* proposes several substantial principles for comparative legal studies between ANE and biblical laws. According to him, three salient points regarding a comparative study between ANE and biblical laws should be note:[1]

(1) It should remain neutral as to the degree of "reality" represented by these laws. In other words, the question of whether any given case ever occurred, was likely to occur, or even *could* occur should be ignored.

(2) It should disregard the issue of enforcement, namely, the question of whether the norms represented by these cases were ever forced, or they were intended or possibly to be enforced.

(3) It should avoid deliberations with respect to the actual purpose and function of these laws in their original social and historical contexts. The concern

---

1 J. J. Finkelstein, *The Ox That Gored* (Philadelphia: The American Philosophical Society, 1981), 7–20.

should center on conceptual framework and moral standard implied in the normative prescriptions which these law collections explicitly set out.[2]

With respect to any given legal topic in Sumerian or Akkadian, there are considerable variations both in substantive legal prescription and in expansiveness or economy of expressions. Even so, the range of topics and the phraseology employed remains relatively uniform throughout these legal corpora.[3] Similarly, although the scope of the laws in the Covenant law book is extremely limited, in comparison with the cuneiform legal corpora, much of its substance reflects the legal thoughts and expressions of much earlier time, possibly even earlier than the Mosaic era itself (i. e., thirteenth – twelfth centuries B.C.).[4] Hence, the comparative study on the single topic of slave law between the ANE and the biblical legal corpora is legitimately comparable. The legal thoughts, the expressions, and the values and interests that the laws promoted and protected will still be at the center stage of the following discussion.

Terminology of Slave and the Slave Systems in the ANE

There is some confusion and misunderstanding in the previous works concerning the terminology and the categorization of ANE slaves. In the past, the distinction of ANE slaves was based on the ideas of redemption from a cultural anthropological perspective,[5] by which two kinds of slaves are defined—debt slave and chattel slave. A debt slave refers to a temporary slave, who is eligible for redemption, while a chattel slave refers to a permanent slave, who retains no individual right of redemption.[6] However, recent studies show that this categorization overlooks the complexity of the ANE slave and economic issues, and thus do not fairly reflects the ANE "slave system." E. D. Lago and C. Katsari propose the term "slave system" to refer to the complexity of slavery. "Slave system" expresses an institution based on the "slave mode of production" and a system of labor—in the economic and society of those regions, countries, and states that were interconnected parts of unified market area. (Hereafter, we will adopt

---

2 Ibid., 16.
3 Ibid., 18.
4 Ibid., 17.
5 Ignace J. Gelb, "Definition and Discussion of Slavery and Serfdom," *UF* 11 (1980): 283–284.
6 R. Thurnwald, "Sklave," in *Reallexikon der Vorgeschichte, XII* (ed. Max Ebert; Berlin: W. de Gruyter, 1928), 210–212; Bernard J. Siegel, "Some Methodological Considerations for a Comparative Study of Slavery," *American Anthropologist, n. s.,* 49, no. 3 (1947): 357–392.

"slave system" to denote the slave institutions of the ANE).[7] To portray a vivid picture of slave history, the terminology of *slave* in the ANE languages will be discussed. Thereafter, some recent studies on ANE slaves will be synthesized to uncover additional forms of *human bondage*. Slavery is a form of human bondage that is assumed to be the major social blot to human rights; however, it is not the only way to deprive humans of freedom and dignity. A more faithful description of other forms of human bondage in the ANE laws will be presented to demonstrate the fundamental problem of disrespect for human rights.

The Terms for Slave in the ANE

In some ANE languages, the term "slave" is not reserved for a bounded slave only. In ancient Mesopotamia, the terms for male slave (Akk. *wardu*; Sum. *urdu*, *ìr*) and female slave (Akk. *amtu*; Sum. *géme*) are also used to designate individuals who practice various occupations that are socially inferior in position. For example, officials are called "slaves," high-officials are called "slaves" of the king, and kings themselves are known as "slaves" of a god.[8] In particular, royal courtiers are referred as "the gentlemen, slaves of the king." Even "slave of the

---

7 E. D. Lago and C. Katsari suggest that historians and historical sociologists have commonly used the term "system" to describe a complex set of factors that allowed the economy and society of a particular culture to operate. Depending on the time and place, a "system" would be defined by the existence of specific sets of relationships between different economic operators (such as elites, laborers, or merchants) and between them and different types of institutions (such as the state, the king or emperor, the banks, etc). Dal Lago Enrico and Constantina Katsari, "The Study of Ancient and Modern Slave Systems: Setting an Agenda for Comparison," in *Slave Systems: Ancient and Modern.* (ed. Enrico Dal Lago and Constantina Katsari; Cambridge: Cambridge University Press, 2008), 3–5

8 Ignace J. Gelb, "Quantitative Evaluation of Slavery and Serfdom," in *Kramer Anniversary Volume: Cuneiform Studies in Honor of Samuel Noah Kramer* (ed. Barry L. Eichler, Jane W. Heimerdinger, and Åke W. Sjöberg; Verlag Butzon & Bercker Kevelaer: Neukirchener Verlag Neukirchen-Vluyn, 1976), 196; idem, "Definition and Discussion of Slavery and Serfdom," *UF* 11 (1980): 284. See also Raymond Westbrook, "Mesopotamia: Old Babylonian Period," in *A History of Ancient Near Eastern Law* (ed. Raymond Westbrook; vol. 1; Leiden: E. J. Brill, 2003), 380; Kathryn Slanski, "Mesopotamia: Middle Babylonian Period," in *A History of Ancient Near Eastern Law* (ed. Raymond Westbrook; vol. 1; Leiden: E. J. Brill, 2003), 486; Carlo Zaccagnini, "Mesopotamia: Nuzi," in *A History of Ancient Near Eastern Law* (ed. Raymond Westbrook; vol. 1; Leiden: E. J. Brill, 2003), 584. In administrative documents, the same term *geme* is used to refer to female workers, not necessarily slaves. See Bertrand Lafont, and Raymond Westbrook, "Mesopotamia: Neo-Sumerian Period (UR III)," in *A History of Ancient Near Eastern Law* (ed. Raymond Westbrook; vol. 1; Leiden: E. J. Brill, 2003), 198.

palace" might sometimes refer to a free man who is in the service of the king. The term "slave" is also used as a modest form of self-reference.[9]

This is similar to the usage of the Hebrew עֶבֶד, which may serve to be a denotation of slave or servant of a master, a king, or God, or to be a humble self-reference.[10] I. J. Gelb indicates the difficulty of classifying slaves in the ANE:[11]

> The term 'slave' can be discussed, but not defined. The ancient codes which treat so extensively of the institution of slavery, never bothered to define it, probably because it was impossible to do so. This is true of the Sumerian, Babylonian, and Assyrian laws, as it is of the Hittite laws and the Old Testament.

For example, Gelb notes some Mesopotamian instances in which a man sold himself, his wife, or children into slavery where these people are not considered to be in the same category as chattel slaves who can be bought or sold again. They are called "slave" just like the individuals sold for indebtedness or held as pledges for debts.[12]

In addition to the ambiguity of defining a slave, the characteristics of chattel slave vary according to areas and periods. Gelb indicates that chattel slaves are employed full-time in a menial domestic capacity constituting a minor labor force in the "primitive societies" of ancient Mesopotamian. They are mainly found in the private sector, in the Ancient Near East, Mycenaean and Homeric Greece, later Sparta, India, China, etc., but in productive type of force in Athens, Rome, and Americas.[13]

M. A. Dandamaev also observes that while slaves were largely foreigners (particularly war captives) only a small number of them were turned into chattel slaves. The rest were settled on the land as palace and temple serfs.[14] The serfs, although closely akin to slaves, occupied an intermediate position between freeman and slaves. They were the major force in state and temple households in Egypt, Asia Minor, Mesopotamia, and Achaemenid Iran. However, in later periods the role of such labor force decreased appreciably (especially from the third and the second millennia), while the role of slave labor increased in

---

9 Westbrook, "Mesopotamia: Old Babylonian Period," 380.

10 For example, officials (Gen 40:20; 2Kgs 22:12), YHWH's servants and prophets (Deut 9:27; 24:29; 34:5; Ps 18:1; Isa 20:3; Job 1:8; Jer 7:25), self-reference (Gen 33:14; 2 Sam 26:18 – 19), and the special Servant (in Isaiah 42 – 53).

11 Ignace J. Gelb, "Definition and Discussion of Slavery and Serfdom," *UF* 11 (1980): 283.

12 Gelb, "Definition and Discussion of Slavery and Serfdom," 284.

13 Ibid., 294.

14 In the later periods, prisoners of war were more widely used in the construction of canals and the building of roads, palaces, and temples. Dandamaev, "Slavery," *ABD* 6:59.

importance.[15] Therefore, a comparison of the number of the semi-free serfs to that of chattel slaves in ANE is relatively negligible.[16]

Bearing in mind the above information, one should circumspectly observe the divergent social backgrounds and slave categories in the comparison of ANE slave laws. Due to the copious amount of scholarship on this topic and the space limit of this study,[17] the legal topics and issues in this study will be primarily limited to those laws that correspond to the biblical slave laws, i.e., debt-servitude, escaped slave, and chattel slave.

The Roles of the Household and Merchant in the Economic and Slave Systems

To study the ANE slave systems, we should first explain what "household" (Sumerian *é*; Akkadian, *bîtum*) means. In the third millennium B. C., the new style of city-states of Sumer replaced the earlier urban style of temple-towns and rose in the river-valleys of Middle and Northern Mesopotamia.[18] A country of city-states usually had a fortified city which seated the central government, some smaller towns with some administrative bodies around, and a larger number of scattered household communities.[19] As a result, the inhabitants rarely lived and worked within a unit of a nuclear family (i.e., father, wife, and children). Rather, the operating unit was that of a *household* (including not only the nucle-

---

15 Dandamaev, *ABD* 6:58.

16 Ignace J. Gelb, "Quantitative Evaluation of Slavery and Serfdom," in *Kramer Anniversary Volume: Cuneiform Studies in Honor of Samuel Noah Kramer* (ed. Barry L. Eichler, Jane W. Heimerdinger, and Åke W. Sjöberg; Kevelaer: Verlag Butzon & Bercker, 1976), 195.

17 Isaac Mendelsohn, *Legal Aspects of Slavery in Babylonia, Assyria and Palestine: A Comparative Study (3000 – 500 B.C.)* (Williamsport: Bayard, 1932); idem, *Slavery in the Ancient Near East: A Comparative Study of Slavery in Babylonia, Assyria, Syria, and Palestine from Middle of the Third Millennium to the End of the First Millennium* (Westport: Greenwood Press, 1978); Muhammad A. Dandamaev, *Slavery in Babylonia: From Nabopolassar to Alexander the Great (626 – 331 B.C.)* (ed. Marvin A. Powell and David B. Weisberg; trans. Victoria A. Powell; DeKalb: Northern Illinois University Press, 1984); idem, "Slavery," *ABD* 6:58 – 65; Gregory C. Chirichigno, "The Social Background to Debt-Slavery in Mesopotamia," in *Debt-Slavery in Israel and the Ancient Near East* (Sheffield: JSOT, 1993), 30 – 54;

18 Chirichigno, *Debt-Slavery in Israel and the Ancient Near East*, 31– 32. See also Adam Falkenstein, *The Sumerian Temple City* (Los Angeles: Undena, 1974), 3 – 21.

19 Falkenstein, *The Sumerian Temple City*, 4.

ar family but also other relatives and work force, such as grandparents, uncles, cousins, hired labors, debt-slaves, and chattel slaves).[20]

According to Gelb, this picture probably did not change much even after the unification of the state in the Sargonic period. The only difference was that there became one capital city and fifty cities with provincial governments. In such an economy, the capital city and the state formed a cohesive unit. The life of the state was intrinsically connected to that of the capital city. Small peasantry was part of the familial "household" communities, which were basically composed of kinship groupings.[21] Aside from small settlements of shepherds and semi-nomadic people, there may not have been any villages of independent peasants.

The term "household" was an economic unit rather than merely a residential one. It may refer not only to a small family or private unit (i.e., a larger familial household) but also to a larger public household (e.g., temple and palace). These households, both private and public, usually held lands and owned trading businesses, and hence require a significant amount of laborers for agricultural and construction works. This economic system of households therefore, necessitated slave trading and its presence in turn facilitated the slave system. This is corroborated by historical evidence where for example, beginning in the Early Dynastic and Sargonic Periods, slaves had been owned and traded by these two private and public households.[22]

The officials of the temple and palace households, who were called "merchants" (Sumerian, *dam-gar*; Akkadian, *tamkārum*), played an important role in the temple and palace economy in most periods.[23] The term "merchant" occurs in several slave laws in the Law of Hammurabi (LH 116, 118,119, and 281). These merchants were not only officials employed by the monarchy, but also private entrepreneurs. They were the agents involved in the sale of slaves in the

---

20 Ignace J. Gelb, "Household and Family in Early Mesopotamia," in *State and Temple Economy in the Ancient Near East* (ed. Edward Lipiński; vol. 1; Louvain: Departement Oriëntalistiek, 1979), 2.

21 The population that lived in the ANE was based on the concept of lineage systems that generally distinguish three stages of kinship: first, the small lineage (e.g., nuclear family); second, lineage proper (e.g., clan); third, maximal lineage (e.g., tribe). The tribe was responsible for the protection of the social and territorial rights of its inhabitants. See also Chirichigno, *Debt-Slavery in Israel and the Ancient Near East*, 32–33.

22 Gelb indicates that the two main types of households, public and private, sometimes overlap. A familial one may own its patrimonial land and household and at the same time possess the right of usufruct in public land and household. Gelb, "Household and Family in Early Mesopotamia," 4–5.

23 Chirichigno, *Debt-Slavery in Israel and the Ancient Near East*, 38.

temple and palace households, and who also used their capital assets to act on behalf of the states.[24] According to M. C. Astour's study on the merchant class of Ugarit, they belonged to the upper class owning the largest land estates, and surrounding the throne as advisors and administrators.[25] One should also know that the case of the Ugarit is quite representative of the complicated systems of slave trading, politics, and economy in the ANE.

W. W. Hallo stresses that in the early Old Babylonian period (ca. 2000–1800 B. C.), the temple economy absorbed a considerable proportion of what is called the GNP in today's understanding.[26] G. C. Chirichigno suggests that the temple, palace, and lager private households held many advantages over other smaller independent groups that brought about increases in social stratification and debt-slavery.[27] More precisely, these privileged people opened up opportunities for money-lending operations which in turn imposed burdensome monetary demands upon the disadvantaged.[28] For example, when free persons were in financial duress, they might enter into the slavery through a sale that was initiated either by their family members who had authority over them (parents or husbands) or by themselves. To examine in further detail how the ANE slave systems function, the following discussion will investigate the Early Dynastic and Sargonic periods (ca. 3000–2200 B. C.), Neo-Sumerian (ca. 2112–2002 B. C.), Old Assyrian (ca. 1950–1840 B. C.), Old Babylonian (ca. 1894–1595 B.C.), Middle Babylonian (ca. 1532–1000 B. C.), Middle Assyrian (ca. 1500–1000 B. C.), Nuzi (ca. 1450–1340 B. C.) in Mesopotamia, and the Hittite Kingdom (ca. 1650–1180 B. C.), some cases in Alalakh, Ugarit, Emar, etc. (these four areas were prosperous in Late Bronze period, during about 1500–1000 B.C.) in Anatolia & Levant.[29]

---

24 William W. Hallo, "God, King, and Man at Yale," in *State and Temple Economy in the Ancient Near East* (ed. Edward Lipiński; vol. 1; Louvain: Departement Oriëntalistiek, 1979), 103. Scholars have debated whether the Babylonian merchants, as well as the Ugarit ones are primary state agents or free entrepreneurs. See the discussion in Michael C. Astour, "The Merchant Class of Ugarit," in *Gesellschaftsklassen im Alten Zweistromland und in den angrenzenden Gebieten; XVIII. Rencontre assyriologique internationale, München, 29. Juni bis 3. Juli 1970* (ed. Dietz Otto Edzard; München: Verlag der Bayerischen Akademie der Wissenschaften, 1972), 26.
25 Astour, "The Merchant Class of Ugarit," 26.
26 Hallo, "God, King, and Man at Yale," 104.
27 Chirichigno, *Debt-Slavery in Israel and the Ancient Near East*, 35.
28 Operating money-lending business is characteristic of Babylonian merchants. Astour, "The Merchant Class of Ugarit," 26.
29 The primary reason for these selections is based on the criteria that they mostly preserve law collections and texts refer to slavery. The dates of the periods are referred from the chronological charts of Martha T. Roth, *Law Collections from Mesopotamia and Asia Minor* (Atlanta: Scholars

The Acquisition of Slaves in the ANE

The first and the most frequently mentioned type of enslavement is the sales of children by parents, typically due to debt or hardship.[30] In the Neo-Sumerian period, documents show that primarily women (especially widows) sold their children. Among some examples include: A mother and a grandmother selling a boy, fathers selling daughters, and both parents selling a son.[31] An extant document shows that a mother sold her son but died before the case was settled, which resulted in the payment going directly to the son. Since the son remained a slave, the price probably was paid out again to the mother's creditor.[32] There were also cases that one sold his wife, or relative(s).[33] Examples of selling oneself were common in most periods.[34] In a time of famine, entering slavery could be a way to ensure survival. In the Middle Assyrian period, an Assyrian girl was sold to forestall a dire situation from occurring and later redeemed.[35] In the Middle Babylonian period, a girl was purchased as a wife where part of her purchase price was food for her parents.[36]

In the ANE slave systems, child born to a female slave also belonged to her owner.[37] As a result, in Old Babylonian slave-sale documents, a slave was occasionally noted as "houseborn," which from a purchaser's perspective is a desirable status that would be less encumbered with the claims of third parties or claims of freedom.[38] There were various legal statements to assure the transactions were legal. Many slave sale documents of Emar (including cases of self-

---

Press, 1997), and Raymond Westbrook, ed., *A History of Ancient Near Eastern Law* (2 vols.; Leiden: E. J. Brill, 2003).

30 Lafont and Westbrook, "Mesopotamia: Neo-Sumerian Period (UR III)," 199; Westbrook, "Mesopotamia: Old Babylonian Period," 381; Zaccagnini, "Mesopotamia: Nuzi," 585; Sophie Lafont, "Mesopotamia: Middle Assyrian Period," in *A History of Ancient Near Eastern Law* (ed. Raymond Westbrook; vol. 1; Leiden: E. J. Brill, 2003), 531.

31 Lafont and Westbrook, "Mesopotamia: Neo-Sumerian Period (UR III)," 199.

32 Ibid., 199.

33 Westbrook, "Mesopotamia: Old Babylonian Period," 381; Zaccagnini, "Mesopotamia: Nuzi," 585.

34 Lafont and Westbrook, "Mesopotamia: Neo-Sumerian Period (UR III)," 199; Westbrook, "Mesopotamia: Old Babylonian Period," 381; Zaccagnini, "Mesopotamia: Nuzi," 585.

35 Sophie Lafont, "Mesopotamia: Middle Assyrian Period," in *A History of Ancient Near Eastern Law* (ed. Raymond Westbrook; vol. 1; Leiden: E. J. Brill, 2003), 531–532.

36 Slanski, "Mesopotamia: Middle Babylonian Period," 499.

37 Raymond Westbrook, "The Female Slave," in *Gender and Law in the Hebrew Bible and the Ancient Near East* (ed. Victor H. Matthews, Bernard M. Levinson, and Tikva Frymer-Kensky; Sheffield: Sheffield Academic Press, 1998), 220.

38 Westbrook, "Mesopotamia: Old Babylonian Period," 382.

sale and sales by others) emphasize that the transaction is voluntary. However, R. Westbrook suggests that their consent must sometimes have been fictional.[39] C. Zaccagnini describes that "[s]ales of wives, children, relatives, or oneself, due to financial duress, are a recurrent feature of the Nuzi socio-economic scene, which is characterized by an overall process of impoverishment of the peasant family groups, mainly as a result of the fiscal burden exerted by the central state apparatus."[40]

In addition to the type of family members sold due to financial difficulties, the second source of slaves came from defaulters of debts or contracts as well as criminals that were consigned to slavery by the courts. Multiple instances show that the court had the power to impose slavery as a contractual penalty on a guarantor, or a non-payment debtor.[41] There are cases where crime victims were entitled to enslave the family of the culprit.[42] In one instance, an Emar court adjudged that the thief must become a slave of the owner who suffered that loss. However, the thief instead compensated the owner by giving his sister as a slave in his place. In another Emar case, after obtaining a judgment for debt, a plaintiff appealed in front of the king, who then assigned the debtor to him as a slave.[43] Elsewhere, in adoptive contracts, a typical penalty upon the adoptee for dissolving the adoption is to be sold as a slave.[44] Such examples illustrate the possible circumstances that free persons could be enslaved when an individual became involved in a legal action.

Following this brief survey, a significant implication should be noted. In view of various economic and social factors that cause a free citizen to become a slave, the categories of slave should not be simply understood as debt slave, temporary and conditional, and chattel slave, permanent and unconditional. The redemption and termination of an enslaved *status* (not a class) depended on the *contracts* and *statuses* noted in the beginning when one enters the enslavement. Therefore, the treatment and legal status of slaves varied from contract to contract. Furthermore, slave sales are often associated with other forms of contracts: debt, loan, adoption, and marriage. That is, the sale of per-

---

39 Raymond Westbrook, "Anatolia and the Levant: Emar and Vicinity," in *A History of Ancient Near Eastern Law* (ed. Raymond Westbrook; vol. 1; Leiden: E. J. Brill, 2003), 665.
40 Zaccagnini, "Mesopotamia: Nuzi," 585.
41 Lafont and Westbrook, "Mesopotamia: Neo-Sumerian Period (UR III)," 199; Westbrook, "Mesopotamia: Old Babylonian Period," 381.
42 Ibid., 199. See also Harry A. Hoffner Jr. "Slavery and Slave Laws in Ancient Hatti and Israel," in *Israel: Ancient Kingdom or Late Invention* (ed. Daniel I. Block; Nashville: B&H, 2008), 133–134.
43 Westbrook, "Anatolia and the Levant: Emar and Vicinity," 665.
44 Westbrook, "Mesopotamia: Old Babylonian Period," 381–382.

sons may come from one of these kinds of contracts. This demonstrates that in addition to cases involving debt slave and chattel slave, other types that implicated the sale of persons could become latent forms of human bondage, which may also abuse freedom and human dignity yet have rarely been discerned. In the ensuing paragraphs, the redemption and termination of enslavement, legal status and treatment of slaves, and other categories of human bondage will be discussed.

Redemption and Termination of Enslavement

In general, if a slave sale is transacted for reasons involving a debt or a loan, redemptive conditions would be included in the contract. It thus follows that a debt slave is *contingent on the existence of the debt* and the terms may either be *fixed* or *fluid*. LH 117, a law which has long been thought as a parallel law to Exod 21:2, stipulates a fixed term of debt-servitude for three years. In the Old Assyrian period, the possible redemption is limited in time, ranging from one month to four years. After that, the debt slaves could be sold by the creditor/owner at will, even abroad if one desired to do so.[45] If the debtor failed to meet his due payment in time, he could become the owner's property as a chattel slave.[46]

Chattel slaves could also be sold due to a similarly impoverished situation, but as an *outright* sale. Even so, in the Middle Babylonian period, native born children sold by their parents were still identified as "Babylonian born," so subject to be freed by a royal decree.[47] Some cases required specific caveats to avoid claims of redemption by third parties. By implication, without such conditions a chattel slave sale could still be redeemable.[48] Certain cases indicate that the manumission of a slave means restoration to one's former owner.[49] There are a few cases where a slave has redeemed himself.[50] Although they are rare,

---

45 Klaas R. Veenhof, "Old Assyrian Period," in *A History of Ancient Near Eastern Law* (ed. Raymond Westbrook; vol. 1; Leiden: E. J. Brill, 2003), 449.

46 J. N. Postgate, *Fifty Neo-Assyrian Legal Documents* (Warminster: Aris & Phillips, 1976), 29.

47 No evidence attests that this kind of decree was ever issued. Slanski, "Mesopotamia: Middle Babylonian Period," 499–450.

48 Westbrook, "Mesopotamia: Old Babylonian Period," 382.

49 Ibid., 384.

50 Veenhof, "Old Assyrian Period," 449.

cases of manumission are attested. Westbrook indicates that in Emar, direct evidence of irredeemable chattel slaves is absent.[51]

Some Neo-Assyrian slave sale contracts demonstrate that even a chattel slave sale may not be perpetually irredeemable. However, to revoke a chattel slave contract inevitably involves a lawsuit, just as a commercial dispute today. These contracts, regardless of sale or redemption, usually follow a standard formula. Below is the formula of a slave sale contract in the Neo-Assyrian period:

> X (the buyer) has contracted and taken Y (the slave), for Z (the amount of payment)....
>
> The money is paid completely. That man/woman/those people is/are purchased and taken. Revocation, lawsuit (or) litigation are void.[52]
>
> Whoever in the future, at any time, lodges a complaint,....He shall contest in his lawsuit, but shall not succeed.[53]
>
> Likewise, the contracts for redemption follow a resemble formula,
>
> X (the redeemer/debtor) has contracted and *released* Y (the slave), for Z (the amount of payment)....
> The money is paid completely. That man/woman/those people is/are purchased and taken. Revocation, lawsuit (or) litigation are void.
> Whoever in the future, at any time, lodges a complaint, shall pay W (the amount of payment) to redeem the man.[54]

A slave redemption contract, according to K. L. Younger, Jr. and J. N. Postgate, is often characterized by the verb *paṭāru* "to set loose, to release."[55] Despite the scant examples at hand, the extant conveyances show that slave sale was common in ANE and an ANE chattel slave was not necessarily permanent and unredeemable.

---

51 Westbrook, "Anatolia and the Levant: Emar and Vicinity," 664.
52 K. Lawson Younger, Jr. "Contracts: Neo-Assyrian Contracts," in *The Context of Scripture III* (ed. William W. Hallo, and K. Lawson Younger, Jr.; New York: E. J. Brill, 2003), 258–260.
53 Younger, Jr. "Contracts: Neo-Assyrian Contracts," 258–259, 261.
54 Ibid., 260.
55 Postgate, *Fifty Neo-Assyrian Legal Documents*, 29, 49; Younger, Jr. "Contracts: Neo-Assyrian Contracts," 260. Also a private talk with K. L. Younger, Jr.

Legal Status and Treatments of Slaves

While chattel slaves are regarded as property that could be sold, hired, pledged, and inherited, they were in due time granted limited rights.[56] In the Early Dynastic and Sargonic periods, a slave could witness a contract or have the right to sell a foundling into slavery. They could also contest his or her slave status against their masters.[57] The same is true for the later Neo-Sumerian period, when a slave could appear before the court to conduct their cases, calling witnesses and testifying on their own behalf. They could conclude a valid marriage.[58] In the Hittite period, even though chattel slaves could be treated as their master wished when they were at fault, some slaves were allowed to own property and pay betrothal money (HL 34) or fine (HL 95, 97). R. Haase thus suggests that these Hittite slaves are more like "servants" or "semi-free" labors.[59]

Female chattel slaves were often regarded as special economic assets, since they could bear children.[60] They could become their masters' concubines, and if they bore children for their masters they might obtain redemption when the debts were paid.[61] In addition, female slaves sometimes could be given as gifts.[62] In the Nuzi area, female chattel slave were the objects of a flourishing foreign trade carried out by private merchants.[63]

To prevent slaves from escaping, in the Middle Assyrian period, measures including the fastening of a metal chain about the waist were allowed. A distinc-

---

56 R. Westbrook indicates that laws did not generally distinguish between social classes. A notable exception is LH, in which a distinction sometimes made between a gentleman (*awīlu*, many scholars translate this word as *free person* or *free citizen*), and a commoner (*muškēnu*). See Raymond Westbrook, "The Character of Ancient Near Eastern Law," in *A History of Ancient Near Eastern Law* (ed. Raymond Westbrook; vol. 1; Leiden: E. J. Brill, 2003), 40; idem, "Mesopotamia: Old Babylonian Period," 377–378. Roth suggests that the term *awīlu* "used for (1) the general, nonspecific, 'person' as subject of a law provision, and for (2) a member of the highest privileged class, in contrast to a member of the *muškēnu*-class or to a slave." *muškēnu* designates "a class of protected persons with lesser rights and privileges." See Roth, *Law Collections from Mesopotamia and Asia Minor*, 268.
57 Claus Wilcke, *Early Ancient Near Eastern Law*, 54; idem, "Mesopotamia: Early Dynastic and Sargonic Periods," in *A History of Ancient Near Eastern Law* (ed. Raymond Westbrook; vol. 1; Leiden: E. J. Brill, 2003), 158–160.
58 Lafont and Westbrook, "Mesopotamia: Neo-Sumerian Period (UR III)," 199.
59 Richard Haase, "Anatolia and the Levant: The Hittite Kingdom," in *A History of Ancient Near Eastern Law* (ed. Raymond Westbrook; vol. 1; Leiden: E. J. Brill, 2003), 632.
60 Westbrook, "The Female Slave," 220.
61 Westbrook, "Mesopotamia: Old Babylonian Period," 381.
62 Lafont, "Mesopotamia: Middle Assyrian Period," 531.
63 Zaccagnini, "Mesopotamia: Nuzi," 585.

tive mark called *abbuttu* is placed on slaves in Old Babylonian period. The exact nature of *abbuttu* is disputed. M. T. Roth translates it as "hairlock."[64] G. R. Driver and J. C. Miles believe this mark is branded, incised, or tattooed in the flesh, on the forehead or the hand.[65] M. E. J. Richardson interprets it "the mark of a slave."[66] Westbrook assumes it may have been a distinctive hairstyle, a brand, or a mark. He suggests that in contractual penalty clauses, such a marking often precedes the sale. Thus the mark may be an indication that the person would become a chattel slave, not subject to redemption.[67] LE 51–52 and LH 226–227 all mention the slave with *abbuttu*, and these laws show that this is a mark indicating that the slave is a property belonging to his/her master. In LE 51–52, *abbuttu* is mentioned with fetters and shackles as the essential preventative means of escape.

Some rituals are performed in acquiring and releasing slaves. In the Early Dynastic and Sargonic periods, nine sale documents attest that after the sale of persons (and possibly also of animals), one must "cross over the wooden stick (*giš-gana*)."[68] According to P. Steinkeller, this ritual symbolizes the transfer of the sold from the *protestas* of the seller to that of the buyer.[69] In one particular case where a governor that purchased from a judge a family consisting of the head, his wife, two daughters, and two brothers required the purchased slaves to practice the ritual.[70]

Pertaining to the release of a slave, there are two basic acts that are symbolically performed: the cleansing of the slave's forehead by pouring oil on his head to symbolize purification, and the breaking of a vessel to signify nullification.[71]

These rituals are different from that of Ex 21 and Dt 15, which is held when the slave is willing to become a permanent slave. The slave's voluntary participation is the key element in the performability of the ceremony. However, these ANE rituals are principally initiated by the masters.

---

64 Martha T. Roth, *Law Collections from Mesopotamia and Asia Minor* (Atlanta: Scholars Press, 1997), 124.
65 G. R. Driver and John C. Miles, *The Babylonian Laws* (vol. 1; Oxford: Clarendon, 1952), 422.
66 M. E. J. Richardson, *Hammurabi's Laws: Text, Translation and Glossary* (Sheffield: Sheffield Academic Press, 2000), 107, 137, 396.
67 Westbrook, "Mesopotamia: Old Babylonian Period," 382.
68 Piotr Steinkeller, *Sale Documents of the Ur-III-Period* (Stuttgart: F. Steiner Verlag Wiesbaden, 1989), 34–39.
69 Steinkeller, *Sale Documents of the Ur-III-Period*, 39.
70 Claus Wilcke, "Mesopotamia: Early Dynastic and Sargonic Periods," in *A History of Ancient Near Eastern Law* (ed. Raymond Westbrook; vol. 1; Leiden: E. J. Brill, 2003), 159.
71 Meir Malul, *Studies in Mesopotamian Legal Symbolism* (Neukirchen-Vluyn: Neukirchener Verlag, 1988), 40–76.

More Forms of Human Bondage

In addition to chattel slave and debt slave, there are still other kinds of human bondage. As we have observed, one could sell his/her family members or oneself into an adoption, or marriage, or to be a human pledge. An adoption can sometimes be redeemed, while a marriage sale is usually unredeemable. Strictly speaking, the taking of a person as a pledge for a debt or loan is not a sale. Rather, it is in essence bondage. A. Testart observes that debt slavery is a form of bondage that results from the debtor's insolvency. However, slavery was not the only form of bondage used to deal with insolvency. Not every bondsman/bondswoman or every insolvent debtor who was forced to work for his creditor is a slave, nor can one be considered as a slave from the mere fact of such constrain.[72] Debt could be a cause for one to become a slave, a pawn, or a labor to pay debt, yet debt was by no means the only avenue to slavery. Gambling loss could also result in these three modes of bondage.[73]

Differences between Pawning for Debt and Debt Servitude

Taking person(s) as pledges, suretyship, or into a joint liability of co-debtors for a debt/loan was common in the ANE world.[74] One of the most frequent forms of human bondage, pawning, has been confused with debt slavery in past scholarly discussions in the fields of anthropology and law. However, Testart indicates that pawning and debt slavery are two entirely different institutions in ancient world. According to him, slavery is:[75]

> an existing status that differentiates it from social categories. The legal content of this status has varied from one society to another, but is everywhere based on a common principle: in one way or another, a slave is an outcast.

---

72 A. Testart, "The Extent and Significance of Debt Slavery," *Revue française de sociologie* (Supplement: Annual English Edition) 43 (2002): 175–176.

73 Ibid., 175.

74 Raymond Westbrook, "The Old Babylonian Period," in *Security for Debt in Ancient Near Eastern Law* (ed. Raymond Westbrook, and Richard Lewis Jasnow; Leiden: E. J. Brill, 2001), 63. See also other discussions on the security in various periods in this edited book, Raymond Westbrook and Richard Lewis Jasnow, eds. *Security for Debt in Ancient Near Eastern Law* (Leiden: E. J. Brill, 2001): Klaas R. Veenhof's "The Old Assyrian Period," Katheleen Abraham's "The Middle Assyrian Period," Carlo Zaccagnini's "Nuzi," Tikav Frymer-Kensky's "Israel," Karen Radner's "The Neo-Assyrian Period," Joachim Oelsner's "The Neo-Babylonian Period," and Joseph Manning's "Demotic Papyri."

75 Testart, "The Extent and Significance of Debt Slavery," 176.

In ancient societies, a slave is excluded from both kinship ties and citizenship. Debt slavery is a situation in which a free human being barters his/her freedom for resources.[76] In this sense, a debt slave is not a free person. This is the general foundation for debt slavery takes: A debt should be guaranteed by the debtor's person. However, this security could be backed by one or more persons (i. e., his children, wife, or slaves) in the place of the debtor. Through these guarantees, such person(s) could be forced to work for the creditor.[77] At the end of one's period of slavery, the debt slave is released by a fixed or fluid term as was previously mentioned.

On the matter of pawning, Testart explains that it refers to an ancient institution which is sometimes called "hostage," or less frequently, "pledge." Pawning is decisively distinct from slavery, as a pawn is legally a free person, while a debt slave is not. In addition, a pawn is not excluded from his/her kinship structure. Pawns continue to keep their names. They retain their lineages and may still participate in lineage councils and the management of lineage affairs and rituals. They are allowed to marry and have legitimate children. Lastly, every pawned person is immediately freed upon clearing the debt.[78]

Nevertheless, pawning represents a particularly heavy form of servitude, because the pawn's labor and the services of all kinds performed by him/her do not go toward reimbursing the debt for which he/she is pawned.[79] According to Testart, the complexity of the pawn's situation is due to the fact that *legally* he/she remains a free person and they retain their place in the kinship structure with all the consequences thereby implied by enjoying kinship rights.[80] Thus, while a pawn and a debt slave may both live in the master's home, and work for his/her creditor, a pawn's labor is not counted toward clearing his/her debt.

In some Old Babylonian contracts, the legal formula clearly indicates that one party is a human pledge for a loan,[81]

A slave, X (his/her name), is given as a pledge (*ana mazzazānūtim izzaz*) from Y for Z (the amount of payment)

X has pledged himself voluntarily to Y for Z (the amount of payment). Y has paid Z (that amount of payment) for his debt (*iḫiltišu*). When X brings the silver, he may take (himself) away.

---

76 Ibid., 178.
77 Ibid., 179.
78 Ibid., 176–177.
79 Ibid., 176–177.
80 Ibid., 186.
81 Westbrook, "The Old Babylonian Period," 65.

The above investigation of such ANE slave systems provides the background for understanding the ANE slave laws and other forms of human bondage. To identify laws that may refer to other forms of human bondage from slave laws is important. In the past, slavery has been a form of human bondage seen as the most degrading towards human rights. However, other forms of human bondage may also disrespect human dignity and freedom. There are some laws in the categories of pledge, loan, debt, adoption, and marriage, which do not contain the term "slave," yet also relate to other forms of human bondage. We shall examine these forms in the following section.

The Grouping Methods of the ANE Laws

In order to survey ANE slave laws and other forms of human bondage in the ANE legal corpora and compare them with the biblical slave laws, this study summarizes the biblical and the ANE laws in a table in appendix A, "A Compilation of Biblical and Cuneiform Law Collections" (which categorizes laws from the three biblical and six cuneiform legal collections into one hundred and thirty three legal concepts, following an alphabetic order in English).[82] The table omits a few extant laws because of the damage state of some original texts (e. g., LL 20).[83] The job of sorting the laws unavoidably brings about difficulties. A certain degree of subjectivity is inevitable; however, the rearrangement process reveals several important connotations, which may contribute the field of comparative study between biblical and ANE laws.

---

[82] Neo-Babylonian Laws (LNB) are excluded in the table for the following reasons: (1) Its fifteen provisions are concerned only with the class of free person, *amēlu*. (2) The slave, *amēluttu*, is mentioned as personal property in only one law (LNB 6), but is not the subject of any law. Martha T. Roth, *Law Collections from Mesopotamia and Asia Minor* (Atlanta: Scholars Press, 1997), 144–145. In 2010 symposium, "Slaves and Households in the Near East," held by the University of Chicago, the Oriental Institute, Krisitin Kleber presented a paper, "Slave, Serf, and Freeman: A Neo-Babylonian Perspective," providing some new observations about the categories of personal status in Neo-Babylonian society, especially on the temple slave, *širkutu*. In the case of ancient Egypt, although there is little evidence for slavery in the Old Kingdom, there are apparently "unfree" persons, whose personal rights and mobility seem to have been restricted. See Richard Jasnow, "Old Kingdom and First Intermediate Period," in *A History of Ancient Near Eastern Law* (ed. Raymond Westbrook; vol. 1; Leiden: E. J. Brill, 2003), 117–118.

[83] For certain items, Hasse's categories were consulted, but some are in disagreement. There is however little difference between Hasse's chart and this research; perhaps some laws are denominated by different titles. The difference between Haase and the chart in appendix A is that Haase excludes biblical laws, which contain a large amount of religious and ritual laws. See R. Haase, *Keilschriftrechtliches* (Leonberg: Im Selbstverlag des Verfassers, 1998), 43–56.

Three categories, *Marriage, Sexual crimes and prohibitions*, and *Slave Laws*, are vital subjects in ANE daily life. In the table, they are therefore categorized with various sub-categories. For example, *Marriage* laws are listed from item numbers 64 to 72 with the *legal topics* of *Engagement and marriage contract, Slave marriage, Widow marriage*, and *Levirate marriage*. Likewise, items 110 – 114 are subject to the category of *Slave Laws*, which can be further classified into three major legal topics: *Slave escape, Slave purchase and management*, and *Debt servitude*.

Certain difficulties must be anticipated in the process of categorizing these ancient laws. One prominent issue is that some laws cannot be neatly fitted into any proper categories. For example, LH 153 concerns a woman having her husband killed on account of another male, which can be classified as "killing of a man, murder" or equally viably as "adultery." Similarly, Deut 24:1– 4 thematically is a law regarding "remarriage," but at the same time, it also relates to the issue of "divorce."[84]

The original method of grouping in the ANE law collections has its own logic. LE 54–58 is a typical example illustrating the ancient compiler's logic of how these ancient laws are grouped together.

> LE 54 *If an ox is a gorer and the ward authority so notify its owner, but he fails to* keep his ox in check *and it* gores a man *and thus causes his death*, the owner of the ox shall weight and deliver 40 shekels of silver.
> LE 55 If it gores a slave and thus causes his death, he shall weight and deliver 15 shekels of silver.
> LE 56 *If a* dog is vicious *and the ward authorities so notify its owner, but he fails to* control his dog *and it* bites a man *and caused his death*, the owner of the dog shall weight and deliver 40 shekels of silver.
> LE 57 If it bites a slave and thus causes his death, he shall weight and deliver 15 shekels of silver.
> LE 58 *If a* wall is buckling *and the ward authority so notify its owner, but he does not* reinforce his wall *and the* wall collapses *and thus causes the death* of a member of the awīlu-class—it is a capital case, it is decided by a royal edict.

LE 54–55 can be labeled as "goring ox," and LE 54–58 as "incidental death" (killed by domestic animals or incidental events), or label LE 58 as "architecture," which actually closely parallels with Deut 22:8 and LH 229. The formulaic phrases (in italics) in the above block texts show that the laws in LE 54–58 were conceptually deemed as a group by their ancient compiler. It shows that, rather

---

84 Therefore, some laws are overlapped in two legal concepts in Hasse's chart and the one of this research.

than the so called "subject matter" with certain thematic concepts, the ANE laws are also arranged by formulaic language.

Originally, LH 229 was grouped in a set of laws that concerned architecture and incidental death in LH 228–233. However, reading LH 229 within a larger context may shed a new light to the law. The group of LH 215–240 can be viewed as a series of laws with reference to commercial activities—"architecture and payment," "boat business and payment." In view of this, LH 228–233 is one of the sub-groups regarding "architecture" and its relative payment regardless of a wage, or a pecuniary recompense for an incidental death caused by construction. Another illustration indicates the significance of the formulaic phrase in grouping is HL 37 and 38:

> HL 37 If anyone elopes with a woman, and *a group of supporters* goes after them, if 3 or 2 men are killed, *there shall be no compensation.*
> HL 38 If persons are engaged in a lawsuit, and *some supporter goes* to them, if a litigant becomes furious and strikes the supporter, so that he dies, *there shall be no compensation.*

According to their subject matters, HL 37 can be identified as "kidnapping, abduction or elopement," and HL 37–38 as "accidental death." However, their original juxtaposition is certainly not because of our understanding of "accidental death," but because of the key formulaic phrase *a group of* (or *some*) *supporter(s) goes after them.* This implies that if there is a didactic purpose for the laws, it is advising people to refrain from facilitating crimes. In other words, the "formulaic phrases" in the ancient laws represent the "relational/concrete logic" that the ancient people held. They concerned "what people do" and the consequences that would occur.

The ANE laws, like the biblical laws, use a concatenation of ideas, key words, and phrases, and motifs to form smooth changes between sub-units and various topical units. These grouping devices show that some of these laws might have been orally transmitted. This has been proposed by J. Bottéro's suggestion that the ancient Mesopotamians knew such rules and passed them on by word of mouth. He asserts that "they learned and furthered the sciences in the same way that all of us learn grammar and arithmetic at a young age: by memorizing examples of conjugated verbs or declined words, and of multiplied or divided numbers."[85]

Although most laws do fall into a topically coherent order either by subject matter or formulaic phrase, still, a few appear to be abrupt. For example, LH

---

85 Jean Bottéro, *Mesopotamia: Writing, Reasoning, and the Gods* (Chicago: The University of Chicago Press, 1992), 178.

144–149 refer to various women's rights in marriage, especially for a *nadītu*. LH 148–149 concerns that if a woman becomes ill and allows her husband to marry another woman, she shall *reside* at quarters her husband constructs and her husband shall continue to support her. If she should not agree to *reside* at her husband's house, she may leave with the value of her dowry. LH 150 then shifts to the topic of a wife's inheritance right, and following this, LH 151–152 concerns a woman who is allowed to *reside* at a man's house with her husband's agreement by abiding contract and some rules about debt issues. LH 150 can be viewed as discrete if we understand it in terms of a different issue (a wife awarded property from her husband) being inserted into the group of LH 144–152, which is an illustration of a wife's right when some unfortunate things may happen in her life. One can also regard LH 144–152 as a series of laws regarding *a wife's right* no matter good or bad. This appears to be the logic as to how this group of laws is compiled.

Similarly, the controversial arrangement of Exod 21:37–22:3 [Eng. 22:1–4] may also be explained by a thematic concept or formulaic phrase in a larger context. Exod 22:1 appears to be an illogical insertion in terms of the subject matter of *theft of animal*. However, if Exod 21:37–22:3 is seen as a group which coheres under the theme of *theft* theme, then Exod 22:1 in this group is consistent with this same theme. This is the biblical example to show that a similar grouping method that is consonant with the ANE styles is in view. The logic of grouping depends on how large a context is included. One should seek to follow the ancient compiler's flow of thoughts, not ours. It is, therefore, not necessary to suppose that these biblical verses must present how a sequential event occurs with its resolutions, as D. Daube proposed.[86] U. Cassuto and B. Childs both agree to retain the sequence of MT for "the verses focus attention on the more important problem relating to theft, namely, the loss of life through a resultant act of violence. The law seeks to guard the lives of both parties involved."[87] If readers can take off such modern conceptual lenses, one would hesitate to jump to conclude that some arrangements are *illogical, random,* or later redactions.[88] Instead, one is freed to recognize that a thematic unit of laws may communicate the value and the interest that the compiler intends to promote and protect. The ensuing paragraphs will focus on slave laws and other laws related to human bondage, and

---

86 David Daube, *Studies in Biblical Law* (New York: Ktav Publishing House, 1969), 89–98.
87 See Brevard S. Childs, *The Book of Exodus* (Philadelphia: Westminster, 1974), 474. Also see U. Cassuto, *A Commentary on the Book of Exodus* (Jerusalem: Magnes, 1967), 218–283.
88 J.J. Finkelstein asserts that "these law collections were not logically organized, and the cases chosen for inclusion are often random." J. J. Finkelstein "Amisaduqa's Edict and the Babylonian Law Codes," *JCS* 15 (1961): 91.

from the groupings and arrangements one would see how Israel's ancient neighbors' viewed slaves and slavery in their own cultures and societies.

Categories and Interpretations on ANE and Biblical Slave Laws

In order to illustrate various slave laws and laws related to slaves, the laws from the table of "A Compilation of Biblical and Cuneiform Law Collections" (appendix A) are sorted, and presented with English translated texts in the table of "Biblical and ANE Laws Related to Slave Issues" (appendix B).[89] The selected "slave laws" either explicitly refer to "slave" in their wording—male slave *urdu* and female slave *géme* in Sumerian, male slave *wardu* and female slave *amtu* in Akkadian.[90]

The qualified slave laws are classified into three *legal topics: Slave Escape, Slave Purchase and Management*, and *Debt-servitude and Other Forms of Human Bondage*. Laws within the same legal topic are further distinguished into various *legal issues*. Laws will be additionally divided into various *situations*. There is an exception in that the *Slave Escape* laws are divided into two opposing positions: One promotes and protects the rights of the slave and the other guards the rights of the master.[91]

Laws of Slave Escape

The laws of *Slave Escape* can be divided into two positions: Deut 23:16–17 is the only law that is aimed at protecting a runaway slave. All other ANE *Slave Escape* laws side with the masters. In this context, *Slave Escape* laws that protect a master's right can be further classified under the following three legal issues: (1) "Rewards of Returning a Runaway Slave" (LU 17; LH 17; HL 22–24), (2) "Punishments for Not Re-

---

89 The English translation excludes those biblical texts that have been discussed in previous chapters, such as Exod 21:2–6, 7–11; Lev 25:39–55; and Deut 15:12–18, 23:16–17. The English translation of the ANE legal texts are cited from Martha T. Roth, *Law Collections from Mesopotamia and Asia Minor* (Atlanta: Scholars Press, 1997).

90 There are two Sumerian words for male slave, *urdu* and *ìr*. See Claus Wilcke, *Early ancient Near Eastern Law: A History of Its Beginnings; the Early Dynastic and Sargonic Periods* (Winona Lake: Eisenbrauns, 2007), 53.

91 Chapter three has earlier discussed laws with vague or opposing *positions*, which mostly occur in biblical laws with theological connotations. Since these kinds of vague and opposing cases are rare, a level of *position* in this categorizational system is not suggested.

turning Runaway Slave" (LL12–13; LE 49–50; LH 16, 18, 19, 20), and (3) "Prohibitions against a Slave Crossing through the Main City Gate" (LE 51, 52; LH 15).

Rewards of Returning a Runaway Slave (LU 17; LH 17; HL 22–24)
and Punishments for Not Returning Runaway Slave
(LL 12–13; LE 49–50; LH 16, 18, 19, 20)

These laws demonstrate that the ancient Mesopotamian and Hittite surroundings oppose slave-harboring. For example, LU 17, LH 17, and HL 22–24 request slave masters to provide monetary prizes (about 2–3 shekels of silver per slave) to those who return runaway slaves. The punishments for slave-harboring vary—a slave for a slave, reparation, charge of theft, or even a death penalty. The Laws of Lipit-Ishtar penalize the crime of harboring fugitive slaves in two ways: a slave for a slave or fifteen shekels of silver if the convict has no slave to give back. In the Laws of Eshnunna, harboring a runaway slave is a crime of theft (LE 50). The Laws of Hammurabi reward a person returning a fugitive slave with two shekels of silver (LH 17), while failure to do so may entail the death penalty (LH 16, LH 19). LH 20 even anticipates the situation when an apprehended runaway slave flees custody. The one who fails to return the slave has to swear an oath to the god to the slave's owner to vouch the capturer's innocence.

Prohibition against a Slave Crossing through the Main City-gate
(LE 51, 52; LH 15)

In order to prevent slave escape, these laws prohibit slave from crossing the main-city gate. LE 51, 52 addresses any slave,[92] but LH 15 addresses only the palace and commoner's slave. LE 51, 52 are prohibitions without penalty, but the one who violates LH 15 will face the death penalty. Driver and Miles explain that LH 15 is particularly strict because the offender is aiding and abetting against the king.[93]

The Laws of Hammurabi have a severe penalty with regard to the slave escape. In the following survey, one will repeatedly see that the Laws of Hammurabi sentences those who violate an owner's property right to a slave the penalty of death or other severe punishments. This is hardly a surprise in light of the evi-

---

92 Albrecht Götze, *The Laws of Eshnunna* (New Haven: Dept. of Antiquities of the Government of Iraq and the American Schools of Oriental Research, 1956), 131.
93 Driver and Miles, *The Babylonian Laws*, vol. 1, 106.

dence presented earlier in this chapter that during that period of time, slave trade was a prosperous business in the temple and palace households, and slaves were regarded as merchandise to merchants and as property to the owners. The lawgivers apparently positioned with the slave traders and owners to protect their own economic interests.

The Grouping and Arrangement of Slave Escape Laws

LU 17, LH 17, and HL 22–24 are the laws of "Rewards of Returning a Runaway Slave." LU 17 is located in the group of LU 8–28, where each law features the formulaic phrase, "weigh and deliver." It is thus obvious that the law is in a group that concerns payments.[94] For example, LU expresses no interest in slave's right, but only about payments in various situations.

In this study, although the laws of LH 15–20 are classified into three slave issues, they are in fact arranged in a series of sequential scenes of the escape of a slave.

- LH 15 relates to the issue of assisting a slave in escape (e.g., crossing the main-city gate).
- LH 16 concerns slave-harboring.
- LH17 rewards a person who returns a fugitive slave.
- LH 18 further regulates the situation if the seized slave refuses to identify his owner.
- LH 19 reiterates the death penalty for the one who retains and possesses the seized slave.
- LH 20 covers the contingency of a slave slipping away during the custody of the person who has seized him.

In the larger context, LH 14–24 can be considered as a group of laws that deal with critical criminal offenses. LH 14 is about kidnapping, LH 15–20 is a series of laws about slave escape, LH 21 concerns burglary, and LH 21–24 relates to robbery. The sentence for kidnapping, assisting and harboring a runaway slave, break-in, and robbery are all punished by death. It shows that slave-harboring is as serious a crime as that of kidnapping or robbery in the eyes of the lawgiver and the society.

Likewise, HL 22–24, the preceding laws of HL 19–21 (Rewards of Returning Runaway Slave), is a group of laws pertaining to abduction. This also demon-

---

94 The Laws of Ur-Namma contains about thirty laws. Among them, about twenty have this formulaic phrase.

strates that slave escape is regarded as a heinous crime. LL12–14 (LL12–13, Punishments for Not Returning Runaway Slave) can also be identified as a small group of laws that concerns slave escape. The arrangement of LL 12–14 is noticeably similar to those of LH 15–20 and LH 278–282, which will be discussed in the next section. There is also a law (LL 14) regarding a slave who contests his slave status against his master. Unlike LH 18 and LH 282 (in which both laws have the slaves listed as defendants), LL 14 discusses a different scenario.[95] This arrangement of LL12–14 may imply the reason for slave escape: A master could have already received a payment of redemption yet refused to release a slave. The probable cause behind this group of laws may drive its listeners to think of injustice. LE 49–52 is also a group of laws that tackles the issue of slave escape. However, there is no clear connection between these laws and the laws surrounding them. The only possible connection may be compensational reparation, which is always the most pivotal concern in ANE laws.

Slave Purchase and Management

The laws under the topic of *Slave Purchase and Management* are concerned with seven primary legal issues: (1) Discipline of a Rebellious Slave (LU 25–26, HL173b), (2) Unlawfully Taking Possession of a Slave (LE 40, LH 7), (3) Protection of a Slave Purchaser's Right" (LH 278–282, MAL C+G1),[96] (4) Violations against Another Person's Slave Property Rights and Punishments (LU 8, LE 31, Lev 19:20–22, LH 199, Exod 21:20–21, 26–27, LH 205, LH 226–227, LE 55, 57, LH 252, Exod 21:32, LH 231, LL f, and LH 213–214), (5) Marital Issues Related to a Slave (LU 4–5; HL 31–36, 175; LH 146–147), (6) Adoption Related to a Slave Woman (LE 33–35), and (7) Special Cases of Slave Release (LL 14, 25–26).

Further examination of these seven legal issues reveals further details. For example, under "Violations against Another Man's Slave Property Rights and Punishments," there are nine situations regarding this issue: (1) Raping another man's female slave (LU 8, LE 31), (2) Sexual intercourse with another man's betrothed slave woman (Lev 19:20–22), (3) Injuring another man's slave (LH 199), (4) Injuring one's own slave (Exod 21:20–21, 26–27), (5) Injuring of a free man by a slave (LH 205), (6) Intentionally and unintentionally cutting off a slave's hairlock (LH 226–227), (7) Incidental death of a slave caused by an animal biting or

---

95 LL 14 will be further discussed in the legal topic of slave purchase and management.
96 MAL C+G1 contains broken texts but from some of the terms, it can be identified as a similar law about the right of a slave buyer.

goring (LE 55, 57, LH 252, and Exod 21:32), (8) Incidental death of a slave caused by a builder's negligence (LH 231), (9) Incidental miscarriage or death of a slave woman caused by striking (LL f; LH 213–214).

Under "Marital Issues Related to a Slave," (the fifth item), two different situations are covered (1) Slave marriages to different social classes (LU 4–5; HL 31–36, 175), and (2) A slave woman bearing children in place of her mistress (LH 146–147).

Discipline of a Rebellious Slave (LU 25–26, HL173b)

On the disciplining of rebellious slaves, LU 25 specifically concerns a situation when a female slave curses someone who acts under the authority of her mistress—she is to be punished by scouring her mouth with one sila of salt. LU 26 is about a slave woman who strikes the person under the authority of her mistress.[97] HL 173b stipulates that if a slave rebels against his owner, he shall go into a clay jar. These three laws show that slaves are expected to be submissive while rebellious behaviors against persons or owners in the positions of authoritative will be subject to discipline by severe treatments.

Unlawfully Taking Possession of a Slave (LE 40; LH 7)

LE 40 and LH 7 are classified as "unlawful taking possession of a slave," but they can also be put into the category of *theft*, because in both laws, a slave is listed among other merchant items such as—animals (e.g., ox, sheep, donkey), and metals (e.g., gold, silver). These two laws concern a buyer who cannot provide proof or contract of his purchase, under which such a failure constitutes proof of theft. Similar to the issue of harboring a slave in LE 50 (where regards slave-harboring as theft, but provides no punishment) and LH 17 (in which regulates slave-harboring is a capital crime), LE and LH each follows their own legal logic and principles of punishment: LE 40 also claims that without a proof of slave purchase, it is a behavior of theft yet does not provide punishment. According to LH 7, the one who holds a slave without purchasing proof should be sentenced to death.

---

97 The following text is broken.

Protection of a Slave Purchaser's Right (LH 278–282; MAL C+G1)

LH 278–282 is a group of stipulations that protect the rights of a slave buyer. They are similar to the modern concept of protection for the consumer's right. For example, LH 278 provides for a situation where a man who buys a slave or a slave woman who is unfortunately befallen by epilepsy after the purchase. If the purchase is made within the one-month period, the buyer can return the slave to his seller and the buyer can get full refund of the original price.[98] In another law, LH 279 pertains to the satisfaction of a slave sale: If a buyer has a claim on the slave he purchases, the seller should satisfy the claim.

LH 280–281 is a set of laws regarding international slave trading and protection for the slave dealer's right when he buys slave(s) from abroad (possibly from a foreign dealer):[99] If the dealer A is traveling within the territory of that country, the original owner B of the slave(s) identifies the slave(s) as his property and the slave(s) are the natives of this country, the slave(s) shall be released without any payment. However, if the slaves are natives of another country, the dealer A shall declare before the god(s) the amount of the silver that he weigh, and the original owner B shall give the amount of the silver to the dealer A so that B can redeem his slaves.[100] In this sense, LH 280–281 can be reckoned as the forerunner of international commercial disputes today. The slave(s) could be runaway or stolen from the original owner B and be traded to the market with the coincidence that the dealer A happened to buy him/her from the market. This law shows that slave trading was a well developed market in ancient Mesopotamia.

A vital issue that cannot be overlooked in ancient slave trade is the purchase contract or proof. LH 282 is a law pertaining to a slave who denies his master's ownership. If a charge was filed against the slave's denial and it was proven, his master shall cut off his ear. Concerning this law, Driver and Miles discuss wheth-

---

98 M. E. J. Richardson' translation of LH 278, "If a man has bought a slave or a slave girl and, before they have finished the first month, sickness has struck them down, he shall return them to the seller and the purchaser shall take back any silver he has paid." M. E. J. Richardson, *Hammurabi's Laws: Text, Translation and Glossary* (Sheffield: Sheffield Academic Press, 2000), 117.

99 In LH 282, the law calls the man "the merchant."

100 Driver and Milers have a different interpretation about this law. They regard the term *mārū mātim* as "native Babylonian," so the slaves have to be released without payment. However, the meaning of the term, according to Roth and Richardson, is merely "native inhabitant." In addition, the context also shows that the differences of dealing these situations are mainly based on whether the slave is a native of the country where the buyer is currently staying or if the slave is a native of another country. See Roth, *Law Collections from Mesopotamia and Asia Minor*, 132; Richardson, *Hammurabi's Laws*, 220; Driver and Miles, *The Babylonian Laws*, vol. 1, 482–489.

er LH 282 is to be read as a part of LH 280 – 281.[101] Although LH 282 and LH 280 – 281 seem to be heterogeneous, the laws in the last group of the Laws of Hammurabi, LH 278 – 282, do share some similar features. These last four laws, 278, 279, 280 – 281, and 282, not only have *slaves* as their common subject matter, but also the theme of protection for the slave purchaser's right. For example, there is an implication in LH 282 of the possibility of a slave daring to refuse his master's ownership of him because he thinks that his master does not keep his sale contract.

Violations against Another Person's Slave Property Rights and Punishments (LU 8, LE 31, Lev 19:20 – 22, LH 19, Exod 21:20 – 21, 26 – 27, LH 205, LH 226 – 227, LE 55, 57, LH 252, Exod 21:32, LH 231, LL f; LH 213 – 214)

The laws regarding "Violations against Another Man's Slave Property Rights and Punishments" can be classified into these diverse categories: sexual offense, injury, and accidental, and incidental death. These stipulations apparently indicate that the ANE laws regard slaves as property and their concerns are mostly about the master's property right.

Raping Another Man's Female Slave (LU 8; LE 31)

LU 8 and LE 31 address a common problem of raping another person's female slave. Should this happen, the offender shall weigh and deliver five shekels (LU 8) or twenty shekels (LE 31) of silver as compensation for the master. The difference between these two is that LU 8 notes that the slave woman is a virgin, while LE 31 stresses that the female slave remains the property of the master. Both laws parallel other cases in their own law books (LU 6 and LE 26 respectively), but the parallel ones concern the rape of a freeman's daughter who is betrothed. The two cases of LU 6 and LE 26 also both carry a death sentence. Other analogous stipulations in various ANE law collections (such as LH 130 and MAL A 12), show that the crime of raping a betrothed woman is always punishable by death. Raping a female slave carries a fine of five shekels of silver, but raping a freeman's daughter leads to capital punishment. In the first case, raping a slave woman is regarded as a tort. These laws show that a slave is mostly regarded as chattel in ANE laws.[102]

---

101 Driver and Miles, *The Babylonian Laws*, vol. 1, 482, 489 – 490.
102 Jacob Milgrom, *Leviticus 17 – 22: A New Translation with Introduction and Commentary* (New York: Doubleday, 2000), 1665.

Sexual Intercourse with Another Man's Betrothed Slave Woman (Lev 19:20 – 22)
The law of Lev 19:20 – 22 addresses a man who has sexual intercourse with a betrothed slave woman. In this case, the man and the slave woman should not be
put to death, because she has not yet been released. The man is required to bring
guilt offering to YHWH and the priest shall make atonement for him and his sin
will then be forgiven.[103] B. A. Levine suggests that Exod 21:7 – 11 is the legal background for this law that accounts for situations where Israelite girls were sold by
their fathers due to extreme deprivation. When the girl reaches a marriageable
age, her master was required to do one of the three things: marrying her himself,
designating her as his son's wife, or allowing her to be redeemed. The last option
provides the possibility that she could be redeemed by another man who wished
to take her as wife. For Levine, the girl is called שִׁפְחָה (a female slave, previously
discussed in chapter three) which refers to an Israelite female slave. This situation is the background to Lev 19:20 – 22.[104]

Upon review, though Levine's suggestion is plausible, it is not clear if the
slave woman exclusively denotes an Israelite girl. The text itself provides the
legal background: Due to the ambiguous status of this slave girl (who is betrothed but not yet been freed), her owner has no right to receive compensation.[105]
Her status also contributes to the man's lenient punishment, being spared the
death penalty.[106]

Scholars have long noticed that the betrothed slave girl is not considered to
be as blameworthy as her paramour. M. F. Rooker illustrates the possible pathos
of the slave girl:[107]

> Being a slave, the woman may have felt she had little recourse in resisting a male who was
> a freeman and thus more powerful both in social and economic spheres. That the freeman
> must bear responsibility is suggested by the fact that the female slave was not required to
> bring the guilt offering sacrifice.

N. Kiuchi suggests that the slave girl is regarded as the possession of another
man who has betrothed her, so her behavior does not constitute adultery. The of-
fence is expiated by offering the reparation offering for what is in view is the

---

103 For some biblical scholars, this law has often been regarded as an insertion of P material in
H. See Milgrom's discussion. Ibid., 1665 – 1677. See also Erhard S. Gerstenberger, *Leviticus: A
Commentary* (Louisville: Westminster John Knox, 1996), 274.
104 Baruch A. Levine, *Leviticus* (Philadelphia: Jewish Publication Society, 1989), 131.
105 John E. Hartley, *Leviticus* (Dallas: Word, 1992), 319.
106 Nobuyoshi Kiuchi, *Leviticus* (Downers Grove: InterVarsity, 2007), 356.
107 Mark F. Rooker, *Leviticus* (Nashville: Broadman & Holman, 2000), 260.

breaking of an oath between the slave girl and her finance.[108] In spite of this, Lev 19:20 – 22 cannot be counted as a parallel law to the previous raping case in LU 8 and LE 31. LU 8 and LE 31 can be viewed as parallel; Lev 19:20 – 21, on the other hand, is not.

Injuring Another Man's Slave (LH 199)

LH 199 addresses a man who blinds the eye or breaks the bone of another man's slave. If it happens, he shall compensate one-half of that slave's value to the owner. However, a similar damage that is incurred on another man (who is not a slave) in LH 196 – 197 leads to *lex talionis* (an eye for an eye). For an injured slave, the offender has to pay only reparation.

Injuring One's Own Slave (Exod 21:20 – 21, 26 – 27)

While Exod 21:20 – 21 claims to punish an Israelite master who strikes a slave to death, there is ambiguity regarding the punishment. N. Sarna indicates that according to rabbinic tradition, the stem of the verb נקם means the death penalty, which is also supported by the witness of the SP, and should be read as מוֹת יוּמָת (he should be put to death).[109] The law further suggests: Should the beaten slave survive the next day, considering that some further conditions may arise so that the master's striking may not be the direct cause to kill the slave. The master thus avoids being accused as a murderer. On the other hand, striking a slave to death at the scene signifies that the owner intends to kill, so his behavior should be regarded as a crime.

The group of laws in Exod 21:23 – 28 has been considered to be the type of *lex talionis*.[110] However, the punishment in Exod 21:26 – 27 applies neither the principle of *lex talionis* nor the general pecuniary compensation in the way that most ANE laws do with regard to a slave who has been injured by his master or other third parties.[111] Exod 21:26 – 27 goes beyond *lex talionis:* It commands the master

---

108 Kiuchi, *Leviticus*, 319.

109 Nahum M. Sarna, *Exodus* (New York: the Jewish Publication Society, 1991), 124.

110 See Bernard S. Jackson, "Problem of Exod 21:22– 5, lus Talionis." *VT* 23, no. 3 (1973): 273 – 304; John Van Seters, "Some Observations on the lex Talionis in Exod 21:23 – 25," in *Recht und Ethos im Alten Testament–Gestalt und Wirkung: Festschrift für Horst Seebass zum 65. Geburtstag* (ed. Stefan Beyerle, Günter Mayer, and Hans Strauss. Neukirchen-Vluyn: Neukirchener, 1999), 27 – 37.

111 Shalom M. Paul, "The Laws of the Book of the Covenant," in *Studies in the Book of the Covenant in the Light of Cuneiform and Biblical Law* (Leiden: E. J. Brill, 1970), 77–78.

to *release* the injured slave while also recognizing that because the slave is the owner's בְּכַסְפּוֹ (Exod 21:23–28) the owner himself could not be punished. However, outside of Israel, the release of an injured slave is an idea that most ANE slave owners would never have considered. In the ANE surroundings (as seen in LH 199), a slave's injury is regarded as a matter of property damage, which requires only pecuniary compensation. B. S. Childs points out that the law obviously seeks to prevent any kind of mistreatment towards slaves by lumping together all injuries indiscriminately. Here the slave is thus regarded as "an oppressed human being." For this reason the loss of a tooth represents an act of abuse as well as the loss of an eye. [112]

The laws of Exod 21:20–21 and 26–27 express the highest ethics concerning the treatment of slave that even a chattel slave should be treated as a person, rather than as a property.[113] This law attests that, in addition to the Hebrew slave manumission laws of Ex 21, Lev 25, and Dt 15, the biblical slave laws over all possess a higher humanitarian respect for them as human beings than their ANE counterparts.

Injuring of a Free Man by a Slave (LH 205)
LH 205 regulates that if a slave strikes another man's cheek, his ear shall be cut off. This punishment is severe in order to prevent slaves from being disobedient.

Intentional and Unintentional Cutting off a Slave's Hairlock (LH 226–227)
LH 226–227 mentions scenarios of the intentional and unintentional cutting of a slave's hairlock. Without the consent of the slave's owner, the barber who cuts off the slave's hairlock shall have his hand be cut off. If the barber acts on some wrong information, then that man who misleads the barber shall be killed and hung. The barber shall be released upon his oath that "I didn't knowingly shave it off." Ostensibly, this law protects a slave master's property right, because the hairlock is the sign for identifying a chattel slave. In the modern legal sense, the law represents the idea of preventing arrogation. The severity of the punishment allows us to understand the strength of the Laws of Hammurabi with regard to the protection of one's slave property right.

---

112 Brevard S. Childs, *The Book of Exodus: A Critical, Theological Commentary* (Philadelphia: Westminster 1974), 473.

113 J. H. C. Wright notes, "[n]o other ancient Near Eastern law has been found that holds a master to account for the treatment of his own slaves'. H. Christopher Wright, *Old Testament Ethics for the People of God* (Downers Grove: InterVarsity Press, 2004), 292.

Incidental Death of a Slave Caused by an Animal Biting or Goring
(LE 55, 57; LH 252; Exod 21:32)

LE 55, 57; LH 252; and Exod 21:32 have an analogous legal issue. Regarding a slave who is bitten by an animal and thus causes the slave's death (by a dog in LE 57 and by a known goring ox in LE 55, LH 252 and Exod 21:32). LE 55 and LE 57 both demand the owner of the ox or dog to pay fifteen shekels of silver to the slave's owner, while LH 252 asks the ox's owner to pay twenty shekels of silver. However, in Exod 21:32, in addition to a payment of thirty shekels of silver, it requires that the animal shall be stoned.

The mention of the fate of the goring ox in Exodus stands out, given that its ANE counterparts have no such concern.[114] To euthanize the goring ox that kills a human being is the primary treatment in the biblical laws concerning these cases. Exod 21:28–32 particularly distinguishes two circumstances: (1) Exod 21:28 refers to an accidental case, therefore no punishment is to be meted on its owner. (2) In Exod 21:29–32, where the incident is regarded as a crime. Here, the emphasis is on when the owner is aware of the potential danger, but he still does not confine the known gorer. In this case, he is an intentional murderer, and is liable of negligent homicide. He is to be sentenced to death or if a כֹּפֶר (ransom) is demanded, he shall pay it to redeem his life. A. Phillips notices that כֹּפֶר "is only mentioned once in the *Mishpatim* when an ox known by its owner to have a propensity to gore kills a man or a woman (Ex. 21:30)."[115]

These above cases can be compared to Exod 21:12, which concerns a person who strikes an individual so that he dies, the punishment to the striker being death. If the larger context of Exod 21:12–36 is considered, it provides a better understanding and context to the command in Exod 21:32 where the ox that gores a slave is stoned to death. Here, Exod 21:12 serves as an introductory law that presents the spirit for the following laws: Whoever intentionally causes a loss of human life, regardless of their social status; the only just punishment is death. Therefore, in the laws that concern striking a slave that leads to death and a human being killed by a known goring ox, the killers (the master or the known gorer) have to be put to death. Phillips notes that "[t]he fact that under biblical law, even death caused by an animal requires exaction of the death penalty, confirms its mandatory nature."[116] Exodus possesses the same central value as Deuteronomy promotes for its law book: the protection of human life.

---

114 The detailed comparative study between the cuneiform and biblical versions of the laws of the goring ox is found in J. J. Finkelstein's discussion. Finkelstein, *The Ox That Gored*, 20–39.
115 Anthony Phillips, "The Decalogue: Ancient Israel's Criminal Law," *JJS* 34, no. 1 (1983): 12.
116 Ibid., 12.

The ANE laws on the other hand advocate a well-established pecuniary system of compensation in dealing with various disputes (including slave issues). When a known goring ox kills a freeman, both LE 54 and LH 252 (the circumstances of LE 54–55 and LH 251–252 are exactly parallel) simply count it as an accident. The penalty is the same pecuniary compensation as when the victim is a slave, only the amounts are higher—forty shekels of silver in LE 54 and thirty in LH 251. There is neither concern between distinctions of intentional or unintentional of killing, nor of the treatment of the animal that kills.

Based on their concern for the same legal issue (slave management) and similarity of situations (a slave's death caused by a known goring ox), LE 55, 57; LH 252; and Exod 21:32 may be the *closely parallel* laws between biblical and ANE slave laws.

Yet, in spite of these close parallels, the biblical laws regarding the goring ox definitely speak to something higher that promotes an inner value that is to be upheld: They distinguish "criminal intent" between the intentional and unintentional killing of a *human life* by an ox,[117] as well as even a *slave's* life.[118] Finkelstein observes that from the goring ox cases, the biblical view strikingly contrasts with its ANE neighbors. According to Finkelstein, "[i]n Mesopotamia no qualitative discontinuity was perceived between the phenomenon of man and any other phenomena of the natural universe."[119] However, "[i]n the biblical view whatever concerns man belongs to a realm of experience that is *qualitatively* removed from, and superior to, anything involving the rest of the experiential universe. The biblical laws of the goring ox offer an eloquent statement of this distinctive world view."[120]

Incidental Death of a Slave Caused by a Builder's Negligence (LH 231)

This law belongs to a set of law (LH 228–233) which is concerned the incidental death caused by a builder's unsound work. The punishments are varied: If the victim is a householder, the builder shall be killed (LH 229). If it causes the death of a householder's son, the builder's son shall be killed (LH 230). In LH

---

117 Num 35:6–34; Deut 4:41–42; 19:1–13.

118 A. Phillips suggests that "ancient Israel distinguished between crimes and torts, the former always demanding the exaction of the death penalty by the community, the latter payment of damages to the injured party." Phillips, "The Decalogue: Ancient Israel's Criminal Law," 1. See also his discussion in *Ancient Israel's Criminal Law: A New Approach to the Decalogue* (Oxford: Basil Blackwell, 1970), 158–159.

119 Finkelstein, *The Ox That Gored*, 39

120 Ibid., 39.

231, when the victim is a slave, the law asks the builder to pay the householder a slave of comparable value for the dead slave. This law again shows that the ANE laws typically switch sentences from capital crime to pecuniary compensations when the victim of death or injury is a slave.

Incidental Miscarriage or Death of a Slave Woman Caused by Striking (LL f; LH 213–214)

LL f and LH 213–214 are similar laws regarding a man who strikes another man's pregnant slave woman and thereby causes a miscarriage or death of the slave woman. Should this occur, that man shall pay five (in LL f) or two shekels (in LH 213) of silver for the death of the fetus and twenty shekels of silver if that slave woman dies (in LH 214). If a similar circumstance occurs to a commoner-class's pregnant wife, the offender will be fined a higher sum, five and thirty shekels of silver, for her fetus and her life, respectively (in LH 211–212). However, if the similar circumstance occurs to a freeman's woman/daughter and she dies, the punishment applies the principles of *lex talionis* (in LL e and in MAL A 50, that man shall be killed; in LH 210, that man's daughter shall be killed).[121]

The case of *accidental* miscarriage in Exod 21:22–24 does not include a slave woman. There the punishment depends on the situation: If the only loss is the fetus, the one responsible shall be fined as the woman's husband demands and the judges determine. If there is any further injury on this woman, the punishment is by the principles of *lex talionis*.[122] One should note that Exod 21:22 arises in a particular scenario when two men in scuffle inadvertently strike a pregnant woman. None of the above ANE laws of miscarriage mention such a special circumstance. Most of the protases of these ANE laws start with "if a

---

121 Other similar ANE laws regarding miscarriage, such as SLEx 1–2; MAL A 21, 50–52 also express no concerns of slave women. SLEx stands for the abbreviation of "A Sumerian Laws Exercise Tablet." See Roth, *Law Collections from Mesopotamia and Asia Minor*, 42–43. SLEx 1–2 concerns two different situations—if a man "jostles" and if a man "strikes" another man's daughter and causes miscarriage. The case of "jostle" will be fined 10 shekels of silver, and the case of "strike" 20 shekels of silver. MAL A 21, 50–52, the man who strikes a woman and causes a miscarriage in different social classes/status (e. g., the *awīlu*-class in MAL A 21, a prostitute in MAL 52) will be punished with different amounts of money according to the circumstance. In MAL A 50, the man pays a fine for the fetus and his wife shall be treated the same as the victim of the case. If that woman dies, the man shall be killed.
122 Discussions about the interpretations and problems between the case of miscarriage and the application of principles of *lex talionis* see E. A. Speiser, "Stem *PLL* in Hebrew," *JBL* 82, no. 3 (1963): 301–306; Paul, "The Laws of the Book of the Covenant," 70–76; and Bernard S. Jackson, "Problem of Exod 21:22–5 (ius talionis)," *VT* 23, no. 3 (1973): 273–304.

man strikes another man's wife/woman/daughter." These ANE laws give an impression that the harm is without a cause. MAL A 51 states, "if a man strikes another man's wife who does not raise her child, causing her to abort her fetus, it is a punishable offense; he shall give 7,200 shekels of lead." It seems that a man can rightfully strike another man's pregnant wife for her irresponsible motherhood. Although the principles of punishment in Exod 21:22–24 appear to be similar to the ANE laws, the biblical law obviously does not directly reproduce these foreign laws. Rather, it distinguishes "criminal intent" (i.e., intentional and unintentional) in events regarding the loss of a human life and infuses its own considerations here. (See also laws in Exod 21:18–19, 20–21, 28–36; Num 35: 9–28; Deut 4:41–43; 19:1–13).

Marital Issues Related to a Slave (LU 4–5; HL 31–36, 175; LH 146–147)

While marriage is a common and important issue, only the Hittite Laws (HL 31–36) provide a group of marriage laws that involves either a male slave or female slave. However, earlier in this chapter, it was stated that the slaves in the Hittite Laws may not be considered a pawn or a labor working to pay off one's debt, but as semi-free servants. Under this legal issue, there are two situations that relate to slaves: slave marriages to different social classes, and a slave woman bearing children in the place of her mistress.

Slave Marriages to Different Social Classes (LU 4–5; HL 31–36, HL 175)

LU 4 and LU 5 regulate a male slave's marriage under two different circumstances: LU 4 applies when he marries a female slave and LU 5 becomes effective when if he marries a native woman. LU 4 regulates that the female slave cannot be released with him on account of this marriage. This is probably due to their different individual contracts or may be similar to the situation in Exod 21:3–4 where the wife is provided by his master. LU 5 seems to command that the male slave and native woman couple shall place one male child in the service of his master and he becomes his master's paternal estate. Following the broken text,[123] it further explains that "a child of the native woman will not be owned by the master, he will be pressed into slavery."

HL 31–36 is a group of marital laws that involves slaves. It belongs to a larger group of marriage issues in HL 26–36. The statement of the law in HL 31 reads more like a story than a law. It begins with a Hollywood-like love story but ends

---

123 LU 5 contains some broken text in the middle of the law.

with a sad divorce. A free man and a female slave fall in love and live together. They marry, make a house, and have children. But afterwards they either become estranged or each finds a new marriage partner, and so they separate. According to the law, "they shall divide the house equally, and the man shall take the children, with the woman taking one child." Though story-like, the subject matter of this law in fact is not about a marriage or a slave, but a divorce settlement. This law provides an ideal concept rather than a law that must be reinforced, because it assumes that the couple has more than one child, and so each can take at least one child when they divorce. However, there is a detail in this law that promotes equality in this marriage of unequals (in class/status) that is prominent—both parties have an equal right to take children and the common property they have had during their marriage. Though the texts of HL 32–33 are broken, their content can be inferred. They appear to share the same principle as HL 31. HL 32 seems to address the situation of a divorce between a male slave and a free woman while, HL 33 concerns a divorce that occurs between a male slave and a female slave.

While HL 31–33 proposes an equal spirit of sharing property and children in divorce, they do not mention whether this marriage changes the socio-economic class of the slave. HL 34–36 provides further information about unequal class marriages but the texts are not clear. HL 34 appears to say that when a male slave marries a slave woman, she would still remain in slavery. R. Hasse translates HL 34 "a steward" rather than "a slave," and notes that HL 35 has two different versions. His translated version of HL 35 is "if a shepherd or a 'steward' abducts a free woman and does not give the betrothal payment, she will become unfree after three years."[124] The version of HL 35 that Roth translates is "if a herdsman [takes] a free woman [in marriage], she will become a slave for (only) 3 years."[125] The text in HL 36 reads "[i]f a slave man takes a free young man and acquires him as a son-in-law, no one shall free him from slavery." Similar to HL 35, HL 175 mentions that "if either a shepherd or a foreman takes a free woman in marriage, she will become a slave after either two or four years. They shall ... her children, but no one shall seize their belts."

These laws appear to declare that a marriage would not change one's class or status as a slave, whereby the slave moves upward in standing. However, when a free woman marries a slave, a herdsman, a shepherd, or a foreman

---

Haase, "Anatolia and the Levant: The Hittite Kingdom," 634.

The reader shall note that full square brackets [ ] mark restorations to broken text in the original, while the parentheses ( ) enclose material added into the English translation. See Roth, *Law Collections from Mesopotamia and Asia Minor*, 222, and 239 n. 26.

(who is a semi-free man),[126] she would become a slave. In HL 34–36, there is no statement regarding whether a free man who marries a slave woman would result in his status or class being changed. It is possible that when a freeman buys a female slave as wife, it automatically belongs to the domain of a different set of laws. The arrangement of the group of laws in HL 31–36 is interesting and it may explain why this group of laws begins with a *romantic* statement: "If a free man and a female slave are lovers and...." It may be a more *emotionally engaging* reminder for a free woman to be careful of choosing to marry a slave man. The cost means that her social status changes while that of her slave husband remains. Unless the couple is true lovers, HL 31–36 seems to discourage a free woman from marrying a slave man.

A Slave Woman Bearing Children in Place of Her Mistress (LH 146–147)

LH 146–147 is a law that recalls to mind the story of Sarah and Hagar in Genesis 16:

> If a man marries a *nadītu* (priestess) and she gives a slave woman to her husband,[127] and the slave woman then bears children, after which that slave woman aspires to equal status with her mistress—because she bore children, her mistress will not sell her; the mistress shall place upon her the slave-hairlock, and she shall reckon her with the slave women. If the slave woman does not bear children, her mistress shall sell her.

This law suggests a similar spirit that was observed earlier on the marital issue—that bearing a child would not promote the slave woman's status, hence she would remain in the same slave status and be required to signify this in the hairlock.

Adoption Related to a Slave Woman (LE 33–35)

LE 33 is a law regarding a slave woman that defrauds her child's adopter and gives her child to someone else. When this child grows up and should the adopter (master) find the child, the adopter shall seize and take that child away. The circumstance and background surrounding LE 34–35 however is ambiguous. It appears to describe a slave woman of the palace who gives her children to a com-

---

126 Haase, "Anatolia and the Levant: The Hittite Kingdom," 634.
127 *Nadītu*, "[a] member of a group or class of Old Babylonian temple dedicatees, with special inheritance privileges and economic freedoms; some groups lived in cloisters or compounds, others married but were not permitted to bear children; Sumerian lukur." Roth, *Law Collections from Mesopotamia and Asia Minor*, 271.

moner for adoption—that when this occurs, the palace shall remove the son or daughter she gave from the roll. In turn, the adopter shall restore the equal value of the child for the palace. These adoptive laws appear to express the idea that children born to a slave woman in a palace belong to the property of the palace, which holds the right to sell them or give them to be adopted.

Special Cases of Slave Release (LL 14, 25–26)

LL 14 and LL 25–26 provide those rare but significant examples that show there still exist some ANE slave laws that concern the slave's rights and protection. LL 14 states that if a slave contests his bonded status against his master whereby it is proven that his master has been compensated for his slavery two-fold, that slave shall be freed. On the other hand, the LL 25–26 is concerned about the issue of "inheritance" rather than that of the slave: that if a man's married wife and his slave woman both bear him a child, then the slave woman shall be freed and his estate shall not be divided between the slave woman's child versus the children of the master. However, if his wife dies and then he marries the slave woman who had borne him children, then the children of the slave woman is considered equal to a native free-born children and they can share the estate. During the Sumerian period, LL25 indicates that a slave woman could be freed by bearing children for his master.

The Grouping and Arrangement of Slave Purchase and Management Laws

As a whole, the Laws of Hammurabi, as well as the Hittite Laws, are two structured and organized law books. The latter contains fourteen legal topics.[128] The laws regarding slave purchases and management are diverse, ranging from categories such as payment, theft, tort, marriage, and adoption. The only two large groups with a clear slave theme that belong to LH and HL are: "Protection of Slave Purchaser's Right" in LH 278–282, and "Slave Marriage with Different Social Classes" in HL 31–36.

With regard to the first group, Driver and Miles believe that LH 278–282 has a slight connection with the group of laws that precede it (i.e., LH 268–273), which concern the hire of men and the rent of beasts in agriculture. LH 274 addresses the wages of craftsmen, while LH 275–277 regulates the renting of ships. However, there is a marked absence of regulations on a general law of sale (which is the most striking omission from these law collections), Driver and

---

128 See Roth's discussion. Roth, *Law Collections from Mesopotamia and Asia Minor*, 215.

Miles suggest that while there is perhaps a certain *familiaritas* between sale and hire, the connection between the set of slave laws in LH 278–282 with its preceding groups is weak. The final groups in LH 268–282 are added as an appendix to the main body of the Laws.[129]

A final large section of the Laws of Hammurabi, LH 215–282, has one obvious and major topic—commercial laws for free professionals and businesses. They are broken down into the following: LH 215–225 deals with physician and medical businesses, LH 226–227 for barbers, LH 228–233 for builder and construction, LH 234–240 boat manufacture and business, 241–252 ox rental business (250–252 are laws of ox goring), 253–277 agricultural workers hiring and animal renting, and the last group, 278–282 the dealer and the purchase of slave trade. The slave sale in this law book is thus one of many business matters addressed. The inclusion of slave sale in commercial laws demonstrates that the Laws of Hammurabi considers the slave sale as a significant economic activity. However, no humanitarian concerns for slaves are found in the ANE slave purchase and management laws.

Debt Servitude and Other Forms of Human Bondage

In past sociological and anthropological studies, the line between debt servitude and pawning (human pledge) was blurred. The same situation also occurs in comparative legal studies of the ANE and biblical laws. For example, LH 114–119 have been wrongly identified as a group of debt-slave laws and subsequently misused to conduct comparative studies with the biblical slave laws, such as Exod 21:2–11.[130] Among them, LH 117 is commonly considered as the prototype of Exod 21:2. In spite of the fact that G. C. Chirichigno has distinguished LH 114–116 as the laws about human pledge from LH 117–119 in his 1993 publication,

---

129 Driver and Miles, *The Babylonian Laws*, vol. 1, 478–479.

130 I. Mendelsohn, "The Conditional Sale into Slavery of Free-Born Daughters in Nuzi and the Law of Ex. 21: 7–11," *JAOS* 55, no. 2 (1935): 194; Henri Cazelles, *Études sur le code de l'alliance* (Paris: Letouzey et Ané, 1946), 150; Robert North, *Sociology of the Biblical Jubilee* (Rome: Pontifical Biblical Institute, 1954), 59–60; Hans Jochen Boecker, *Law and the Administration of Justice in the Old Testament and Ancient East* (Minneapolis: Augsburg 1980), 158–159; Innocenzo Cardellini, *Die biblischen Sklaven-Gesetze im Lichte des keilschriftlichen Sklavenrechts: Ein Beitrag zur Tradition, Überlieferung und Redaktion der alttestamentlichen Rechtstexte* (Königstein: Peter Hanstein Verlag, 1981), 245–246;

Debt-Slavery in Israel and the Ancient Near East,[131] his effort did not completely dissuade old scholarly perceptions (e. g. D. P. Wright still assumes that LH 114 – 119 is a set of debt servitude laws in his most recent book, *Inventing God's Law*).[132]

Debt servitude, human distraint, and human pledge are three different types of methods that implicate people with a debt to pay or loan to offer. Before we proceed further, the above terms will be defined.

Distraint, in general legal usage, refers to "the seizure of another's property to secure the performance of a duty"[133] while a pledge is "a bailment or other deposit of personal property to a creditor as security for a debt or obligation."[134] A human distraint is to be taken *after* a loan is foreclosed, while a human pledge is taken *at or before* the commencement of a loan. Individuals who enter into any of these three kinds of contracts that involve degrees of human bondage usually live and work in the creditor's house for a certain length of term depending on the stipulations of the debt or loan. When a person is taken into debt-servitude, his service pays off the debt. Hence, when his service term is due, he can be re-leased without any further payment. Sociologically, he or she is temporary alien-ated with his/her family and kinship linage. On the other hand, human distraint and pledge are different from debt-servitude. Their redemption depends on the *loan or debt being repaid*, but not on *the service at the creditor's house*. Socially, they however remain linked to their family and kinship lineage. Westbrook de-scribes its nature as follows [italics mine]:

> At first sight, the situation of a free person given in pledge to a creditor was identical to slavery: the pledge lost his personal freedom and was required to serve the creditor, who exploited the pledge's labor. *Nonetheless,* the relationship between pledge and pledge hold-er remained one of contract, not property. Since the creditor did not own the pledge, he could not alienate him, nor did property of the pledge automatically vest in the creditor. It was in the nature of a pledge that it could be redeemed by payment of the debt, at which point the human pledge would go free. During the period of his service, *failure by the pledge to fulfill his duties led to contractual penalties, not punishment under the general disciplinary powers of a master.*

---

131 Driver and Miles also distinguish 113 – 116 and 117 – 119 as two different sets of laws. See Chirichigno, *Debt-Slavery in Israel and the Ancient Near East*, 61 – 72; Driver and Miles, *The Babylonian Laws*, vol. 1, 209.
132 David P. Wright, *Inventing God's Law: How the Covenant Code of the Bible Used and Revised the Laws of Hammurabi* (New York: Oxford University Press, 2009), 151.
133 "Distress," *Black's Law Dictionary*, 487.
134 "Pledge," *Black's Law Dictionary*, 1175.

Therefore, one should note that persons who enter into either one of these forms of human bondage would not become the property of the creditor, but human distraint and pledge could potentially become the creditor's property when the debt/loan fails to be paid off. These are the three forms of human bondage that prevail in ANE world and laws. Previously, scholars uncovered and distinguished them by the detection of certain specific phrases of *loan* or *debt*. There are other laws that contain no such specific phrases, yet are embedded in the contexts of laws that address human distraint or pledge. Since the detection of specific phrases has its limits; therefore, in addition to searching for specific terms, this study suggests paying equal attention to the contexts of the laws (that describes relationships regarding debt security, debt, debtor, and creditor). Following this proposal, a categorization of such laws in appendix B in the table "Biblical and ANE Laws Related to Slave Issues" shows the following:
–   LE 22–24 and LH 114–116 are laws regarding human distraint.
–   LH 117 is the only ANE debt-servitude law.
–   LH 118–119 more likely concern human pledge by nature, which is similar with other human pledge laws in MAL A 39, 44, 48; C+G 2–3, 7.

In the following section, these above laws will be discussed in detail.

Human Distraint (LE 22–24; LH 114–116)

LE 22–24 are laws that have not been included in the category of human distraint in previous discussions. An analysis shows that LE 22 does not have the key verb *nepûm* (to distrain) as used in LE 23–24, while the immediate context indicates that this is a controversial case about illegal human distraint as found in LH 114. It addresses the case of an individual that is not implicated in a debt relationship, yet illegally takes the other man's slave woman. In such a case, the slave woman's owner shall swear no claim against him and then the distrainer shall compensate the value of the slave woman to the distrainee. LE 23 envisages that if this kind of illegal distraint occurred and the slave woman dies in that man's house, then the illegal distrainer shall replace her with two slave women to the distrainee. LE 24 also addresses a similar circumstance to LE 23. The only distinction is that the distrainee in view is a commoner. In this case, the illegal distraint becomes a capital offense.

LH 114–116 is a series of laws about illegally and legally taking a human distraint (*nipûtum*) on an account of debt dispute. LH 114 concerns the case of a man who takes another man's family member as distraint that is not implicated in a debt relationship. In this case, that distrainer shall be fined twenty shekels of silver to be paid to the distrainee. LH 115–116 discusses the treatments of a legal distraint's death under two special circumstances—when the distraint dies due to natural causes or to physical abuse during his residency in the distrainer's house.

While Chirichigno distinguishes LH 114–116 from LH 117–119 as laws that concern the seizing of human distraint, he also sees that both groups of laws envisage the defaulting of a *ḫubullûm* loan.[135] According to Driver and Miles, *ḫubullûm* "denotes not a mere loan of accommodation but an advance for some commercial purpose such as a loan of money or grain to enable a farmer to sow his land for the following harvest."[136] J. Huehnergard understands *ḫubullûm* to be a debt with interest.[137] Though the real nature of this loan may be unknown, from the description of these laws and the usage of *nipûtum* in LH 114–116, one should understand that LH 114–119 deals with three different methods of resolving a loan:

– LH 114–116 concerns various controversial scenarios of taking human distraint.
– LH 117 refers to debt-servitude.
– LH 118–119 is another option to make the loan by surrendering the debtor's slaves as pledge.

From the above observation, one sees that the common concern of LH 114–119 is that they deal with the relationship between debt security, debt, debtor, and creditor in various situations.

Debt-servitude (LH 117)

LH 117 states that if a man is indebted and thus puts his wife, his son, or his daughter into a *kiššātim* (debt-servitude),[138] they shall serve in their buyer's house for three years and then released in the fourth year. Similar to the Hebrew indebted slave laws in Dt 15, Ex 21, and Lev 25, the debt slave in LH 117 works for a certain period of time to pay off his/her debt.

---

135 Chirichigno, *Debt-Slavery in Israel and the Ancient Near East*, 61.
136 Regarding this loan, see Driver and Miles, *The Babylonian Laws*, vol. 1, 209–210, and Chirichigno, *Debt-Slavery in Israel and the Ancient Near East*, 61–62.
137 Huehnergard, John. *A Grammar of Akkadian* (Winona Lake: Eisenbrauns, 1997), 497.
138 *kiššātim* occurs only in plural form. Roth and J. Huehnergard both understand this word as "debt-servitude." Richardson considers it as "bound-service" See, Roth, *Law Collections from Mesopotamia and Asia Minor*, 103; Huehnergard, John. *A Grammar of Akkadian* (Winona Lake: Eisenbrauns, 1997), 502; Richardson, *Hammurabi's Laws*, 79.

Human Pledge (LH 118–119; MAL A 39, 44, 48; C+G 2–3, 7)

In LH 118, if the debtor in the same indebted situation of LH 117 yet gives a male or female slave as a replacement of his family members, the merchant has the right to extend the term and sell the debtor's slave. The next law, LH 119 envisages another circumstance: if the slave woman that the debtor gives has already borne him children, the master of the slave woman shall return that money that the merchant has lent him and redeem his slave woman. These two laws appear to be the sub-cases of LH 117.[139]

Based on their key terms, Chirichigno divides LH 117–119 into two types of loan—*kiššātim* and *kaspim*. LH 117 is the type of *kiššātim* that the debtor's dependents work in the creditor's house to pay off the debt toward their release in the fourth year. Although LH 118 also mentions the type of debt servitude with *kiššātim*, instead of his dependents, the debtor sells his slaves into the debt servitude for *kaspim* (lit., money, silver), which constitutes a *kaspim* loan. The right of a *kaspim* loan that is warranted to the merchant implies that upon the sale, he has assumed the possession of the slave that is sold. Unless the debtor pays off his debt and redeems the slave by the due date, the merchant may legally exercise ownership as he wills.[140] Nonetheless Chirichigno concludes that while the two transactions are different, the ultimate outcomes may be the same since in both cases there is the possibility that the debtor would never be able to redeem his family members.[141] Chirichigno's conclusion about the outcomes of these two types of loan is inconsistent with his distinction between them.

For example, if LH 117 involves debt-servitude, the debt slave would work in the creditor's house to pay off the debt. A debt slave in principle would not become the creditor's property during the term of service. To pay off a debt to redeem one's debt security occurs only in cases of surrendered pledges or distraints, but not in the cases of debt-servitude. LH 117–119 do not explicitly explain that it is due to the nature of different loans that requires different types of debt security, or that it is different loans that warrants creditors or merchants to have different rights. Given that LH 118 indicates that the merchant can extend the term and has the right to sell the slave and that LH 119 implies that the debt-security is taken at the commencement of the loan, the slaves surrendered in this loan are a human pledge in nature. The laws tell their readers that the debtor can choose the ways in which he prefers to pay off his debts,

---

139 Theophile J. Meek, "A New Interpreation of Code of Hammurabi §§ 117–119," *JNES* 7, no. 3 (1948): 180–183.
140 Chirichigno, *Debt-Slavery in Israel and the Ancient Near East*, 69–71.
141 Ibid., 71–72.

be it to surrender whatever he has under debt-security or some other means. Even if these laws refer to different loans, the debtor's can still choose options such as debt-servitude and human pledge, or giving his slaves to work to pay off debt (but risk losing his slave property when he cannot pay off the debt by foreclosure). This should be the prime message that LH 117–119 promote.

Other laws such as MAL A 39, 44, 48; C+G 2–3, 7 all regulate human pledges. However, based on the term *šapartu* (pledge), Chirichigno includes MAL A 44, C+G 2–3, 7 to be in this category,[142] and indicates that these laws belong to another kind of human pledge for a *šapartu* loan. He suggests that MAL A 44, C+G 2–3, 7 deals with the treatment of human pledges who have either been acquired by the creditor after the foreclosure of a *šapartu* loan or those who are in residency as pledges in a creditor's house.[143]

In fact, MAL A 39 and 48 both mention taking a human pledge, using the same term *šaparte* (pledge) as in MAL A 44.[144] The major concern of MAL A 39, 44, 48 is the legal position of persons who have been pledged due to a debt.[145] According to P. Koschaker, the verbal root *šapāru* (to send), used as a legal form, denotes a thing or a person "being sent" to the house of the creditor. He suggests that this kind of loan is similar to a "pawn" in English, and thus the creditor holds the hypothec.[146] Although A 39 and 48 each have complicated conditions, they both present a similar circumstance in which a creditor has given or intends to give a girl as a pledge to someone to be a wife (with subsequent legal problems).

Elsewhere, A 44 also treats the issue of a human pledge. Unlike Koschaker, Driver and Miles categorize A 39 and 44 as the same form of loan, *kī šaparte*, and A 48 as *kī ḫubulli*.[147] They conclude that "it appears that in these laws, when it is that a pledge is residing in the creditor's house, it must be presumed that he is in fact there and in the possession of the pledge."[148] As one surveys the previous arguments, this dispute regarding the types of loans may never come to a unan-

---

142 Ibid., 72–85.

143 Chirichigno suggests that in the *ḫubullûm* loan, a distraint is not seized until a loan is foreclosed by the debtor, but the *šapartu* loan contracts a human pledge that is generally taken by the creditor at the commencement of a loan transition to be a substitute security for a loan. Chirichigno, *Debt-Slavery in Israel and the Ancient Near East*, 72–73.

144 "šaparte," *CAD* 17:428–430.

145 Godfrey Rolles Driver and John C. Miles, *The Assyrian Laws* (Darmstadt: Scientia Verlag Aalen, 1975), 271.

146 Paul Koschaker, *Neue keilschriftliche Rechtsurkunden aus der El-Amarna-Zeit* (Leipzig: S. Hirzel, 1928), 96–116; See also "šapāru," *CAD* 17:430–449.

147 Driver and Miles, *The Assyrian Laws*, 271–273.

148 Ibid., 273.

imous agreement. However, the message of these laws is clear: A 39 and 48 both imply that when the debt is foreclosed, the distraint would become the property of the creditor, and the latter has the right to sell or deal with the fate of the distraint, including marry a girl distraint to a man.

The Grouping and Arrangement of Debt-Servitude and Human Bondage Laws
Three salient points may be drawn from the above examinations on the ANE laws of debt-servitude and human bondage:

(1) Among the ANE slave laws, only LH 117 deals with debt-servitude, in which the family members work off debt and have to be released after a three-year service. LH 118 implies that if it is *a slave* who steps in to replace his debt-master in the same indenture of *kiššātim* as in LH 117, the term of service yet can be extended and he/she may be sold. Therefore, even though LH 118 uses *kiššātim*, it is not a debt-servitude in a real sense. It means that *a slave* who enters *kiššātim* will become a pawn (human pledge).

(2) Other laws related to debt either address human distraint (e. g., LE 22–24; LH 114–116, 118–119) or human pledge (e. g., MAL A 39, 44, 48; C+G 2–3). These laws are pessimistic because such individuals may eventually become the creditors' property and be sold.

(3) The nature of various loans (detected through studying usages of specific terms) do not sufficiently explain the nature of loans in these laws even though numerous scholars such as Driver and Miles, Chirichigno and others have made attempts. These laws mainly concern the relationship between debt, debt-security, debtor, and creditor, but not about the types of loan.

Among these laws, LH 114–119 can be classified as those that pertain to debt. The fact that LH 117 is arranged in the midst of LH 114–119 signifies that the compiler considers debt servitude as a viable solution to resolving debts. People may have options to decide the solutions to their debts. On the other hand, if viewed from a larger context, LE 22–24 can be counted as part of LE 19–24, a set of laws about loan and interest.

MAL A laws deal almost exclusively with females who are victims or principals.[149] However, the issue of slavery is not the main concern in the Middle Assyrian Laws. Yet, even when some of these laws do not directly address slave issues, these human distraint and pledge laws may be sufficiently influential in their application to adversely affect human dignity and freedom.

---

149 Roth, *Law Collections from Mesopotamia and Asia Minor*, 153.

Discerning the Similarities and Differences between ANE and Biblical Slave Laws with the Legal Categorizational System

As we conclude this study, we see that biblical versus ANE slave laws are in fact quite different. Though they may contain some of the same legal topics, they have completely different positions, legal issues, or situations in view.

For example, Deut 23:16 – 17 holds a completely different position to the rest of the ANE slave laws where it opposes to the entire ANE concept and the laws in the legal topic of *Slave Escape*. Regarding *Slave Purchase and Management*, though three biblical laws (i.e., Lev 19:20 – 22, Exod 21:20 – 21, 26 – 27, and Exod 21:32) may share similar legal issues on the matter of "Violations against Another Person's Slave Property Rights and Punishments" with some ANE stipulations. *Only* Exod 21:32 shares the same situation with LE 55, 57, and LH 252. At best, Exod 21:32 can be regarded as the *closest parallel* to the ANE stipulations.

Other examples such as Lev 19:20 – 22 (having sexual intercourse with another man's betrothed slave woman) and Exod 21:20 – 21, 26 – 27 (injuring one's own slave), while sharing similar legal issues with other ANE slave sexual and injury laws address different situations:

–   Lev 19:20 – 22 also does not parallel LU 8 and LE 31 (raping another man's slave woman) even though it can be categorized as dealing with a similar legal issue.
–   Exod 21:20 – 21, 26 – 27 (injuring one's own slave) should not be reckoned to parallel the laws in LH 199 (injuring another man's slave) or LH 205 (injuring a free man by a slave).[150] Even though the laws of Exod 21:20 – 21, 26 – 27 have a similar legal issue with LH 199, they hold a strong humanitarian spirit that is never found in the ANE laws. In Exod 21:20 – 21 the Israelite master who strikes his slave and he dies on the same day is regarded as having committed a capital crime, and the master has to be put to death. In Exod 21:26 – 27, the Israelite master who blinds the eye or knocks out a tooth of a slave should free the slave. These two laws in Exodus demonstrate that the biblical slave laws, while defining the chattel slave as property, nevertheless advocate treating the slave as a dignified person.[151] Furthermore, the biblical

---

150 As discussed in chapter three, without the emphasis on ethnic identity, the slaves referred in Exod 21:20 – 21, 26 – 27, as well as Exod 21:32 and Lev 19:20 – 22 are most likely to be chattel slaves that the Israelites purchase from foreigners. See discussion in page 116 of this study.
151 Westbrook and B. Wells suggest that "[s]laves were property that could be bought and sold, exploited for their labor, and, in the case of women, exploited also for their sexual and reproductive capacity. At the same time, the law recognized the humanity of slaves. For example, they could marry and have legitimate children. The two concepts of a slave, as property and as a

slave laws do not list slaves alongside other forms or categories of merchandise. There are also no slave marks to put on the slaves. On the other hand, slaves in the ANE laws are treated as property (things). Pecuniary compensation is the only way to deal with damages or losses of a slave's property, even when a human life is at stake. There is no ANE slave law that deals with the same issue of "injuring one's own slave" as in Exod 21:20 – 21, 26 – 27. Perhaps this is because chattel slaves are regarded as *property* rather than persons. This issue will be further discussed in chapter five.

Lastly and most importantly, biblical laws also do not provide any legal basis for human distraint and pledge. The pledge laws in the Pentateuch, Exod 22:25 – 26 [Eng. 22:26 – 27] and Deut 24:6, 10 – 13, allow the taking of a poor man's cloak as a pledge but the creditor has to return it to the debtor before sunset. The book of Job and the prophetic books also mention only cloaks and animals to be pledged (e. g., Job 22:6; 24:3, 9; Isa 36:8; Ezek 18:7, 12, 16; 33:15). There is no biblical law about human distraint, but a case is attested in one of the Elisha's stories (2 Kgs 4:1). Though it does not concern human pledge, another law that expresses its sympathetic concern of the human dignity of the underprivileged is Deut 24:10 – 11, where an Israelite creditor is forbidden to enter into the debtor's house. Even a debtor possesses dignity in the privacy and sanctity of his home.

Most remarkably, the above investigation reveals that in the numerous ANE slave laws, debt-servitude is mentioned in only one law, LH 117. Therefore, LH 117 is the only law that can be reasonably regarded as *parallel* to the debt slave laws of Ex 21, Lev 25, and Dt 15. When comparing only the length of servitude between LH 117 and the biblical ones (three years versus six years), one may conclude that the former is more humanitarian. However, the emphases of strong humanitarian concerns, such as benign treatment, provision, and theological motivation of manumission embodied in the three biblical laws are absent in LH 117. Although the lack of mentioning the spirit and method of treatment to the debt slaves does not necessarily mean that the Babylonian masters would thus treat their debt slaves harshly, the biblical debt slave laws noticeably speak of their humanitarian concerns and provide "to-do" lists to reflect their concerns. The regulations in Ex 21 and Dt 15, and the protective institution in Lev 25, prevent the socially powerful from creating debts and furthering permanent forms of human bondage. This study is not claiming that biblical law is superior to others. There

---

person, often came into conflict." Raymond Westbrook and Bruce Wells. *Everyday Law in Biblical Israel: An Introduction* (Louisville: Westminster John Knox, 2009), 55.

exist different stances of legal philosophy between the biblical and the ANE laws, which will be further discussed in chapter five.

In summary, one can conclusively say that
- The *closely parallel* slave laws between biblical and ANE laws are Exod 21:32 with LE 55, 57; LH 252;
- Some *parallels* exist between the debt servitude laws in Ex 21, Lev 25, and Dt 15 with LH 117.
- Other laws may be classified into similar categories of legal topic but in their details, they may actually advocate different approaches (e. g., different *positions*). While some can be classified as having similar legal issues, they actually address diverse situations and *dissimilar* cases.

The above conclusions lead us back to review one of the purposes of this study— to contribute to comparative legal study between the ANE and biblical laws. This was done by using a standard of the legal categorizational system, which allows one to discern degrees of similarities and differences between ANE and biblical laws. This system was also used to respond to scholarly assertions of duplication and abolishment of laws between the ANE and biblical legal corpora. Through this method of comparison, even where two laws that could be identified as parallel, each may still have its own emphasis in the *Volksgeist* of its own context. Although the legal categorizational system can be fruitfully used to compare legal topics, issues, and situations, the humanitarian concerns that the biblical slave laws directly or indirectly promote is incomparable.

At the conclusion of the above survey of ANE laws on slavery, it is appropriate at this juncture to think about whether poverty is truly the primary cause that leads a person into enslavement, or whether there are other social and political issues involved. A survey of slavery between the ANE and the modern world will show that, from the ANE times to the modern epoch, from the privileged Mesopotamian merchants to present-day ruling political or tribal classes, the pattern of enslavement remains intact: a brother sells his brother; a brother oppresses his brother. Slavery systems exist, regardless of place or time, with an unchanged theme—socially powerful people oppress their own socially powerless fellows.

A Survey of Slavery between the ANE and the Modern World

According to the Slavery Convention signed at Geneva on 25th September 1926, slavery is defined as the following:[152]

> (1) Slavery is the status or condition of a person over whom any or all of the powers attaching to the right of ownership are exercised.
> (2) The slave trade includes all acts involved in the capture, acquisition or disposal of a person with intent to reduce him to slavery; all acts involved in the acquisition of a slave with a view to selling or exchanging him; all acts of disposal by sale or exchange of a slave acquired with a view to being sold or exchanged, and, in general, every act of trade or transport in slaves.

In sociological studies, freedom and subjugation are generally considered as basic criteria that are used to define enslavement. "Slavery is a system that legally and socially designates 'slave' as being entirely under the control of those termed 'masters'."[153] "A condition of subordination and domination involving forced labor and servitude, which has been present from the dawn of civilization; it is a condition made possible through distinguishing insiders and outsiders, creating social groups who are possible to enslave, to dominate, and to make use."[154]

At the level of personal relations, O. Patterson offers a preliminary definition: "Slavery is the permanent, violent domination of natally alienated and generally dishonored persons." His definition is based on Frederick Douglass' famous remark, that:[155]

> A man without force is without the essential dignity of humanity. Human nature is so constituted that it cannot do long, if the signs of power do not arise.

Patterson's definition has often been applied and discussed in recent sociological studies. Contrastive definitions taken from an understanding of property and personal relations concern two of the most controversial and interrelated topics today—the treatment of slaves as property or as a person, and the power structure between human societies from the dawn of civilization up to present times.

---

152 "Slavery Convention Signed at Geneva on 25th September 1926," n. p. [cited 20 September 2010]. Online: http://www2.ohchr.org/english/law/pdf/slavery.pdf.
153 Tim Lockley, "Slavery," *Encyclopedia of Social Theory*, 549–551.
154 Ron Eyerman, "Slavery," *The Cambridge Dictionary of Sociology*, 554–556.
155 Patterson, Orlando. *Slavery and Social Death: A Comparative Study* (Cambridge: Harvard University Press, 1982), 13.

As Gelb has suggested that although it is commonly recognized that there are three social classes in the Mesopotamian and the ANE, (i.e., free citizen, semi-free serf, and chattel slave), it may in fact distinguish just two classes: the master class and the rest of the population.[156]

To understand notions and practices of slavery in the modern world, J. K. Thornton's provides a brilliant account. In his examination on the slave trade between Africans and Europeans in 1400–1800, he concludes that Africans controlled the nature of their interactions with Europe. Despite the prevailing view, Europeans did not possess sufficiently overwhelming military power to force Africans to participate in any type of trade in which their leaders did not wish to engage. Therefore all African trade with the Atlantic, including the slave trade was voluntary.[157] Thornton finds that a fundamental starting point for understanding the entire slave system (the slave trade and the process of acquisition of slaves) in Africa was that it had long been accepted and practiced even before the arrival of the Europeans. The system was such that it placed great importance on the legality of slavery for a political agenda, and that relatively large numbers of people were likely to be slaves at any given time.[158] Because the process of acquisition, transfer, and the sale of slaves were under the control of African states and elites, the ruling classes were able to protect themselves from the social and demographic impact of the European invasion and shift problems they were having onto the considerable social dislocations of the poorer members of their own societies.[159] Africans and Europeans were co-conspirators in slavery.

In another recent study, Testart illustrates two examples of how a punishment system was well developed and organized by a higher dominant class to enforce more people to become slaves. One example involved the tradition of an Indian tribe living in what is considered northwestern California today and the other in southern Zambia. In his study, both societies assumed highly devel-

---

156 The distinction of three classes is a general category. Still, different areas and periods may have dissimilar situations. Regarding the ancient social classes, see Dandamaev, *Slavery in Babylonia*, 44–45; Raymond Westbrook, "The Character of Ancient Near Eastern Law," in *A History of Ancient Near Eastern Law* (ed. Raymond Westbrook; vol. 1; Leiden: E. J. Brill, 2003), 36–38; Wilcke, *Early Ancient Near Eastern Law*, 51–52.

157 John K. Thornton, *Africa and Africans in the Making of the Atlantic World, 1400–1800* (Cambridge: Cambridge University Press, 1998), 7, and particularly chapter three "Slavery and African Social Structure," and chapter four "The Process of Enslavement and the Slave Trade."

158 Ibid., 98. They did slave trade in order to obtain the necessary military technology (guns and horses) to defend themselves from any enemy.

159 Ibid., 7.

oped systems of fines and hostage-taking for offenses that seem extremely incredible for modern people.

In the native Indian culture, whoever breaks a taboo, offends a man, accidently causes a fire, or destroys wealth, is required to provide compensation in the form of an appropriate payment. If he is unable to pay, he will be put into a form of bondage. The conditions these people are subject to are by no means lenient. They could be transferred from one master to another as payment for life or as a dowry. They may be forced to work or face death if they attempted to flee. If a man under bondage is married to a woman of the same condition, their children belong to the master.[160] In the case of Zambia, if a guest is not familiar with the women present, or takes things that he erroneously thinks he has been allowed to take, he has to reimburse the value to the host. If he refuses or cannot pay, he will be seized. If no family claims for him, he will be held captive or sold as a slave.[161]

Testart uses these two examples to show that slavery is an institution that is in fact operated by the socially powerful and that slavery is a game that they play to gain more wealth and power. He concludes that "[s]uch systems are well-organized, with their own logic, and we find them in many societies in Africa and elsewhere."[162] He further concludes that at present, this is still the major reason for slavery around the world.[163] According to Testart, this type of slavery may be called "internal-domestic slavery," which in fact is the primary category that has long existed in the history of human slavery.[164] The hard truth is that enslavement in human history and its connection to debt is a means of oppression that can be imposed upon or enforced by the socially powerful where the weaker may become a debt slave, a pledge, distraint, and eventually, a chattel slave.

Another more recent investigation on modern slavery by E. B. Skinner also reveals similar findings. Traveling for four years among twelve countries, Skinner recorded interviews with over a hundred slaves, slave dealers, and survivors. In addition, he witnessed various kinds of human bondages (e. g., labor or sex slaves). In his research, Skinner testifies that there are more slaves in the world today than at any time in history, but only less visible compared to ancient

---

160 Testart, "The Extent and Significance of Debt Slavery," 173–174.
161 Ibid., 174.
162 Ibid., 174.
163 Ibid., 192.
164 Regarding some detailed account of this internal-domestic type slavery, see Edwin William Smith and Andrew Murray Dale, *The Ila-Speaking Peoples of Northern Rhodesia* (vol. 1; New Hyde Park: University Books, 1968), 398–412.

times.[165] In one example, he sarcastically comments that any individual could departure from the UN Secretariat in New York, hail a taxi, take a flight, and within five hours of departure, buy a slave that is a healthy boy or girl with a negotiable price in Haiti.[166] To sum up, in the 2000's, today's version of modern slavery also derives from the same prototype that was present in the ANE, where a (Haitian) broker sells his (Haitian) brothers and sisters to another (Haitian) higher class owner or foreigners.[167]

It is believed that the first and the most common cause that results in the enslavement of a human being is often poverty. However, the ugly reason as to why slavery has never vanished from human societies tells us a different story—the glaring absence of the concepts and practice of *peoplehood* and *brotherhood* may be the fundamental factors that a man buys and enslaves another.[168]

Though the Bible is an ancient book, the humanitarian concerns found in the laws of Exodus, Leviticus and Deuteronomy with regard to slave laws not only stands out in positive contrast to the ANE concept of slavery, it also serves as an exemplar for today. On the matter of brotherhood, Ex 21, Dt 15 and Lev 25 sympathetically highlights this notion in treatments that affect a brother debt slave as well as humanitarian concerns to other non-Israelite slaves. Taken as a whole, the biblical laws advocate a consistent concern for the good of humanity: to protect human life and dignity with essential provisions and rights to survive on YHWH's land.

Summary and Conclusion

Six conclusions can be made at the end of this study:

First, in the first part of this chapter, recent scholarly studies on the terminology of "slave" and the slave systems of the ANE world were presented where a distinction based on redemption (namely the dichotomy between chattel slave and debt slave), is called into question. This is because the availability of

---

165 Skinner presents the book in a narrative style. E. Benjamin Skinner, *A Crime So Monstrous: Face-to-Face with Modern-Day Slavery* (New York: Free, 2008).

166 Ibid., 1–9.

167 Skinner, *A Crime So Monstrous*, 1–9.

168 The term "peoplehood" is recently used in some sociological and anthropological studies. In this study, peoplehood describes "what is a human being and what is the proper way that a human being should live, and how they should be treated." See also Allen Dwight Callahan, Richard A. Horsley, and Abraham Smith, "Introduction: The Slavery of New Testament Studies," *Semeia* 83–84 (1998): 1; John Lie, *Modern Peoplehood* (Cambridge: Harvard University Press, 2004).

redemption is regulated by individual contracts and to divide slaves into only categories such as indentured and chattel, temporary and permanent are over-simplistic, and fails to account for all elements of various slave systems in the ANE. Contexts such as the household system provide us a useful background to better understand the ANE slave systems and slave laws. Another context is slave trading (where it is a significant economic activity in ancient Mesopotamia), that must also be taken into account as a reflection in the Slave Laws in Laws of Hammurabi.

Second, the compilation of ancient laws sheds light into the comparative legal study between the biblical and ANE laws and redresses some prevailing misconceptions. The most outstanding method of grouping legal materials in the ANE law books are by the detection of formulaic phrases and thematic issues. By these two techniques, the compilers effectively communicate the didactic values and ideas of their society. Previous scholarly attempts to use insertion theory are entirely unnecessarily even if redactions had taken place. This study has shown that ANE slave laws, when understood in their original grouping categories, have little concern for slave rights for in their legal perspective a slave is a piece of property rather than a person. Among the ANE slave laws, only these five units LE 49–52, LH 15–20, HL 22–24, LH 278–282, and LH 117–119 are identically formed groups that have evident slave motifs.[169] The central concern of those laws is mainly to protect the property and purchase rights of the owner. On the other hand, while biblical slave laws do allow chattel slaves, they have to be treated as a person in YHWH's land.

Third, slavery is hardly the only form of bondage that disrespects human dignity and freedom in the ANE world. There are many forms of human bondage that deprive the socially weak of their freedom and dignity. Human distraint and the pledge are two other forms of human bondage which may, and have been, cunningly developed to bind people into permanent chattel slavery. On the other hand, the biblical laws do not provide a legal basis for oppression. More particularly, the Deuteronomic laws favor the socially weak in dealing with a loan or pledge. Likewise, Ex 21, Lev 25 and Dt 15 build up a social protective network to prevent permanent human bondage.

Fourth, this study has suggested a consistent principle in reading ANE laws—appreciating the *entire* context of a law. Laws mostly describe relationships and obligations between related parties and objects. For these ancient

---

169 LE 49–52, LH 15–20, and HL 22–24 are about *Slave escape*, LH 278–282 is clearly a group of laws that deals with *Slave purchase* while LH 117–119 are a set of laws that deals with the resolation of a loan by giving debt servitude and human pledge.

casuistic laws, examining a single term or verse is insufficient to expound the spirit or the concern of a law. Rather, the context, including its location in a group or a larger context in its immediate group(s) is the better approach.

Fifth, the use of the legal categorizational system to understand the biblical and ANE laws reveal obvious differences. Though these ancient laws may share similar legal topics, they hold different positions, issues, or situations. Among them, the *closely parallel* slave laws between biblical and ANE are Exod 21:32 with LE 55, 57 and LH 252. The next closest parallel is the debt servitude laws of Ex 21, Lev 25, and Dt 15 to LH 117. Others are only similar in the level of the various legal issues discussed. Taken as a whole, biblical slave laws consistently hold to a higher humanitarian concern. The demands in Exod 21:20 – 21; 26 – 27 find no parallel in similar ANE laws. The humanitarian thought that the biblical slave laws promote is beyond comparison.

Finally, the notions and practices of peoplehood and brotherhood that Deuteronomy emphasizes are significant and crucial ethical values that can provide insights to the problems of enslavement and disrespect of human rights. In next chapter, how the different theology and character of lawgivers between the One and Only God, YHWH versus the kings or deities of ANE that could decisively influence laws and the promotion of human rights are discussed.

5 The Laws and the Concepts of Human Rights in the ANE Law Books and in Deuteronomy

In the previous three chapters, this study has presented distinctive humanitarian concerns in the biblical slave laws, which are beyond comparison. This chapter will discuss the possible rationales behind the laws that led to these differences between the biblical and the ANE laws. Then, according to the understanding of the rationales behind the laws, this chapter will illustrate the concept of human rights in Deuteronomy. In view of that, the first step will examine the different cosmologies between the Bible and the ANE based on J. J. Finkelstein's study.[1] The second step will seek to understand the different worldviews presented in the biblical and the ANE law books. This examination will apply P. G. Hiebert's definition of worldview in the three dimensions: cognitive, affective, and evaluative.[2] The third comparative study will employ E. Fox-Decent's theory to understand the different positions of morality shaping in laws held by the biblical and ANE laws.[3] This comparison will focus on the book of Deuteronomy and the ANE law collections with a tripartite presentation,[4] given that the presentation also expresses its lawgiver's attitude toward humanitarian concerns. The final section of this chapter then will depict the concept of human rights in Deuteronomy and answer the question of whether God is a necessary figure in respecting and protecting human rights.

The Differing Cosmologies of the Bible and the ANE

The cosmology of the Bible begins with Genesis 1, where God's creation and the unique position of human beings in the universal scheme are expressed. Human beings were created in God's image. The rest of creation is ruled over by the agency of human beings with God's blessings and authorization. The universe of the Bible is thus to be seen as human-centered. Human beings are the

---

1 J. J. Finkelstein, *The Ox That Gored* (Philadelphia: The American Philosophical Society, 1981).
2 Paul G. Hiebert, *Transforming Worldviews: An Anthropological Understanding of How People Change* (Grand Rapids: Baker Academic, 2008).
3 Evan Fox-Decent, "Is the Rule of Law Really Indifferent to Human Rights," *Law and Philosophy* 27 (2008): 533–581.
4 A law book consists of hree parts: prologue, legal corpus, and epilogues.

focus and apex of the universe. The hierarchical order of the universe is: God, human beings, and the rest of creation.[5]

On the other hand, an investigation on ANE cosmology first reveals that there exists no such single "canonical" or "systematic" exposition of its cosmic viewpoint. J. J. Feinkelstein professes: "the Mesopotamians provide no such statement is actually a logical concomitant of their own pluralistic and multi-dimensional response to such themes." He suggests that the investigator must create his/her own synthesis to "extract anything resembling a coherent cosmological 'system' out of varied and often 'contradictory' sources deriving from various localities within the 'cuneiform world' and spanning a period of more than two thousand years."[6] What follows will first discuss Finkelstein's synthesis on the comparative study of cosmology between the Bible and Mesopotamia. His presentation provides a preliminary angle to understand the different cosmologies between these two cultures.[7]

Observing the essence of polytheism from their varied and colorful mythological sources, Finkelstein suggests that a Mesopotamian view of the universe is that it is sustained and ruled by a large and infinite number of independent forces. "The truly major deities are very few in number and the domains which they govern or with which they are identified comprise the three primary

---

5 Finkelstein, *The Ox That Gored*, 7–8.

6 Ibid., 8.

7 The reason for discussing Finkelstein's study is because he also deals with comparative legal study on the laws of the goring ox and suggests that worldview is the factor that influences the difference of humanitarian concerns in the laws. Rarely have scholars studied how different worldviews would influence peoples' legislation and the ethical values behind the laws. However, most scholars who devote themselves to the comparative study of ethics, cosmology, and worldview between the ANE and the Bible agree that ethics are motivated by theologies (esp. polytheism versus monotheism). As G. Buccellati suggests, "[i]n the polytheistic system, values are coterminous with the perception of the absolute; and conversely, their violation is a sin not in the sense of a personal offense against fate or any god in particular but, rather, in the sense of a breach that affects the harmony of a global order embodied by fate as the underlying nature of things." On the other hand, "[i]n Israel, values also are coterminous with the divine world, but only because they are posited by the explicit will of God, to such an extent that the will of God becomes the supreme value that can be perceived by humans, all the more so whenever it defies the canons of reasonable expectations." See Giorgio Buccellati, "Ethics and Piety in the Ancient Near East," in *Civilizations of the Ancient Near East* (ed. Jack M. Sasson; vol. 3; New York: Simon & Schuster Macmillan, 1995), 1691. See also Loren R. Fisher, "Creation at Ugarit and in the Old Testament," *VT* 15, no. 3 (1965): 313–324; Richard J. Clifford, "Cosmogonies in the Ugaritic Texts and in the Bible," *Or* 53, no. 2 (1984): 183–201; David Toshio Tsumura, *Creation and Destruction: A Reappraisal of the Chaoskampf Theory in the Old Testament* (Winona Lake: Eisenbrauns, 2005); and Rebecca Sally Watson, *Chaos Uncreated: A Reassessment of the Theme of "Chaos" in the Hebrew Bible* (Berlin: Walter de Gruyter, 2005).

regions of the visible or tangible universe: the celestial, the atmospheric, and the chthonic."[8] Therefore, the Mesopotamian gods were independent and limited in authority or power at one and the same time. No speculation ever arrived at the notion of the absolute omnipotence of any single deity.[9] This quality differentiates the "immanence" that characterizes Mesopotamian deity from the "transcendence" which characterizes the God of the Bible.[10] In addition, "the anthropomorphic conception of deity in Mesopotamia served to reinforce the limitations already implied in the identification of a particular god with a specific sphere of the objective universe." Therefore, "[b]eing restricted, or unable to realize themselves fully as individual personalities, the gods could not give their undivided attention to the concerns of mankind, since the cosmic equilibrium required them to keep an eye upon each other."[11] Within such a power structure of deities, Mesopotamian cosmological literature never suggested or implied that humanity was destined to have dominion over nature, the mandate which Genesis 1 emphasizes and reiterates. Instead, humankind was created to relieve the intolerable burden of the ANE oppressed gods.[12]

In contrast to the ANE gods, the God of the Bible—while transcending the experiential universe—is seen as omnipotent within it with human beings occupying the center of his attention. Unlike his Mesopotamian counterparts, "he has no peers to be watched; he is thus free to give his undivided attention to the affairs of mankind, taking constant cognizance of its conduct and being ever solicitous of its welfare, individually and collectively."[13] The God of the Bible, speaks, commands, and expresses his moods in direct discourse and in explicit language. He is "the image of man magnified to infinite dimension."[14]

Finkelstein is convinced that "[i]t is not that the Mesopotamian thinkers held a truly low estimate of man's place in the cosmic scheme, or that they were oblivious of his uniqueness within the visible order of nature,[15]" but that they hold a different concept of cosmology from that of the Bible. Therefore, he suggests that the question "What is Man?" is biblical, not Mesopotamian.[16] With this comparative study of cosmology in mind, when Finkelstein compares the laws of the

---

8 Finkelstein, *The Ox That Gored*, 9.
9 Ibid., 9.
10 Ibid., 10.
11 Ibid., 10.
12 Ibid., 12.
13 Ibid., 11.
14 Ibid., 12.
15 Ibid., 12.
16 Ibid., 13.

goring ox between the biblical and cuneiform versions, he notices that biblical law holds an attitude of moral priorities to human life. When a legal issue is related to human life, biblical laws treat it as the issue with a "Law of Persons" rather than with a "Law of Things."[17] He indicates, "nobody's life, even that of a would be burglar, may be taken with impunity solely in defense of property; the issue of life or death, or homicide, overrides any question of guilt related to the wrongful taking of mere 'things'."[18] He wraps up a conclusion on his comparative legal study of the goring ox, which is similar to that of this study on slave laws: Their respective literary units disclose a disparity in outlook between them that far outweighs their admittedly close formal resemblances. They are divergent in the way that "the two different civilizations apprehend and classify experience, that we can detect the underlying rationales that are responsible for the divergence in the substantive rulings applicable to identical sets of circumstance."[19]

From the ANE cosmology, Finkelstein explains the humanitarian concern of biblical law as a result of the Bible's *worldview* which has a higher estimation on human beings. However, the ANE laws do not treat *all* human beings according to their cosmology as Finkelstein puts forth, "[i]n Mesopotamia no qualitative discontinuity was perceived between the phenomenon of man and any other phenomena of the natural universe."[20] From the preceding study of slave laws, the ANE commonly differentiates freeman and slave (especially, a chattel slave). The former is regarded as a *person*, yet the later is often assumed as a *thing*. On the contrary, the biblical laws deem *all* human beings as *person* and intend to preserve human life with ethical considerations, even if it is a life of a chattel slave (e. g., Exod 21:20, 32), a burglar (e. g., Exod 22:2 [Eng 22:3]), or a suspected murderer (e. g., Deut 19:3). This attitude goes beyond the idea of human-centered cosmology, but articulates its concern for human rights.[21]

---

17 The "Law of Persons" and the "Law of Things" are two terms that Finkelstein uses to distinguish biblical laws that revolve about "persons" and merely "things." Finkelstein, *The Ox That Gored*, 25, 38 – 39.
18 Ibid., 38.
19 Ibid., 39.
20 Ibid., 39.
21 In his recent work, "Slavery and Slave Laws in Ancient Hatti and Israel," H. A. Hoffner compares and examines the Hittite slave practices and biblical slave laws and concludes that "although slavery was never abolished in the Old Testament, in principle Israelites were to treat their slaves humanely and with compassion, based on their status as bearers of the image of God." Harry A. Hoffner Jr. "Slavery and Slave Laws in Ancient Hatti and Israel," in *Israel: Ancient Kingdom or Late Invention* (ed. Daniel I. Block; Nashville: B&H, 2008), 130.

Differentiating the values (prices) of human life and punishments against the same crime based on social class/status in a law collection suggests that the attitude of the lawgiver or the collective sense of the society lacked the concept of equality of human life.[22] One should note that the starting point for establishing the concept of human rights is based on equal value of *all* human lives.[23] To regard every human being equally as a *person* is the basic criterion that can defend human freedom, dignity, and rights.[24] Hence, the first rationale

---

22 Some may argue that the ox goring laws in Exod 21:29–32 show an unequal valuation of human lives. Exod 21:29–31 regulates that if a known ox that gores kills a free person, the ox and the ox owner both have to be killed. In the same case of a slave's death, however, as described in Exod 21:32, the ox owner pays thirty shekels of silver to the slave's owner and only the ox has to be put to death; the owner is exempt from the death penalty. See discussions in Shalom M. Paul, "The Laws of the Book of the Covenant," in *Studies in the Book of the Covenant in the Light of Cuneiform and Biblical Law* (Leiden: E. J. Brill, 1970), 83; and Cheryl B. Anderson, "The Construction of Identity in the BC and DL," in *Women, Ideology, and Violence: Critical Theory and the Construction of Gender in the Book of the Covenant and the Deuteronomic Law* (New York: T and T Clark International, 2004), 52. However, one should notice that Exod 21:30 also remarks that "if there is a ransom imposed on him (the owner), he shall give whatever is imposed on him." This means that this incidental event is allowed to be *conditioned with some* pecuniary compensation. Therefore (as previously discussed in chapter four), the punishment for one who causes the loss of any human life (regardless of whether it is a free person or a slave's life) remains the same—the one who kills has to be killed (here, the ox has to be put to death), and any pecuniary compensation is paid by the ox owner for his due negligence.

23 J. H. C. Wright notes, "equality before the law for all social groups, including alines and immigrants, is made explicit in Exodus 12:49, Leviticus 19:34 and Numbers 15:16." See J. H. Christopher Wright, *Old Testament Ethics for the People of God* (Downers Grove: InterVarsity Press, 2004), 310.

24 The first article of UDHR, "[a]ll human beings are born free and equal in dignity and rights. They are endowed with reason and conscience and should act towards one another in a spirit of brotherhood" implies this basic recognition that all human beings are regarded as persons. UDHR is a long-time effort inspired from historical experiences. The debates of contemporary human rights have rarely reviewed this original point, since UDHR is assumed as a universal and international value. The contemporary debated issues of human rights are often incorporated into political initiatives, which have led to more complicated issues. This study will not touch upon these contemporary debates of human rights, but will discuss the basic concepts of human rights (as suggested in chapter one, liberty, equality, and fraternity) that can be adduced from comparative legal studies. One can read some recent publications about the contemporary issues on human rights, such as, Eugene Kamenka, and Alice Erh-Soon Tay, *Human Rights* (New York: St. Martin's, 1978); Ellen Frankel Paul, Fred Dycus Miller, Jr., and Jeffrey Paul, eds. *Human Rights* (Oxford: Basil Blackwell, 1984); Laura K. Egendorf, ed. *Human Rights: Opposing Viewpoints* (San Diego: Greenhaven, 2003); M. Bucar and Barbra Barnett, eds. *Does Human Rights Need God?* (Grand Rapids: Eerdmans, 2005); James W. Nickel, *Making Sense of Human Rights* (Malden: Blackwell, 2007).

behind the laws, which leads to the difference, is the absence of the concept concerning equality of human lives.[25]

Different Worldviews Presented between the Biblical and the ANE Law Books

Finkelstein's understanding of the different cosmologies and worldviews cannot satisfactorily explain the difference. This may be limited by his examination of only the laws of goring ox and the concept of "worldview." It is more likely that the ANE laws themselves represent their worldview, as mentioned in chapter one that: (1) The ANE laws belong to a common legal culture that shares a legal ontology. (2) The laws often shape social and economic factors, not vice versa. Therefore, the following discussion suggests applying the definition of "worldview" proposed by Hiebert to understand the worldviews presented in the laws and the law books.

In his new book, *Transforming Worldviews: An Anthropological Understanding of How People Change*, Hiebert indicates three problems with the term "worldview" that has been used. First, because of its roots in philosophy, it focuses on the cognitive dimensions of cultures and does not deal with the affective and moral dimensions, which are equally important. Nor does it deal with how these three dimensions of being human relate to one another. Second, the term often gives priority to sight or view over hearing or sound.[26] Hiebert explains,[27]

> All cultures use both sight and sound, but in most, sound is the dominant sensory experience. Spoken words are more immediate, relational, and intimate than printed ones. Written words are impersonal, detached from specific contexts, and delayed. Scripture says that in the beginning God spoke and the world came into being. In many societies spoken words have the powers of magic and curse or blessing.

The third problem, according to Hiebert, is that it applies both to individuals and to communities.[28] Based on A. F. C. Wallace's study,[29] he suggests that "the dominant worldview in cultures is shaped greatly by power and the social dynamics

---

25 With regard to how cosmology may influence the concept of the eqality of human lives will be another field of study, which is beyond the scope of the present study.
26 Hiebert, *Transforming Worldviews*, 15.
27 Ibid., 15.
28 Ibid., 15.
29 A. F. C. Wallace, "Revitalization Movements," *American Anthropologist* 58 (1956): 264–281.

of the community.[30] He thus provides his definition of "worldview" used in his book: the "fundamental cognitive, affective, and evaluative presuppositions a group of people make about the nature of things, and which they use to order their lives."[31]

From the previous examination on slave laws, Hiebert's definition of "worldview" could better explain the humanitarian concerns present in the biblical laws yet absent in the ANE ones. Two differences are observed: First, the ancient law book is a form of expression that represents its worldview shaped by the social dynamics of the ancient communities. For example, the ANE law books reflect the values of the hierarchical, merchant, and household systems in their societies. On the other hand, the biblical laws are built on the foundation of YHWH's redemption and his covenantal relationship with the Israelites. Second, the ANE laws are principally *written* words (the third person voice of statements—impersonal, detached from specific contexts, and delayed) and have no persuasive motive clauses to enrich their expression in affective and evaluative dimensions. On the contrary, the two distinctive features of the biblical laws that are completely absent and different from the ANE laws are its use of the second person voice and motive clauses (particularly the pattern language used in the Deuteronomic laws). Both elements shape the affective (e. g., *your* brother—brotherhood) and evaluative (e. g., morality—peoplehood) dimensions. Most importantly, they are reinforced by the lawgiving God's own *spoken* words.

Nonetheless, one should note that the prologues and epilogues in the ANE law books are presented in the first person voice of the lawgivers' *spoken* words, which directly express their attitudes toward human beings. In addition, some edicts and acts also suggest the ANE lawgivers' concerns about the socially weak and the release of slaves. Therefore, these prologues, epilogues, edicts and acts should be further examined and compared to the presentation of God's spoken words in Deuteronomy.

The Lawgivers' Spoken Words in the ANE

It is interesting that in the epilogue of the Laws of Hammurabi, the king of Hammurabi proclaimed his concern toward human beings and his contributions of providing protection and justice for his people:[32]

---

30 Hiebert, *Transforming Worldviews*, 15.

31 Ibid., 15.

32 The English translation of the texts is cited from Martha T. Roth, *Law Collections from Mesopotamia and Asia Minor* (Atlanta: Scholars Press, 1997), 133.

> I am Hammurabi, noble king. I have not been careless or negligent toward humankind, granted to my care by the god Enlil, and with whose shepherding the god Marduk charged me. I have sought for them peaceful places, I removed serious difficulties, I spread light over them....The great gods having chosen me, I am indeed the shepherd who brings peace, whose scepter is just.

Likewise, in the prologue of the Laws of Ur-Namma, the king of Ur-Namma also declared his attitude toward the socially weak: "I did not deliver the orphan to the rich. I did not deliver the widow to the might."[33] In addition to LU and LH, the Laws of Lipit-Ishtar (hereafter LL) also contain a prologue and epilogue.[34] LU, LL, and LH are the only three ANE law books that contain prologues and epilogues. Theses prologues and epilogues usually include three major features: (1) A self-praise of the king's benevolence, achievements, and contributions for all the people and cities under his reign. (2) A declaration of his kingship is appointed and his power is granted by divine authority. (3) An emphasis on his role as guardian and protector of justice and the socially weak.

With respect to the nature of these prologues and epilogues, scholars have different understandings. For example, from the epilogue of the LH, Finkelstein infers that LH was compiled in the last years of Hammurabi's reign after he had accomplished all of the conquests enumerated in the prologue.[35] He concludes that the function of the LH law book with its stylized prologue and epilogue serves as a representative of a literary genre, a royal *apologia*, and its primary purpose was "to lay before the public, posterity, future kings, and, above all, the gods, evidence of the king's execution of his divinely ordained mandate to have been 'the Faithful Shepherd' and the '*šar mīšarim*'."[36] S. M. Paul agrees with Finkelstein and states that "Mesopotamian legal corpora, with their personal prologue and epilogue frames, are primarily reports to the gods delivered by the king in order to vindicate his royal office of *šar mēšarim*."[37] On the other hand, R. Westbrook disagrees with Finkelstein's proposal. He argues,[38]

---

33 Ibid., 16. LU preserves only the prologue and fewer than forty laws.
34 Ibid., 24–26, 33–35.
35 J. J. Finkelstein, "Ammisaduqa's Edict and the Babylonian 'Law Codes,'" *JCS* 15 (1961): 91–104.
36 Ibid., 103. *šar mīšarim*, "king of justice."
37 Here, Paul transliterates *mēšarim* instead of *mīšarim*. The latter yet is used by most scholars. Shalom M. Paul, "Cuneiform Proloues and Epilogues,"in *Studies in the Book of the Covenant in the Light of Cuneiform and Biblical Law* (Leiden: E. J. Brill, 1970), 26. See also Wiseman, D. J. "Laws of Hammurabi Again." *JSS* 7, no. 2 (1962): 166.
38 Raymond Westbrook, "Biblical and Cuneiform Law Codes," *RB* 92, no. 2 (1985): 250.

The prologue and epilogue, which are vital to the purpose of the royal inscription, are missing in the cuneiform codes later than Codex Hammurabi, and probably also in Codex Eshnunna (which slightly antedates it). Since we possess copies of these codes that originally provided a complete version of the text, and not an extract (with the possible exception of the Neo-Babylonian Laws), there is no reason for them to have omitted the prologue and epilogue if they existed.

Considering J. Klíma's suggestion,[39] Westbrook proposes that "the legal corpus already existed as an independent unit with an independent purpose and was sometimes inserted into a frame, as in Codex Hammurabi, in order to be applied to a new purpose, that of the royal *apologia*."[40] In view of the above discussion, while the composition and the function of the prologues and epilogues in these ancient law books may remain debated, there seems no reason, however, to suggest that the ANE people (the kings, the lawgivers, the jurists, or the compilers) had no idea at all about having sympathy for the socially weak in their societies.

In addition to the prologues and epilogues in the ANE law books, some edicts and acts also indicate that the ANE kings announced releases of debts or slaves.[41] For example, the *mīšarum* edicts were royal proclamations intended to release private debts and some forms of public taxes. The *mīšarum* edicts were normally proclaimed in the first year of a new king's reign.[42] The particular *andurārum* act of granting freedom to slaves is linked to the *mīšarum* edicts by its appearance in pars. 20 and 21 of *Ammisaduqa*'s edict.[43] On this, J. Hamilton suggests that "[t]he apodosis of par. 20 reads: 'because the king has established the *mīšarum* for the land, he [i.e. the debt-slave] is released, his freedom is established.' In par. 20 of Ammisaduqa's edict the connections between debt, slavery, and

---

39 J. Klíma suggests that the tripartite division of the law book (prologue, legal corpus, and epilogue) were formulated by two different authors: the legal corpus was by jurists and the prologue and epilogue were by the temple or court poets. See J. Klíma, "Gesetze," *RIA* 3: 243–255.

40 Westbrook, "Biblical and Cuneiform Law Codes," 251. See also Jeffries M. Hamilton's discussion in *Social Justice and Deuteronomy: The Case of Deuteronomy 15* (Atlanta: Scholars, 1992), 56–62.

41 Moshe Weinfeld, *Social Justice in Ancient Israel and in the Ancient Near East* (Minneapolis: Fortress, 1995), 48–56; Hamilton, *Social Justice and Deuteronomy*, 48–53.

42 Hamilton, *Social Justice and Deuteronomy*, 48–49. See also F. R. Kraus, *Ein Edikt des Königs Ammi-Saduqa von Babylon* (Leiden: E. J. Brill, 1958); Niels Peter Lemche, "Andurārum and Mīšarum: Comments on the Problems of Social Edicts and Their Application in the Ancient Near East," *JNES* 38, no. 1 (1979): 11–22.

43 In its most general sense, the word *andurārum* and the acts which employ it simply indicate release. See Hamilton, *Social Justice and Deuteronomy*, 53–54.

freedom are clear."[44] The concept that a king is responsible for practicing justice was prevalent in the ANE, as well as in the Bible.[45] Therefore, the ancient law-givers/kings did possess the concepts of acting graciously and practicing justice for the poor and slaves, even though these prologues, epilogues, edicts, and acts were for political propaganda.

The issue in view, then, is that the lawgivers' humanitarian concerns are not embodied in their laws. This phenomenon may be explained by, as Westbrook suggests, the possibility that they were originally independent units to be compiled to serve for a new purpose (the royal apologia). However, this current tripartite composition of the ANE law books should be regarded as an integral whole that this final form we receive is also a presentation of its worldview, as well as its *Volksgeist*. They should be treated in the same way as this study treats the book of Deuteronomy.

In comparison with the presentations in the book of Deuteronomy and its legal corpus, two salient points are observed: (1) The first person voice address by the lawgivers in the prologues and epilogues neither has the intention to establish relationship, interact with, and have dialogue with their legal subjects,[46] nor to shape their morality or ethical values. (2) The third person voice of ANE laws provides almost no inspiration for morality shaping, providing no interpersonal relationship for the legal subjects to meditate and to shape their brotherhood and peoplehood. This presentation reveals that the ANE laws do not hold the view that the law is a vehicle for carrying out the function of morality shaping.

The Lawgivers' Spoken Words in Deuteronomy

On the other hand, Deuteronomy holds the concept that the law is supposed to shape its legal subjects' morality and conduct. Therefore, not only does the legal writing apply various rhetorical techniques (such as the calls of brotherly empa-

---

44 Cited from Hamilton, *Social Justice and Deuteronomy*, 54. See also Raymond Westbrook, "Social Justice in the Ancient Near East," in *Social Justice in the Ancient World* (ed. K. D. Irani and Morris Silver; Westport: Greenwood, 1995), 154–160.

45 Weinfeld, *Social Justice in Ancient Israel and in the Ancient Near East*, 25–33.

46 Applying E. Fox-Decent's definition, "legal subjects" refers to persons who interact with the lawgivers. It denotes a wider class of persons than "citizens." Anyone affected by an exercise of the lawgiver's power (presumably the state authority, etc.), including non-citizens within or outside the state's territorial jurisdiction. According to Fox-Decent, lawgivers and legal subjects stand in a relationship of reciprocity. This relationship of reciprocity has an important fiduciary dimension. See Fox-Decent, "Is the Rule of Law Really Indifferent to Human Rights," 536, 543.

thy, the use of the second person voice, and the persuasive motive clauses with pathos, ethos, and logos), the book of Deuteronomy also presents a covenantal relationship between YHWH and his people. This format exposes its strong intention that the lawgiver desires to have relationship, interaction, and dialogue with his legal subjects. Furthermore, as mentioned in chapter two, the central theme of the chiastic framework is the preservation of human lives where the laws within this framework intend to shape attitudes toward the socially weak and suggests an interpersonal relationship for this community.

The three elements, the covenantal relationship, the chiastic framework, and the highly rhetorical phrasing expressed in the laws, reveal that Deuteronomy perceives that laws can bear the function of shaping morality based on a *reciprocal* relationship with God. Therefore, the second rationale behind the laws that leads to the absence of humanitarian concerns in the ANE laws is that they do not consider shaping morality by laws.

The ensuing passages will further apply Fox-Decent's theory to demonstrate that the presentation of the three-elements in Deuteronomy is the legitimate way to promote human rights in laws.

The Different Position on Morality Shaping in Deuteronomy

Studies in legal philosophy demonstrate that there are also different positions with regard to the use of the law as a tool for morality shaping and the promotion of human rights. A broad range of scholars contend that the rule of law is indifferent to human rights. They view law and the rule of law in strictly instrumental terms, lacking any necessary connections to morality.[47] For example, J. Raz points out that "[t]he law may, for example, institute slavery without violating the rule of law."[48] This perspective is called "no-rights thesis," claiming that the rule of law is compatible with slavery and other gross violations of human rights.[49] The ANE slave laws can be regarded as this kind of law. For their law-

---

47 Fox-Decent, "Is the Rule of Law Really Indifferent to Human Rights," 533.
48 Cited from Fox-Decent, "Is the Rule of Law Really Indifferent to Human Rights," 533. On this view, Fox-Decent writes "[l]aw can guide conduct because human beings have cognitive and volitional capacities which permit them to interpret, comprehend and follow rules. However, merely noting a connection between the rule of law and human agency does not show, without more, that the rule of law constrains the ends to which law can be put." Fox-Decent, "Is the Rule of Law Really Indifferent to Human Rights," 534. See also Joseph Raz, "The Rule of Law and Its Virtue," in *The Authority of Law: Essays on Law and Morality* (Oxford: Oxford University Press, 2009), 221.
49 Fox-Decent, "Is the Rule of Law Really Indifferent to Human Rights," 533.

givers or cultures, slave laws do not violate their understanding of humanitarian concerns.

Some scholars, such as C. Murphy for example, defend that the rule of law has non-instrumental moral value, while suggesting that respecting human rights is not part of the ideal.[50] Against the idea of "no-right thesis," E. Fox-Decent argues that the rule of law can be a tool for respecting human rights, as well as human dignity and rights for freedom from slavery.[51]

Fox-Decent's argument is based on two theories: L. Fuller's idea of "internal morality of law"[52]and the Kantian concept of human agency—that in relevant circumstances, human agency has substantive implications for human rights.[53] Fox-Decent suggests that these circumstances are all those in which lawgivers and legal subjects interact with one another. According to him, the lawgivers and legal subjects stand in a relationship of reciprocity. This relationship has an important fiduciary dimension.[54] The fiduciary relationship is *trust*-like in nature, just like a parent-child relationship in which both are entrusted to each other with an unattainable consent.[55] However, trust is simply a moral concept that mediates relations between parties. Trust does not reveal the characteristics that legislation and administration must have in order to comply with the rule of law. Therefore, Fox-Decent suggests, in addition to trust, *freedom* and *dignity* are

---

50 Ibid., 533. See also Colleen Murphy, "Lon Fuller and the Moral Value of the Rule of Law," *Law and Philosophy* 24 (2005): 239, 261–262.

51 Fox-Decent, "Is the Rule of Law Really Indifferent to Human Rights," 534–581.

52 Fuller's theory has long been debated and applied in the studies of law and morality. Fuller believes that law is necessarily subject to morality. His understanding of law is regarded as being conceptually functionalist, which implies that nothing can count as law unless it is capable of performing law's essential function of guiding behavior. In order to perform this function, a system of rules must satisfy the eight principles: The rules (1) must be expressed in general terms, (2) must be publicly promulgated, (3) must be prospective in effect, (4) must be expressed in understandable terms, (5) must be consistent with one another, (6) must not require conduct beyond the powers of the affected parties, (7) must not be changed so frequently that the subject cannot rely on them, and (8) must be administered in a manner consistent with their wording. See Lon L. Fuller, *The Morality of Law* (New Haven: Yale University Press, 1969), 49–94. See also the discussion in Kenneth Einar Himma, "Natural Law," *Internet Encyclopedia of Philosophy*. n.p. [cited 22 January 2011]. Online: http:// http://www.iep.utm.edu/natlaw/.

53 Immanuel Kant and H. J. Paton, *The Moral Law: Kant's Groundwork of the Metaphysic of Morals* (New York: Barnes & Noble, 1967).

54 "The fiduciary nature of the relationship places lawgivers under a legal as well as moral obligation to respect the agency of the people subject to their powers. The content of the obligation is to govern in accordance with the rule of law." Fox-Decent, "Is the Rule of Law Really Indifferent to Human Rights," 536.

55 Ibid., 546–550.

two precepts that are significant for this relationship and the capacity of morality in law.[56]

Following Fuller's eight principles of law, Fox-Decent argues that when the rule of law assumes the internal morality of law, it entails a commitment to the view that the law regards persons as free, self-determining, and responsible agents, and that they possess inherent dignity in virtue of their autonomy.[57] He suggests that respect for agency is what distinguishes law from other forms of rules which guide human conduct.[58] The subject's self-determined participation in legal order reflects a liberal concept of autonomy.[59] The idea that legal subjects are free implies that they can engage in purposive action. The capacity to engage in purposive action implies that person can obey or disobey the law.[60]

According to Fox-Decent, in those societies that slavery is deemed as acceptable, a slave is not regarded as a person. "Legal subjects may possess rights whereas slaves generally do not because slave-owning societies do not count slaves as persons and legal subjects."[61] These societies assume that slaves are not legal persons, but *agents*, whose rights are severely restricted or denied. On this, Fox-Decent argues that this restriction and denial violates the fiduciary relationship between the lawgivers and the legal subjects:[62]

> On the fiduciary view of the rule of law, the fiduciary principle authorises state power exclusively for the purpose of securing legal order on behalf of each agent who is subject to such power. At a minimum, establishing legal order on behalf of every agent entails that each must have the possibility of acquiring rights which can enshrine and protect their respective interests. Otherwise, such interests would be entirely vulnerable to the power and caprice of others. In other words, each agent must be treated and regarded as a *person* [italic, mine], and this because each agent is equally free and self-determining, and so each agent is an equally valid subject of the fiduciary authorisation of public authority. As a principle of legality, the fiduciary principle has no capacity to discriminate arbitrarily between agents who, in virtue of the state–subject fiduciary relationship, enjoy equal status vis-à-vis the state as co-beneficiaries of the rule of law.

Fox-Decent concludes that the chief purpose of law is "to enable people to interact with one another within the limits of the congenial environment established by a lawful regime of secure and equal freedom, an environment which enables

---

56 Ibid., 550.
57 Ibid., 550–551.
58 Ibid., 553.
59 Ibid., 554.
60 Ibid., 556.
61 Ibid., 564.
62 Ibid., 564–565.

each to *choose* and *pursue* [italics, mine] his/her conception of good independently of the power of others."[63] He expounds that,[64]

> It is not the person's actual conception of the good, nor his/her actual possession of rights and obligations that underlies agency and dignity. Those are entirely contingent matters. Instead, it is the capacity of the person to *choose* and *pursue* [italic, mine] his/her own conception of the good that reflects his/her status before the law as an autonomous and self-determining being worthy of respect...Therefore, a person's status before the law does not lie in the particularities of what he/she does, but rather in something about the kind of being he/she is."

For Fox-Decent, the conception of viewing all agents as persons without discrimination and respecting a person as a free and self-determining being is the critical factor that warrants that the law can command respect for human rights.[65]

In Fox-Decent's discussion, the term "lawgiver" is presumptively a state authority and his theory is based on the principles of modern political democracy and legal theories. Nonetheless, the book of Deuteronomy is perfectly representing Fox-Decent's theory. The covenantal relationship, the legal chiastic framework, and its legal writing are purposefully constructed and designed to reflect this position that laws can bear the function of shaping morality and promoting human rights based on a *reciprocal* relationship with God. The following will discuss these three elements based on Fox-Decent's theory.

First, the covenantal relationship articulates the *reciprocal* relationship with fiduciary dimension between YHWH (lawgiver) and his people (legal subjects). This relationship demands the legal subjects (the Israelites) to recognize and trust that YHWH is the One and Only God, who redeemed, guided, and fought for them in history (Deuteronomy 1–3). The lawgiver YHWH promises to continue his protection and provision as long as the legal subjects persist in revering him as the One and Only God (Deuteronomy 4–11; Deut 26:16–30).

Moreover, this covenantal relationship is also established on the basis of regarding the legal subjects as free and self-determining persons who have the capacity and freedom to *choose* to obey or disobey laws (e. g., 30:15–18) and to *pursue* his/her own conception of the good that reflects his/her status before the law as an autonomous and self-determining being worthy of respect (e. g., 30:19. Note the use of the verb בחר).

---

63 Ibid., 576. In his article, Fox-Decent uses the pronoun "she" or "her" to refer to a person. The citations and quotations here and the following replace all the uses of "she" or "her" with "he/she" and "his/her."
64 Ibid., 576.
65 Ibid., 576.

Second, from the chiastic framework of the Deuteronomic legal corpus, one can see that since the central theme of the law book is preserving human life the laws in this framework regard *all* agents as persons: A non-premeditated murderer is regarded as a person who has the *rights* to stay in asylum (19:4–7). A war captive woman who married an Israelite is assumed as a person who has *rights* to be freely released and not to be sold if her husband does not love her any more (21:10–14). A runaway chattel slave is supposed to be treated as a person who has *rights* to choose his place to live and not to be extradited and mistreated (23:16–17). In ancient worlds, murderers, war captives, chattel slaves were often treated as things rather than persons. Here, Deuteronomy not only regards them as persons, but also entitles them to legal rights.[66]

As the laws for the socially weak, the Levite, the alien, the orphan, and the widow have *rights* to be satisfactorily fed every three years (14:28–29; 26:12–13). The poor Israelites have *rights* to be freed from their debts, avoid usury, and to be loaned again whenever they have needs (15:1–11; 23:19–20). The Hebrew indentured slaves have *rights* to be released with dignity and provision after six-year debt servitude (15:12–15). In addition, the most remarkable thing is that there are laws that command respecting the underprivileged's dignity and consider these respectful actions as the underprivileged's *rights* (24:6, 10–13, 14–15, 17–18, 19–21; 25:3)!

Third, the rhetorical techniques of the use of the second person voice, the persuasive motive clauses, and the emphasis on brotherhood in laws have been discussed in chapter two, while one significant point needs to be addressed. These rhetorical techniques are indications that the lawgiver *believes* that his legal subjects have the capability to meditate and respond to his words. In fact, the whole book of Deuteronomy not only emphasizes that all the commands in this book are God's *spoken* words, but also repeatedly stresses on "listening/obeying" to these words.[67] The trust in his legal subjects' capability of listening, meditation, making decisions, and taking responsibility is the foundation that YHWH can direct his people about his concerns for human rights. As Fox-Decent suggests, a person who has such freedom and dignity can do the above reactions so as to respect and protect human rights.

---

66 See also discussion in Wright, *Old Testament Ethics for the People of God*, 312–314.
67 For examples, Deut 4:1; 5:1; 6:4; 7:12; 9:1; 11:3, 27, 28; 12:28; 13:4, 17; 15:4; 28:1, 2, 13, 15, 45, 62; 29:4, 19; 30:2, 8, 9, 12, 13, 17, 20; 31:11, 12, 13, 28, 30; 32:1, 44.

The Concept of Human Rights in Deuteronomy

In the book of Deuteronomy, although YHWH regards all agents in his land as persons and respects all his legal subjects as free, dignified, and self-determining human beings, he reiteratively recalls their attention to their *limits* and *dependence* on him as human beings. The memory of slavery, mentioned throughout the book of Deuteronomy, is one of the most striking reminders: It is YHWH, who redeemed, protected, and fought for these runaway Egyptian slaves. The One and Only God, who listened, talked, and loved these originally menial Hebrews, establishes the relationship with them and gives them divine blessings. This historical and theological foundation of their peoplehood is affectively expressed in Deuteronomy 4–11.[68] The passages in these chapters explain that the freedom and dignity they are now entitled to as persons is the work of YHWH, not what they had done or who they were (e.g., 7:7–11; 8:2–5). Therefore, the concepts of peoplehood and human rights are correlated under such a theology, as A. D. Callahan, R. A. Horsley, and A. Smith note that,[69]

> Slavery is a species of social murder. It reduced human life to a travesty of itself, sacrifices human beings on the altar of violent desire. And slavery teaches us what freedom really is. We have never known freedom without it. The paradigmatic *magnalium Dei* in the Bible is the liberation of slaves. The rupture of the Egyptian slave regime by a rag-tag Hebrew underclass, that ancient huddled mass yearning to be free, was the beginning of freedom. The freedom of that mixed multitude was the beginning of peoplehood. And the interdictions delivered to this delivered people, the revelation of the Law at Sinai, the beginning of an alternative political-economic-religious order, inclusive of human rights: all defined by the previous experience of slavery.

As a result, the concept of human rights that Deuteronomy promotes is based on YHWH's redemption and sovereignty within a covenantal relationship. One may ask whether this is the criterion for respecting human rights. In other words, does "human rights" need God as the essential figure to get involved? Deuteronomy would answer this question as "yes" in terms of "validity."[70] Respecting and

---

68 Especially those passages exhort them to retrospect their history and do comparison with other nations.

69 Allen Dwight Callahan, Richard A. Horsley, and Abraham Smith, "Introduction: The Slavery of New Testament Studies," *Semeia* 83–84 (1998): 1.

70 "The question of validity" is proposed by L. Kolakowski and developed by M. J. Perry. Perry doubts whether human rights can be pursued and achieved on a non-religious ground. He explains, "to doubt that any non-religious ground can bear the weight of the claim that every human being has inherent dignity and its inviolable is not to doubt that a non-believer can both affirm that every human being has inherent dignity and live her life accordingly." See Leszek

defending human rights require moral strength and convictions.[71] Deuteronomy proclaims that one who reveres YHWH by obeying his words under his covenantal relationship could assume moral strength and convictions, because YHWH and his words are the universal origins and norms of righteousness and justice (e. g., 4:6 – 8; 32:5).[72] On the contrary, one who goes astray to follow pagan deities would fall into moral corruption (e. g., 18:9 – 13).

Meanwhile, the command of utterly destroying the seven Canaanite peoples (Deut 7:1– 2) calls for an explanation when discussing human rights in Deuteronomy. Does it mean that a non-Israelite/a non-believer is not a human being? Are these peoples not human lives that YHWH determines to protect? A significant theological point has to be addressed: YHWH destroys and expels *any* person who worships other pagan deities and disobeys his words *in his land*, including the Israelites. Deut 8:20 has answered this question: "Like the peoples that YHWH destroyed before you, so you shall perish; because you would not listen to the voice of YHWH your God." Deuteronomy 7 has to be read with Deuteronomy 28, where it articulates that no Israelite can subsist on YHWH's land without revering him and obeying his words.[73] It is remarkable that Deuteronomy 28 ends this paragraph with the theme of slavery (Deut 28:68, also cf. Neh 9:36a—"Behold! We are slaves today!"): The Israelites would lose their freedom and dignity as persons if they refused to revere YHWH and obey his words.

Summary and Conclusion

The first three sections of this chapter compare the different cosmologies, worldviews, and positions on the function of morality shaping in law between the ANE and the Bible to understand the rationales behind the laws that lead to the different presentations of humanitarian concerns. Two different rationales are observed.

The first is the lack of the concept of equal human lives. While the different ANE cosmology provides a certain cognitive dimension for understanding its

---

Kolakowski, *Religion, If There Is No God...: On God, the Devil, Sin, and Other Worries of the So-Called Philosophy of Religion* (New York: Oxford University Press, 1982), 191– 192; Michael J. Perry, *Toward a Theory of Human Rights: Religion, Law, Courts* (Cambridge: Cambridge University Press, 2007), 15.

71 See the discussion in Perry, *Toward a Theory of Human Rights*, 14– 29.

72 32:4—"He is the Rock! His work is perfect, for all his ways are just. A faithful God who does no wrong, righteous and upright is he!"

73 See also the chart of the land and the symbolism of the argraian products in chapter two.

worldview, it cannot satisfactorily explain the absence of humanitarian concerns in the ANE laws. The ANE laws do not regard *all* human beings as the same *equal* persons in the universal scheme, but discriminately place value on human lives with different prices and degrees of punishments based on their social classes/statuses. On the contrary, the biblical laws regard *all* human lives equally as *persons*.

The second reason is that the ANE lawgivers/cultures do not hold the view that laws should bear the function of morality shaping. The examination demonstrates that while the ANE lawgivers express their humanitarian concerns in the prologues and epilogues of their law books, these speeches, while using the first person voice, have no intent to establish relationship with their legal subjects, interact with them, or to shape their morality. The third person voice of the ANE laws provides no interpersonal relationship (moral dimension) for their legal subjects to meditate and to interact with one another. On the other hand, Deuteronomy holds the position that laws can bear the function of morality shaping and promoting human rights based on a *reciprocal* relationship with God.

The entire book of Deuteronomy is purposefully constructed and designed to reflect this position. With the covenantal relationship, YHWH can interact with his legal subjects, shape their peoplehood, and promote the ethical values and his humanitarian concerns. This reciprocal relationship is based on the concept that all legal subjects are free and dignified persons and all agents are regarded as persons, including slaves, suspected murderers, and war captives.

Deuteronomy on the one hand recognizes that its legal subjects are free and dignified persons; on the other hand, it asserts their limits and dependence. Therefore, the concept of human rights in Deuteronomy is built on YHWH's redemption and sovereignty. For Deuteronomy, human rights needs God to be the essential figure to get involved because respecting and defending human rights require moral strength and convictions. Deuteronomy proclaims that one who reveres YHWH by obeying his words under his covenantal relationship could assume moral strength and convictions, because YHWH and his words are the universal origins and norms of righteousness and justice. In this way, by obeying his words and laws, Israel would also learn of God's character and in turn be shaped not only in their moral development and betterment of interpersonal relationships with the slaves in Israelite society, but as to function as whole moral persons. In becoming such persons, the ethos of God's laws would hopefully permeate the hearts of the Israelite so that they would truly be God's people, in *spirit* and in *deed*.

6 Conclusion: Summary, Contributions, and Further Avenues of Research

Law without (what I call) religion degenerates into mechanical legalism.
Religion without (what I call) law loses its social effectiveness.[1]

Law has to be believed in, or it will not work.
It involves not only man's reason and will,
but his emotions, his intuitions, and commitments,
and his faith.[2]

This study has presented a multidimensional examination involving a comparative legal study between the biblical and the ANE slave laws. It not only compared analogous laws, but also rhetorical techniques, methods of law grouping, structures, and arrangements of law collections, as well as the rationale of legal philosophy behind laws and law books. In addition, by incorporating a proposed legal categorizational system, this multidimensional comparative study arrived at the following conclusion: The degree of similarity between the biblical and the ANE slave laws is limited to certain legal topics and issues. It is not an exaggeration to note that they are fundamentally different, given that the biblical laws hold two diverse rationales of legal philosophy in comparison to the ANE laws: (1) *all* agents are regarded as *persons* and should be treated accordingly. (2) *all* legal subjects are seen as *free, dignified*, and *self-determining* human beings. Hence, both chattel and debt slaves are regarded as persons and should be treated as unbound persons with dignity. In addition to these two extraordinary legal philosophies, the biblical laws often distinguish an offender's "criminal intent," by which a criminal's rights are also considered. Based on these two distinctive legal philosophies and also the distinction of criminal intent, the biblical laws are able to articulate YHWH's humanitarian concerns in a way that is fundamentally different than those of the ANE laws (e.g. see in particular, the two slave laws in Deuteronomy 15:12–18 and 23:16–17 which outstandingly represent YHWH's compassion for human rights).

In previous comparative legal studies between the biblical and the ANE laws, scholars mostly focused on their similarities and developed theories based on these resemblances. However, the humanitarian concerns of the biblical slave laws and their abundant rhetorical techniques that were laced with persuasive modes in the Deuteronomic slave laws rarely received commensurate at-

---

1 Berman, Harold J. *The Interaction of Law and Religion* (Nashville: Abingdon, 1974), 11.
2 Ibid., 14.

tention. With regards to comparative studies of biblical and ANE slave laws, the literary review in chapter one showed that previous studies attempted to explain similarities by literary dependence and differences by their historical settings. However, this ignored the fact that legal transplants were common in ancient societies since the earliest human history. In light of this, any similarity between various laws do not necessarily represent later or direct evidence of borrowing. Hence (following R. Westbrook, W. W. Hallo, A. Watson, and K. L. Younger's approaches on comparative studies), even when one considers that biblical laws and other ANE laws belonged to a common legal culture that shared a legal ontology, each legal corpus in a specific society could develop laws within its own *Volksgeist*. It was in this manner that this study aimed to distinguish any such similarities and dissimilarities to pursue an understanding of underlying values promoted within these slave laws and the interests they protected.

To do so, certain innovative methodologies were crucial to this task. This study suggested five methods of doing comparative legal studies with respect to these ancient laws: (1) A classification of biblical and ANE laws to provide a more inclusive base for surveying slave laws and other forms of human bondage. (2) A legal categorizational system to discern degrees of analogy. (3) Examinations on methods of law grouping and structures of law books to understand the ancient compilers' logic of arrangements, didactic intentions, and the values these laws promoted. (4) Explorations on rationales of legal philosophies behind laws (such as cosmologies, worldviews, and positions of morality that was shaped in the laws) to uncover the fundamental ethos that the laws legislated. (5) Rhetorical analyses of the laws to read their phraseology, syntaxes, and contexts as originally written. Finally, these methods, in varying degrees of emphasis, were applied throughout various chapters of this study to appreciate these laws and comprehend their promotion of human rights.

The manner of their examination unfolded in chapter two with an exegetical study of the Deuteronomic slave laws (illuminated by an exploration of the structure and theological theme of the Deuteronomic law book). It reviewed and evaluated past and common approaches on the arrangement of Deuteronomic laws (e. g., the "association of elements" and "Decalogue correspondence") and discussed their limitations. Consequently, a "chiastic framework" was therefore suggested to satisfactorily explain the current settings and locations of the two slave laws.

It was argued that the central theme of the chiastic framework (in Deut 19:1–21:9) is YHWH's determination to protect all human lives on his promised land. Within this framework, Deuteronomy presented YHWH's humanitarian concerns with a combined theological and sociological theme. The most significant feature of this theme is that YHWH, land, and law are indivisible. The agrarian products from the land are the significant symbols of YHWH's blessings that reflected Israel's obedience to YHWH's laws. The responsibility of the Israelite is to revere YHWH as the One and Only God by obeying his laws and sharing their blessings to the socially weak. From this perspective, this study contends that Deuteronomy does not view the land that was promised to Israel to be merely conditional, but the book elucidates the promise by characterizing the *land* and *law* together with a combined theological and sociological meaning. In this study, the two slave laws are the representatives of the combined theological and sociological theme of the law book: they aim at unconditionally protecting the underprivileged in YHWH's land as well as to address the most basic of human rights—to live freely without fear and with substantial provision regardless of one's status, gender, and ethnicity.

An exegesis of indentured Hebrew slave laws in Deut 15:12–18 also showed that this law is embodied with a basic spirit of human rights. The collocation of עִבְרִיָּה/עִבְרִי and אָחִיךָ are not tautologous even though both terms are ethnic in sense. The phrase אָחִיךָ הָעִבְרִי אוֹ הָעִבְרִיָּה is used to illustrate an inherent concept of *fraternity*, evoking the listeners' affection of sympathy to sway their rational (logos) and emotional (pathos) senses into compliance with the law. The idea of *equality* in Deut 15:12–18 is based on one's experience of YHWH's redemption and understanding of selflessness so that one can truly treat one another with equality while Deut 15:16–18 promotes an intrinsic value that explicates *liberty* for all those who are under YHWH's redemption and covenant – that *all* slaves should go out of service in the seventh year unless the slave is willing to stay.

In a discussion of the motive clauses in Deut 15:15, 18, it was observed that Deuteronomy applies various formulated phrases, which consist of specific vocabularies that can be regarded as a "pattern language." This Deuteronomic pattern language is a deliberate design which relates YHWH to his people and his humanitarian concerns.

A study of the fugitive slave law in Deut 23:16–17 revealed that this law also reflected the combined theological and sociological theme that was found in Deut 15:12–18. When a foreign slave runs away from his/her master and enters into YHWH's land, he/she is no longer considered as a slave, but as a resident alien. YHWH's land is an asylum not only for escaped slaves from Egypt, but also for any other non-Hebrew slave fugitives. The land promise includes freedom and human dignity for anyone who enters into this territory. Deut 23:16–17 thus challenges the entire community to recognize that YHWH is the real Master of the Land.

The values that the two Deuteronomic slave laws promoted are explicit: Slavery, for any Israelite, is a means of requiting debt, not a destiny. There is no permanent, abused, or involuntary slave to be allowed in YHWH's land.

Following chapter two, the next chapter was dedicated to a comparative study between the biblical slave laws in Exod 21, Lev 25, and Dt 15. While differences between these laws were obvious, this study argued that the explanations for these differences did not necessitate any literary dependence, changes of social background, or suppression/abrogation of a later law to a former one. This chapter however suggested three approaches to interpret their differences and similarities: rhetorical analysis, examinations of legal categorizational system, and reading the law in its own context.

From a rhetorical analysis, it was argued that Dt 15 and Ex 21 shared the same rhetorical technique (e.g., the polyvocality of the combined discourses) to maintain the same attitude concerning regulations of permanent slaves. The combined discourses expounded the lawgiver's intention to help readers understand his attitude toward the underprivileged and his concern about human rights. Likewise, Lev 25 not only shared some similar linguistic features with Dt 15, it also used other rhetorical skills to present the same humanitarian concerns as Dt 15. In this context, any interpretation of Lev 25 should consider the logic of an idealistic protective system in Leviticus 25. The manumission law in Lev 25 expresses nothing about a forty-nine years long debt-service, because it assumes that if a particular issue (e.g., land redemption and sufficient supplement) in the earlier stages had been resolved, the successive stage needs not have taken place. The Jubilee was the last *recourse* of this social protective system: none should be retained in bondage in the Jubilee year.

The three laws were further compared by the legal categorizational system, which was a tangible way to demarcate the degrees of similarity and difference. This system distinguished laws in three levels of similarities and differences—*topic*, *issues*, and *situations*. Laws within the same legal topic were further distinguished into different legal issues. Under one legal issue, laws were additionally divided into various *situations*. This system suggests the standard of analogy as such: laws in the same legal topic and under a similar legal issue can be considered as *parallel*. Laws that have a similar situation can be regarded as *closely parallel*. Outside of this system, laws may have only *similar* legal topics or *similar* legal issues. Under this legal categorizational system, these slave laws can be understood in another manner. They are similar in three ways: (1) They have the same *legal topic* of *Debt-servitude*. (2) Their primary *legal issue* concerns the same one regarding Hebrew debt slave manumission, and (3) Their *legal style* (casuistic primary law) and *substance* (release with various conditions) are similar. They are *parallel* laws but differ in varying degrees of emphasis.

A closer examination and evaluation of other passages using the legal categorizational system suggested that Exod 21:7–11 should be regarded as an independent law with a different legal topic. Even though it refers to a law concerning the sale of an Israelite daughter into a marriage contract, it does not fall under the same legal topic of *Debt-servitude* in Exod 21:2–6. Therefore, the parallels between Ex 21, Lev 25, and Dt 15 should exclude Exod 21:7–11.

Furthermore, it is argued that to read a law within its entire context in a corpus provides a vastly superior understanding of its underlying values rather than readings of a single verse or word. The former approach better avoids any misconstrual of the intents or values of a law. Historical examples of various misinterpretations of these three slave laws that resulted from partial readings can be seen in (1) the change of viewpoints from buyer (Exod 21:2) to seller (Deut 15:12), (2) assertions that the laws destroy the marriage concept and family ties (Exod 21:3–4), that male slaves can be used for reproduction, and that the laws protect only the owner's profit, (3) claims that Dt 15 supersedes Ex 21 to allow a female slave to have the same right to leave and that Lev 25 abolishes Dt 15 to forbid Hebrew slaves to become permanent slaves, (4) assumptions that Lev 25 maintains a forty nine year enslavement, and so on. This study concludes that when one reads the law in its own context, such issues would be reasonably solved and the laws be appropriately interpreted.

Elsewhere, chapter four investigated a number of ANE slave laws and compared them with the biblical ones. From terminology studies and examinations of the slave systems in the ANE, it was suggested that the traditional distinction between a debt slave (as temporary) versus a chattel slave (as permanent), failed to account for all elements of various ANE slave institutions as the availability of redemption was based on contract by contract, but not limited to the types of slave that many modern scholars tend to assume.

This study also classified the laws of six ANE legal collections and three biblical law books (Covenant, Leviticus, and Deuteronomy) into a compilation, which shed light into the area of comparative legal study between the biblical and ANE laws as well as addressing some prevailing misconceptions. It showed that the grouping of legal materials in the ANE law books can be done by detecting formulaic phrases and thematic issues. By the use of these two techniques, the ANE compilers were able to effectively communicate the values and ideas of their society didactically. Because of this, the previous attempts to use insertion theory are unnecessarily even if redactions had taken place. This study demonstrated that ANE slave laws, when understood in their original grouping categories, have little concern for slave rights for in their legal perspective a slave is a piece of property (a thing) rather than a person. One can see that among the ANE slave laws, only LE 49–52, LH 15–20, HL 22–24, LH 278–282, and LH 117–119 are identically formed groups that show evidence of slave motifs. As a whole, the major concern of those laws is to protect the property and purchase rights of the owner. On the other hand, while biblical slave laws do allow chattel slaves, these slaves were required to be treated as a person in YHWH's land.

In chapter four, it was argued that slavery is hardly the only form of bondage that disrespects human dignity and freedom in the ANE world as there existed many forms of human bondage that deprived the socially weak of their freedom and dignity. For example, human distraints and pledges were two other forms of human bondage cunningly developed to bind people into permanent, chattel slavery. In contrast, the biblical laws do not provide any legal basis for such kinds of oppression. The Deuteronomic laws for example favor the socially weak in dealing with a loan or pledge. Likewise, Ex 21, Lev 25 and Dt 15 build up a social protective network to prevent permanent human bondage.

A consistent principle in reading the ANE slave laws was also suggested for their interpretation, i.e., appreciating the *entire* context of a law. The approach is that slave laws mostly describe relationships and obligations between related parties and objects. For these ancient casuistic laws, examining a single term or verse (a method often used by ANE comparative legal scholars) is insufficient to expound the spirit or the concern of a law. Rather, due considerations such as its location in a group or within a larger context in its immediate group(s) is a better approach.

The use of the tabulation of the ANE and biblical laws and the legal categorizational system to compare the biblical and ANE laws revealed significantly obvious differences between these two sets of laws. Though the biblical slave laws and their ANE counterparts may share similar legal topics, they may actually be referring to different positions, issues, or situations. Of them all, the slave laws that most closely parallel biblical and ANE laws are Exod 21:32 with LE 55, 57 and LH 252. The next closest parallel is the debt servitude laws of Ex 21, Lev 25, and Dt 15 to LH 117. Others are only similar in the level of the various legal issues discussed. Surveyed as a whole, biblical slave laws consistently hold to a higher humanitarian concern (i.e., the demands in Exod 21:20–21; 26–27 find no parallel in similar ANE laws). The humanitarian ethos that the biblical slave laws promote finds no comparison in the ANE laws. However, no claims are made here that biblical laws are superior to other ANE laws for the reason that the ANE and biblical laws are based on different legal philosophies of morality in the shaping of their laws.

Following this, chapter five thus explored and compared the different cosmologies, worldviews, and positions on the function of moralities that shape the ANE versus biblical laws to understand the logic behind these laws that led to differences in humanitarian concern. While the differences in ANE cosmology provide a certain cognitive dimension for understanding its worldview as reflected in its laws, this does not fully explain the absence of humanitarian concerns in the ANE laws. Two different rationales were observed. The first is the differing notions of equality in regarding all human beings as persons.

The second point of logic found in the ANE lawgivers/cultures is that they probably do not believe that laws should bear a function of shaping morality. The examination in chapter five showed that while the ANE lawgivers express their humanitarian concerns in the prologues and epilogue sections of their law books, these speeches, while using the first person voice, have no intentions of establishing any relationship with their legal subjects, whether in terms of interacting with them, or in shaping their morality. In addition, the third person voice of the ANE laws provides no interpersonal relationship (moral dimension) for their legal subjects to meditate and to interact with one another. On the other hand, Deuteronomy holds that laws can function in terms of working to shape morality and promote human rights based on a *reciprocal* relationship with God.

By deploying Fox-Decent's theory, this study concludes that the entire book of Deuteronomy is purposefully constructed and designed to reflect this position. In the covenantal context of the book, YHWH is identified as that *personal* monarch that establishes a reciprocal relationship so that he can interact with his legal subjects relationally to shape their peoplehood and promote the ethical values of his humanitarian concerns. A reciprocal relationship in this arrangement is also seen in the book where all legal subjects are free and dignified persons and all agents are regarded as persons, including slaves, suspected murderers, and war captives. While Deuteronomy recognizes that its legal subjects are free and dignified persons, it does stipulate their limits and dependence. Thus, while the concept of human rights in Deuteronomy is built on YHWH's redemption and sovereignty, the rights of humans need God to be the essential figure and key agent of action because respecting and defending these rights requires a requisite moral strength and conviction to do so in the midst of human weakness. Deuteronomy is convinced that the one who reveres YHWH by obeying his words under his covenantal relationship could assume the effective source of moral strength and convictions, because YHWH and his words are the universal origins and norms of righteousness and justice. In this way, by obeying his words and laws, Israel would also learn of God's character and in turn be shaped not only in their moral development and betterment of interpersonal relationships with the slaves in Israelite society, but to function as whole moral persons. In becoming such persons, the ethos of God's laws would hopefully permeate the hearts of the Israelite so that they would truly be God's people, in *spirit* and in *deed*.

The Import of This Study for Biblical Comparative Legal Studies

This research has sought to present a different approach to the comparative legal studies between the biblical and the ANE laws in comparison to traditional approaches such as the source critical model or historical setting method. Accordingly the contributions of this study can be summarized as falling mainly into the following seven areas below.

First, chapter one observed that "legal transplant" activities have been common since the earliest era of human history. Similarities between two laws do not necessarily represent the reproduction of a later law to a former law. Two similar laws may both derive from a third common legal source. In human history, people have long borrowed laws from other societies/cultures, significantly changed certain details in the process of making them into their own new laws. In this respect, two laws might have a similar subject matter, yet in fact reflect a different ethos or value. This perspective thus suggests to biblical comparative legal scholars to consider that any similarities between laws (e. g., inner-biblical or extra-biblical) do not have to be explained merely by notions of literary dependence or read as evidence of direct borrowing.

Second, this research indicates that the most obvious difference between the biblical and ANE laws is the former's use of various unique rhetorical techniques, which are completely absent in the latter. They include the use of the second person address, the combined discourses, and the motive clauses. These techniques often convey persuasive modes of pathos, ethos, and logos to touch the listeners' hearts to empathize with the socially weak and to comply with the laws. In addition, the biblical laws often distinguish "criminal intent" in most criminal laws to clarify intentional or unintentional crimes of killing a person – an advanced jurisprudential concept that also finds no parallel in the ANE laws. These rhetorical techniques and the distinction of "criminal intent" demonstrate that not only do the biblical laws hardly replicate laws from other legal sources directly; they also revised these laws and voiced them with their own spirit, values, and theological motivation. These significant differences have seldom been closely investigated and discussed. Historically, similarities between the laws have attracted the most attention and have been frequently emphasized as the evidence of direct borrowing.

Third, the tabulations of "A Compilation of Biblical and Cuneiform Law Collections" (appendix A) and "Biblical and ANE Laws Related to Slave Issues" (appendix B) classifies slave laws into three categories: *Slave Escape*, *Slave Purchase and Management*, and *Debt-servitude and Other Forms of Human Bondage*, which presented the first level of comparison as a *legal topic*. Taken in conjunction with the legal categorizational system, the degrees of analogy between the biblical and the ANE laws can be more objectively discerned and compared. The use of such categories in combination with a legal categorizational system is suggested as a promising method for use in future comparative legal studies between these ancient casuistic laws.

Fourth, in surveying the rhetorical techniques in Deuteronomic slave laws, this study observes pattern language in the book which is a deliberate design to relate YHWH to his people and his humanitarian concerns. The three major features of this Deuteronomic pattern language are the following: (1) It is YHWH-related. (2) It often serves as a motive clause and this motive clause usually carries strong persuasive modes that attempt to convey pathos, ethos, and logos. (3) It conceptually links similar laws and commandments together, often with an intention to highlight humanitarian concerns. It is proposed that the Deuteronomic pattern language can be the basis for further discussions, development and research in studying these laws.

Fifth, a principle, *reading a law in its context*, was introduced and deployed as a hermeneutic throughout the comparisons of both the biblical and the ANE laws. This approach overcomes many previous misunderstandings and biased explanations that mostly resulted from a partial reading of a law with a single word, phrase, or verse. In so doing, these readings did not treat these ancient laws as legislative texts or as a type of "legal genre". On the other hand, the exploration and reading of a law in its larger context and its grouping with external others in this study reveal a number of significant insights in which to understand the values and the interest that these ancient laws intend to promote and protect. In addition, this research also indicates that a misunderstanding of past studies of these slave laws also noted that the manner in how one would use or abuse a law does not necessarily represent the function or the purpose of a law.

Sixth, this study is concerned with propinquity in doing comparative study in the manner that Younger proposes.[3] For example, the comparisons made in this study were limited to the biblical and ANE laws, not in comparison with the contemporary laws or the advanced concepts of human rights today. In using this manner of comparison to their ancient counterparts, it was noted that the biblical laws do express humanitarian concerns and some basic concepts of equality of human worth, dignity and rights in Deuteronomy while similar concerns and concepts find no parallels in their ancient counterparts. How-

---

3 K. Lawson Younger, Jr. "The 'Contextual Method': Some West Semitic Reflections," in *The Context of Scripture III* (ed. William W. Hallo and K. Lawson Younger, Jr.; New York: E. J. Brill, 2003), xxxvii.

ever, when Younger's approach is not followed, unjust critiques of the biblical slave laws often prevail in scholarship as a result of comparing biblical laws with contemporary concepts and conditions. In a recent example, C. B. Anderson argued that "certain biblical laws ignore the specific circumstances and interests of women, non-Israelites (especially the Canaanites), and the poor, and that consideration of these situations challenges some of the ethical principles commonly drawn from the Old Testament."[4] Anderson's critique is unsound. In comparison to their ancient counterparts, the biblical laws extraordinarily express more concerns for the needs and the rights of the socially weak, even including the slaves, the captives, and criminals who commit unintentional killing of a human being. Chapter five also indicated that YHWH destroys and expels *any* person, including an Israelite, who worships other pagan deities and disobeys his words *in his land* (Deut 8:20).[5]

Seventh, the conclusions regarding the biblical laws' humanitarian concerns and the concept of human rights were also drawn by examining the legal philosophies between the biblical and the ANE law books. It was noted that the lawgivers of the ANE laws do express their humanitarian concerns in the prologues and epilogues in some of their law collections and edicts. However, they seem to hold to the position that the law need not bear the function of shaping morality; therefore the laws themselves were not written with humanitarian concerns in mind. The book of Deuteronomy holds to an opposite position and thus articulates its humanitarian concerns and the concepts of human rights.

---

4 Cheryl B. Anderson, "Biblical Laws: Challenging the Principles of Old Testament Ethics," in *Character Ethics and the Old Testament* (ed. M. Daniel Carroll R. and Jacqueline E. Lapsley; Louisville: Westminster John Knox, 2007), 38.
5 One may consider thinking about how many Israelites perished in YHWH's anger when they did the same things as the Canaanites did in the Golden Calf event in Exodus 32 and the Shittim adultery event in Numbers 25. In fact, they were eventually destroyed and expelled out of the Promised land as the Canaanites when they went astray to follow pagan deities in the sixth centuray B. C.

Appendix A: A Compilation of Biblical and Cuneiform Law Collections

Italics represent unique laws or legal concepts that occur only in the biblical law collections.

	Sumerian		Babylonian		Assyrian	Hittite	Israelite
	LU	LL	LE	LH	MAL	HL	
1. Abortion (also miscarriage)	d–f			209–214	A 21, 50–53		
2. Accusation (or blaspheme, slander)	13, 14	17, 33		1, 2, 127, 131–132	A 2, 17–19; N 1, 2		Exod 23:1–3, 6–9; Lev 19:11–12; Deut 19:15–21
3. Adoption			32–35?	185–193			
4. Accidental death (a man killed by domestic animals—ox, dog, or accidental events)			54–58	228–233		37, 38	Exod 21:28–32
5. Architecture			58?	228–233			Deut 22:8
6. Alimony contract			32?				
7. Arson						98–100, 105–106	
8. Body injury (1)— *lex talionis*				195, 196–197	A 7		Exod 21:23–25; Lev 24:19–20; Deut 25:11–12

	Sumerian		Babylonian		Assyrian	Hittite	Israelite
	LU	LL	LE	LH	MAL	LU	
9. Body injury (2)—pecuniary compensation	18–22		42–47	198–208	A 7–9,	7–18	Exod 21:18–19; 26–27
10. Border violation					B 8, 9, 19, 20	168–169	Deut 19:14
11. Businessman				100–107		5	
12. Buying			15, 38–41	C	C+ G 2–4		
13. Cattle which has knocked				250–252			
14. Commercial Law			15				
15. Community		7?		112 ?	B 1–5 O 5		
16. Competence	32						
17. Contract, break of		20b	48	42–44		145–149	
18. Culture/Agriculture						101–113	
19. *Cursing God or ruler*							*Exod 22:28*
20. Defamation, slander					A 2, 17–19		Deut 22:13–19
21. *Delaying of offerings*							*Exod 22:29–30*
22. Distraint	3		22–24	241			
23. Divorce	9–11	30	59	137–143	A 36–38	26–27	Deut 24:1–4
24. Doctor, physician, go to see a doctor						10	

	Sumerian		Babylonian		Assyrian	Hittite	Israelite
	LU	LL	LE	LH	MAL	HL	
25. Domestic animal, safeguard			54–58?		C+ G 4–6		Exod 21:28–36; Deut 25:4?

26. Damage to property	10	59, 244–248		74, 75, 77a-78, 86–90, 98–100, 107, 109, 113	Exod 22:5–6; Lev 24:21a,
27. Damage to animal-caused by animal	53–57	57–58, 250–252		60–62, 79, 90	Exod 21:33, 34–36
28. *Eating the torn in the field*					*Exod 22:31*
29. Employment	7, 8	100–107, 253–258, 261, 263		42, 200b	Exod 23:10–12; Deut 24:14–15
30. Female innkeeper	15, 41				
31. *Festivals*		108–111			*Exod 23:14–17; Lev 23:1–44; Deut:16:1–17*
32. Fields, lease and cultivation	30–32	42–58	B 10–15, 19, 20	39	
33. Field, sale					Lev 25:23–28
34. Field, taxes	18	36–41	B 6–7		
35. Find, trove				45, 71, 60–62?	Exod 23:4–5
36. Gardens	7–10	59–66			Deut 22:9
37. Goring ox	54–55	250–252	B 12, 13		Exod 21:28–32, 36–37 [Eng. 21:35–36]
38. *Handling of peace offering*					*Lev 19:5–8*
39. *Honor the elderly*					*Lev 19:32*
40. *Holy people to Yahweh*					*Lev 18:24–30; Deut 14:1–21; 23:9–14*
41. House, sale and redemption	39				Lev 25:29–34
42. House, Guarding	60				

			MAL	Bible
43. Husband's right of treating his wife	21–27, 31, 32			Deut 21:15–17
44. Inheritance, property distribution	16–18	137–143, 150, 151–152? 162–184	MAL A 42, 43, 57–59; A 25–29, 41, 46, B 1–5, O 3; 173; 25; 6, 27	
45. Insubordination to rulers				
46. Irrigation, Water Right				
47. Jubilee				Lev 25:8–22
48. Judge, corrupt		5		
49. Judgment of God		2	A 22	
50. Juridical offices and Institutions: priests and judgers' duties				Deut 17:8–13; 21:1–9;
51. Kidnapping, abduction or elopement				Exod 21:16; Deut 24:7
52. Killing of a man (1)—murder [1]	26	15	A 10?	Exod 21:12; Lev 24:17, 21b; Num 35:16–21
53. Killing of a man (2) —accidentally		153, 207/8, 210, 212, 214, 218, 219, 229, 251	1–6, 19–21, 37	Exod 21:13–14; Num 35:22–28
54. *King's duties*				Deut 17:14–20
55. Lease		42–47		
56. *Leviticus*				Deut 18:1–8
57. *Limits on flogging*				Deut 25:1–4
58. Loan and debts (1)—regular case	20–24	48–52	A 44	Lev 25:35–55; Deut 15:1–6; 23:19–20; 24:6, 10–13

59. Loan and debts (2)— no usury							*Exod 22:25–27; Lev 25:35–37; Deut 23:19–20*
60. Loan and debts (3)— shemittah law							*Deut 15:1–6*
61. Love your neighbor as yourself							*Lev 19:17–18*
62. Magic, wizardry and sorcery				2	A 47	44b, 111, 163, 170, 180,	*Exod 22:18; Lev 19:31; 20:6–8, 27; Deut 18:9–14*
63. Magic, wizardry and sorcery				2	A 47	44b, 111, 163, 170, 180	*Exod 22:18; Lev 19:31; 20:6–8, 27; Deut 18:9–14*
64–72. Marriage law							
64. Engagement, marriage contract/agreement and compensation of breaking off marriage contract	15	11, 29	17–18, 25–28	128, 156, 159–161	A 30, 31, 322, 43, 48	28–30	
65. Slave marriage	4–5					31–36, 175	
66. Widow marriage					A33–35		
67. Levirate marriage				193	A 30		Deut 25:5–10
68. Priest/Priestess marriage				178–184			Lev 21:7, 13–14
69. Remarriage forbidden							*Deut 24:1–4*
70. Wife's provision while husband's away (e.g. in prison, missing, death...)			29–30	133–136	A36, 45, 46		
71. Marry a captive woman							Deut 21:10–14
72. Polygamy		28	144–149				Exod 21:7–11?

	Sumerian		Babylonian		Assyrian	Hittite	Israelite
	LU	LL	LE	LH	MAL	HL	
73. Miqtum[1]							
74. Military duty and soldier's property/marriage protection		15, 16		26–38			Deut 20:5–8; 24:5
75. Miscarriage				209–214	A 21, 50–52	17, 18	
76. Miscellaneous law: mixture of diverse elements, Transvestism							Lev 19:19; Deut 22:5–7, 9–11
77. Monotheism: no other gods, destruction of the cults of other gods, beware of false prophets, and idolatries							Exod 22:20; 23:13; Lev 26:1–2 Deut 12:2–4; 13:1–13; 17:1–7
78. Oath				227, 240	A 22	75	
79. Oil for the lamp before Yahweh							Lev 24:1–4
80. Pledge			22–24	113–119, 241	A 39, 44, 48, C+G 2, 3, 4, 7	76, 164–165	Deut 24:6
81. Prices			1–11, 14, 18 A-24	241–277		1–18, 25, 178–188	
82. Priest, requirements							Lev 21:1–24
83. Prostitution forbidden							Lev 19:29; Deut 23:17–18
84. Property Loads		18					
85. Release all the debts at the end of seven years							Deut 15:1–6
86. Real estate, sale of					B 6–7		

87. Rent, lease	5, 7, 34–37	4, 9	242–249, 268–271	144, 150–152	
88. *Restriction on entry into the Assembly of Yahweh*					*Deut 23:1–8*
89. Reward, paying			215–217, 220–283	150–161	
90. Reputation of the son				171	
91. Repurchase right	39				
92. Robbery			22–24		
93. Ritual regulations				163–167	
94. *Ritual: oil of lamp, bread and pure incense*					*Lev 24:1–9*
95. *Sabbatical year*					*Lev 25:1–7*
96. Sabbath					
97. *Sacrifices: no blemish*					*Lev 22:17–33; Deut 17:1*
98. *Sacrifice to Yahweh: the right places*					*Deut 12:5–32*
99. *Sacrifice to Molek*		M 1, 2	234–240		*Lev 18:21; 20:1–5*
100. Ship, boat					
101–109 Sexual crime and Prohibited sexual relation					
101. Adultery (1)—general cases	7	A13–16, 23–24	127, 129, 153	196–197	*Lev 18:20; 19:20–22; Deut 22:20–21; Num 5:11–31; Deut 22:13–21, 22*
(2)—suspicious of marital infidelity		A22	131–132		
102. Bestiality			187–188, 199, 200a		*Exod 22:19; Lev 18:23; 20:15–16*

Item						Scripture
103. Incest			154–158		189–195a	Lev 18:6–18; 20:11–12, 17, 19–21; Deut 22:30
104. *Homosexuality*						*Lev 18:22; 20:13*
105. Rape	6, 8	26, 31	130	A 12, 55		Deut 22:23–29
106. Seduction	7					
107. Sexual attack, harassment				A 9, 12, 55 / A 20	197–198	Deut 22:23–27, 28–30
108. Sodomy						
109. *With menstruating woman*						*Lev 17:18*
110–114 Slavery laws						
110. *Slave escape (1)— protecting runaway slaves*						*Deut 23:16–17 [Eng. 21:15–16]*
111. Slave escape (2)—Demanding returning runaway slaves	17	12–13	49–52	15–20	22–24	
112. Slave Purchase and Management	4–5, 8, 25–26,	31, 33–35, 40, 55, 57	7, 19, 146–147, 205, 213–214, 252, 278–282	C+G 1	31–36, 173b, 175	Exod 21:20–21, 26–27, 31; Lev 19:20–22
113. Debt-servitude			117			Exod 21:2–6; Lev 25:39–55; Deut 15:12–18
114. Other form of human bondage (also pledge, distraint)		22–24	114–116, 118–119	A 39, 44, 48, C+G 2, 3, 7		
115. *Social justice*						*Exod 23:1–9; Lev 19:11–16, 35–36; Deut 25:13–16*

116. Soil right	7, 8						Exod 22:7–15
117. Storage, custody, deposit		36, 37	52–58	113, 120–126, 259–260	B 10–15, 19, 20; C+G 9–11		
118. Suppression				112, 113	C+G 3, M 3		
119. *Transgenerational punishment forbidden*							*Deut 24:16*
120. Taxes, tithe	18						*Deut 12:6,11, 17; 26:1–15*
121. Tariffs	28, 29	1, 2					
122. Testimony, false			3, 4				
123. Theft, burglary	9	12–13, 36–37	6–14, 21, 25, 253–255, 259–260		A 1, 3–6; C+G 6, 8, F 1, 2	57–59, 63–70, 81–85, 93–97, 101–104, 110, 119–143 200b	Exod 21:37–2:3 [Eng. 22:1–4]
124. *Training contract*							
125. Treatment of parents—striking, cursing and rebellious against parents			192–193, 195				Exod 21:15, 17; Lev 19:32; 20:9; Deut 21:18–21
126. *Treatment of minority (foreigners, widow, orphan, and poverty)*							*Exod 22:21–27; 23:9; Lev 19:9–10, 33–34; Deut 15:7–11; 24:14–15, 19–22*
127. *Treatment of dead body on the tree*			57, 58, 253–256, 264–267		F 2		*Deut 21:22–23*
128. Unfaithful herdsman or shepherd							

129. Unauthorized person, order of			C+G 4–6	*Deut 23:21–23*
130. *Vow*				*Deut 20:1–22*
131. *Warfare*				
132. Water Law	53–56		B 17,18 162	
133. Wet-nurse-contract	32	194		

[1] "Miqtum" is a member of a social or economic class of persons possibly under royal patronage. See M. T. Roth, *Law Collections from Mesopotamia and Asia Minor* (Atlanta: Scholar Press, 1997), 271.

Appendix B: Biblical and ANE Slave Laws and ANE Laws Related to Slave Issues

The texts of the ANE slave laws are cited from Martha T. Roth, *Law Collections from Mesopotamia and Asia Minor* (Atlanta: Scholars Press, 1997). The texts of Exod 21:2–11; Lev 25 39–55; Deut 15:12–18, are not reproduced here.

Notations and symbols appear in the following texts:

[ ] Full square brackets mark restorations to broken text in the original.
< > Half square brackets mark modern insertion of text omitted by the ancient scribe.
( ) Parentheses enclose material added to the English translation.
... Ellipses mark untranslatable text or a gap.

Slave escape		
1. Slave escape— protecting runaway slaves (Deut 23:16–17 [Eng. 21:15–16])		
2. Slave escape— returning runaway slaves	(1). Rewards of Returning a Runaway Slave (LU 17; LH 17; HL 22–24)	LU 17 If [a slave or (?)] a slave women [...] venture beyond the borders of (his or) her city and a man returns (him or) her, the slave's master shall weigh and deliver [x] shekels of silver to the man who returned (the slave). LH 17 If a man seizes a fugitive slave or slave woman in the open country and leads him back to his owner, the slave owner shall give him 2 shekels of silver. HL 22a If male slave runs away, and someone brings him back, if he seizes him nearby, his owner shall give shoes to the finder. 22b. If he seizes him on the near side of the river, he shall pay 2 shekels of silver. If on the far side of the river, he shall pay him 3 shekels of silver. HL 23a If a male slave runs away and goes to the land of

Luwiya, his owner shall pay 6 shekels of silver to whomever brings him back. 23b. If a male slave runs away and goes into an enemy country, whoever brings him back shall keep him for himself.

HL 24 If a male or female slave runs away, the one at whose hearth the slave owner finds him/her shall pay one month's wages: 12 shekels of silver for a man, 6 shekel's of silver for a woman.

(2). Punishments for Not Returning Runaway Slave (LL 12–13; LE 49–50; LH 16, 18, 19, 20)

LL 12 If a man's female slave or male slave flees within the city, and it is confirmed that the slave dwelt in a man's house for one month, he (the one who harbored the fugitive slave) shall give slave for slave.

LL 13 If he has no slave, he shall weigh and deliver 15 shekels of silver.

LE 49 If a man should be seized with a stolen slave or a stolen slave woman, a slave shall lead a slave, a slave woman shall lead a slave woman.

LE 50 If a military governor, a governor of a canal system, or any person in a position of authority seizes a fugitive slave, fugitive slave woman, stray ox, or stray donkey belonging either to the palace or to a commoner, and does not lead it to Eshnunna but detains it in his house and allows more than one month to elapse, the palace shall bring a charge of theft against him.

LH 16 If a man should harbor a fugitive slave or a slave woman of either the palace or of a commoner in his house and not bring him out at the herald's public proclamation, that householder shall be killed.

LH 18 If that slave should refuse to identify his owner, he shall lead him off to the palace, his circumstances shall be investigated, and they shall return him to his owner.

LH 19 If he should detain that slave in his own house and afterward the slave is discovered in his possession, that man shall be killed.

LH 20 If the slave should escape the custody of the one who seized him, that man shall swear an oath by the god to the owner of the slave, and he shall be released.

(3). Prohibition against a Slave Crossing through the Main City-gate (LE 51, 52; LH 15)

LE 51 A slave or a slave woman belonging to (a resident of) Eshnunna who bears fetters, shackles, or a slave hairlock will not exit through the main city-gate of Eshnunna without his owner.

LE 52 A slave or a slave woman who has entered the main city-gate of Eshnunna in the safekeeping of only a foreign envoy shall be made to bear fetters, shackles, or a slave hairlock and thereby is kept safe for his owner.

LH 15 If a man should enable a palace slave, a palace slave woman, a commoner's slave, or a commoner's slave woman to leave through the main city-gate, he shall be killed.

Slave Purchase and Management

1. Discipline to a Rebellious Slave (LU 25–26, HL173b)

LU 25 If a slave woman curses someone acting with the authority of her mistress, they shall scour her mouth with one sila of salt.

	LU 26 If a slave woman strikes someone acting with the authority of her mistress, […].	
	HL 173b If a slave rebels against his owner, he shall go into a clay jar.	
2. Unlawfully Taking Possession of a Slave (LE 40; LH 7	LE 40 If a man buys a slave, a slave woman, an ox, or any other purchase, but cannot establish the identity of the seller, it is he who is a theft.	
	LH 7 If a man should purchase silver, gold, a slave, a slave woman, an ox, a sheep, a donkey, or anything else whatsoever, form a son of a man or from a slave of a man without witnesses or a contract—or if he accepts the goods for safekeeping—that man is a thief, he shall be killed.	
3. Protection of a Slave Purchaser's Right (LH 278–282; MAL C+G1	LH 278 If a man purchases a slave or a slave woman and within his one-month period epilepsy then befalls him, he shall return him to his seller and the buyer shall take back the silver that he weighed and delivered.	
	LH 279 If a man purchases a slave or slave woman and then claims arise, his seller shall satisfy the claims.	
	LH 280 If a man should purchase another man's slave or slave woman in a foreign country, and while he is traveling about within the (i. e., his own) country the owner of the slave or slave woman identifies his slave or slave woman—if they, the slave and slave woman, are natives of the country, their release shall be secured without any payment.	
	LH 281 If they are natives of another country, the buyer shall declare before the god the amount of silver that he weighed and the owner of the slave or slave woman shall give to the merchant the amount of silver that he paid, and thus he shall redeem his slave or slavewoman.	
	LH 282 If a slave should declare to his master, "You are not my master," he (the master) shall bring charge and proof against him that he is indeed his slave, and his master shall cut off his ear.	
	MAL C+G 1[…] their owner […] and if the buyer [declares, "…"] which I redeemed […," he shall give a slave for x] shekels of lead and a slave woman for 14,400 shekels of lead […]; and if the one who receives should declare, ["…"]; he shall swear an oath before the god and as much as […] he shall take […]	
4. Violations against Another Person's Slave Property Rights and Punishments (LU 8, LE 31, Lev 19:20–22, LH 19, Exod 21:20–21, 26–27, LH 205, LH 226–227, LE 55,	(1). Raping Another Man's Female Slave (LU 8; LE 31)	LU 8 If a man acts in violation of the rights of another and deflowers the virgin slave woman of a man, he shall weight and deliver 5 shekels of silver.

57, LH 252, Exod 21:32, LH
231, LL f; LH 213–214)

LE 31 If a man should de-
flower the slave woman of
another man, he shall weigh
and deliver 20 shekels of silver, but the slave woman remains the property of the
master.

(2). Sexual Intercourse with
Another Man's Betrothed Slave
Woman (Lev 19:20–22)

Lev 19: 20 If a man has sexual
relations with a woman who is
a slave, designated for another man but not ransomed
or given her freedom, an inquiry shall be held. They shall
not be put to death, since she
has not been freed.
Lev 19:21 He shall bring his
guilt offering to the LORD to
the doorway of the tent of
meeting, a ram for a guilt offering.
Lev 19:22 the priest shall also
make atonement for him with
the ram of the guilt offering
before the LORD for his sin
which he has committed, and
the sin which he has committed will be forgiven him.

(3). Injuring Another Man's
Slave (LH 199)

LH 199 If he should blind the
eye of an *awīlu*'s slave or
break the bone of an *awīlu*'s
slave, he shall weigh and deliver one-half of his value (in
silver).

(4). Injuring One's Own Slave
(Exod 21:20–21, 26–27)

Exod 21:20 If a man strikes
his male or female slave with
a rod and he dies at his hand,
he shall be punished.
Exod 21:21 If, however, he
survives a day or two, no
vengeance shall be taken; for
he is his property.
Exod 21:26 If a man strikes
the eye of his male or female
slave, and destroys it, he shall
let him go free on account of
his eye.

	Exod 21:27 and if he knocks out a tooth of his male or female slave, he shall let him go free on account of his tooth.
(5). Injuring of a Free Man by a Slave (LH 205)	LH 205 If an *awīlu*'s slave should strike the cheek of a member of the *awīlu* class, they shall cut off his ear.
(6). Intentional and Unintentional Cutting off a Slave's Hairlock (LH 226–227)	LH 226 If a barber shaves off the slave-hairlock of a slave not belonging to him without the consent of the slave's owner, they shall cut off that barber's hand.
	LH 227 If a man misinforms a barber so that he then shaves off the slave hairlock of a slave not belonging to him, they shall kill that man and hang him in his own doorway; the barber shall swear, "I didn't knowingly shave it off," and he shall be released.
(7). Incidental Death of a Slave Caused by an Animal Biting or Goring (LE 55, 57; LH 252; Exod 21:32)	LE If it gores a slave and thus causes his death, he shall weigh and deliver 15 shekels of silver.
	LE 57 If it bits a slave and this causes his death, he shall weigh and deliver 15 shekels of silver.
	LH 252 If a man's slave (who is fatally gored), he shall give 20 shekels of silver.
	Exod 21:32 If the ox gores a male or female slave, the owner shall give his *or her* master thirty shekels of silver, and the ox shall be stoned.
(8). Incidental Death of a Slave Caused by a Builder's Negligence (LH 231)	LH 231 If it shall cause the death of a slave of the householder, he shall give to the householder a slave of comparable value for the slave.

(9). Incidental Miscarriage or Death of a Slave Woman Caused by Striking (LL f; LH 213–214)	LL f If a …strikes the slave woman of a man and causes her to lose her fetus, he shall weigh and deliver 5 shekels of silver. LH 213 If he strikes an *awīlu*'s slave woman and thereby causes her to miscarry her fetus, he shall weigh and deliver 2 shekels of silver. LH 214 If that slave woman should die, he shall weigh and deliver 20 shekels of silver.
5. Marital Issues Related to a Slave (LU 4–5; HL 31–36, 175; LH 146–147)	(1). Slave Marriages to Different Social Classes (LU 4–5; HL 31–36, HL 175)	LU 4 If a male slave marries a female slave, his beloved, and that male slave (later) is given his freedom, she/he will not leave (or: be evicted from?) the house. LU 5 If a male slave marries a native woman, she/he shall place one male child in the service of his master; the child who is placed in the service of his master, his paternal estate,…the wall, the house, […]; a child of the native woman will not be owned by the master, he will be pressed into slavery. HL 31 If a free man and a female slave are lovers and live together, and he takes her as his wife, and they make a house and children, but afterwards either they become estranged or they each find a new marriage partner, they shall divide the house equally, and the man shall take the children, with the woman taking one child. HL 32 If a male slave [takes] a [free] woman in marriage, [and they make a home and

children, when they divide their house], they shall divide their possessions [equally, and the free woman shall take] most of [the children], with [the male slave taking] one child.

HL 33 If a male slave takes a female slave in marriage, [and they have children,] when they divide their house, they shall divide their possessions equally. [The slave woman shall take] most[t of the children,] with the male slave [taking] one child.

HL 34 If a male slave pays a brideprice for a woman and takes her as his wife, no one shall free her from slavery.

HL 35 If a herdsman [takes] a free woman [marriage], she will become a slave for (only) 3 years.

HL 36 If a slave pays a brideprice for a free young man and acquires him as a son-in-law, no one shall free him from slavery.

HL 175 If either a shepherd or a foreman takes a free woman in marriage, she will become a slave after either two or four years. They shall...her children, but no one shall seize their belts.

(2). A Slave Woman Bearing Children in Place of Her Mistress (LH 146–147)

LH 146 If a man marries a *nadītu*, and she gives a slave woman to her husband, and she (the slave) then bears children, after which that slave woman aspires to equal status with her mistress—because she bore children, her mistress will not sell her; she shall place upon her the

	slave-hairlock, and she shall reckon her with the slave women. LH 147 If she does not bear children, her mistress shall sell her.
6. Adoption Related to a Slave Woman (LE 33 – 35)	LE 33 If a slave woman acts to defraud and gives her child to a woman of the *awīlu-class*, when he grows up should his mater locate him, he shall seize him and take him away. LE 34 If a slave woman of the palace should give her son or her daughter to a commoner for raring, the palace shall remove the son or daughter whom she gave. LE 35 However, an adopter who takes in adoption the child of a slave woman of the palace shall restore (another slave of) equal value for the palace.
7. Special Cases of Slave Release	LL 14 if a man's slave contests his slave status against his master, and it is proven that his master has been compensated for his slavery two-fold, that slave shall be freed. LL 25 If a man marries a wife and she bears him a child and the child lives and a slave woman also bears a child to her master; the father shall free the slave woman; the children of the slave woman will not divide the estate with the children of the master. LL 26 If the first-ranking wife dies and after his wife's death he marries the slave woman (who had borne him children), the child of his first-ranking wife shall be his (primary) heir; the child whom the slave woman bore to her master is considered equal to a native free-born son and they shall make good his (share of the estate).

Debt-servitude
LH 117 If an obligation is outstanding against a man and he sells or gives into debt service his wife, his son, or his daughter, they shall perform service in the house of their buyer or of the one who holds them in debt service for three years; their release shall be secured in the fourth year. Exod 21:2 – 6; Lev 25:39 – 55; Deut 15:12 – 18

Other form of human bondage	
Human Distraint (LE 22 – 24; LH 114 – 116)	LE 22 If a man has no claim against another man but he nonetheless takes the man's slave woman as a distress, the owner of the slave woman shall swear an oath by the god: "you have no claim against me;" he (the distrainer) shall weigh and deliver silver as much as is the value(?) of the slave woman. LE 23 If a man has no claim against another man but he nonetheless takes the takes the man's slave woman as a distress, detains the distress in his house, and causes her death,

he shall replace her with two slave women for the owner of the slave woman.

LE 24 [If...], he shall bring [a slave woman]; if he has no slave woman, he shall instead weigh and deliver 10 shekels of silver; if he has no silver, he shall give him whatever of value he has.

LH 114 If a man does not have a claim of grain or silver against another man but distrains a member of his household, he shall weigh and deliver 20 shekels of silver for each distrainee.

LH 115 If a man has a claim of grain or silver against another man, distrains a member of his household, and the distranee dies a natural death while in the house of her or his distrainer, that case has no bas no basis for a claim.

LH 116 If the distrainee should die from the effects of a beating or other physical abuse while in the house of her distrainer, the owner of the distrainee shall charge and convict his merchant, and if (the distrainee is) the man's son; if the man's slave, he shall weigh and deliver 20 shekels of silver; moreover, he shall forfeit whatever he originally gave as the loan.

Human Pledge (LH 118–119; MAL A 39, 44, 48; C+G 2–3, 7)	LH 118 If he should give a male or female slave into debt service, the merchant may extend the term (beyond three years), he may sell him; there are no grounds for a claim.

LH 119 If an obligation is outstanding against a man and he therefore sells his slave woman who has borne him children, the owner of the slave woman shall weigh and deliver the silver which the merchant weighed and delivered (as the loan) and he shall thereby redeem his slave woman.

MAL A39 If a man should give one who is not his own daughter in marriage to a husband—if (this situation arose because) previously her father had been in debt and she had been made to reside as a pledge—and a prior creditor should come forward, he (i.e., the prior creditor) shall receive the value of the woman, in full, from the one who gives the woman in marriage; if he has nothing to give, he (i.e., the prior creditor) shall take the one who gives the woman in marriage. However, if she had been saved from a catastrophe, she is clear for the one who saved her. And if the one who marries the woman either caused a tablet to be...for him or they have a claim in place against him, he shall [..] the value of the woman, and the one who gives (the woman) [...]

MAL A 44 If there is a Assyrian man or an Assyrian woman who is residing in a man's house as a pledge for a debt, for as much as his value, and he is taken for the full value (i.e., his value as pledge does not exceed that of the debt), he (the pledge holder) shall whip (the pledge), pluck out (the pledge's) hair, (or) mutilate or pierce (the pledge's) ears.

MAL A 48 If a man <wants to give in marriage> his debtor's daughter who is residing in his house as a pledge, he shall ask permission of her father and then he shall give her to a husband. If her father does not agree, he shall he shall not give her. If her father is dead, he shall ask permission of one of her brothers and the latter shall consult with her (other) brothers. If one brother so desire he shall declare, "I will redeem my sister within one month;" if he should not redeem her within one month, the creditor, if he so please, shall clear her of encumbrances and shall give her to a husband, [...] according to [...] he shall give her [...]

MAL C+G 2 [If a man] sells to another man [either a man's son] or a man's daughter who is residing [in his house] either for a silver (debt?) or as [a pledge], or sells [anyone else] who is residing in his house, [and they prove the charges against him], he shall forfeit his silver; [...] he shall give his/its [...] to the owner of the property; they shall strike him [x blows with rods]; he shall perform the king's service for 20 days.

MAL C+G 3 [If a man] sells into a foreign land [either a man's son] or a man's daughter who [is residing in his house] either for a silver (debt?) or as a pledge, and they prove the charges against him and find guilty, he shall give his/its [...] to the owner of the property; they shall strike him [x blows with rods]; he shall perform the king's service for 40 days. But if the man whom he sells dies in the foreign land, he shall make full payment for a life. He may sell into a foreign land an Assyrian woman who had been taken for full value (i.e., the value as pledge does not exceed that of debt).

MAL C+G 7 [If...] or anything else that is staying in the house of an Assyrian as a pledge [...] and the term (of the loan) elapses [...]; if the silver (owed) amounts to as much as its/his value [...]; if the silver (owed) does not amount to as much as its/his value [...] he shall acquire and he shall take [..] he made abandon, the capital sum of the silver [..] there is not [...]

Bibliography

Alexander, Christopher, Sara Ishikawa, and Murray Silverstein. *A Pattern Language: Towns, Buildings, Construction.* New York: Oxford University Press, 1977.

Alexander, Christopher. *The Timeless Way of Building.* New York: Oxford University Press, 1979.

Alt, Albrecht. "The Origins of Israelite Law." Pages 79–132 in *Essays on Old Testament History and Religion.* Translated by R. A. Wilson. Sheffield: JSOT, 1989.

Anderson, Cheryl B. "Biblical Laws: Challenging the Principles of Old Testament Ethics." Pages 37–49 in *Character Ethics and the Old Testament.* Edited by M. Daniel Carroll R. and Jacqueline E. Lapsley. Louisville: Westminster John Knox, 2007.

——. "The Construction of Identity in the BC and DL." Pages 51–76 in *Women, Ideology, and Violence: Critical Theory and the Construction of Gender in the Book of the Covenant and the Deuteronomic Law.* New York: T and T Clark International, 2004.

Andreasen, Niels Erik. "Festival and Freedom: A Study of an Old Testament Theme." *Interpretation* 28, no. 3 (1974): 281–297.

Astour, Michael C. "The Merchant Class of Ugarit." Pages 99–111 in *Gesellschaftsklassen im Alten Zweistromland und in den angrenzenden Gebieten; XVIII. Rencontre assyriologique internationale, München, 29. Juni bis 3. Juli 1970.* Edited by Dietz Otto Edzard. München: Verlag der Bayerischen Akademie der Wissenschaften, 1972.

Aurelius, Erik. "Der Ursprung des Ersten Gebots," *Zeitschrift für Theologie und Kirche* 100.1 (2003): 1–21.

Averbeck, Richard E. "Law." Pages 113–138 in *Cracking Old Testament Codes.* Edited by D. Brent Sandy and Ronald L. Giese, Jr. Nashville: Broadman & Holman, 1995.

Barker, Paul A. *The Triumph of Grace in Deuteronomy: Faithless Israel, Faithful Yahweh in Deuteronomy.* Carlisle: Paternoster, 2004.

Barr, J. "Ancient Biblical Laws and Modern Human Rights." Pages 21–33 in *Justice and Holy: Essays in Honor of Walter Harrelson.* Edited by Douglas A. Knight and Peter J. Paris. Atlanta: Scholar, 1989.

Bartor, Assnat. *Reading Law as Narrative: A Study in the Casuistic Laws of the Pentateuch.* Atlanta: Society of Biblical Literature, 2010.

——. "The Representation of Speech in the Casuistic Laws of the Pentateuch: The Phenomenon of Combined Discourse." *Journal of Biblical Literature* 126, no. 2 (2007): 231–249.

Beckman, Gary. "Hittite Treaties and the Development of the Cuneiform Treaty Tradition." Pages 279–301 in *Deuteronomistischen Geschichtswerke.* Edited by Markus Witte, Konrad Schmid, Doris Prechel, and Jan Christian Gertz. Berlin: Walter de Gruyter, 2006.

Bellefontaine, Margaret Elizabeth. "A Study of Ancient Israelite Laws and Their Function as Covenant Stipulations." Ph.D. diss., University of Notre Dame, 1973.

Bendor, Shunya. *The Social Structure of Ancient Israel: The Institution of the Family (beit 'ab) from the Settlement to the End of the Monarchy.* Jerusalem: Simor, 1996.

Bennett, Harold V. *Injustice Made Legal: Deuteronomic Law and the Plight of Widows, Strangers, and Orphans in Ancient Israel.* Grand Rapids: Eerdmans, 2002.

Berman, Harold J. *The Interaction of Law and Religion.* Nashville: Abingdon, 1974.

Boecker, Hans Jochen. *Law and the Administration of Justice in the Old Testament and Ancient East.* Minneapolis: Augsburg 1980.

Bottéro, Jean. *Mesopotamia: Writing, Reasoning, and the Gods.* Translated by Zainab Bahrani and Marc Van De Mieroop. Chicago: University of Chicago Press, 1992.

Botterweck, G. Johannes, and Helmer Ringgren, eds. *Theological Dictionary of the Old Testament.* Translated by John T. Willis. 13 vols. Grand Rapids: Eerdmans, 1974–2004.

Braulik, George. "Das Deuteronomium und die Menschenrechte." *Theologische Quartalschrift* 166 (1986): 8–24.

——. *Deuteronomium 1–16, 17.* Würzburg: Echter Verlag, 1986.

——. *Deuteronomium II, 16, 18–34, 12.* Wurzburg: Echter, 1992.

——. "Deuteronomy and Human Rights." *Skrif en kerk* 19 (1998): 207–229.

——. "Haben in Israel auch Frauen geopfert? Beobachtungen am Deuteronomium. " Pages 19–28 in *Zur Aktualität des Alten Testaments: Festschrift für Georg Sauer zum 65 Geburtstag.* Edited by Siegfried Kreuzer and Kurt Lüthi. Frankfurt am Main: Peter Lang, 1992.

——. "The Sequence of the Laws in Deuteronomy 12–26 and in the Decalogue." Pages 313–335 in *A Song of Power and the Power of Song: Essays on the Book of Deuteronomy.* Edited by Duane L. Christensen. Winona Lake: Eisenbrauns, 1993.

Brichto, Herbert Chanan. "Religion Is about Freedom, Human Rights, and Individual Autonomy." *American Baptist Quarterly* 19, no. 4 (2000): 307–308.

——. "The Hebrew Bible on Human Rights." Pages 215–233 in *Essays on Human Rights: Contemporary Issues and Jewish Perspectives.* Edited by David Sidorsky, Sidney Liskofsky and Jerome J. Shestack; Salo W. Baron,...et al. Philadelphia: Jewish Publication Society of America, 1979.

Bruckner, James K. *Exodus.* Peabody: Hendrickson, 2008.

Brueggemann, Walter. *Deuteronomy.* Nashville: Abingdon Press, 2001.

——. *Old Testament Theology: An Introduction.* Nashville: Abingdon, 2008.

——. *The Land: Place as Gift, Promise, and Challenge in Biblical Faith.* Minneapolis: Fortress, 2002.

Brugger, Winfried. "The Image of the Person in the Human Rights Concept." *Human Rights Quarterly* 18 (1996): 594–611.

Bucar, Elizabeth M., and Barbra Barnett, eds. *Does Human Rights Need God?* Grand Rapids: Eerdmans, 2005.

Buccellati, Giorgio. "Ethics and Piety in the Ancient Near East." Pages 1685–1696 in *Civilizations of the Ancient Near East.* Edited by Jack M. Sasson. Vol. 3. New York: Simon & Schuster Macmillan, 1995.

Bultmann, C. *Der Fremde im antiken Juda.* Göttingen: Vandenhoeck & Ruprecht, 1992.

Bush, George. *Notes on Exodus.* Minneapolis: James and Klock, 1976.

Callahan, Allen Dwight, Richard A. Horsley, and Abraham Smith. "Introduction: The Slavery of New Testament Studies." *Semeia* 83–84 (1998): 1–15.

Cairns, John W., and Olivia F. Robinson, eds. *Critical Studies in Ancient Law, Comparative Law and Legal History: Essays in Honour of Alan Watson.* Oxford: Hart, 2001.

Cardellini, Innocenzo. *Die biblischen Sklaven-Gesetze im Lichte des keilschriftlichen Sklavenrechts: Ein Beitrag zur Tradition,Überlieferung und Redaktion der alttestamentlichen Rechtstexte.* Königstein: Peter Hanstein Verlag, 1981.

Carmichael, Calum M. *The Laws of Deuteronomy.* Ithaca: Cornell University Press, 1974.

——. "The Three Laws on the Release of Slaves." *Zeitschrift für die alttestamentliche Wissenschaft* 112 (2000): 509–525.

Cassin, René. *Amicorum discipulorumque liber. IV, methodologie des droits de l'homme.* Paris: Pédone, 1972.

Cassuto, Umberto. *A Commentary on the Book of Exodus.* Jerusalem: Magnes, 1967.

Cazelles, Henri. "Droit Public dans le Deutéronome." Pages 99–106 in *Das Deuteronomium: Entstehung, Gestalt und Botschaft.* Edited by Norbert Lohfink. Leuven: University Press, 1985.

——. *Études sur le code de l'alliance.* Paris: Letouzey et Ané, 1946.

——. "The Hebrews." Pages 1–28 in *Peoples of Old Testament Times.* London: Oxford University, 1973.

Childs, Brevard S. *The Book of Exodus: A Critical, Theological Commentary.* Philadelphia: Westminster, 1974.

Chirichigno, Gregory C. *Debt-Slavery in Israel and the Ancient Near East.* Sheffield: JSOT, 1993.

Cholewiński, Alfred. *Heiligkeitsgesetz und Deuteronomium: Eine vergleichende Studie.* Rome: Biblical Institute Press, 1976.

Christensen, Duane L. *Deuteronomy 1:1–21:9.* Nashville: Thomas Nelson, 2001.

——. *Deuteronomy 21:10–34:12.* Nashville: Thomas Nelson, 2002.

——. "Form and Structure in Deuteronomy 1–11." Pages 135–144 in *Das Deuteronomium: Entstehung, Gestalt und Botschaft.* Edited by N. Lohfink. Leuven: University Press, 1985.

Clements, R. E. *Exodus.* Cambridge: Cambridge University Press, 1972.

Clifford, Richard J. "Cosmogonies in the Ugaritic Texts and in the Bible." Orientalia 53, no. 2 (1984): 183–201.

Cole, Robert Alan. *Exodus: An Introduction and Commentary.* Downers Grove: InterVarsity, 1973.

Cotterrell, Roger. *The Sociology of Law: An Introduction.* London: Butterworths, 1992.

——. "Comparatists and Sociology." Pages 131–153 in *Comparative Legal Studies: Traditions and Transitions.* Edited by Pierre Legrand and Roderick Munday. New York: Cambridge University Press, 2003.

Craigie, Peter C. *The Book of Deuteronomy.* Grand Rapids: Eerdmans, 1976.

Crüsemann, Frank. *The Torah: Theology and Social History of Old Testament Law.* Minneapolis: Fortress, 1996.

Dandamayev, Muhammad A. "Slavery." Pages 58–65 in vol. 6 of *The Anchor Bible Dictionary.* Edited by Noel Freedman. 6 vols. New York: Doubleday, 1992.

——. *Slavery in Babylonia: From Nabopolassar to Alexander the Great (626–331 B.C.).* Edited by Marvin A. Powell and David B. Weisberg. Translated by Victoria A. Powell. DeKalb: Northern Illinois University Press, 1984.

Daube, David. *Studies in Biblical Law.* New York: Ktav Publishing House, 1969.

Davies, Gwynne Henton. *Exodus.* London: S.C.M. Press, 1967.

Deeley, Mary Katharine. "The Rhetoric of Memory: A Study of the Persuasive Function of the Memory Commands in Deuteronomy 5–26." Ph.D. diss., Northwestern University, 1989.

Deng, Francis Mading. *Tradition and Modernization: A Challenge for Law among the Dinka of the Sudan.* New Haven: Yale University Press, 1986.

De Vaux, R. *Ancient Israel: Its Life and Institutions.* Translated by John McHugh. Grand Rapids: Eerdmans, 1961.

"Distress." Page 487 in *Black's Law Dictionary.* Edited by Byran A. Garner. St. Paul: West Group, 1999.

Douglas, J. D., ed. *The New Bible Dictionary.* Grand Rapids: Eerdmans, 1965.

Dozeman, Thomas B. *Commentary on Exodus.* Grand Rapids: Eerdmans, 2009.

Driver, Godfrey Rolles, and John C. Miles, eds. and trans. *The Babylonian* Laws. Vol. 1. Oxford: Clarendon, 1952.

——. *The Assyrian Laws.* Darmstadt: Scientia Verlag Aalen, 1975.

Driver, S. R. *A Critical and Exegetical Commentary on Deuteronomy.* Edinburgh: T.& T. Clark, 1896.

Durham, John I. *Exodus.* Waco: Word, 1987.

Egendorf, Laura K., ed. *Human Rights: Opposing Viewpoints.* San Diego: Greenhaven, 2003.

Ellison, H. L. *Exodus.* Philadelphia: Westminster, 1982.

——. "The Hebrew Slave: A Study in Early Israelite Society." *Evangelical Quarterly* 45 (1973): 30.

Enrico, Dal Lago, and Constantina Katsari. "The Study of Ancient and Modern Slave Systems: Setting an Agenda for Comparison." Pages 3–31 in *Slave Systems: Ancient and Modern.* Edited by and Enrico Dal Lago and Constantina Katsari. Cambridge: Cambridge University Press, 2008.

Eyerman, Ron. "Slavery." Pages 554–556 in *The Cambridge Dictionary of Sociology.* Edited by Bryan S. Turner. Cambridge: Cambridge University Press, 2006.

Fabry, Heinz-Josef. "Deuteronomium 15: Gedanken zur Geschwister-Ethik im Alten Testament." Pages 92–111 in *Zeitschrift für altorientalische und biblische Rechtsgeschichte.* Edited by Echart Otto. Vol. 3. Wiesbaden: Harrassowitz, 1997.

Falkenstein, Adam. *The Sumerian Temple City.* Los Angeles: Undena, 1974.

Falk, Ze'ev W. "Exodus 21:6." *Vetus Testamentum 9,* no.1 (1959): 86–88.

——. "Hebrew Legal Terms: II." *Journal of Semitic Studies* 12.2 (1967): 241–244.

Feeley-Harnik, Gillian. "Is Historical Anthropology Possible? The Case of the Runaway Slave." Pages 95–126 in *Humanizing America's Iconic Book: Society of Biblical Literature Centennial Addresses 1980.* Edited by Gene M. Tucker and Douglas A. Knight. Chico: Scholars, 1982.

Fensham, F. Charles. "New Light on Ex 21:6 and 22:7 from the Laws of Eshnunna." *Journal of Biblical Literature* 78, no. 2 (1959): 160–161.

Fields, A. Belden, and Wolf-Dieter Narr. "Human Rights as a Holistic Concept." *Human Rights Quarterly* 14 (1992): 1–20.

Finkelstein, J. J. "Amisaduqa's Edict and the Babylonian Law Codes." *Journal of Cuneiform Studies* 15 (1961): 91–104.

——. *The Ox That Gored.* Philadelphia: The American Philosophical Society, 1981.

Fisher, Loren R. "Creation at Ugarit and in the Old Testament." *Vetus Testamentum* 15, no. 3 (1965): 313–324.

Fox-Decent, Evan. "Is the Rule of Law Really Indifferent to Human Rights." *Law and Philosophy* 27 (2008): 533–581.

Frankena, R. "The Vassal-Treaties of Esarhaddon and the Dating of Deuteronomy." Pages 122–154 in *25:1940–1965; Oudtestamentlich Werkgezelschap in Nederland.* Leiden: E. J. Brill, 1965.

Freedman, David Noel, ed. *Anchor Bible Dictionary.* 6 vols. New York: Doubleday. 1992.

Frymer-Kensky, Tikav. "Anatolia and the Levant Israel." Pages 975–1066 in *A History of Ancient Near Eastern Law.* Edited by Raymond Westbrook. Vol. 2. Leiden: E. J. Brill, 2003.

——. "Israel." Pages 251–263 in *Security for Debt in Ancient Near Eastern Law.* Edited by Raymond Westbrook, and Richard Lewis Jasnow. Boston: E. J. Brill, 2001.

Fuller, Lon L. *The Morality of Law*. New Haven: Yale University Press, 1969.

Gane, Roy. *Leviticus, Numbers*. Grand Rapids: Zondervan, 2004.

Gelb, Ignace J. "Definition and Discussion of Slavery and Serfdom." *Ugarit-Forschungen* 11 (1980): 283–297.

——. "From Freedom to Slavery." Pages 81–92 in *Gesellschaftsklassen im Alten Zweistromland und in den angrenzenden Gebieten; XVIII. Rencontre assyriologique internationale, München, 29. Juni bis 3. Juli 1970*. Edited by Dietz Otto Edzard. München: Verlag der Bayerischen Akademie der Wissenschaften, 1972.

——. "Household and Family in Early Mesopotamia." Pages 1–97 in *State and Temple Economy in the Ancient Near East*. Edited by Edward Lipiński. Vol. 1. Louvain: Departement Oriëntalistiek, 1979.

——. "Quantitative Evaluation of Slavery and Serfdom." Pages 195–207 in *Kramer Anniversary Volume: Cuneiform Studies in Honor of Samuel Noah Kramer*. Edited by Barry L. Eichler, Jane W. Heimerdinger, and Åke W. Sjöberg. Kevelaer: Verlag Butzon and Bercker, 1976.

Gemser, Berend. "The Importance of the Motive Clause in Old Testament Law." *Vetus Testamentum Supplements* (1953): 50–66.

Gerstenberger, Erhard S. "Covenant and Commandment." *Journal of Biblical Literature* 84, no. 1 (1965): 38–51.

——. *Leviticus: A Commentary*. Louisville: Westminster John Knox, 1996.

Ginzberg, Eli. *Studies in the Economics of the Bible*. Philadelphia: Jewish Publication Society of America, 1932.

Gispen, Willem Hendrik. *Exodus*. Grand Rapids: Zondervan, 1982.

Glass, Zipporah G. "Land, Slave Labor and Law: Engaging Ancient Israel's Economy." *Journal for the Study of the Old Testament* 91 (2000): 27–39.

Gnuse, Robert. *You Shall Not Steal*. Maryknoll: Orbis, 1985.

Gordon, Cyrus Herzl. *A New Parallel to Deuteronomy 21:11–12*. Jerusalem, 1935.

——. "ELOHIM in its Reputed Meaning of Rulers, Judges." *Journal of Biblical Literature* 54, no. 3 (1935): 139–144.

Götze, Albrecht. *The Laws of Eshnunna*. New Haven: Dept. of Antiquities of the Government of Iraq and the American Schools of Oriental Research, 1956.

Greenberg, Moshe. "Biblical Attitudes toward Power: Ideal and Reality in Law and Prophets." Pages 101–112 in *Religion and Law: Biblical-Judaic and Islamic Perspectives*. Edited by Edwin B. Firmage, Bernard G. Weiss, and John W. Welch. Winona Lake: Eisenbrauns, 1990.

Greengus, Samuel. "Biblical and ANE Law." Pages 242–251 in vol. 4 of *Anchor Bible Dictionary*. Edited by David Noel Freedman. 6 vols. New York: Doubleday, 1992.

——. "Legal and Social Institutions of Ancient Mesopotamian." Pages 469–484 in *Civilizations of the Ancient Near East*. Edited by Jack M. Sasson. Vol. 1. New York: Charles Scribner's Sons, 1995.

——. "Some Issues Relating to the Comparability of Laws and the Coherence of the Legal Tradition." Pages 60–87 in *Theory and Method in Biblical and Cuneiform Law: Revision, Interpolation and Development*. Edited by Bernard M. Levinson. Sheffield: Sheffield Academic Press, 1994.

——. "The Selling of Slaves: Laws Missing from the Hebrew Bible?" *Zeitschrift für altorientalische und biblische Rechtgeschichte* 3 (1997): 1–11.

Grimmelsman, H. Joseph. *The Book of Exodus: A Study of the Second Book of Moses with Translation and Concise Commentary.* Cincinnati: The Seminary Book Store, 1927.

Grosz, Katarzyna. "Bridewealth and Dowry in Nuzi." Pages 193–206 in *Images of Women in Antiquity.* Edited by Amélie Kuhrt and Averil Cameron. Detroit: Wayne State University Press, 1983.

Gunneweg, Antonius H. J., *Geschichte Israels bis Bar Kochba.* Stuttgart: W Kohlhammer, 1972.

Haase, Richard. "Anatolia and the Levant: The Hittite Kingdom." Pages 227–251 in *A History of Ancient Near Eastern Law.* Edited by Raymond Westbrook. Vol. 1. Leiden: E. J. Brill, 2003.

——. *Keilschriftrechtliches.* Leonberg: Im Selbstverlag des Verfassers, 1998.

——. "Mesopotamia: Nuzi." Pages 619–656 in *A History of Ancient Near Eastern Law.* Edited by Raymond Westbrook. Vol. 1. Leiden: E. J. Brill, 2003.

Halberstam, Chaya. "The Art of Biblical Law." *Prooftexts* 27, no. 2 (2007): 345–364.

Hallo, William W., and K. Lawson Younger, Jr., eds. *Context of Scripture.* 3 vols. New York: E. J. Brill, 2003.

Hallo, William W. "Biblical History in Its Near Eastern Setting: the Contextual Approach." Pages 1–16 in *Scripture in Context: Essays on the Comparative Method.* Edited by Carl D. Evans, William W. Hallo, and John B. White. Pittsburgh: Pickwick, 1980.

——. "Compare and Contrast: The Contextual Approach to Biblical Literature." Pages 1–30 in *The Bible in the Light of Cuneiform Literature: Scripture in Context III.* Edited by William W. Hallo, Bruce William Jones, and Gerald L. Mattingly. Lewiston: Pickwick, 1990.

——. "God, King, and Man at Yale." Pages 99–111 in *State and Temple Economy in the Ancient Near East.* Edited by Edward Lipiński. Vol. 1. Louvain: Departement Oriëntalistiek, 1979.

Hamilton, Jeffries M. *Social Justice and Deuteronomy: The Case of Deuteronomy 15.* Atlanta: Scholars, 1992.

Harrelson, Walter. *The Ten Commandments and Human Rights.* Philadelphia: Fortress, 1980.

Hartley, John E. *Leviticus.* Dallas: Word, 1992.

Helck, Wolfgang. "Die Bedrohung Palästinas durch einwandernde Gruppen am Ende der 18 und am Anfang der 19 Dynastie." *Vetus Testamentum* 18, no. 4 (1968): 472–480.

Hiebert, Paul G. *Transforming Worldviews: An Anthropological Understanding of How People Change.* Grand Rapids: Baker Academic, 2008.

Himma, Kenneth Einar. "Natural Law," *Internet Encyclopedia of Philosophy.* No pages. Cited 22 January 2011. Online: http:// http://www.iep.utm.edu/natlaw/.

Hoffner, Harry A. Jr. "Slavery and Slave Laws in Ancient Hatti and Israel." Pages 130–155 in *Israel: Ancient Kingdom or Late Invention.* Edited by Daniel I. Block. Nashville: B&H, 2008.

Hoftijzer, Jacob. "Exodus 21:8." *Vetus Testamentum* 7, no. 4 (1957): 388–391.

Horton, Fred L. "A Reassessment of the Legal Forms in the Pentateuch and Their Functions." Pages 347–396 in *One Hundred Seventh Annual Meeting Seminar Papers.* Vol. 2. Atlanta: SBL, 1971.

Huber, Wolfgang. "Human Rights and Biblical Legal Thought." Pages 47–63 in *Religious Human Rights in Global Perspective.* Edited by John Witte, Jr. and Johan D. van der Vyver. Hague: Martinus Nijhoff, 1996.

Huehnergard, John. *A Grammar of Akkadian.* Winona Lake: Eisenbrauns, 1997.

Irani, K. D., and Morris Silver, eds. *Social Justice in the Ancient World.* Westport: Greenwood, 1995.

Ishay, Micheline R. *The History of Human Rights: From Ancient Times to the Globalization Era.* Berkeley and Los Angeles: University of California Press, 2004.

Jackson, Bernard S. "Gender Critical Observations on Tripartite Breeding Relationships in the Hebrew Bible." Pages 39–52 in *A Question of Sex? Gender and Difference in the Hebrew Bible and Beyond.* Edited by Deborah W. Rooke. Sheffield: Sheffield Phoenix Press, 2007.

——. "Problem of Exod 21:22–5, Ius Talionis." *Vetus Testamentum* 23, no. 3 (1973): 273–304.

——. "Revolution in Biblical Law: Some Reflections on the Role of Theory in Methodology." *Journal of Semitic Studies* 50 (2005): 83–115.

——. "Some Literary Features of the Mishpatim." Pages 235–242 in *"Wünschet Jerusalem Frieden": Collected Communications to XIIth Congress of Int'l Org for Study of the Old Testament, Jerusalem, 1986.* Edited by Matthias Augustin and Klaus D. Schunck. Frankfurt am Main: Peter Lang, 1988.

——. *Studies in the Semiotics of Biblical Law.* Sheffield: Sheffield Academic Press, 2000.

——. *Wisdom-Laws: A Study of the Mishpatim of Exodus 21:1–22:16.* Oxford: Oxford University Press, 2006.

Jackson, Bernard S., and Trevor F. Watkins. "Distraint in the Laws of Eshnunna and Hammurabi." Pages 407–419 in *Studi in onore di Cesare Sanfilippo* Rome/Miland: Giuffrè, 1982.

Janzen, Waldemar. *Exodus.* Waterloo: Herald, 2000.

Japhet, Sara. "The Relationship between the Legal Corpora in the Pentateuch in Light of Manumission Laws." Pages 63–89 in *Studies in Bible.* Edited by Sara Japhet. Jerusalem: Magnes, 1986.

Jasnow, Richard. "Old Kingdom and First Intermediate Period." Pages 93–140 in *A History of Ancient Near Eastern Law.* Edited by Raymond Westbrook. Vol. 1. Leiden: E. J. Brill, 2003.

Jepsen, Alfred. *Untersuchungen zum Bundesbuch.* Stuttgart: W. Kohlhammer, 1927.

Joüon, Paul, and T. Muraoka. *A Grammar of Biblical Hebrew.* Roma: Editrice Pontificio Istituto Biblico, 2008.

Kaiser, Otto. *Introduction to the Old Testament: A Presentation of Its Results and Problems.* Translated by John Sturdy. Minneapolis: Augsburg, 1975.

Kaiser, Walter C. "The Law of Deuteronomy." Pages 127–137 in *Toward Old Testament Ethics.* Grand Rapids: Zondervan, 1983.

Kamenka, Eugene, and Alice Erh-Soon Tay. *Human Rights.* New York: St. Martin's, 1978.

Kant, Immanuel, and H. J. Paton. *The Moral Law: Kant's Groundwork of the Metaphysic of Morals.* New York: Barnes & Noble, 1967.

Kaufmann, Stephen A. "A Reconstruction of the Social Welfare Systems of Ancient Israel." Pages 277–286 in *In the Shelter of Elyon.* Edited by Boyd Barrick and John R. Spencer. Sheffield: JSOT, 1984.

——. "The Structure of the Deuteronomic Law." *MAARAV* 1, no. 2 (1978–1979): 105–158.

Kaufmann, Yehezkel. *The Religion of Israel: From Its Beginnings to the Babylonian Exile.* Translated by M. Greenberg. New York: Schocken, 1972.

Keil, C. F., and F. Delitzsch. *The Pentateuch.* Translated by James Martin. Vol. 3. Grand Rapids: Eerdmans, 1949.

Kitchen, Kenneth A. "Ancient Orient, 'Deuteronism,' and the Old Testament." Pages 1–24 in *New Perspectives on the Old Testament.* Edited by J. Barton Payne. Waco: Word, 1970.

——. *On the Reliability of the Old Testament.* Grand Rapids: Eerdmans, 2003.

——. *The Bible in Its World: The Bible and Archaeology Today.* Exeter: Paternoster, 1977.

——. "The Fall and Rise of Covenant, Law and Treaty." *Tyndale Bulletin* 40 (1989): 118–135.

Kiuchi, Nobuyoshi. *Leviticus.* Downers Grove: InterVarsity, 2007.

Kline, Meredith G. "Hebrews." Pages 457–458 in *The New Bible Dictionary.* Edited by J. D. Douglas. Grand Rapids: Eerdmans 1965.

——. *The Structure of Biblical Authority.* Grand Rapids: Eerdmans, 1972.

Knight, Douglas A. "The Ethics of Human Life in the Hebrew Bible." Pages 65–88 in *Justice and the Holy: Essays in Honor of Walter Harrelson.* Edited by Douglas A. Knight and Peter J. Paris. Atlanta: Scholars, 1989.

Knauf, Ernst Axel. "Observations on Judah's Social and Economic History and the Dating of the Laws in Deuteronomy," *The Journal of Hebrew Scriptures* 9, a.18 (2009): No Pages. Cited: 17 November 2013. Online: http://www.jhsonline.org/Articles/article_120.pdf.

Kohler, Ludwig, Walter Baumgartner, Johann Jakob Stamm, and M. E. J. Richardson, eds. *The Hebrew and Aramaic Lexicon of the Old Testament.* 2 vols. Leiden: E. J. Brill, 2001.

Kolakowski, Leszek. *Religion, If There Is No God...: On God, the Devil, Sin, and Other Worries of the So-Called Philosophy of Religion.* New York: Oxford University Press, 1982.

Koschaker, Paul. *Neue keilschriftliche Rechtsurkunden aus der El-Amarna-Zeit.* Leipzig: S. Hirzel, 1928.

Kratz, Reinhard G. *The Composition of the Narrative Books of the Old Testament.* Translated by John Bowden. New York: T&T Clark, 2005.

——. *One God, One Cult, One Nation: Archaeological and Biblical Perspectives.* Berlin: Walter de Gruyter, 2010.

Kraus, F. R. *Ein Edikt des Königs Ammi-Saduqa von Babylon.* Leiden: E. J. Brill, 1958.

Lafont, Bertrand, and Raymond Westbrook. "Mesopotamia: Neo-Sumerian Period (UR III)." Pages 183–226 in *A History of Ancient Near Eastern Law.* Edited by Raymond Westbrook. Vol. 1. Leiden: E. J. Brill, 2003.

Lafont, Sophie. "Ancient Near Eastern Laws: Continuity and Pluralism." Pages 91–118 in *Theory and Method in Biblical and Cuneiform Law: Revision, Interpolation and Development.* Edited by Bernard M. Levinson. Sheffield: Sheffield Academic Press, 1994.

——. "Mesopotamia: Middle Assyrian Period." Pages 521–563 in *A History of Ancient Near Eastern Law.* Edited by Raymond Westbrook. Vol. 1. Leiden: E. J. Brill, 2003.

Lasserre, Guy. "Lutter contre la paupérisation et ses conséquences: Lecture rhétorique de Dt 15/12–18." *Études théologiques et religieuses* 70 (1995): 481–492.

Legrand, Pierre. "*The Impossibility of 'Legal Transplants'*," *Maastricht J. European and Comparative Law* 4 (1997): 111–124.

——. "The Same and the Different." Pages 240–311 in *Comparative Legal Studies: Traditions and Transitions.* Edited by Pierre Legrand and R. J. C. Munday. Cambridge: Cambridge University Press, 2003.

Legrand, Pierre, and R. J. C. Munday, eds. *Comparative Legal Studies: Traditions and Transitions.* Cambridge: Cambridge University Press, 2003.

Lemche, Niels Peter. "Andurārum and Mīšarum: Comments on the Problems of Social Edicts and Their Application in the Ancient Near East." *Journal of Near Eastern Studies* 38, no. 1 (1979): 11–22.

——. "The Hebrew Slave: Comments on the Slave Law Ex 21:2–11." *Vetus Testamentum* 25, no. 2 (1975): 129–144.

——. "The Manumission of Slaves—the Fellow Year—the Sabbatical Year—the Jobel Year." *Vetus Testamentum* 26, no. 1 (1976): 38–59.

Lenchak, Timothy A. *Choose Life! A Rhetorical-Critical Investigation of Deuteronomy 28,69–30,20*. Roma: Editrice Pontificio Istituto Biblico, 1993.

Leuchter, Mark. "The Manumission Laws in Leviticus and Deuteronomy: The Jeremiah Connection." *Journal of Biblical Literature* 127, no. 4 (2008): 635–653.

Levine, Baruch A. *Leviticus*. Philadelphia: Jewish Publication Society, 1989.

Levine, Etan. "On Exodus 21,10 'onah and Biblical Marriage." Pages 133–164 in *Zeitschrift für altorientalische und biblische Rechtsgeschichte*. Edited by Eckart Otto. Vol. 5. Wiesbaden: Harrassowitz, 1999.

Levinson, Bernard M., and Eckart Otto, eds. *Recht und Ethik im Alten Testament: Beiträge des Symposiums 'Das Alte Testament und die Kultur der Moderne' Anlässlich des 100. Geburtstags Gerhard von Rads (1901–1971) Heidelberg, 18.–21. Oktober 2001*. Münster: Lit Verlag, 2004.

Levinson, Bernard M. "The Birth of the Lemma: The Restrictive Reinterpretation of the Covenant law book's Manumission Law by the Holiness Code (Leviticus 25:44–46)." *Journal of Biblical Literature* 124, no. 4 (2005): 617–639.

——. "The Case for Revision and Interpretation within the Biblical Legal Corpora." Pages 37–59 in *Theory and Method in Biblical and Cuneiform Law: Revision, Interpolation and Development*. Edited by Bernard M. Levinson. Sheffield: Sheffield Academic Press, 1994.

——. "The 'Effected Object' in Contractual Legal language: The Semantics of 'If You Purchase a Hebrew Slave' (Exod. XXI 2)." *Vetus Testamentum* 56, no. 4 (2006): 485–504.

——. "The Manumission of Hermeneutics: The Slave Laws of the Pentateuch as a Challenge to Contemporary Pentateuchal Theory." Pages 283–284 in *Congress Volume Leiden 2004*. Edited by André Lemaire. Boston: E. J. Brill, 2006.

Lie, John. *Modern Peoplehood*. Cambridge: Harvard University Press, 2004.

Limburg, James. "Human Rights in the Old Testament." Pages 20–26 in *The Church and the Rights of Man*. Edited by Alois Müller and Norbert Greinachherceds. New York: Seabury, 1979.

Lindenberger, James M. "How Much for a Hebrew Slave? The Meaning of Mišneh in Deut 15:18." *Journal of Biblical Literature* 110, no. 3 (1991): 479–498.

Lipiński, Edward. "L''esclave Hébreu'." *Vetus Testamentum* 26, no. 1 (1976): 120–124.

Lockley, Tim. "Slavery." Pages 549–551 in *Encyclopedia of Social Theory*. Edited by Austin Harrington, Barbara L. Marshall, and Hans-Peter Müller. New York: Routledge, 2006.

Lohfink, Norbert. *Das Hauptgebot: Eine Untersuchung Literarischer Einleitungsfragen zu Dtn 5–11*. Roma: Pontificio Instituto Biblico, 1963.

——. "Fortschreibung? Zur Technik von Rechtsrevisionen im deuteronomischen Bereich, erllrtert an Deuteronomium 12, Ex 21,2–11 und Dtn 15,12–18." Pages 127–171 in *Das Deuteronomium und seine Querbeziehungen*. Edited by T. Veijola. Helsinki: Göttingen, 1996.

——. "Gibt es eine deuteronomistische Bearbeitung im Bundesbuch." Pages 91–113 in *Pentateuchal and Deuteronomistic Studies*. Louvain: Leuven University Press, 1990.

Malul, Meir. *Studies in Mesopotamian Legal Symbolism*. Neukirchen-Vluyn: Neukirchener Verlag, 1988.

——. *The Comparative Method in Ancient Near Eastern and Biblical Legal Studies*. Kevelaer: Butzon & Bercker; Neukirchen-Vluyn: Neukirchener Verlag, 1990.

Matthews, Victor H. "The Anthropology of Slavery in the Covenant law book." Pages 119–135 in *Theory and Method in Biblical and Cuneiform Law: Revision, Interpolation and Development*. Edited by Bernard M. Levinson. Sheffield: Sheffield Academic Press, 1994.

McCarthy, Dennis J. *Treaty and Covenant: A Study in Form in the Ancient Oriental Documents and in the Old Testament.* Rome: Pontifical Biblical Institute, 1981.

McConville, J. G. *Law and Theology in Deuteronomy.* Sheffield: Sheffield University Press, 1984.

——. *Deuteronomy.* Downers Grove: InterVarsity 2002.

McDonald, N. *Deuteronomy and the Meaning of 'Monotheism.'* Tübingen: J. C. B. Mohr, 2003.

Meek, Theophile J. "A New Interpretation of Code of Hammurabi §§ 117–119." *Journal of Near Eastern Studies* 7, no. 3 (1948): 180–183.

Mendelsohn, Isaac. *Legal Aspects of Slavery in Babylonia, Assyria and Palestine: A Comparative Study (3000–500 B.C.).* Williamsport: Bayard, 1932.

——. *Slavery in the Ancient Near East: A Comparative Study of Slavery in Babylonia, Assyria, Syria, and Palestine from Middle of the Third Millennium to the End of the First Millennium.* Westport: Greenwood Press, 1978.

——. "Slavery in the OT." Pages 383–391 in vol.1 of *The Interpreter's Dictionary of the Bible.* Edited by George Arthur Buttrick. 4 vols. Nashville: Abingdon, 1962.

——. "The Conditional Sale into Slavery of Free-Born Daughters in Nuzi and the Law of Ex. 21: 7–11." *Journal of the American Oriental Society* 55, no. 2 (1935): 190–195.

——. "The Family in the Ancient Near East." Pages 144–160 in *The Biblical Archaeologist Reader.* Edited by David Noel Freedman and Edward F. Campbell. Vol. 3. Garden City: Anchor, 1970.

Mendenhall, George E. *Law and Covenant in Israel and the Ancient Near East.* Pittsburgh: The Biblical Colloquium, 1955.

——. "Ancient Oriental and Biblical Law." *Biblical Archaeologist* 17, no. 2 (1954): 26–46.

——. "Covenant Forms in Israelite Tradition," *Biblical Archaeologist* 17, no. 3 (1954): 50–76.

Merendino, R. P. *Das deuteronomische Gesetz: Eine literarkritische, gattungs-und überlieferungsgeschichtliche Untersuchung zu Dt 12–26.* Bonn: P. Hanstein, 1969.

Merrill, Eugene H. *Deuteronomy.* Nashville: Broadman & Holman, 1994.

Meyers, Carol L. *Exodus.* Cambridge: Cambridge University Press, 2005.

Milgrom, Jacob. *Leviticus 17–22: A New Translation with Introduction and Commentary.* New York: Doubleday, 2000.

——. *Leviticus 23–27: A New Translation with Introduction and Commentary.* New York: Doubleday, 2001.

Miller, Patrick D. "Gift of God: Deuteronomic Theology of the Land." *Interpretation* 23, no. 4 (1969): 451–465.

Milsom, S. F. C. *Historical Foundations of the Common Law.* London: Butterworths, 1969.

Mitchell, H. G. "The Use of the Second Person in Deuteronomy." *Journal of Biblical Literature* 18 (1899): 61–109.

Morrow, William S. *Scribing the Center: Organization and Redaction in Deuteronomy 14:1–17:13.* Atlanta: Scholars, 1995.

Müller, David Heiner. *Die Gesetze Hammurabis und ihr Verhältnis zur mosaischen Gesetzgebung sowie zu den XII Tafel.* Wien: Alfred Hölder, 1904.

Murphy, Colleen. "Lon Fuller and the Moral Value of the Rule of Law." *Law and Philosophy* 24 (2005): 239–262.

Murphy, James Gracey. *A critical and Exegetical Commentary on the Book of Exodus: With a New Translation.* Andover: Warren F. Draper, 1881.

Na'aman, Nadav. "Ḫabiru and Hebrews: The Transfer of a Social Term to the Literary Sphere." *Journal of Near Eastern Studies* 45, no. 4 (1986): 271–288.

Napier, Bunyan Davie. *The Book of Exodus.* Richmond: John Knox, 1963.

Nelson, Richard D. *Deuteronomy: A Commentary.* Louisville: Westminster John Knox, 2002.

——. "A Response to Thomas C. Römer, The So-Called Deuteronomistic History," *The Journal of Hebrew Scriptures* 9 a.17 (2009): No Pages. Cited 17 November 2013. Online: http://www.jhsonline.org/Articles/article_119.pdf.

Nicholson, Ernest W. *God and His People: Covenant and Theology in the Old Testament.* New York: Oxford University Press, 1986.

Nickel, James W. *Making Sense of Human Rights.* Malden: Blackwell, 2007.

Nihan, Christophe. "The Holiness Code between D and P: Some Comments on the Function and Significance of Leviticus 17–26 in the Composition of the Torah." Pages 81–122 in *Das Deuteronomium zwischen Pentateuch und deuteronomistischem Geschichtswerk.* Edited by Eckart Otto and Reinhard Achenbach. Göttingen: Vandenhoeck & Ruprecht, 2004.

North, Robert. *Sociology of the Biblical Jubilee.* Rome: Pontifical Biblical Institute, 1954.

Noth, Martin. *Exodus: A Commentary.* Translated by J. S. Bowden. Philadelphia: Westminster, 1962.

Oosthuizen, Martin J. "Deuteronomy 15:1–18 in Socio-Rhetorical Perspective." *Zeitschrift für altorientalische und biblische Rechtsgeschichte* 3 (1997): 64–91.

Örücü, E., and David Nelken, eds. *Comparative Law: A Handbook.* Oxford and Portland: Hart, 2007.

Otto, Eckart. *Das Deuteronomium im Pentateuch und Hexateuch.* Tübingen: Mohr Siebeck, 2000.

——. *Das Deuteronomium: Politische Theologie und Rechtsreform in Juda und Assyrien.* Berlin: De Gruyter, 1999.

——. "Exkurs: Das Deuteronomium als Quelle des Bundesbuches? Zu einer These von John Van Seters," in *Gottes Recht als Menschenrecht: Rechts und literaturhistorische Studien zum Deuteronomium.* Wiesbaden: Harrassowitz, 2002.

——. "False Weights in the Scales of Biblical Justice: Different Views of Women from Patriarchal Hierarchy to Religious Equality in the Book of Deuteronomy." Pages 128–146 in *Gender and Law in the Hebrew Bible and the Ancient Near East.* Edited by Victor H. Matthews, Bernard M. Levinson, and Tikva Frymer-Kensky. Sheffield: Sheffield University Press, 1998.

——. *Gottes Recht als Menschenrecht: Rechts und literaturhistorische Studien zum Deuteronomium.* Wiesbaden: Harrassowitz, 2002.

——. "Human Rights: The Influence of the Hebrew Bible." *Journal of Northwest Semitic Languages* 25 (1999): 1–20.

——. "Programme der Sozialen Gerechtigkeit: Die Neuassyrische (an-)durāru-Institution Sozialen Ausgleichs und das Deuteronomische Erlassjahr in Dtn 15." *Zeitschrift für altorientalische und biblische Rechtsgeschichte* 3 (1997): 26–63.

——. Review of Van Seters, *A Law Book for the Diaspora: Revision in the Study of the Covenant law book,* RBL (2004): No Pages. Cited 17 January 2010. Online: http://www.bookreviews.org/pdf/3929_3801.

——. *Theologische Ethik des Alten Testaments.* Stuttgart: W. Kohlhammer, 1994.

——. "Vom Bundesbuch zum Deuteronomium: Die deuteronomische Redaktion in Dtn 12–26." Pages 260–278 in *Biblische Theologie und gesellschaftlicher Wandel: für Norbert Lohfink SJ.* Edited by Georg O. S. B. Braulik, Walter Groß, and Sean McEvenue. Herder: Freiburg, 1993.

——. *Wandel der Rechtsbegründungen in der Gesellschaftsgeschichte des antiken Israel: eine Rechtsgeschichte des „Bundesbuches" Ex XX 22-XXIII 13*. Leiden: E.J. Brill, 1988.

Patrick, Dale. "Casuistic Law Governing Primary Rights and Duties." *Journal of Biblical Literature* 92, no. 2 (1973): 180–184.

——. *Old Testament Law*. Atlanta: John Knox, 1985.

——. "Studying Biblical Law as a Humanities." *Semeia* 45 (1989): 27–47.

Patterson, Orlando. *Slavery and Social Death: A Comparative Study*. Cambridge: Harvard University Press, 1982.

Paul, Ellen Frankel, Fred Dycus Miller, Jr., and Jeffrey Paul, eds. *Human Rights*. Oxford: Basil Blackwell, 1984.

Paul, Shalom M. *Studies in the Book of Covenant in the Light of Cuneiform and Biblical Law*. Leiden: E. J. Brill, 1970.

Perry, Michael J. *Toward a Theory of Human Rights: Religion, Law, Courts*. Cambridge: Cambridge University Press, 2007.

Person, Raymond F. Jr., R. D. Nelson, S. L. McKenzie, E. Otto, and Y. Amit. "In Conversation with Thomas Römer, *The So-Called Deuteronomistic History: A Sociological, Historical, and Literary Introduction* (London: T. & T. Clark, 2005)." *The Journal of Hebrew Scriptures* 9, a.17 (2009): No Pages. Cited: 17 November 2013. Online: http://www.jhson line.org/Articles/article_119.pdf

Phillips, Anthony. *Ancient Israel's Criminal Law: A New Approach to the Decalogue*. Oxford: Basil Blackwell, 1970.

——. "The Attitude of Torah to Wealth." Pages 148–163 in *Essays on Biblical Law*. New York: Sheffield Academic Press, 2002.

——. "The Decalogue: Ancient Israel's Criminal Law." *Journal of Jewish Studies* 34, no. 1 (1983): 1–20.

——. "The Law of Slavery: Exodus 21:2–11." *Journal for the Study of the Old Testament* 30 (1984): 51–66.

"Pledge." Page 1175 in *Black's Law Dictionary*. Edited by Byran A. Garner. St. Paul: West Group, 1999.

Polzin, Robert. *Moses and the Deuteronomist: A Literary Study of the Deuteronomic History*. New York: Seabury 1980.

Postgate, J. N. *Fifty Neo-Assyrian Legal Documents*. Warminster: Aris & Phillips, 1976.

Pressler, Carolyn. *The View of Women Found in the Deuteronomic Family Laws*. Berlin: W. de Gruyter, 1993.

——. "Wives and Daughters, Bond and Free: Views of Women in the Slave Laws of Exodus 21:2–22." Pages 147–172 in *Gender and Law in the Hebrew Bible and the Ancient Near East*. Edited by Victor H. Matthews, Bernard M. Levinson, and Tikva Frymer-Kensky. Sheffield: Sheffield Academic Press, 1998.

Preuss, Horst Dietrich. *Deuteronomium*. Darmstadt: Wissenschaftliche Buchgesellschaft, 1982.

Radmacher, Earl D. "Liberty and Freedom in the Old Testament." Pages 128–143 in *America in History and Bible Prophecy*. Edited by Thomas S. McCall. Chicago: Moody 1976.

Raz, Joseph. "The Rule of Law and Its Virtue." Pages 210–229 in *The Authority of Law: Essays on Law and Morality*. Oxford: Oxford University Press, 2009.

Regt, L. J. de. "Word Order in Different Clause Types in Deuteronomy 1–30." Pages 152–172 in *Studies in Hebrew and Aramaic Syntax: Presented to Professor J Hoftijzer on the*

Occasion of His Sixty-Fifth Birthday. Edited by H L. Murre-Van den Berg K. Jongeling, and Lucas Van Rompay. Leiden: E J Brill, 1991.

Reider, Joseph. *Deuteronomy.* Philadelphia: JPS, 1937.

Reimer, Haroldo. "A Time of Grace in Order to Begin Anew: The Sabbatical Year in Exodus 21:2–11 and Deuteronomy 15:1–18." Pages 71–88 in *God's Economy: Biblical Studies from Latin America.* Edited by F. Ross Kinsler, and Gloria Kinsler. Maryknoll: Orbis Books, 2005.

――. "Un Tiempo de Gracia para Recomenzar: El año Sabático en Exodo 21, 2–11 y Deuteronomio 15, 1–18." *Revista de interpretación bíblica latino-americana* 33 (1999): 31–47.

Reventlow, Henning Graf. *Das Heiligkeitsgesetz formgeschichtlich Untersucht.* Neukirchen: Neukirchener Verlag, 1961.

Richardson, M. E. J. *Hammurabi's Laws: Text, Translation and Glossary.* Sheffield: Sheffield Academic Press, 2000.

Rodd, Cyril S. *Glimpses of a Strange Land: Studies in Old Testament Ethics.* Edinburgh: T & T Clark, 2001.

Rofé, Alexander. "The Arrangement of the Laws in Deuteronomy." *Ephemerides theologicae lovanienses* 64, no. 4 (1988): 265–287.

Rogerson, J. W., ed. *Theory and Practice in Old Testament Ethics.* New York: T & T Clark, 2004.

Römer, Thomas. *The So-Called Deuteronomistic History: A Sociological, Historical, and Literary Introduction.* London: T. & T. Clark, 2005.

Rooker, Mark F. *Leviticus.* Nashville: Broadman & Holman, 2000.

Rosen, Lawrence. "Beyond Comparison." Pages 493–510 in *Comparative Legal Studies: Traditions and Transitions.* Edited by Legrand, Pierre and R. J. C. Munday. Cambridge: Cambridge University Press, 2003.

Rostow, Eugene. *The Sovereign Prerogative: The Supreme Court and the Quest for Law.* Westport: Greenwood, 1962.

Roth, Martha T. *Law Collections from Mesopotamia and Asia Minor.* Atlanta: Scholars Press, 1997.

――. "The Law Collection of King Hammurabi: Toward an Understanding of Codification and Text." Pages 9–31 in *La Codification des Lois dans L'Antiquité: Actes du Colloque de Strasbourg 27–29 Novembre 1997.* Edited by Edmond Lévy. Paris: De Boccard, 2000.

Sakenfeld, Katharine Doob, ed. *The New Interpreter's Dictionary of the Bible.* 5 Vols. Nashville: Abingdon, 2006.

Sarna, Nahum M. *Exodus.* Philadelphia: The Jewish Publication Society, 1991.

Sasson, Jack M., John Baines, Gary Beckman, and Karen S. Rubinson, eds. *Civilizations of the Ancient Near East, Vol 1 and 2.* Peabody: Hendrickson, 2000.

Scheil, V. *Code des Lois (droit privé) de Hammurabi.* Paris, 1902.

Schenker, Adrian. "Affranchissement d'une Esclave selon Ex 21:7–11." *Biblica* 69, no. 4 (1988): 547–556.

――. "The Biblical Legislation on the Release of Slaves: The Road from Exodus to Leviticus." *Journal for the Study of the Old Testament* 78 (1998): 23–41.

Schulz, Hermann. *Das Todesrecht im Alten Testament: Studien zur Rechtsform der Mot-Jumat-Satze.* Berlin: A. Topelmann, 1969.

Seitz, Gottfried. *Redaktionsgeschichtliche Studien zum Deuteronomium.* Stuttgart: Verlag W. Kohlhammer, 1971.

Siegel, Bernard J. "Some Methodological Considerations for a Comparative Study of Slavery." *American Anthropologist, n. s.*, 49, no. 3 (1947): 357–392.

Skinner, E. Benjamin. *A Crime So Monstrous: Face-to-Face with Modern-Day Slavery.* New York: Free, 2008.

Slanski, Kathryn. "Mesopotamia: Middle Babylonian Period." Pages 485–520 in *A History of Ancient Near Eastern Law.* Edited by Raymond Westbrook. Vol. 1. Leiden: E. J. Brill, 2003.

"Slavery Convention Signed at Geneva on 25th September 1926." No Pages. Cited 20 September 2010. Online: http://www2.ohchr.org/english/law/pdf/slavery.pdf.

Smith, Edwin William, and Andrew Murray Dale. *The Ila-Speaking Peoples of Northern Rhodesia.* Vol. 1. New Hyde Park: University Books, 1968.

Smith, J. M. Powis. *The Origin and History of Hebrew Law.* Westport: Hyperion, 1990.

Sonsino, Rifat. *Motive Clauses in Hebrew Law: Biblical Forms and Near Eastern Parallels.* Chico: Scholars, 1980.

Speiser, E. A. "Stem *PLL* in Hebrew." *Journal of Biblical Literature* 82, no. 3 (1963): 301–306.

Sprinkle, Joe M. *Biblical Law and Its Relevance: A Christian Understanding and Ethical Application for Today of the Mosaic Regulations.* Lanham: University Press of America, 2006.

Steiner, Franz. "Enslavement and the Early Hebrew Linage System: An Explanation of Genesis 47:29–31; 48:1–16." Pages 21–25 in *Anthropological Approaches to the Old Testament.* Edited by Bernhard Lang. Philadelphia: Fortress, 1984.

Steinkeller, Piotr. *Sale Documents of the Ur-III-Period.* Stuttgart: F. Steiner Verlag Wiesbaden, 1989.

Stuart, Douglas K. *Exodus.* Nashville: Broadman & Holman, 2006.

Talmon, Shemaryahu. "The 'Comparative Method' in Biblical Interpretation—Principles and Problems." Pages 320–356 in *Essential Papers on Israel and the Ancient Near East.* Edited by Frederick E. Greenspahn. New York: New York University Press, 1991.

Testart, A. "The Extent and Significance of Debt Slavery." *Revue française de sociologie* (Supplement: Annual English Edition) 43 (2002): 173–204.

Thiele, Edwin R. *The Mysterious Numbers of the Hebrew Kings.* Grand Rapids: Zondervan, 1983.

Thornton, John K. *Africa and Africans in the Making of the Atlantic World, 1400–1800.* Cambridge: Cambridge University Press, 1998.

Thurnwald, R. "Sklave." Pages 209–228 in *Reallexikon der Vorgeschichte, XII.* Edited by Max Ebert. Berlin: W. de Gruyter, 1928.

Tigay, Jeffrey H. *Deuteronomy.* Philadelphia: Jewish Publication Society of America, 1996.

Toulmin, Stephen Edelston. *The Use of Argument.* London: Cambridge University Press, 1958.

Tsevat, Matitiahu. "Alalakhiana." *Hebrew Union College Annual* 29 (1958): 109–134.

——. "The Hebrew Slave According to Deuteronomy 15:12–18: His Lot and the Value of His Work, with Special Attention to the Meaning of מִשְׁנֶה." *Journal of Biblical Literature* 113 (1994): 587–595.

Tsumura, David Toshio. *Creation and Destruction: A Reappraisal of the Chaoskampf Theory in the Old Testament.* Winona Lake: Eisenbrauns, 2005.

Turnham, Timothy John. "Male and Female Slaves in the Sabbath Year Laws of Exodus 21:1–11." *Society of Biblical Literature Seminar Papers* 26 (1987): 545–549.

Uitti, Roger William. "The Motive Clause in Old Testament Law." Ph.D. diss., Lutheran School of Theology at Chicago, 1973.

Van Cangh, Jean Marie. "Le Jubilé biblique: Un Temps Marqué Ouvrant un Temps Neuf." *Science et esprit* 53 (2001): 63–92.

Van der Ploeg, J. P. M. "Slavery in the Old Testament." Pages 72–87 in *Congress Volume: Uppsala, 1971.* Leiden: E. J. Brill, 1972.

VanGemeren, Willem. *New International Dictionary of Old Testament Theology & Exegesis.* 4 vols. Grand Rapids: Zondervan, 1997.

Vanhoozer, Kevin J. *Is There a Meaning in This Text? The Bible, the Reader, and the Morality of Literary Knowledge.* Grand Rapids: Zondervan, 1998.

Van Seters, John. *A Law Book for the Diaspora: Revision in the Study of the Covenant Code.* New York: Oxford University Press, 2003.

——. "Law of the Hebrew Slave: A Continuing Debate." *Zeitschrift für die alttestamentliche Wissenschaft* 119 (2006): 169–183.

——. "Some Observations on the lex Talionis in Exod 21:23–25." Pages 27–37 in *Recht und Ethos im Alten Testament–Gestalt und Wirkung: Festschrift für Horst Seebass zum 65. Geburtstag.* Edited by Stefan Beyerle, Günter Mayer, and Hans Strauss. Neukirchen-Vluyn: Neukirchener, 1999.

——. "The Law of the Hebrew Slave." *Zeitschrift für die alttestamentliche Wissenschaft* 108 (1996): 534–546.

Vasholz, Robert I. "A Legal 'Brief' on Deuteronomy 23:16–17." *Presbyterion* 17 (1991): 127.

Veenhof, Klaas R. "Old Assyrian Period." Pages 431–483 in *A History of Ancient Near Eastern Law.* Edited by Raymond Westbrook. Vol. 1. Leiden: E. J. Brill, 2003.

Veijola, Timo. "Deuteronomismusforschung zwischen Tradition und Innovation (I)." *Theologische Rundschau* 67 (2002): 273–327.

——. "Deuteronomismusforschung zwischen Tradition und Innovation (II)." *Theologische Rundschau* 67 (2002): 391–424.

——. "Deuteronomismusforschung zwischen Tradition und Innovation (III)," *Theologische Rundschau* 68 (2003): 1–44.

VerSteeg, Russ. *Early Mesopotamian Law.* Durham: Carolina Academic Press, 2000.

Viberg, Åke. *Symbols of Law: A Contextual Analysis of Legal Symbolic Acts in the Old Testament.* Stockholm: Almqvist & Wiksell International, 1992.

Vogt, Peter T. *Deuteronomic Theology and the Significance of Torah: A Reappraisal.* Winona Lake: Eisenbrauns, 2006.

von Rad, Gerhard. *Deuteronomy: A Commentary.* Philadelphia: Westminster, 1966.

——. *The Problem of the Hexateuch and Other Essays.* New York: McGraw-Hill, 1966.

Vriezen, Th. C. *An Outline of Old Testament Theology.* Newton: C. T. Branford, 1970.

Wallace, A. F. C. "Revitalization Movements." *American Anthropologist* 58 (1956): 264–281.

Walton, John H. "Deuteronomy: An Exposition of the Spirit of the Law." *Grace Theological Journal* 8. no. 2 (1987): 213–225.

Watson, Alan. *Legal Transplants: An Approach to Comparative Law.* Athens: University of Georgia Press, 1993.

——. "Legal Transplants and European Private Law." *Electronic Journal of Comparative Law* 4, no. 4 (2000): No Pages. Cited 17 February 2009. Online: http://www.ejcl.org/44/art44–2.html.

——. *Society and Legal Change.* Edinburgh: Scottish Academic Press, 1977.

——. *Sources of Law, Legal Change, and Ambiguity.* Philadelphia: University of Pennsylvania University Press, 1984.

Watson, Rebecca Sally. *Chaos Uncreated: A Reassessment of the Theme of "Chaos" in the Hebrew Bible*. Berlin: Walter de Gruyter, 2005.

Watts, Fraser. "Human Dignity: Concepts and Experiences." Pages 247–262 *in God and Human Dignity*. Edited by R. Kendall Soulen and Linda Woodhead. Grand Rapids: Eerdmans, 2006.

Watts, James W. "Rhetorical Strategy in the Composition of the Pentateuch." *Journal for the Study of the Old Testament* 68 (1995): 3–22.

Weinfeld, Moshe. *Deuteronomy and Deuteronomic School*. Winona Lake: Eisenbrauns, 1992.

——. *Deuteronomy 1–11*. New York: Doubleday, 1991.

——. "Freedom Proclamations in Egypt and in the Ancient Near East." Pages 317–327 in *Pharaonic Egypt: The Bible and Christianity*. Edited by Sarah Israelit-Groll. Jerusalem: Magnes, 1985.

——. "Sabbatical Year and Jubilee in the Pentateuchal Laws and Their Ancient Near Eastern Background." Pages 39–62 in *Law in the Bible and in Its Environment*. Edited by Timo Veijola. Göttingen: Vandenhoeck & Ruprecht, 1990.

——. *Social Justice in Ancient Israel and in the Ancient Near East*. Minneapolis: Fortress, 1995.

——. "Social Justice in the Ancient Near East." Pages 149–163 in *Social Justice in the Ancient World*. Edited by K. D. Irani and Morris Silver. Westport: Greenwood, 1993.

Weingreen, Jacob. *From Bible to Mishna: The Continuity of Tradition*. New York: Holmes & Meier, 1976.

Weippert, Manfred. *The Settlement of the Israelite Tribes in Palestine: A Critical Survey of Recent Scholarly Debate*. Translated by James D. Martin. London: SCM, 1971.

Wellhausen, Julius. *Die Composition des Hexateuchs und der historischen Bücher des Alten Testaments*. Berlin: W. de Gruyter, 1963.

Wells, Bruce. "The Covenant Law Book and Near Eastern Legal Traditions: A Response to David P. Wright." *MAARAV* 13, no. 1 (2006): 85–118.

Wenham, Gordon J. *The Book of Leviticus*. Grand Rapids: Eerdmans, 1979.

Westbrook, David A. "Theorizing the Diffusion of Law: Conceptual Difficulties, Unstable Imaginations, and the Effort to Think Gracefully Nonetheless." *Harvard International Law Journal* 47 (2006): 489–505.

Westbrook, Raymond. "Jubilee Laws," *Israel Law Review* 6 (1971): 209–226.

——. *Studies in Biblical and Cuneiform Law*. Paris: J. Gabalda, 1988.

——. "The Character of Ancient Near Eastern Law." Pages 1-90 in *A History of Ancient Near Eastern Law*. Edited by Raymond Westbrook. Vol. 1. Leiden: E. J. Brill, 2003.

——. "The Development of Law in the Ancient Near East: Slave and Master in Ancient Near Eastern Law." *Chicago-Kent Law Review*, 70 (1995): No pages. Cited 4 November 2009. Online: http://www.lexisnexis.com/us/lnacademic/results/docview/docview.do?do cLinkInd=true&risb=21_T9205617514&format=GNBFI&sort=RELEVANCE&startDocNo=1&re sultsUrlKey=29_T9205616733&cisb=22_T9205617517&treeMax=true&treeWidth=0&csi= 7421&docNo=7.

——. "Anatolia and the Levant: Emar and Vicinity." Pages 657–691 in *A History of Ancient Near Eastern Law*. Edited by Raymond Westbrook. Vol. 1. Leiden: E. J. Brill, 2003.

——. "Biblical and Cuneiform Law Codes." *Revue biblique* 92, no. 2 (1985): 247–264.

——. "Mesopotamia: Old Babylonian Period." Pages 361–430 in *A History of Ancient Near Eastern Law*. Edited by Raymond Westbrook. Vol. 1. Leiden: E. J. Brill, 2003.

——. "Social Justice in the Ancient Near East" Pages 149–163 in *Social Justice in the Ancient World*. Edited by K. D. Irani and Morris Silver. Westport: Greenwood, 1995.

——. "The Female Slave." Pages 214–238 in *Gender and Law in the Hebrew Bible and the Ancient Near East*. Edited by Victor H. Matthews, Bernard M. Levinson, and Tikva Frymer-Kensky. Sheffield: Sheffield Academic Press, 1998.

——. "The Old Babylonian Period." Pages 63–92 in *Security for Debt in Ancient Near Eastern Law*. Edited by Raymond Westbrook and Richard Lewis Jasnow. Leiden: E. J. Brill, 2001.

——. "What Is the Covenant Code?" Pages 15–26 in *Theory and Method in Biblical and Cuneiform Law: Revision, Interpolation and Development*. Edited by Bernard M. Levinson. Sheffield: Sheffield Academic Press, 1994.

Westbrook, Raymond, ed. *A History of Ancient Near Eastern Law*. 2 vols. Leiden: E. J. Brill, 2003.

Westbrook, Raymond, and Bruce Wells. *Everyday Law in Biblical Israel: An Introduction*. Louisville: Westminster John Knox, 2009.

Westbrook, Raymond, and Richard Lewis Jasnow, eds. *Security for Debt in Ancient Near Eastern Law*. Leiden: E. J. Brill, 2001.

Wiener, Harold Marcus. "The Arrangement of Deuteronomy XII-XXVI." Pages 26–36 in *Posthumous Essays*. Edited by Herbert Loewe. London: Oxford University press, 1932.

Wilcke, Claus. *Early ancient Near Eastern Law: A History of Its Beginnings; the Early Dynastic and Sargonic Periods*. Winona Lake: Eisenbrauns, 2007.

——. "Mesopotamia: Early Dynastic and Sargonic Periods." Pages 141–181 in *A History of Ancient Near Eastern Law*. Edited by Raymond Westbrook. Vol. 1. Leiden: E. J. Brill, 2003.

Wiseman, D. J. "Laws of Hammurabi Again." *Journal of Semitic Studies* 7, no. 2 (1962): 161–172.

Wolff, Hans Walter. "Masters and Slaves: On Overcoming Class-Struggle in the Old Testament." *Interpretation* 27, no. 3 (1973): 259–272.

Work, Telford. *Deuteronomy*. Grand Rapids: Brazos, 2009.

Wright, Christopher J. H. *Deuteronomy*. Peabody: Hendrickson, 1996.

——. *Old Testament Ethics for the People of God*. Downers Grove: InterVarsity Press, 2004.

——. "What Happened Every Seven Years in Israel? Old Testament Sabbatical Institutions for Land, Debts and Slaves Part II." *Evangelical Quarterly* 56 (1984):193–201.

Wright, David P. *Inventing God's Law: How the Covenant Code of the Bible Used and Revised the Laws of Hammurabi*. New York: Oxford University Press, 2009.

——. "The Laws of Hammurabi as a Source for the Covenant Collection." *MAARAV* 10 (2003): 11–87.

——. "The Laws of Hammurabi and the Covenant Code: A Response to Bruce Wells." *MAARAV* 13, no. 2 (2006): 211–260.

Yaron, Reuven. "Matrimonial Mishaps at Eshnunna." *Journal of Semitic Studies* 8, no. 1 (1963): 1–16.

Yoffee, Norman, and George L. Cowgill, eds. *The Collapse of Ancient States and Civilizations*. Tucson: University of Arizona Press, 1988.

Younger, K. Lawson, Jr. "The 'Contextual Method': Some West Semitic Reflections." Pages xxxv-xlii in *The Context of Scripture III*. Edited by William W. Hallo, and K. Lawson Younger, Jr. New York: E. J. Brill, 2003.

——. "Contracts: Neo-Assyrian Contracts." Pages 258–265 in *The Context of Scripture III*. Edited by William W. Hallo, and K. Lawson Younger, Jr. New York: E. J. Brill, 2003.

Zakovitch, Yair. *For Three... and for Four: The Pattern of the Numerical Sequence Three-Four in the Bible*. Jerusalem: Makor, 1979.

Zaccagnini, Carlo. "Mesopotamia: Nuzi." Pages 565–617 in *A History of Ancient Near Eastern Law*. Edited by Raymond Westbrook. Vol. 1. Leiden: E. J. Brill, 2003.

Index of Authors

Index of Scripture References

29:19 179
29:24 34
30:2 55, 179
30:3-4 75
30:8 55, 179
30:9 179
30:10 55
30:11 55
30:12 179
30:13 179
30:16 55
30:17 179
30:19 63
30:20 55, 179
31:11 179
31:12 55, 179
31:13 55, 179
31:28 179
31:30 179
32:1 179
32:5 181
32:44 179
32:46 55
33:1 18
33:9 55
34:4 35
34:5 116
34:11 34

Joshua
8 13

1 Samuel
6:3 50
17:25 46
18:25 94

2 Samuel
1:22 50
4:3 45
26:18-19 116

2 Kings
4:1 157
14:5-6 16, 19, 20
14:6 19
22:12 116

2 Chronicles
8:7-9 109

Nehemiah
5 109
9:36 181

Job
1:8 116
22:6 157
22:9 50
24:3 157
24:9 157
39:5 46

Psalms
7:5 50
18:1 116
25:3 50

Proverbs
3:32 56
11:1 56
11:20 56
12:22 56
15:8 56
15:26 56
16:5 56
17:15 56
20:10 56
20:23 56

Ecclesiastes
2:7 71

Isaiah
14:2 107
16:14 105
20:3 116
21:16 105
36:8 157
42-53 116
55:11 50

Jeremiah
7:25 116
14:3 50